This is one of the very few books available in English to present a comprehensive interpretation of the philosophy of Simone Weil and how her thought can illuminate issues of contemporary importance such as work, justice, the law, war and peace, and matters of more general moral and theological concern. In addition to focusing on how Weil's thought may apply to social and cultural issues, it offers critical interpretations of the following important notions in her philosophy: reading, decreation, imagination, beauty, God, and contradiction.

SIMONE WEIL'S PHILOSOPHY OF CULTURE

SIMONE WEIL'S PHILOSOPHY OF CULTURE

Readings toward a divine humanity

EDITED AND INTRODUCED BY

RICHARD H. BELL

Frank Halliday Ferris Professor of Philosophy
The College of Wooster, Ohio

Published by the Press Syndicate of the University of Cambridge
The Pitt Building, Trumpington Street, Cambridge CB2 1RP
40 West 20th Street, New York, NY 10011–4211, USA
10 Stamford Road, Oakleigh, Victoria 3166, Australia

First published 1993

Printed in Great Britain at the University Press, Cambridge

A catalogue record for this book is available from the British Library

Library of Congress cataloguing in publication data

Simone Weil's philosophy of culture: Readings toward a divine humanity / edited and
introduced by Richard H. Bell.
p.   cm.
Includes bibliographical references and index.
ISBN 0 521 43263 4 (hardback)
1. Weil, Simone, 1909–1943. 2. Culture – Philosophy – History – 20th century.
1 Bell, Richard H.
B2430.W474S63 1993   194 – dc20 92–11490 CIP

ISBN 0 521 43263 4 hardback

for Rebecca,
and her contemporaries who want
to change the world for the common good;
remember,

'Praise to God and compassion for creatures.
It is the same movement of the heart.'
(Simone Weil, *FLN* 102)

Contents

Notes on contributors

DIOGENES ALLEN is the Stuart Professor of Philosophy at Princeton Theological Seminary. He was educated at Yale and Oxford universities. Besides some fifteen articles devoted to Simone Weil, several of his books (*Three Outsiders, Love, Finding Our Father*, and *Christian Belief in a Postmodern World*) have used or developed her ideas. He is currently working on a major study on spirituality and theology.

MARTIN ANDIC is Associate Professor of Philosophy at the University of Massachusetts, Boston Harbor Campus. He studied at Dartmouth College, Princeton University, and St John's College, Oxford, and has published essays on Plato, Hume, Kierkegaard, and Simone Weil. He is currently preparing a book on Weil's notion of supernatural knowledge, and a commentary on Kierkegaard's *Works of Love*.

RICHARD H. BELL is Frank Halliday Ferris Professor of Philosophy at The College of Wooster, Wooster, Ohio. He is editor of a six-book series on 'Spirituality and the Christian Life' published by The Westminster Press, which includes his book *Sensing The Spirit*. He also edited and introduced *The Grammar of the Heart: New Essays in Moral Philosophy and Theology* (Harper and Row 1988). Recent articles of his have appeared in the journals *Philosophy, Journal of Aesthetics and Art Criticism, Journal of the History of European Ideas*, and *Religious Studies*. Professor Bell is a Life Member of Clare Hall, Cambridge University.

RONALD K. L. COLLINS is on the law faculty of George Washington University, National Law Center, in Washington, D.C., where he teaches commercial law, criminal law, and jurisprudence. He is the co-founder of the Center for the Study of Commercialism, a non-profit interest group in Washington, D.C. Mr Collins holds degrees from the University of California at Santa Barbara and Loyola Law School in California. He served as a judicial fellow to Chief Justice Warren Burger at the United States Supreme Court. He is the editor of *Constitutional Government in America* (1980), has authored numerous articles for scholarly journals, and is the co-author of *The Death of Discourse* (forthcoming).

ANDRÉ A. DEVAUX is emeritus Professor of Philosophy at the Sorbonne, Paris. He was President of the *Association pour l'étude de la pensée de Simone Weil* from 1973 to 1987, and edited the journal *Cahiers Simone Weil*. He has published many distinguished articles on Simone Weil – of most recent note is 'Simone Weil et Blaise Pascal' (1990). Professor Devaux is co-editor of the *Oeuvres Complètes* being published by Gallimard, Paris.

H. L. FINCH is emeritus Professor of Philosophy at Hunter College, City University of New York. He has been a 'student' of the thought of Simone Weil for over thirty years, and has contributed a great deal in the past decade to the proceedings of the American Weil Society. He is, perhaps, best known for his two volume study of Ludwig Wittgenstein.

CLARE B. FISCHER is Aurelia Henry Reinhardt Professor of Religion and Culture at the Starr King School for Ministry, and Chair of Comparative Religion of the Graduate Theological Union in Berkeley, California. She holds advanced degrees in political science, public law, and in religious studies. She is currently completing the book-length study of Simone Weil and theory of work, *Our Mother Country is Hope* (forthcoming from SUNY Press). Professor Fischer has recently written a paper on Simone Weil and Christa Wolf on peace and the meaning of *The Iliad*.

J. P. LITTLE is Lecturer in French at St Patrick's College, Dublin. She is well known for her many studies in twentieth-century French literature with critical guides to Samuel Beckett's *En attendant Godot* and *Fin de Partie*, and Jean Genet's *Les Nègres*. Her book, *Simone Weil: Waiting on Truth* (1988) is part of the Berg Publishers women's series. Simone Weil scholars are indebted to Dr Little's *Simone Weil: A Bibliography* (1973) and *Supplement No. 1* (1979), and to her editing role in the recent collection *Simone Weil: La Soif de l'absolu* (1990).

ANN LOADES is Reader in Theology, University of Durham. Her books include *Kant and Job's Comforters* (1985) and the Scott Holland Lectures, *Searching for Lost Coins* (1987) which includes a chapter on Simone Weil. She recently edited *Feminist Theology: A Reader* (1990). Dr Loades is currently editor of the journal *Theology*.

FINN E. NIELSEN is Senior Lecturer, Department of English, Swedish School of Economics and Business Administration, Helsinki, Finland, as well as on the staff of the Department of Political Science at the University of Helsinki. He received his Ph.D. in political science from the University of California at Santa Barbara (it was here that his association with Ronald Collins began). Mr Nielsen's dissertation was entitled *The Political Vision of Simone Weil*.

D. Z. PHILLIPS is Professor of Philosophy at University College of Swansea, University of Wales and Danforth Professor of the Philosophy of Religion, Claremont Graduate School, Claremont, CA. Three recent books of his are of particular note: *Faith After Foundationalism* (1988), *From Fantasy to Faith* (1991), and *Through a Darkening Glass* (1982). In a number of his books and articles Simone Weil has been a catalyst for moving his own ideas forward. Professor Phillips is editor of the journal *Philosophical Investigations*, and is one of Britain's leading interpreters of Wittgenstein.

PATRICK SHERRY is Reader in Religious Studies at the University of Lancaster, England. He holds advanced degrees in both classical studies and theology. His most recent books are *Spirit, Saints, and Immortality* (1984), and *Spirit and Beauty: Introduction to Theological Aesthetics* (1991). Dr Sherry is co-editor of the three-volume work, *Nineteenth-Century Religious Thought in the West* (Cambridge University Press, 1986).

ERIC O. SPRINGSTED is president and co-founder (with Diogenes Allen) of the American Weil Society. He is Associate Professor of Philosophy and Religion at Illinois College, Jacksonville, Illinois. Professor Springsted's books *Christus Mediator* (1983), and *Simone Weil and the Suffering of Love* (1986), are well known to Simone Weil scholars. He is also author of *Who Will Make Us Wise: How the Church is Failing Liberal Education* (1988). During the summer of 1988 he was engaged in research on the unedited Weil manuscripts at the *Bibliothèque Nationale*, Paris.

ROWAN WILLIAMS is the Bishop of Monmouth in South Wales and formerly Lady Margaret Professor of Divinity and Canon of Christ Church, Oxford University. He has written widely in patristic studies, orthodox theology, and contemporary theology. Among his recent books are: *Arius: Heresy and Tradition* (1987), *Resurrection* (1982), and *The Wound of Knowledge* (1979). Two essays of recent note are his 'Religious Realism', *Modern Theology* (1984), and 'The Suspicion of Suspicion: Wittgenstein and Bonhoeffer' in *The Grammar of the Heart* (1988).

Acknowledgements

Simone Weil said that 'philosophy is *exclusively* an affair of action and practice'. So, too, is the writing of books. Ideas lie fallow without some action upon them, and remain vague or unfamiliar without practice in their use. A lot of the ideas and writings of Simone Weil are unfamiliar to many (especially to the English-speaking world), and the process of making them familiar has been a relatively slow one in her case. This book is designed to make her ideas more familiar and accessible, and also to present them in a clear and critical way. That has taken both the action and practice of a number of people – *action* to raise support to bring people together and to organise the co-operation between institutions and individuals in planning various kinds of gatherings; *practice* of hospitality by many, and listening with some humility, patience, and understanding by scholars whose ideas and interpretations were often challenged and changed as they encountered the world of Simone Weil's philosophy together. So it is the action and practice of many persons that we acknowledge as part of the whole cloth that brought this book about. It was truly a communal affair, and the editor owes his deep gratitude to those named below, and to others who contributed in smaller and kind ways to make this effort a challenging and enjoyable one.

This project on the philosophy of Simone Weil was given life through funds granted by The National Endowment for the Humanities and The College of Wooster. Their generous support occasioned conversation among nearly twenty scholars which bridged two continents over a two-year period, and underwrote consultations of this group in Cambridge, England, and Wooster, Ohio. Special thanks go to Henry Copeland, President of the College of Wooster, for his encouragement and support through the entire project, to John Plummer, Treasurer's Office of the college,

xv

for his judicious and friendly record keeping, and to the American Weil Society and its President, Eric O. Springsted, for their interest and co-operative spirit.

If an impetus for the book came from its funding, its being is the result of dedicated persons who organised the consultations, made them run smoothly, and who were particularly welcoming human beings. We owe a great debt of gratitude to Amy Patterson, secretary to the Departments of Philosophy and Geology at The College of Wooster, and John Garrod, Bursar of Clare Hall, Cambridge University; to Barbara L. Bell, Rebecca Bell, Rachel Johnson, Clarissa Roberts, Laura Caliguiri, Doug Sauer, Scott Nelson, Cameron Maneese, and Gary Thompson – all of whom made the project participants feel at home.

Rachel Johnson and Clarissa Roberts, supported by The Sophomore Scholars Research Experience at The College of Wooster, have also participated whole-heartedly in the editing of this volume, helping in word processing, bibliographic assistance, and indexing. Their work has been skilful and philosophically astute in all respects.

Thanks also to Clare Hall, Cambridge University and its President, Anthony Low, and to The Center of Theological Inquiry, Princeton, New Jersey, and its Director, Daniel Hardy, for providing creative scholarly environments in which work was carried on by me as NEH Project Director and book editor. I was visiting Fellow of Clare Hall for the academic year 1989–1990, and the Center of Theological Inquiry during the summer of 1991.

Among scholars who were either part of the project's conversations or who were consulted on aspects of it, but who were unable to contribute to this volume directly, were Peter Winch, Champaign/Urbana, Illinois, David McLellan, Canterbury, England, Jean-Yves Lacoste, Paris, France, Miklos Vetö, Rennes, France, and David Wilkin, Wooster, Ohio.

RICHARD H. BELL

Princeton, New Jersey
August 1991

Abbreviations for works cited in the text

EL   *Ecrits de Londres et derniéres lettres*, Paris: Gallimard, Coll. Espoir, 1957.

ER   'Essay on the Notion of Reading', trans. by Rebecca Fine Rose and Timothy Tessin, *Philosophical Investigations*, 13:4 (October 1990). Originally published as 'Essay Sur la notion de lecture', *Etudes Philosophiques* (Marseilles), NS, 1 (January–March 1946): 13–19.

FLN   *First and Last Notebooks*, trans. Richard Rees, London: Oxford University Press, 1970.

FW   *Formative Writings: 1929–1941*, edited and trans. by Dorothy Tuck McFarland and Wilhelmina Van Ness, Amherst: The University of Massachusetts Press, 1987.

FWK   'Factory Work', in *The Simone Weil Reader*, edited by George A. Panichas, New York: David McKay Co., 1977.

GG   *Gravity and Grace*, trans. Emma Craufurd, London: Routledge and Kegan Paul, 1972.

IC   *Intimations of Christianity Among the Ancient Greeks*, trans. E. C. Geissbuhler, London: Routledge and Kegan Paul, 1957.

IL   *The Iliad or The Poem of Force*, trans. Mary McCarthy, Wallingford, PA: Pendle Hill Pamphlet, number 91, 1981. This essay is also in *IC* in a different translation.

IP   *Intuitions pré-chrétiennes*, Paris: La Colombe, 1951.

LP   *Lectures on Philosophy*, trans. H. Price with an introduction by Peter Winch, Cambridge: Cambridge University Press, 1978.

LPG   'The Legitimacy of the Provisional Government', trans. Peter Winch, *Philosophical Investigations*, 53 (April 1987).

N   *Notebooks*, trans. Arthur Wills, London: Routledge and
             Kegan Paul, 2 volumes, 1956.
NR   *The Need for Roots*, trans. Arthur Wills, with a preface by
             T. S. Eliot, New York: Harper Colophon Books, Harper
             and Row, 1971.
OL   *Oppression and Liberty*, trans. Arthur Wills and John
             Petrie, Amherst: The University of Massachusetts Press,
             1973.
PSO   *Penseés sans ordre concernant l'amour de Dieu*, Paris:
             Gallimard, 1962.
SE   *Selected Essays: 1934–1943*, trans. Richard Rees, Oxford:
             Oxford University Press, 1962.
SJ   'Are We Struggling for Justice?' trans. Marina Barabas,
             Philosophical Investigations, 53 (January 1987).
SL   *Seventy Letters*, trans. Richard Rees, London: Oxford
             University Press, 1970.
SNLG   *Science, Necessity and the Love of God*, trans. Richard Rees,
             London: Oxford University Press, 1968.
WG   *Waiting for God*, trans. Emma Craufurd, New York,
             Harper Colophon Books, Harper and Row, 1951.

Introduction: divine humanity
Simone Weil's philosophy of culture

Richard H. Bell

> What is good is also divine. Queer as it sounds, that sums up my ethics. Only something supernatural can express the Super-natural.
>
> Ludwig Wittgenstein, 1929.

APPROACHING SIMONE WEIL

In 1973, Megan Terry wrote a play on the life of Simone Weil entitled 'Approaching Simone'. The play was little noticed, but its title has become part of the inherited background for this project. I was introduced to a piece of Simone Weil's several years before this play appeared. Subsequently, each time I read a new piece of this modern French thinker, I was puzzled about how to approach her – as a religious thinker, as political theorist, a philosopher, a classicist, as spiritual guide, or social activist. One reading or another could make reasonable claim to each or all of these approaches. Also, little of the growing secondary literature in English in the 1960s and '70s seemed helpful in gauging how one might most fruitfully 'approach Simone'.

There were a few British philosophers I read who seemed to take her literature seriously as a kind of moral philosophy, but they only made mention or limited use of a select number of her remarks, with little critical appraisal. Seldom was there a more comprehensive attempt to see her philosophy in its larger setting. Most British and American writers who took note of her life and thought approached her as religious thinker, spiritual guide, or social activist. I was still left to ask: 'How are we to "approach Simone", and to what extent would a primarily philosophical reading help us understand her work?'

At the end of their Introduction to *Simone Weil: Formative Writings 1929–1941*, published in 1987, Dorothy Tuck McFarland and

Wilhelmina Van Ness wrote, 'A phenomenal amount of work remains to be done on all Weil's writings, on their content as well as on the linkages and continuities that underlie them.' Because of this 'phenomenal amount of work remaining', the several legitimate approaches, and the character of the literature itself, it became apparent to me that perhaps 'approaching Simone' – even if it were to focus primarily on her philosophy – might best be done in collaboration with others who may have experienced difficulties similar to mine. So it came about that this project was born, and this book nurtured to completion.

The volume has been carefully crafted by a group of scholars working in collaboration on the philosophy of Simone Weil. It began with a simple idea that this extraordinary philosopher may best be approached – perhaps only really understood – by several people in close conversation with one another about central concepts or ideas in her work.[1] Her thoughts are powerful and seductive to any reader who would take up one of her personal letters, a political essay, or a fragment from a notebook. But they are also daunting; they are richly textured from both a literary and a philosophical point of view, and often enigmatic, if not downright inscrutable. We were driven by both the intellectual challenge her work provided us, and the stimulation that our conversations produced.

Our collaboration can be seen as a model of interdisciplinary studies – literary critics, philosophers, political and legal theorists, and theologians were engaged in the conversation. As we looked first from within our own disciplines towards central concepts in Simone Weil, our conversations forced us to enlarge our focus and our own disciplinary perspective. Each essay, in the end, opens out towards other disciplines, and finds a place in the internal analysis of another's essay. Rather than reflecting one mode or another of 'fashionable' criticism, the process became more an exercise in 'recollective' and 'reconstructive' criticism as we listened to, and questioned, one another. Far from detracting from a 'philosophical' critique of her thought, we found our interdisciplinary interrogations focused more clearly the range of what philosophy meant for

[1] The research group that formed was made up of scholars who had for over a decade been producing individual critical pieces on varying aspects of Simone Weil's thought, and who could immediately recognise the potential value of talking together and, by so doing, move study of her work to a 'higher' level. See the 'Notes on Contributors' for details on these scholars.

Simone Weil, and further discovered in the process that philosophy itself became rescued from narrow 'analytic' or 'linguistic' bounds that have constrained it for too long. 'Philosophy', declares Simone Weil, 'is a virtue', and its reward 'joy', and André Devaux notes 'the joy which can be communicated among minds when there reigns a climate of mutual confidence, such as that which brought us together at Cambridge, and then at Wooster'.

Although it is often easier to decipher a great deal of Simone Weil's ideas with the works of Plato and Descartes or Kant (but especially Plato) as background, she may be better read with Socrates in mind, rather than his more systematic pupil. Her conception of doing philosophy, like Socrates', is to see it as a remedial task – as preparing us to see things for which we may be otherwise blinded. Philosophy forces questions more than it gives clear answers. Simone Weil's philosophy is one that interrogates and contemplates our culture; it makes us aware of our lack of attention to words and empty ideologies, to human suffering, to the indignity of work, to our excessive use of power, to religious dogmatisms. Rather than set out a *system* of ideas (like a theory of justice or a theory of the good), Simone Weil uses her philosophical reflections to show us how to *think* about work and oppression, freedom and the good, necessity and power, love and justice – even to think, or not think, about God. In this way we are asked to examine the human condition and learn to discern a way through it.

In her essay, 'The Power of Words', Simone Weil wrote: 'When a word is properly defined it loses its capital letter and can no longer serve either as a banner or as a hostile slogan; it becomes simply a sign, helping us to grasp some concrete reality, or concrete objective, or method of activity. To clarify thought, to discredit the intrinsically meaningless words, and to define the use of others by precise analysis – to do this, strange though it may appear, might be a way of saving human lives' (*SE* 156). How could the Socratic agenda be stated more clearly? It is not just, as Socrates might say, that clarifying thought, discrediting meaningless words, and defining the use of terms by precise analysis, may improve our moral life, even our community, but Simone Weil takes us a step further to say that this may be a way of 'saving human lives'. This is so because of the '*C*apital letter' abuses in the name of power and self-interest we experience today. Simone Weil is specifically attacking what she calls 'vacuous abstractions' in 'our political and social vocabulary:

nation, security, capitalism, communism, fascism, order, authority, property, democracy ... we make these words mean anything what-soever' (*SE* 157). And she concludes this thought by saying:

Our lives are lived, in actual fact, among changing, varying realities, subject to the causal play of eternal necessities, and modifying themselves according to specific conditions within specific limits; and yet we act and strive and sacrifice ourselves and others by reference to fixed and isolated abstractions which cannot possibly be related either to one another or to any concrete facts. In this so-called age of technicians, the only battles we know how to fight are battles against windmills. (*SE* 157)

This last thought of hers points to one of the most striking features in her philosophy. She always turned our focus to the concrete, the changing and varying realities in our lives, and the specific circum-stances that produced them. This is often done through her use of literary examples and in retelling short narratives. Her very 'philo-sophical procedure', Peter Winch notes in his book *Simone Weil: 'The Just Balance'*, 'is to root the concepts which are most important to her in actual, very concrete, features of human life. Although she is no enemy of abstract theoretical considerations, she does not start with these, but with the circumstances of life which gave rise to them.'[2] This feature quickly became clear in our conversations, and is central in all of our essays. We are all concerned to link Simone Weil's conception of God and the 'supernatural' to our ordinary human life, and to focus on the concrete, on specific examples from ordinary life, in both interpreting, and in applying, her philosophy to contemporary problems.

Our approach to Simone Weil is different in this way as well. It sees Simone Weil thinking with, and about, concepts. This is an extension of her concern for 'precise analysis' and the clarification of thought. Although a reader should not think of these concepts as isolated in her thinking (for they are highly interrelated as will become clear), to turn them over and interrogate their use by her, reveals nuances in their meaning that might otherwise be missed. So

---

[2] Peter Winch, *Simone Weil: 'The Just Balance'*, Cambridge: Cambridge University Press, 1989, p. 190. Part of our conversation has been informed by Peter Winch, both as partici-pant in our consultation in Cambridge and through his important work. Our conversation with Winch includes two lengthy reviews of his book by authors in this volume. Cf. critical discussions by Richard H. Bell in *Religious Studies* 26, March 1990, pp. 166–75, and Rowan Williams in *Philosophical Investigations* 14, April 1991, pp. 155–71. Williams notes that the main purpose of Winch's study 'is to make us think *with* Weil, and in so doing to recognise her as a philosopher', and hails it as 'the harbinger of a new generation of Weil scholarship'.

in these essays, one will find focused attention given, in Part I, to the concepts of 'decreation', 'God', the person or the autonomous 'I', 'the impersonal', 'discernment', 'imagination', 'reading', and 'contradiction', and, in Part II, to the concepts of 'rootedness', 'work', 'rights', 'justice', 'love', 'law', 'obligation', 'innocence and affliction', 'beauty', and 'religious pluralism'. Through such concepts a larger picture of Simone Weil's complex world-view emerges. Our conversations have led us to see many subtle connections, and to note these connections as they link to another's essay. This introduction may serve to give the reader some sense of the connectedness of concepts, or provide a preliminary mapping of concepts, in what we have called Simone Weil's philosophy of culture.

Simone Weil was a woman who always thought ahead of herself, who acted with her thoughts, and who demanded no less of her contemporaries and those who might read her sometimes unconnected jottings. Her writings, like her life, ended prematurely – she died in 1943 at 34 years of age. They were as a whole incomplete. But in part, because of their incompleteness, they invite readers to complete them through themselves – through the appropriation of her many insights into their own lives. The reader is forced to 'read' his or her *self* relative to the very specific circumstances in which he or she lives, or relative to concrete actions that are being undertaken. This, too, is a fundamental Socratic characteristic.

UNDERSTANDING SIMONE WEIL

Finding an approach to Simone Weil is an important step towards understanding her and the texts we have which give us access to her way of thinking. But attempting to understand anyone through texts requires 'readings' of those texts, and all readings are from a point of view. Thus to arrive at any common understanding the readings must be somehow shared. Although no *one* reading can be authoritative, our conversations have given us confidence to move towards greater common ground. This common ground is reflected in our essays.

Although it is often argued that Simone Weil's social philosophy reflects an uncompromisingly individualistic point of view stemming from her early anarchistic political outlook, as well as a persistent epistemology that places obstacles in the way of realising any meaningful knowledge of the other, this overlooks the way she

understands the individual in terms of a culture – as formed in a
context by language, traditions, moral and religious practices, and
more. A common consensus in our readings was to see this latter
point very clearly. This is brought out in detail in essays by J. P. Little,
D. Z. Phillips, Diogenes Allen and Eric Springsted. Rowan Williams
is more sceptical as to the success of this aspect of Simone Weil's
project. This point, however, may have easily been lost had we not
reminded each other how carefully she shows the evolution of this
idea through her writing. Winch reveals the movement in her
thought from a Cartesian starting point to a more social view of
language. He writes at the end of his chapter on 'Language':

Here the emphasis is on the role of language in the kinds of life people lead:
the handing down of traditions, the uniting in action and feeling of those
distant from each other, the intimacies of friends and lovers; the discourse
of the soul with itself. Language is part of the essential constitution, so the
suggestion seems to be, of certain distinctive patterns of human life:
patterns formed in the intercourse of people with each other and in their
attempts to see, or give form to their own lives as individuals.[3]

Winch is sure that these ideas were in place, in embryo at least, in
Simone Weil's *Lectures on Philosophy*, and they are clearly developed
in her later writings.

What Winch goes on to do in his book, and which had already
been seen by a number of our group members, sets forward an
approach to her thought from which there seems no turning back –
an approach again which is best understood by keeping Socrates
before our eyes as model philosopher, rather than Plato. Simone
Weil saw a certain 'geometry' to human life.[4] She also saw that
human beings and their societies had distorted this geometry and
thrown it out of balance. Only if we were to seek a balance between
human beings and the natural order in which they live – 'a just
balance' between the two and among human beings in the world –
could the 'geometry' be restored. This balance requires several
things, all of which are reflected in our essays: consent, the power to
refuse, attention to the different readings that human beings give to

---

[3] Winch, p. 58. There is a notable similarity between Simone Weil's view of language and
that of Ludwig Wittgenstein developed independently in the same decade, the 1930s.
Winch makes a great deal of this comparison.

[4] Winch writes: 'The phrase ... from the essay on *The Iliad*: "that interval of hesitation,
wherein lies all our consideration from our brothers in humanity", expresses the possible
growth of a 'geometry' of human life out of certain of our primitive, unreflective reactions to
each other. These reactions are the basis of a possible 'geometry' of human relations', p. 118.

the world and to one another, and an active 'waiting' before God in order to 'draw God down'. Let us explore these things just a bit further.

Consent is fundamental to our human nature; it is 'sacred' says Simone Weil. She gives a graphic example of the violation to our nature that happens in the event that consent is ignored. She writes: 'Rape is a frightful caricature of love without consent. Next to rape oppression is the second horror of human existence. It is a frightful caricature of obedience. Consent is as essential to obedience as it is to love' (*SJ* 3). Because of love's relationship to justice for Simone Weil, consent is also essential to justice, as is shown in my essay.

Our natures as human beings require that we have a certain regard for other human beings, even if such regard requires us to set aside pursuit of our projects, or overcome certain obstacles in such pursuits. This mutual recognition of other human beings comes, in Simone Weil's words, as an 'interval of hesitation, wherein lies all our consideration for our brothers in humanity' (*IL* 14). Such 'intervals of hesitation', Winch notes, can be both of an immediate, unreflective nature, or of a nature that requires more concentrated attention to an object or another human being. This point, says Winch, is 'that the tendency to hesitate in certain circumstances is the seed out of which grow certain kinds of thinking about our fellow human beings'.[5] And, because hesitation is of such a fundamental, almost primordial, nature, it is proper to human knowledge itself. We see this same mechanism working in situations where humans can exercise, or have been denied, their power to refuse. We do not come to such concepts as 'liberty' and 'justice' *after* the fact of tangibly encountering our external world, as many main-line philosophers would argue; rather, Simone Weil is arguing that the very way in which our concepts of human life are formed and applied includes these basic aspirations and values in a very preliminary form – that is, *as* we encounter and 'read' the world we *are* forming our values (see Allen, Phillips, and Andic on this point. Also Winch, chapter 9). We can know another human being only when we recognise for ourselves what being human is.

Part of the recognition of our own humanness lies in the possibility of what Simone Weil calls 'decreation', or in the renunciation of the obstacle of our ego that keeps us from recognising another's situation

---

[5] Winch, p. 108.

except that it might serve our own interest or power. Broader implications of the notion of a 'geometry' of human life are developed in several essays, especially in Little, Williams, Allen, Andic, Devaux, and Springsted.

To advance our understanding of Simone Weil further, as it has emerged from our conversations and is developed through these essays, we must turn to a few central points from the essays themselves. I do not intend a summary of different arguments here, rather, I intend to select what seem to be representative concerns from a few essays. I will then turn to applications of the philosophy of Simone Weil and discuss what new directions they suggest for the thinking of human life in our age.

Although the concept of 'decreation' is one of those near inscrutable notions in Simone Weil, we begin with an essay by J. P. Little on it – not because it is thought to be so impenetrable, but because it is so important in seeing the larger implications of her 'geometry' of human life. In the last months of her life Simone Weil wrote to her friend Maurice Schumann:

I feel an ever increasing sense of devastation, both in my intellect and in the center of my heart, at my inability to think with truth at the same time about the affliction of men, the perfection of God, and the link between the two. (*SL* 178)

As devastating as it seemed to her, she was thinking hard about the link between 'the perfection of God' and 'the affliction of men'. The concept of 'decreation' was at the centre of this linkage.

With this concept we can begin to see the connection between the human order, the order of nature, and what Simone Weil calls the 'supernatural order'. Decreation also focuses our attention on two important themes that run through the essays in this book: (1) how Simone Weil understood the human being, or the *person*, both in this world and in relationship to the supernatural, and (2) how she understood a person's *autonomy* or capacity for freedom and action in the world.

Tied up with decreation are the more traditional notions of God's creation and the human response to it. 'Every idea', says Little, 'to be real, has to find its incarnation.' And the incarnation of the idea of decreation is found in the withdrawing of the self – my becoming non-being – in order to reunite with the being of God. Little summarises this idea in the following way: 'Evil ... is nothing but the distance between God and the creature. Decreation is the suppression of this distance through the death of the autonomous self and the subsequent living presence of the Spirit in the regenerated being.' An important question is who am 'I' as a regenerated being? If I must withdraw from, even destroy, my autonomous self, what role do 'I' – a particular self – have in shaping the world? There is in Simone Weil, says Little, a relentless 'refusal of the anthropocentric perspective', while at the same time wanting to restore a concrete quality of dignity and spirituality to each human being.

Little makes a most original contribution to Weil studies with her analysis of the relationship between 'the soul and decreation' found in a long and very difficult passage from Simone Weil's American notebooks. In this analysis we see the sharpest contrast possible between an autonomous self and a decreated self. We also see the limits to which the notion of a decreated self can be incarnated, and what effects this might have on a world driven by our egos. This sharp contrast, combined with Simone Weil's very understanding of God as 'contradictory', leads Rowan Williams to doubt whether any meaningful concept of a self remains for Simone Weil, and he criticises what he calls 'her difficulties over the love of particulars'.

Williams' reading of Simone Weil, more than anyone else's opens up one of the most difficult notions in her writings to understand, that is: How is *God* to be spoken of. He shows us where Simone Weil has taken us with her conception of God, and, in seeing that, we are brought up short to understand how the absence of God and the absence of the self can co-exist with the presence of God and the presence of the self (or a *subject's* perspective). It is not that this can be simply resolved as strangely paradoxical (this often being a way that readers of Weil explain away difficult notions), rather, it is a stubborn logical and grammatical problem for anyone to think through. Although one might see how God's absence can become a living presence only when we renounce our 'ego-self', it is more difficult to see what a human being is at all if he or she renounces all perspectives from which our world is known. What we know to be human love, even unselfish compassion, loses its grip on the world if 'I' disappear altogether. If 'I'–'not I' become reconstituted through my love for the other, then this love, if true, is really God's love and not 'mine'. Here again we have her 'refusal of an anthropocentric perspective'. Williams offers some possible interpretations – none of which can explain away the difficulties, but each of which offers a number of interesting ways of seeing how her thought actively engages current philosophical and theological questions.

While Williams' analysis may yield negative conclusions about Simone Weil's picture of human nature, these conclusions are counter-balanced in several other essays which attempt to seat the 'subject', or the individual self, and show that an account can be given of what it is to love God *and* the world. This is done through showing the depth of her very analysis and her understanding of this world in all its materiality, and how our attention to this world can have a transformative effect on such issues as human work, justice and love, and the moral reconstitution of human society and community – these three issues, all of which are variations on what Simone Weil calls 'implicit forms of the love of God', are expressed and exercised *through* this world. These counter-balancing issues are taken up respectively by Clare Fischer, myself, and Eric Springsted in our essays in Part II.

The issues set up by J. P. Little and Rowan Williams, in their discussions of decreation and the 'existence' or 'non-existence' of God and the self, are amplified and explored further in the essays in Part I by D. Z. Phillips and Martin Andic. Phillips, for example, takes a different tack from Williams by showing how the concept of God is used in religious practice to form the views of the world human beings have, which incorporate both God's goodness *and* human vulnerability. In fact, Phillips directly challenges one aspect of Rowan Williams interpretation (see pages 88–9 below). Phillips argues that, although there are tensions, even dangers, in the 'unattractive austerity' in some of Simone Weil's remarks which Williams notes, she is not 'turning away' from either the supernatural or the world. Rather, Simone Weil is locating the grammatical context for the meaningful use of both, and their relationship to one another. Phillips shows how 'the concept of God is mediated through the necessities and limitations of human life'. He is concerned about the direction in which Williams' interpretation might take readers of Simone Weil; that it may dissolve the very tension that locates the meaning of God in human life and 'do violence to the grammar of "the divine".' It would, Phillips continues, be a major mistake 'to incorporate the vulnerability of *our relation* to divine love into the grammar of *that divine love itself*. If that is done, we shall fail to see how that love can give a sense to the vulnerability which it could not have otherwise.' Thus the tension between God's unconditional love and our continued vulnerability must remain. In this tension itself, Simone Weil sees 'a legitimate use of contradiction' as 'a sign of truth', as is discussed later in the essay by André Devaux.

I want to remark, finally, relative to our *understanding* of Simone Weil, on her concept of 'reading'. This is touched upon in more or less significant ways by most of the essays in Part I, but explicitly taken up by Diogenes Allen in his essay 'The concept of reading and the Book of Nature', and by Martin Andic in his 'Discernment and the imagination'.

Allen's essay focuses singularly on how we are to understand the ways in which the natural world manifests, or mediates, God's presence according to Simone Weil. Allen asks, with Weil, how can we learn 'to read nature's operations religiously?' To do this, he takes very seriously Simone Weil's analogy between the ordinary act of reading (as in reading a letter) and the reading of nature as this is suggestively worked out in her 'Essay on the Notion of Reading', and in fragments from various later writings. Allen shows how Simone Weil suggests a series of apprenticeships in order to enable us to give more comprehensive readings of the world – each 'higher' or more comprehensive reading enhances our perspective towards a religious reading, or towards one where God becomes more transparent through nature. The point of controversy seen in Little's and Williams' essays is taken up again on the matter of a reader's perspective, be it via self-centred readings or more discerning readings (see Andic on the point of discernment and a 'higher' reading, and on 'non-reading' and perspective or point of view).

Allen's critique, along with the central sections of Andic's study, clearly break new ground. They comprise the most comprehensive and instructive analysis of Simone Weil's concept of reading that is available. Allen's essay offers us a key that unlocks much of Simone Weil's vision of how we can understand our human nature in connection with the created order, and in what sense that created order is connected with a perspective (or non-perspective) of the supernatural that is outside the human and natural orders. Central to this vision, notes Allen, were her experiences with affliction and her religious conversion. The latter experience 'modified her view of how reality is to be known – by being gripped [rather than grasping] – and her view of how individual human value can be sustained'. We will see more, through a variety of applications of Simone Weil's philosophy, of what is required of us to sustain both individual and shared human values.

In the brief concluding essay to Part I, André Devaux catches up many of the difficult issues dealt with above, and sees them all to be a part of Simone Weil's understanding of reality in terms of 'essential contradictions'. Here again the over-arching concern in Simone Weil's thought is linking the natural order with the supernatural. Devaux notes that 'there is a legitimate use of contradiction when the suffering it imposes impels the soul to go higher than the original plane where the opposites were perceived, but to go higher "one must be pulled"'. Resolving essential contradictions, therefore, for Simone Weil, is a question of 'conceiv[ing] of a relationship which transforms contradiction into correlation'. Devaux thus provides a tool for understanding conceptual difficulties such as those which arise when we affirm that God exists and 'necessarily' does not exist, as in the discussion by Williams, and shows the possibility of 'super-imposed readings', explored by Allen and Andic, as a way of seeing how we can love the 'impersonal God' through the 'personal', and the 'personal' through the 'impersonal'. 'Such is "the harmony of opposites"', says Devaux, '... the harmony which consists in "the simultaneous grasping of different things"' (*N* 409).

SIMONE WEIL'S PHILOSOPHY OF CULTURE

Early in 1914, Ludwig Wittgenstein advised his teacher Bertrand Russell – who was about to embark on a lecture-course in America – to take this opportunity 'to tell them your *thought* and not *just* cut and dried results'.[6] The suspicion Wittgenstein had of Russell was that he did not value thought, his own thinking, enough. Wittgenstein had earlier, after attending some lectures in Cambridge of G. E. Moore on psychology, said something similar to Moore. Moore wrote in his diary: '[Wittgenstein] told me these lectures were very bad – that what I ought to do was to say what *I* thought, not to discuss what other people thought; and he came no more to my lectures.'[7] Wittgenstein, himself, believed that integrity and greatness in the academic profession – especially in philosophy – depended on a person doing his or her own thinking, and not resting

---

[6] Ray Monk, *Ludwig Wittgenstein: The Duty of Genius*, New York: The Free Press, 1990, p. 98. Quoted from a letter to Russell from Wittgenstein.

[7] Monk, p. 63.

on others' thoughts. His own *Tractatus* was a brilliant example of a piece of original thought – it was very much a product of his own thinking. Furthermore, Wittgenstein believed that his own work should serve to help others do their own thinking. He wrote in *Culture and Value*: 'I ought to be no more than a mirror, in which my reader can see his own thinking with all its deformities so that, helped in this way, he can put it right.'[8]

It becomes immediately clear to readers of Simone Weil that she, too, did her own thinking. Even if she were criticising another's work, like Descartes or Karl Marx, the stamp of *her* thought was everywhere. Her works also serve as mirrors for us to see our own thinking, especially with all its deformities. It is our job to 'put our thinking right!' This is done, in part, by our thinking with concepts. Another conclusion from reading both Wittgenstein and Weil is that we can no longer be satisfied with 'cut and dried' interpretations, nor can we rest easily if we have not been brought to some thoughts of our own. I believe our collaborative readings and conversations produced a restlessness in each of us, and provided a motivation, even a moral obligation, to think harder about our interpretations and applications of Simone Weil. This is particularly true in our seeing how her thoughts could enable us to have new thoughts – thoughts with a different perspective – about our contemporary cultural situation. The essays in Part II testify to this latter point very clearly.

Eric Springsted's essay is a good example of thinking one's own thoughts with the help of Simone Weil, and applying them to an aspect of contemporary culture. He asks a crucial question for American culture in what may be its waning decades: In the face of our current 'pluralisms' and a 'liberal' morality of the autonomous self held in place only by a fragile external social fabric, how do we put a meaningful life together? Or, as Allen had said, 'how can individual human values be sustained?' He explores Richard Rorty's answer to this question, and points to its limitations. He then proposes a new and radical interpretation of Simone Weil's last London writings, particularly *The Need for Roots*. His thesis is twofold: first, that Simone Weil was not opposed to pluralisms. In fact, given that cultural values are rooted in language, traditions, and, to some extent, local moralities, they are very historically

[8] Ludwig Wittgenstein, *Culture and Value*, ed. G. H. Von Wright, Chicago: University of Chicago Press, and Oxford: Basil Blackwell, 1980, p. 16e.

contingent and variable. This secures the very idea that a global culture, as well as societies with multiple heritages (like American society), will be pluralistic. Furthermore, Springsted supports the view that individual societies may act as vehicles for spirituality and that, if properly rooted in morality, tradition, and truth, they can move towards a spiritual transformation. A second thesis supported by Springsted, and which is consistently upheld throughout most of the essays in this book, is that we form our lives through our human practices, and that for these practices to be meaningful they must be embedded in some concrete reality. This, again, is confirmation of Little's phrase that, for Simone Weil 'every idea, to be real, has to find its incarnation'.

On this second thesis, Springsted argues, the moral part of our lives is rooted in that impersonal, 'uncreated', part of the soul that strives after the good. The striving after the good, however, takes place in a social context, and the context places constraints on the striving. Thus we must do the best we can with our striving to realise the good within the social world. For example, Springsted argues that 'rights' have an important and specific cultural value, and that they link the historically and culturally bound human being with the supernatural virtue of justice through the 'obligations' (moral as well as legal obligations; see also the essay by Collins and Nielsen) that each human being has towards others. This notion he sees as central to understanding *The Need for Roots*. There is some tension between this reading and my interpretation of the distance between 'rights' and 'justice' language in Simone Weil.

Springsted's thesis also takes Peter Winch's contextual interpretation of Simone Weil's philosophy of human action further by giving more shape and substance to the notion of social context itself. He shows how Simone Weil's use of 'supernatural' in connection with moral action and human cultures gives them special significance. Springsted's reading of Weil, on terms like 'God', 'truth', 'justice', and 'love', shows them functioning as 'moral icons' to turn our attention *beyond* our limited public morality.[9] Springsted identifies the 'supernatural' as a centre around which a community can be balanced, and from which it can find motivation for consent. By (or through) being rooted a community draws upon the supernatural. Such a rootedness in culture, Springsted understands as a form of

[9] Springsted's book, *Christus Mediator*, Chico, CA: Scholars Press, 1983, discusses how certain notions in Weil 'mediate' between the supernatural and the natural orders.

primary apprenticeship similar to the apprenticeship in reading noted by Allen. Both Winch and Springsted see the supernatural as embedded in our natural histories, but Springsted's 'supernatural' comes from outside our natural history, and thus is closer to Weil's own emphasis on *incarnation*.

I, too, in 'Reading Simone Weil on rights, justice and love', carry Winch further by developing the notion of justice in connection with love to form what I call 'a new virtue' (a virtue understood as a kind of 'madness' in the eyes of this world) – a supernatural virtue that radically alters the very nature of what it means to be 'striving for the good' within our cultural contexts and communities. Perhaps this 'new virtue' of love and justice is not so far from Springsted's moral icons, 'supernaturally' grounded, which move us beyond the limits of public morality.

Having established the notion of an historically and culturally based context for our human action, it is easier to see the importance of considering Simone Weil's understanding of work (Clare Fischer), the law (Collins and Nielsen), innocence and affliction (Loades), and beauty (Sherry). The essays on these specific notions play a crucial role in rounding out Simone Weil's vision of culture. Simone Weil, for example, envisions 'our age' – and we can say the entire twentieth century – as plagued by human cruelty. Both Ann Loades and H. L. Finch underscore this point. Ann Loades reminds us of why Simone Weil often turned our attention to the *Iliad* and to Greek tragedy, especially to 'Antigone'. 'These texts', Loades says, 'give Simone Weil something of "the density of the real", the density which life offers every day, but which she says "we are unable to grasp because we are amusing ourselves with lies".' And such amusement, Martin Andic shows, is part of how we use our imagination to avoid 'the density of the real'.

In another essay, 'The spirit of Simone Weil's law', Ronald Collins and Finn Nielsen show how her vision of a new society is not conceived in abstraction, but is given to us right down to an account of the place of the subject of law and a specific judicial system. In a very brief summary remark in their essay – an essay that covers a great deal of uncharted territory in Simone Weil – Collins and Nielsen say of her view of law:

Above all, law is a means for transforming the power of arbitrary rule into a system oriented towards the recognition and realisation of human needs, physical and spiritual. Integral to this idea is Weil's notion of obligation.

Since her concept of obligation is two-dimensional, law serves both temporal and transcendental purposes. As to the latter, law is also one means,
along with education, whereby the 'reality *outside* of this world' might be
implanted within the reality *of* this world. From this vantage point, law is
not an end in itself; rather, it points beyond itself.

The connections of her view of law to the whole of her philosophy is
seen clearly in this remark, and we also get a glimpse of how,
through rethinking our notions of law and education, we might
improve the quality of our lives.

The essay by Clare Fischer on 'The civilisation of work' shows a
most urgent and existential argument for the value of applying
Simone Weil's thought to 'our age'. Fischer explores, by comparing
contemporary social philosopher Agnes Heller of the 'Budapest
Circle' with Simone Weil, how their 'joint' critique of work may
open for us possibilities of re-envisioning the world of human work
in such a way that it no longer makes a worker 'homeless'; rather
working in the world becomes transformed to embrace the dignity
of work. A stable world order, thought Simone Weil, requires
meaningful spiritual work, and meaningful spiritual work
requires (according to Weil and supported by Heller): protection
from cruelty, assurance that work will not demean or humiliate a
human being, conditions for greater rational exchange among
workers and between workers and management, a sense of usefulness
to one's society, and some way of making connections between one's
working life and one's family life.

The applicability of these human concerns for the ordinary
worker can be readily seen in the workplaces of Third-World countries, which now resemble the workplaces Simone Weil experienced
sixty years ago. Even in our electronic, micro-chip world, piece-
work has only changed to the degree that the pieces have become
smaller. In the burgeoning service sector of affluent societies, pay
has even lost its meaning as incentive, and demeaning work has
proliferated. The quality of spirituality in work in our post-
industrial setting has only increased the urgency that we make
new diagnoses and find ways to transform the global civilisation of
work.

I want to comment on one final essay from the second Part of this
volume, that is Patrick Sherry's 'On Beauty' – this is not to suggest
that the others which may have been only briefly remarked upon in
this introduction are less worthy. In other essays we see how our

striving for the good within a social context (Springsted, Collins and Nielsen) can mediate the human world with the supernatural, and how justice *with* love can change the human world by transforming human practices to a form of God's love (Bell). These are all examples of what Simone Weil calls *metaxu*. There is, however, a larger order than either society or community and justice and law; this is the order of the world itself in its *beauty*. Sherry says, 'Beauty is more than a creation of God; it is also a *metaxu*, an intermediary which reflects God's nature and attracts the soul to Him: "Thanks to God's wisdom, who has printed on this world the mark of the good, in the form of beauty, one can love Good through the things of this world"' (*FLN* 139). How important it is to see in almost every aspect of Simone Weil's thought that she is trying to show us how 'one can love the Good *through* the things of this world'.

Sherry details how Simone Weil's understanding of beauty as an incarnation of God, and as an attribute of God (as an attribute in which we *see* God), is central to her view of the order of the world and how it can reflect the presence of God in it. He also shows how this diverges from most contemporary philosophical discussions of beauty in aesthetics, where beauty is often totally disregarded or construed merely as an aspect of a thing, like a work of art. The very notion of beauty as a religious concept is an extremely novel idea among twentieth-century philosophers. Her views do, however, direct us towards, and converge with, some new and important developments in theology, namely, theological aesthetics and the revival of Trinitarian theology. Sherry discusses these developments in an informative way.

One interesting remark of Sherry's is that a reason why we have difficulty in attributing beauty to God is 'that we lack a proper vocabulary to support our ascription of beauty to God'. The closest concepts that he can see are 'holiness' and 'true virtue' – both suggested by Jonathan Edwards. The latter, 'true virtue', might help us in understanding Simone Weil's unusual use of the idea of beauty. When she says that 'the beautiful is the experimental proof that the incarnation is possible' (*GG* 137), we might link this up with her new virtue of justice or with friendship, whereby love of one's neighbour or one's friend becomes experimental proof of divine love or of the very presence of God in the world. Such love can be said, with some natural conviction, to be 'beautiful'.

There are, of course, other important concepts in Simone Weil's work that are not explored in these pages. Certain concepts, for example, related to her political philosophy in addition to 'rootedness', 'work', 'rights', 'justice', and 'the law' (taken up here by Springsted, Fischer, Bell, and Collins and Nielsen) are important, such as 'power', 'liberty', and 'oppression' , but these latter concepts have been treated in the recent book, *A Truer Liberty: Simone Weil and Marxism*, by Blum and Seidler (1989).[10] There is one very important notion in Simone Weil that has not been dealt with directly in this book, nor has it been given much extended treatment elsewhere, that should be briefly mentioned, but ultimately left for another conversation. That is her understanding of 'science'. Her discussions of science are found largely in four sources: her early dissertation on 'Science and Perception in Descartes', in *Formative Writings, 1929–1941*, in eight essays on science found in *Science, Necessity, and the Love of God*, in two essays collected in *Intimations of Christianity Among the Ancient Greeks*, and in letters on science to her brother André, which appear in *Sur le science*,[11] but are as yet untranslated.

In the essay 'Classical Science and After,' where we have an overview of her thinking on science, Simone Weil sharply distinguishes classical science (Renaissance through the nineteenth century) from Greek science. The former models itself on work and energy, while the latter models itself on balance or equilibrium, on art and beauty, where 'love, art and science [are] three scarcely separate aspects of the same movement of the soul towards the good' (*SNLG* 16). The subject of Greek science, she says, 'is the relation between order and the conditions for order' (*SNLG* 19). Of classical science, she writes:

Classical science takes as its model for representing the world the relations between a desire and the conditions for its fulfilment, but it suppresses the first term of the relation. This suppression, however, cannot be complete. And that is why classical science bases itself upon linear motion, which is the very image of the project and is the thought of every man who desires to go somewhere, for example, or to seize or hit something or somebody; and upon distance, which is a condition inherent in every desire of a creature

[10] L. A. Blum and V. J. Seidler, *A Truer Liberty: Simone Weil and Marxism*, London: Routledge, 1989, chps. 4, 5, and 7. See also Mary G. Dietz, *Between the Human and the Divine: The Political Thought of Simone Weil*, Totowa, NJ: Rowan and Littlefield, 1988, chps. 3, 4, and 5; and David McLellan, *Simon Weil: Utopian Pessimist*, London: Macmillan, 1989 chapters 4, 5, and 11.

[11] *Sur la Science*, Paris: Gallimard, 1966, contains her student thesis on Descartes, letters to her brother, and later articles on scientific themes.

subjected to time. In such a picture of the world, the good is altogether absent; it is absent to the point where one cannot even find a trace of its absence; for even the deliberately suppressed term of the relation, the term which concerns man, is altogether foreign to the good. Therefore classical science is without beauty; it neither touches the heart not contains any wisdom. (*SNLG* 15f.)

One can see from this passage how central science is to her thinking. She, of course, favours the view of Greek science, and argues that it can interpret the world more wholistically and, she believes, more correctly than classical science.

Of contemporary science – twentieth-century science symbolised by quantum mechanics and relativity theory – she says, 'we don't yet know what it is' (*SNLG* 3); it marks a return to discontinuity – an upsetting idea for classical science. 'Twentieth century science is classical science with something taken away' (*SNLG* 22). There is great caution in her assessment of the value of twentieth-century science, and, of course, her assessment is limited to the perspective we had on contemporary science before World War II.

Her preference for the kind of science which will benefit us most in planning for the future is summed up in this colloquial manner: 'it is frequently more useful to apply to an old countryman rather than to a meteorological institute if one wants to know tomorrow's weather. Cloud, rain, storm, and wind are still today very largely outside the domain where we can replace things with systems defined by ourselves; and who knows if it will not always be so?' (*SNLG* 42).

CONCLUDING REMARKS

By way of summary, I will call Simone Weil's philosophy of culture a form of *pragmatic idealism*. It is *pragmatic* because she asks us continually to discern the character of, and endlessly to struggle against, the debilitating nature of our human world – the ways it humiliates, crushes, politicises, demoralises, and generally destroys the human spirit. It is *idealistic* in that she proposes our only hope in our discernment and struggle is to insinuate the ideal into our real human practices, or, religiously put, to wholly desire the incarnation of divine presence into the everyday actions of our human life – to 'draw God down' into real human affairs. 'Today', wrote Simone Weil, 'after being bemused for several centuries with pride in technical achievement, we have forgotten the existence of a divine

order of the universe. We do not realize that labor, art and science
are only different ways of entering into contact with it' (*OL* 168). It
is this latter point that our 'modern' and 'postmodern' worlds have
forgotten, and it is just that spiritual or divine order that H. L. Finch
argues, in the final essay in this volume, is our only hope for some
form of cultural salvation.

Simone Weil has been characterised as a 'utopian pessimist.'[12]
She was rather more like a 'pragmatic idealist'. Though such
general descriptive notions as these do not really open out her
thought properly (and perhaps risk short-circuiting the hard work
her philosophy demands of its readers), they do give us a place to
begin tracing out themes in her writings. Her idealism, for example,
enables us to see her emphasis on the transcendent, derived from
Plato, and her latter-day Christian mystical strain. The transcendent, however, is only meaningful for her in so far as it is
incarnate in human practices, in the 'readings' we give to one
another as human beings, and in recognising imperatives like
consent, friendship, and love. Thus all that she thinks about, writes
about, and all that she lived towards in her short life was to specific
pragmatic ends; they were aimed at bringing greater peace, justice,
harmony, and beauty into human affairs.

Since every idea, for Simone Weil, has to find its incarnation, and
since in terms of our human practices love of our neighbour is 'proof'
of God's presence in the world, our very humanity, when truly
realised, is an expression of divine love, order, justice, and beauty.
This goes along with her refusal of an anthropocentric perspective.
In fact, in a very real way, when we are not constrained to live a lie,
we have in Simone Weil's philosophy of culture both the hope for,
and the possibility that we can become, in Finch's words, educators
and spokespersons for a 'divine humanity'.

Late in Wittgenstein's life he remarked: 'When you are philo-
sophizing you have to descend into primeval chaos and feel at home
there.'[13] You could hardly find a more accurate description of
Simone Weil's 'philosophising'. There are so many moments that
her way of putting something, or her way of taking you through a
difficult thought, makes you feel at home; there is a flash in which
'the penny drops', when the human order suddenly becomes per-

---

[12] This is the characterisation given Simone Weil by David McLellan in his biography of her,
Simone Weil: Utopian Pessimist.
[13] *Culture and Value*, p. 65e.

spicuous. That happens, however, because you have descended deeply into 'primeval chaos' and surfaced into some new clarity. The 'primeval chaos' of Simone Weil's world is the world of Greek poetry and tragedy and Greek philosophy; it is the world of St John of the Cross and Meister Eckhart; it is the world of a radically incarnational Christology without dogma; it is the world of Descartes, Kant, Racine, Alain and René Le Senne; it is the world of the *Bhagavad-Gita* and Zen Buddhism; it is the world of folklore and mythology; it is the world of resistance and revolution – a search for the Grail through a half century of great human affliction. It is into that chaos that you descend when you read Simone Weil. We believe that this book may serve as a guide through some of that chaos, with the sole aim of making us all feel more at home.

André Devaux affirms Simone Weil's preference for a 'Socratic' oriented philosophy that follows an 'interrogative method' over a systematic one 'whose value consists only in a certain poetic beauty' (*FW* 288). The former kind of philosophy and the one embodied in Simone Weil, says Devaux, is oriented towards 'an intellectual salvation which can be seen as a prelude to spiritual salvation'. This is precisely the method embraced by Simone Weil when she wrote, for a class of secondary-school girls, her essay on 'The Right Use of School Studies with a View to the Love of God'. Here the remedial task of correcting errors, giving undivided attention to a geometry problem and, finally, attending absolutely to a human being caught in the web of life's circumstances carries with it the possibility of a transformation from intellectual to spiritual salvation.

Simone Weil became a citizen of many worlds. Her thought, drawing upon diverse sources in search of the truth, points us both within ourselves and beyond ourselves; it at once collapses into one and keeps in tension the human order and the divine. Furthermore, it has drawn us in our conversations into a more intense contact with *reality* – a *reality* that must not lose sight of the significance of the spiritual. It is in this spirit that Simone Weil might have said with Wittgenstein that 'what is good is also divine. Queer as it sounds, that sums up my ethics. Only something supernatural can express the Supernatural.'

PART I

Readings: the grammar of the divine and the human

CHAPTER I

Simone Weil's concept of decreation

J. P. Little

Simone Weil's idea of decreation is one of great richness and complexity, and appears throughout the writings of her mature years, most particularly in the *Notebooks*. It is also an idea that tends to cause problems for readers of Simone Weil, and one that is most frequently rejected in an assessment of her philosophy as a whole. It has been given serious consideration by a number of scholars, however: Miklos Vetö, in his seminal work *La Métaphysique religieuse de Simone Weil*,[1] sees it as being at the heart of her metaphysics, while noting that the term is a neologism created by Péguy, who used it in a diametrically opposite sense.[2] More recently, Béatrice-Clémentine Farron-Landry, in a series of articles published in the *Cahiers Simone Weil*, brings out the importance of this concept within the framework of her mysticism.[3] Notably, she relates Simone Weil's thinking

[1] Paris: Vrin, 1971, 168pp. In the notes, the abbreviation *CSW* designates the *Cahiers Simone Weil: Revue trimestrielle publiée par l'Association pour l'étude de la pensée de Simone Weil* (Paris, 1978–).

[2] Vetö, *La Métaphysique*, p. 19. It is also used by Gabriel Bounoure in an article on Pierre Reverdy, also giving it a sense very different from that understood by Simone Weil. 'Ce qui avait été espéré de l'opération poétique, une création, la création d'un objet plus réel et plus vrai, n'était qu'une décréation, un exil des choses et un exil de la conscience parmi les choses en morceaux.' 'Pierre Reverdy et sa crise religieuse de 1925–27,' *Mercure de France: Pierre Reverdy (1889–1960)*, 1962, quoted by Andrew J. Rothwell, *Textual Spaces: the Poetry of Pierre Reverdy*, Amsterdam: Rodopi, 1989, p. 178. Rolf Kühn, in 'Le Monde comme texte, Perspectives herméneutiques chez Simone Weil', *Revue de Sciences Philosophiques et Théologiques*, 64 (1980), pp. 509–30, notes its use also by D. de Rougemont, Maurice Blanchot, S. Breton, and P. Ricoeur, and makes convincing parallels (p. 520) with certain aspects of Lagneau's philosophy which were certainly known by Simone Weil. He also traces affinities with Bachelard's *déréalization* and *déconstruction*, J. Monchanin's *décentration* and M. Deguy's *désignification*, as well as, in German, Eckhart's *Entwerdung*, J. G. Fichte's *Entdisparatmachung*, P. L. Berger's *Eng-Entfremdung*, and V. Frankl's *Dereflexion* (p. 511, n. 10). Kühn's article is a fruitful study of several of the themes treated in this volume, notably decreation and reading.

[3] 'Détachement, renoncement et origine du mal selon Simone Weil', *CSW*, 1:2 (June 1979), pp. 71–83; 'Notes introductives sur le vide, ou la nuit obscure selon Simone Weil', *CSW*, 6:3

on the subject to that of the Neptic Fathers, whose writings, dating
from the fourth to the fourteenth century, were assembled in the
eighteenth century under the title *Philocalia*. According to Jacques
Touraille, translator of this volume, their notion of 'hesychia' can
best be rendered by 'decreation'.[4] Georges Charot has also given the
idea attention in his 'La "décréation" comme méthode psychologi-
que de construction de "l'âme créée" chez Simone Weil'.[5]

In the course of this essay, I want to show that, if the idea is
negative in appearance – its very form is clearly negative, and the
emotional charge invested in our perception of the term 'creation'
tolerates with difficulty the privative 'de-' – it is only in appearance,
and through a kind of paradox. Many of Simone Weil's most
striking insights depend on the use of paradox, either explicit or
implicit, and it is of extreme importance not to neglect this in
assessing the value, and indeed the sense, of Simone Weil's ideas.[6]
Thus, for example, access to knowledge of the real is through
recognition of the impossibility of such access. It should be borne in
mind also that, since for Simone Weil decreation was in some
respects only the recognition of the actual status of the created
being, and therefore a way of avoiding error, it was for her, in her
passionate commitment to the truth, a profoundly liberating
experience.

Another indication of the positive force of the idea for Simone
Weil is the way in which many of her most important ideas make no
sense unless the concept of decreation is taken seriously. Her ideas on
beauty, justice, love of one's neighbour, are incomprehensible
without the presupposition of this state. Virtually every area she
touched is implicated here, and it is therefore not possible to retain
these other ideas while rejecting the idea of decreation.

A further reason why the idea is significant is because, paradoxically, it brings out the immense importance of the physical and the
material for Simone Weil. There is perhaps no other area of her
thought where she attempts to come to terms so fully and so sys-

(September 1983), pp. 243–8; 'Décréation: l'attention-hesychia chez Simone Weil, témoin
de l'impossible: I', *CSW*, 12:1 (March 1989), pp. 52–63; 'Décréation: Simone Weil, témoin
de l'impossible (fin)', *CSW*, 12:2 (June 1989), pp. 170–5.

[4] Touraille, article in *Contact, Revue Orthodoxe de Théologie et de Spiritualité*, 33:113, pp. 49–50,
quoted in Farron-Landry, 'Décréation: l'attention-hesychia chez Simone Weil, témoin de
l'impossible', p. 54.

[5] *CSW*, 10:1 (March 1987), pp. 41–53.

[6] See J. P. Little, 'Contribution à une étude de l'usage du paradoxe chez Simone Weil', *CSW*,
2:2 (June 1988), pp. 105–14.

tematically with the material existence of human beings and creation as a whole. It therefore acts as a useful counterbalance to the tendency in some readers to see in Simone Weil a refusal of the physical, of incarnation in its most general sense, and a commitment to the abstract.

The point is immediately illustrated when we turn to the idea itself, and ask what exactly decreation is for Simone Weil. At its most basic level, it is our response to our creation by God, a reflection of the act of creation itself. It will be recalled that for Simone Weil creation is an act, not of expansion on God's part, but of abdication. God in creation, by allowing the existence of other creatures, refuses to be everything (*FLN* 120, 297). Creation is therefore seen in terms of sacrifice, of suffering, of rupture, and the Incarnation and Passion of Christ, far from being opposed as in traditional Christian theology, are merely two aspects of the same process. The separation of God from God in the Incarnation of the Son is a reflection of the original rift created in the divine existence through the coming into being of creatures other than God. It is to the initial act of creation that decreation is a response. I am, says Simone Weil, God's abdication, and the more I insist on being, the more God abdicates (*FLN* 213). To allow the full existence of God once more, it is therefore necessary for me to reproduce God's initial abdication, by refusing to be (*FLN* 213), and by destroying a part of myself. But I can destroy only what belongs to me: everything that I usually regard as belonging to me, which I recognise as an identifiable self, is subject to chance, and can be modified or destroyed without my consent (*FLN* 217), is, in fact, outside my control, everything, that is, except my will as an autonomous being. The gift of free will is itself, she says, creation (*FLN* 211). It is this autonomy alone that must be sacrificed in response to God's initial sacrifice. This is what Simone Weil calls 'moral death', or decreation, the acceptance of everything that is, has been, or will be, independent of my particular desires. Accepting to be a creature and only that is the same as accepting the extinction of the autonomous self (*FLN* 217). It will be obvious that this extinction of the self restores the original unity of God without creation, and in referring to it one comes up against a very real problem of language: how does one refer to a perspective, that is to say, God's perspective pre-creation or post-decreation, that is non-positional and therefore not truly a perspective at all? Our language cannot cope with perception that does not imply a limited perceiver.

The difficulty will be apparent at several points in this essay, where I have adopted terms such as 'non-perspective', 'God's perspective', 'the perspective beyond perspective'.

It is immediately clear that Simone Weil's doctrine of creation has implications far beyond mere speculation. If she posits creation as God's withdrawal, it is only to ask immediately: what is my response to this act? No idea is ever left on the level of mere abstraction, but has implications for our activity in the world. This observation illustrates forcefully the existential nature of Simone Weil's thought, and the way every idea, to be real, has to find its incarnation. Indeed, she claims, we start in our experience of the world, and our perceptions are at the root of our concepts about it.[7] Matter, she says, is the infallible judge of the real in thought (*FLN* 364). It also helps to explain perhaps the form in which so much of Simone Weil's thinking on decreation is expressed. Our human response to God, decreation replying to creation, amounts to an almost necessary reciprocity, a symmetry indicative of Simone Weil's need in this, as in many other areas of her thought, to restore a balance that has been disturbed by the assertion of the autonomous self. Examples abound: the creature, by allowing itself to be created, preferred itself to God. It redeems itself by asking God to destroy it (*FLN* 123). Or again, God abdicated his divine omnipotence and 'emptied' himself. By abdicating our limited human power, we become equal to God in 'emptiness' (*FLN* 297). One might contrast this, however, with Simone Weil's condemnation of attempts to restore a balance on a merely rational level, for example 'The search for balance is bad because it is imaginary' (*N* 140), imagination being a 'filler of voids'.

Many of these formulations relate to an extension of the decreation theme, and one which immediately implies the sense of paradox. It also illustrates the way in which decreation for Simone Weil is related to truth, and to a perception of the real. For, she says, although I believe I am giving up something by consenting to be decreated, in fact this is an illusion, since as a creature I am in fact nothing. Hence, linking again creation and incarnation, 'Adam made us believe that we had being: Christ showed us that we are non-beings' (*FLN* 218). Again, 'To teach us that we are non-being, God made himself non-being' (*FLN* 218). Or: 'For God, sacrifice consists in letting man believe that he has being. For a man, sacrifice

---

[7] See D. Z. Phillips, 'God and Concept-Formation in Simone Weil', in the present volume, pp. 78–80.

consists in recognising that he is non-being' (*FLN* 218). Creation, she says, is 'a fiction of God's'. When we adopt God's perspective, therefore, what appeared to be being is in fact non-being, and accepting the status of creature is recognising this fact. But the very acceptance of this is to accede to a higher reality: 'God created me as a non-being which has the appearance of existing in order that through love I should renounce this apparent existence and be annihilated by the plenitude of being' (*FLN* 96). There is a clear opposition here between 'being' and 'existence', to which I shall have cause to return later. In the meantime it should be noted that, in her consideration of the true nature of the created being, Simone Weil warns against a kind of 'false humility': it is not a question of perceiving that one is nothing in terms of such and such an individual being, but in terms of a created being itself. The rational creature is one who contains the vocation of decreation within him or herself (*N* 275).

The realisation of my true status in the universe is the basis for a new perception of things, and it is this perception that explains in large measure some of Simone Weil's rather terse formulations. The autonomous 'I' is source only of error, and it is in this sense that the impersonal is the only access to the truth. 'I' do not create truth, I can only bring myself into conformity with it. In a mathematical calculation, for example, my individual self only comes into play when I make a mistake. Two plus two equals four, independent of my will or my personality, and it is only if they make five that the result bears my individual stamp. It is the same reasoning that explains her well-known remark 'To say "I" is to lie' (*FLN* 132), in so far as when what I say is conditioned by my individual desires and projections, it cannot be concordant with absolute truth. When I act only as a passage for reality from the outside, whether this be facts about the universe, or reflections on those facts, truth can, at least potentially, be there. On the other hand, 'I am absent from everything which is true, or beautiful, or good. I sin' (*N* 126).

It is important here to appreciate the tone of such formulations: there is no regret, no self-deprecation, only a lucid realisation that, if the incommensurability of the autonomous self and the truth is accepted, one is in fact in the truth, and therefore in the most desirable state possible. That this is not merely a form of playing with ideas is indicated in a related passage in the *Notebooks*, where she speaks of

> The beauty of a landscape just at the moment when nobody is
> looking at it, absolutely nobody . . .
> To see a landscape such as it is when I am not there.
> When I am anywhere, I pollute the silence of earth and sky
> with my breathing and the beating of my heart.   (*N* 423)

The poignant urgency of this exclamation echoes the dying lines of
Racine's Phèdre.[8] (We know that Simone Weil considered Racine
to be in a state of grace when he wrote *Phèdre*.) It also calls to mind in
an interesting way contemporary theories of perception, which take
account of the fact that the object of perception is indeed changed, if
not 'polluted', by the perceiver, as a result of the exchange of energy
between the two. Is it also too fanciful to see in Simone Weil's
preoccupation with purifying the universe from the imperialistic 'I',
a forerunner of much of our present-day thinking on the environment?

Our somewhat tardy concern with the ecology of the planet stems
surely from the same urge to curb the predations of the human ego.
Would not Simone Weil have applauded the current desperate
attempt to save Antarctica, the last true 'wilderness', the last area of
the globe not yet (totally) despoiled by humankind? Simone Weil
frames her point aesthetically, the ecologists scientifically, but their
common inspiration asserts the absolute value of phenomena, irre-
spective of their use to humanity. One could also evoke Gaia theory
at this point, the view of our planet developed by James Lovelock,
which sees the earth as a living organism, a self-sustaining and
interacting whole, in which no individual part is more important
than any other.[9] Thus human life is not privileged over other forms,
and the anthropocentric perspective of even a certain number of the
ecologists – the motive in saving the planet is after all frequently to
conserve it for future generations – simply becomes redundant. Gaia
has no need of human beings, and their disappearance would not
destroy her. They have the same status as any other part of creation.
The same refusal of the anthropocentric perspective is found in
Simone Weil, who emphasises the goodness of material creation, as
part of the Creator's design. Its essential purity and independence
from humankind is underlined in the following passage:

[8] *Phèdre*, act V, scene 7: 'Et la mort, à mes yeux dérobant la clarté,/Rend au jour, qu'ils
souillaient, toute sa pureté.'
[9] James Lovelock, *Gaia, A New Look at Life on Earth*, Oxford: OUP, 1982, and *The Ages of Gaia*,
Oxford, OUP, 1989. This connection suggests to the editor that there would be resonances
between Simone Weil's thinking here and current discussions of 'deep' or 'spiritual' ecology.

I do not in the least desire that I should no longer be able to feel this created world, but that it should not be to me personally that it is made sensible. To me it cannot confide its secret, which is too lofty. But if only I go away, then creation and Creator will be able to exchange their secrets. (*N* 422)

Implicit in these passages, of course, is the idea that viewing a landscape from the absence of perspective brought about by decreation, that is, when 'I' am not there, is at least a theoretical possibility. She cites Giotto and Cézanne as painters who worked from this renunciation of perspective, artists whose autonomous self did not come between the subject to be painted and the result on the canvas. Cézanne's 'Je pars neutre' (I start from a neutral position) is a clear statement of his intentions in this respect. There is a revealing passage in the *Notebooks* which suggests that this distancing of self from the object of perception is both revealer of reality and source of true joy: 'Joy is directed towards an object. I am full of joy at the sight of the sun shining, or the moon over the sea, or a beautiful city, or a fine human being; no "I" obtrudes itself in the fulness of joy'. Suffering, however, is a result of the I-perspective:

On the other hand, 'I' suffer.
Joy is the consciousness of that which is not me *qua* human being. Suffering is the consciousness of myself *qua* nothingness. (*N* 291)

Because the change involved in decreation is one of perspective only, nothing is lost in terms of exterior reality when the creature consents to decreation. This is made clear in Simone Weil's reflections on the nature of necessity. Necessity is an enemy for the person who says 'I', she says (*FLN* 88): the autonomous self keeps us shut into necessity, and we see it only as brutal domination. By renouncing the autonomous 'I', the decreated self passes to 'the other side', and what appeared to be domination becomes docility, obedience (*FLN* 90). From a 'reading' of necessity that interprets it as hostile and malevolent, I pass to a state beyond 'reading', or 'a reading of non-reading', as Martin Andic puts it.[10] God does not 'read', since God has no perspective: reading is always mediated through phenomena, and in a universe where individual creatures have abandoned their autonomy, mediation is not necessary to God.[11]

[10] Martin Andic, 'Discernment and the imagination', in the present volume, below.
[11] On the relationship of reading to perspective, see Diogenes Allen, 'The Concept of Reading and the Book of Nature', *passim*, in the present volume.

It is clear that there is a process of rupture here: the decreated self is radically different from the autonomous 'I', in that the former is total absorption into the divine will, whereas the latter is opposition to that will. Continuity between the two states is supplied, not by the continuance of the autonomous self into the regenerated one, but rather through what Simone Weil terms the 'uncreated part' of the soul, that 'infinitely small' part which, in the soul's natural state, constitutes its relationship with goodness. As Eric Springsted points out,[12] Simone Weil rejects the 'metaphysical self' of the Personalists, on the grounds firstly that persons belong to the realm of necessity, and obey its laws, and secondly, that, through locating what is most precious in a human being in this metaphysical core, the Personalists fail to protect that being as such: Simone Weil was too acutely conscious of the power of affliction not to know that it could, and frequently did, turn a person into a mere object.[13] If, on the other hand, the essential part of a human being is located in the desire for good, the soul's only operation is to consent to that good, a consent which is seen more as a refusal to be discouraged by the pain and apparent confusion of the invading universe, than an act of will *per se*. Simone Weil's image of waiting *en hupomene* conveys much better the active passivity of her spiritual stance than the more muscular concept of willed consent. Simone Weil's belief was that, provided there was no betrayal on the part of the soul, grace and goodness would inevitably descend and operate the regeneration process. This new non-perspective is thus not an 'alternative' reading, but brought about necessarily by the steadfast desire of the uncreated part of the soul turned towards goodness. In this way, Simone Weil's notion of the decreated, regenerated self forms a critique of the Personalists' metaphysical self, being a form of mediation between the good which sustains its being, and necessity in which it continues to operate.

An essential element in this new way of non-reading is our attitude towards time, which is for Simone Weil the most basic, and also the most problematic, form of necessity. It is the realm of the autonomous self *par excellence*, since 'I' cannot help but project back and forth in time, trying to reorganise reality to suit my particular desires. I can change the past in imagination, project my will onto

[12] Eric Springsted, 'Rootedness: culture, and value', in the present volume, below.
[13] Cf. the essay '*The Iliad* or the poem of force' in *Intimations of Christianity among the ancient Greeks*, London: Routledge and Kegan Paul, 1957, pp. 24, 26.

the future, plan and organise as if the future belonged to me. In fact, says Simone Weil, I possess only the present moment, and since this moment cannot be stopped, seized or otherwise prevented from becoming immediately past, I am in a real sense nothing (cf. N 71). All sin, she claims, is an attempt to escape from time (*FLN* 102): the pride of the flesh is the belief that it has power over the future, that being hungry gives it the right to eat, being thirsty the right to drink. Privation teaches that this is not the case, and that the individual is powerless faced with the uncertainty of the future (*FLN* 101). This deliberate fixing of limits to desire is, she says, a source of secret and fulfilling joy, and, characteristically, in another passage she uses again the concept of food as a concrete illustration: eating bread when one is hungry is a form of communion with the universe and its creator, provided that the desire thus satisfied is subordinated to strict limits, and the satisfaction felt as precarious (*FLN* 135). Matter in the form of food, far from being rejected by Simone Weil, can thus become a kind of sacrament. It is important to underline this, since the assumption often made is that Simone Weil was at best indifferent, at worst hostile, to the idea of physical nourishment. On the contrary, it was a matter of considerable importance to her, one on which it was necessary to take a stand: if she felt that it was somehow immoral to eat one's fill, it was precisely because so many people in the world were starving. But at the same time she maintains that you can tell that a society is becoming decadent by the way that it fails to maintain its culinary tradition in a state of purity: she notes with displeasure, albeit ironically, the way in which the English have adulterated their apple '*compote*' by adding custard or gelatine, to make a 'fruit fool' (*SL* 189, 200). In the same way bread, that most basic of Western foodstuffs, can be a matter of great cultural and symbolic importance: as inanimate object, it does not change, but its relationship to the one who eats it is totally different according to the perspective adopted. 'Daily bread' is 'the food of the humble soul' (*FLN* 102), in the sense that we have already noted: humility is the acceptance of creaturely status, and the refusal to grasp at illusory power over the future. That this is a liberating experience is illustrated by the following argument: if one desires a particular thing, one becomes a slave of the sequence of events and conditions. But if one desires simply this sequence, the satisfaction of this desire is unconditional. Loving the world order is therefore the only liberation (*FLN* 143–4).

It is one thing to describe the abolition of perspective that takes place when the soul has been decreated. It is another entirely, however, to give an account of how this happens. It is characteristic of Simone Weil's thinking that she gives many pointers, scattered mainly through the *Notebooks*, as to the process which the soul undergoes in order to be decreated. She was always intensely interested in process: if she appreciated many aspects of social thinkers such as Machiavelli and Marx, it was because they had subjected society to rigorous analysis, to find out how it worked. Her own analysis of industrial society, contained in the essays of *Oppression and Liberty*, is a model of response to the same imperative. In the spiritual domain also she admired St John of the Cross for the way he analysed the stages of the soul's spiritual development. Thus it is not surprising to find her giving a meticulous account of the way in which decreation takes place, in terms of the respective parts of the soul and differing forms of energy which it produces. The account figures in a long passage in the American notebooks, and I shall try now to outline its essential elements. It should be noted, however, that what Simone Weil is constructing here is a myth: she was trying to give form to extremely complex and fertile ideas, and the mythical form is clearly the one she felt most appropriate. There is therefore no question, for her or for her readers, of having to give intellectual assent to these ideas. Like other 'mysteries', they are to be contemplated for the light they throw on the relationship between human beings and God.

THE SOUL AND DECREATION

To draw some of the threads together, then, in Simone Weil's view, the soul is divided into two unequal parts, the natural, 'created' part, and a much smaller, sometimes infinitesimally small part, which she called the 'supernatural' or the 'uncreated' part. In creation, Simone Weil says, God abandoned every being to necessity, except for this uncreated part, which 'is himself'. It is 'the Life, the Light, the Word' (*FLN* 103). This uncreated part has only one function with regard to normal terrestrial life, and that is to consent to every moment of every event that comes along, and to consent to it not only for the present, but indefinitely – or, alternatively, to consent to its immediate and irreparable loss (*FLN* 219–20). The other, natural part of the soul is carried along by events, sustained by what Simone Weil calls 'supplementary energy', or 'animal energy'. If the energy required to sustain the forward movement of the soul in time is more than that available – the implication is that this refers to particularly difficult and unbearable circumstances – the supplementary energy is used up, and the natural part of the soul cries out 'Enough!' What provokes this cry is the laying bare of the other form of energy, what Simone Weil calls 'vegetative energy', that which is used to sustain life itself. It is intolerable that that too should start to be worn away, and the natural part of the soul cries out in protest. The role of the tiny, 'uncreated' part of the soul is then to reply 'I consent to this continuing for ever'. The relationship of the parts of the soul and of the different forms of energy to time is of importance here. Supplementary energy is on the level of time, and that is what allows us to handle difficult situations, by saying 'this won't last more than an hour' (*FLN* 220). This is the energy that projects into the future, that feeds desire and the will. Vegetative energy, on the other hand, is 'beneath' time, so that when supplementary energy is used up, a quarter of an hour seems like eternity, since there is no escape in imagination. Although Simone Weil frequently talks of the divisions of the soul as if they were permanent, she suggests here that it is at this moment that the soul 'divides' – provided, that is, that the entire soul does not associate itself with the cry of revolt produced by the intolerable circumstances.

There are still for Simone Weil two potential escape-routes, such is the soul's tenacious hold on life. Firstly, what she calls the 'spirit of sporting competition', the desire to win over circumstances (of which she accused Roman Stoicism: *FLN* 221) can enable an individual to bear almost anything. Secondly, there is always the possibility of supplementary energy being renewed. If the Prodigal Son had invested his money instead of wasting it on prostitutes, he would never have come home to his father (*FLN* 221). It is important, therefore, that the supplementary energy is entirely used up. At this point the soul makes a choice – Simone Weil's images of paradise or hell clearly represent good and evil – and that choice has eternal consequences. The notion of pure, unconditional good enters the soul, and the soul either accepts or rejects it. If the good is accepted, the soul then starts to deflect the vegetative energy used for sustaining life towards God. This, says Simone Weil, is spiritual death, where the soul is, as it were, consumed in offering to God.

The two parts of the soul then play a different role: the suffering experienced by the natural, 'carnal' part of the soul, which has sinned, is transferred on to the 'eternal' part, which is innocent, and which then suffers on behalf of the natural part, and 'justifies' it, as Simone Weil puts it. What then follows is a mystical reflection of the original act of creation. The composition of the soul as it existed in the finite sphere disappears, and the soul divides into an unlimited and a limiting part. Primordial chaos is reproduced, the 'original waters over which the Spirit moves'. Between the two parts of the soul lies now the totality of time, time being 'the sword that cuts the soul in two'. After that, says Simone Weil, there is 'a new creation', which the soul accepts out of love for other creatures, just as the original creation was a result of God's love. The new creation is a form of incarnation, and those who accept to be created thus are 'born from on high', formed 'of water and the Spirit'.

The word 'decreation' is nowhere used in this account, but it is clear that this is the process that Simone Weil is describing. I have given her account in some detail, because it illustrates both the tremendous fertility of the idea, and some of the problems that accompany it. It is clear that the 'regeneration' of the soul is an ideal state – Simone Weil herself refers to 'perhaps one person saved in a generation' – but nevertheless an ideal capable of producing at least a lesser good. It is also apparent that the being thus produced has a function in the real world, and that physical death is not necessarily envisaged. What also emerges clearly is the innocence of matter: what is being destroyed is the autonomous self, the natural part of the soul, which is sustained by supplementary energy. The body as matter has, in fact, an eminently worthy role, according to Simone Weil, which is to act as a balance, restoring equilibrium between the two parts of the soul (*FLN* 230, 300). Where evil exists, it is not through matter, but through the existence of the autonomous self: she in fact refers to 'God's great crime against us', which is 'to have created us', it is our very existence. Conversely, our great crime against God is to have accepted existence (*FLN* 263). The theme of the crime implicit in creation itself is maintained elsewhere: 'We can exist only as criminals', she declares (*FLN* 263). 'We have stolen a little of God's being to make it ours. God has made us a gift of it. But we have stolen it' (*FLN* 269). What is creation from God's point of view, that is to say, renunciation through love, is sin from the point of view of the creature (*FLN* 211). In a characteristic sequence, she maintains 'Our sin consists in wanting to be, and our punishment is that we believe we possess being. Expiation is desiring to cease to be; and salvation consists for us in perceiving that we are not' (*FLN* 218). In a clear reference to the process outlined above, she suggests that God continually asks us if we want to be created, and we reply 'yes', except for certain individuals whose soul is divided into two parts, where the tiny eternal part of the soul cries 'no'. If the cry is maintained, says Simone Weil, this tiny part grows, and one day invades the whole soul (*FLN* 211). Evil, therefore, is nothing but the distance between God and the creature. Decreation is the suppression of this distance (*N* 342) through the death of the autonomous self and the subsequent living presence of the Spirit in the regenerated being. This regenerated state is thus source of true joy: 'If one finds the fullness of joy in the thought that God *is*, one must find the same fullness in the knowledge that oneself one is not, for it is the same thought' (*N* 291).

Although I believe, as I say, that decreation is not necessarily accompanied by death, it could be an appropriate moment to examine the whole question of death and destruction in relation to Simone Weil's idea (it is surely significant that the above quotation from the *Notebooks* ends '... this knowledge is only bestowed on the sensibility through suffering and death'). Firstly, Simone Weil is emphatic that suicide is a false imitation of decreation, since it is an act of the will. The creature did not create itself, and it is not up to it to destroy itself (*N* 404). It appears that Simone Weil contemplated suicide for herself at one point, in the event of her being totally incapacitated by her illness, but there is no suggestion that she looked on this as a form of decreation.[14] As to her actual death, many hypotheses have been put forward, and it is doubtless impossible to be totally sure of her motivation. In some ways it would, however, seem to be explicable as the very opposite of decreation. She herself was desperate to share the lot of her fellow-countrymen in Occupied France, convinced that to be where the suffering was greatest was both her personal vocation and a contact with reality. This sense of vocation, she says, overrode all her normal human instincts, because on a personal level the idea frightened and horrified her, even though she told Father Perrin that every time she thought of the crucifixion of Christ she committed the sin of envy

[14] Simone Pétrement, *La Vie de Simone Weil*, II, Paris: Fayard, 1973, pp. 206–7.

(*WG* 83), illustrating the depth of her desire, in spite of the demands of her 'lower' self, to be 'in the truth'. But she remained convinced that no one can seek out affliction voluntarily. Obedience to this perceived vocation was an absolute imperative for her, and to appear to ignore it the greatest evil. Participation in a 'front-line' capacity amidst the affliction of war-time could well be read as a situation of potential decreation for her, therefore, where the little supplementary energy she had remaining would gradually be worn away. This situation was not to be hers, however: she was given a 'safe' job in an office, where all too quickly ideological conflicts came to the fore, and she resigned, only partly through her ill-health, feeling she had nothing further to offer in that sphere. It would seem, then, from a certain point of view, that hers was a vocation of decreation that was doomed to be frustrated.

Looked at in another perspective, however, an office job in London could be interpreted as potentially the most decreative situation of all: if in a sense she could not 'choose' to put herself in a situation of great danger, because the animal part of her refused such peril, she was even less capable of 'choosing' relatively safe London as a place to spend the war, since it seemed so contrary to what she saw as her vocation. True decreation, in her own terms, must mean the abandonment of I-centred acts of will, and hence the acceptance of what is, including situations from which there is apparently no escape. It is at least arguable that there was for her more I-saying left in a dangerous situation than in a relatively safe one. To say this, however, involves recognising the paradox that the I that willed the situation in which it would be fulfilled was also the I that would be destroyed by it. In fact, so intense and so consistent was her sense of vocation to be where the affliction was greatest, and so intimate the working-out of its implications in real-life situations, that it is perhaps not possible to reach a clear conclusion to the matter.[15]

Much clearer is the situation regarding the death of other people, and destruction in general. The acceptance of death is a necessary part of consent to the order of the world, a form of detachment which should be practised quite consciously, so that, for example,

[15] For other interpretations of her death, see Pétrement, II, pp. 501–4, and Maurice Schumann, *La Mort née de leur propre vie*, Paris: Fayard, 1974, pp. 61–106, and 'L'Expérience religieuse de Simone Weil' in *Simone Weil: La Soif de l'absolu*, edited by J. P. Little and A. Ughetto, Marseille: Sud, 1990, pp. 33–4.

Simone Weil says that when thinking of an absent loved one, one should think of them as possibly dead (N 218). In other words, death here is merely part of the world-order to which the decreated soul consents, and is in no way to be sought for its own sake. Destruction, on the other hand, is not something to which one consents, and is always and everywhere wrong. It is never any more than a 'false imitation of decreation' (N 247), the 'extreme opposite of decreation' (N 342). In terms of other people, the conscious or unconscious moral destruction present in throwing others into a state of affliction is totally evil in Simone Weil's view. Decreation can take place only from the inside, and the greatest crime one can commit against a fellow human being is to destroy his or her autonomy from the outside, so that he or she is no longer in a position to consent to the process of decreation. A long analysis in the Marseilles *Notebooks* (N 337–9) of what happens when an individual's autonomous self is destroyed from the exterior shows the importance she attached to this idea, while illustrating the clarity of her insight into the whole matter of affliction. It is the anguish of extreme affliction that causes the exterior destruction of the self, she says, and for those who are in this state one can do absolutely nothing. It is not, however, possible to tell from the outside, without possessing supernatural discernment, whether the self is completely dead. The process goes through several stages: when the self is merely wounded, there ensues a fierce struggle, like an animal fighting for its life. But when the self is half dead, its suffering is so great that it wants to be finished off, it becomes apathetic to the outside world. A gesture of pure love on the part of another can in fact waken it at this point, but it is likely to produce such pain that the reaction is one of anger and hatred rather than gratitude. Hence, says Simone Weil, the apparently inexplicable acts of vengeance by afflicted people against their benefactors. If, on the other hand, the gesture has not been perfectly pure, the awakened self receives yet another wound, and once more the reaction is one of hatred. It is impossible to tell one reaction from the other. When the self has been truly killed from the outside, a loving gesture has no effect at all on the individual concerned. Such individuals allow themselves to be the object of attention in the way a dog or a cat would, attaching themselves like a dog, or merely taking advantage of the situation like a cat. In either case the afflicted individual sucks dry the source of the attention with no scruples at all.

It is impossible to mistake the accuracy of tone of this analysis. It arises from personal experience on the part of Simone Weil herself, and close and empathic observation of those around her. The whole passage reveals the horror Simone Weil felt when a human being was deprived of consent, and reinforces her revulsion at various other situations in which there is a similar deprivation, slavery and rape being two of the instances which recur most often in her thinking. It is not difficult to see why rape should have been such a source of revulsion to her: she saw the sexual act as inseparable from love, the ultimate gift of oneself to another, but love was possible only where consent was given. In the domain of human relationships, to take what was not freely offered was the ultimate crime, resulting in the destruction of the moral being of the individual, the infinitely small but precious capacity for consent. The important point to note is that this destruction is, in Simone Weil's view, the exact opposite of decreation. In spite of the horror implicit in certain stages of the decreative process, Simone Weil was convinced that, unlike the fruits of destruction, there was joy to be found in it, in that it revealed reality, this because reality becomes apparent only when the individual, desiring self has ceased to operate. There is thus a common bond between joy and pain: she was persuaded that 'there is as much sacrifice and renunciation at the bottom of joy as at the bottom of pain' (*FLN* 235), sacrifice, that is, of the autonomous self. But it is a sacrifice that is consented to. In another passage in the *Notebooks* she underlines the importance of joy as a means of access to reality, suggesting that, without this revelation, the experience of suffering remains negative:

In order to find reality in suffering, the revelation of reality must have come to one through joy. Otherwise life is nothing but a more or less evil dream.

One must manage to discover a still fuller reality in suffering, which is emptiness, nothingness.

Likewise one must greatly love life, so as to be able to love death even more. (*N* 291)

In the same way, Simone Weil defines sadness as 'a weakening of the feeling of reality. It is a wrong kind of decreation, on the level of the imagination' (*N* 266). Sadness here seems to correspond for Simone Weil to some feeling of deprivation on the part of the desiring self, and such deprivation is not to be confused with the process of decreation. Simone Weil's views on joy and sadness are thus yet another illustration of the importance of the impersonal in her thought. In all areas, the personal was a limiting factor, subject to whim and restricted in perspective, whereas access to the impersonal was access to truth itself.

Since there is therefore no question of intervening in the decreative process of others, what attitude should we take towards them? The answer in a sense is clear from her own life and the choices she made. But much of her thinking on the subject depends on achieving a state of non-perspective either implicit or explicit, and it could be useful at this point to consider precisely how this is worked out. In Simone Weil's view, human relationships, like anything else, are amenable to rational analysis. Firstly it must be said that the abandonment of perspective is of extreme importance to her in the treatment of fellow human beings, precisely because of her pessimism regarding our 'natural' relationships with our neighbours. Since these are subject to necessity, sometimes our treatment of them will be beneficial, sometimes harmful, but always as a result of chance, and not in conformity with good. On a natural level, she says, we love in a cannibalistic way. 'Thanks to their companionship, their words, or their letters, we get comfort, energy, and stimulation from the people we love. They affect us in the same way as a good meal after a hard day's work. So we love them like food. It is indeed an anthropophagous love' (*FLN* 284–5). We love, therefore, in response to a need, for what we can obtain from the other. From a certain point of view, she is obviously right: the more urgently we desire another human being, the more difficult it is to consider that individual's interest before our own, and the more the relationship can be called a 'cannibalistic' one. From the perspective beyond perspective, however (Simone Weil uses the word 'detachment' here), we learn to love the hunger in the loved one, and not the food that he offers us in response to our own hunger (*FLN* 286). To do this there must be a moment in our approach to another individual when we halt, when we look instead of eating.[16] In the normal course of events, says Simone Weil, eating and looking are two different processes, although we call both of them loving. Any hope of salvation is only for those who have managed to look for a certain length of time instead of eating (*FLN* 286).[17] Again, as in the act of

---

[16] In her essay on the *Iliad*, Simone Weil speaks of 'that interval of hesitation wherein lies our consideration for our brothers in humanity' (quoted by Richard Bell, 'Reading Simone Weil on Rights, Justice, and Love', in the present volume, below).

[17] The reference here is to the two birds in the *Mundaka* Upanishad, 3.1.1–2, and *Svetasvatara*, 4.6, one of whom eats while the other watches. Sri Aurobindo's reading essentially reflects

creation itself, the emphasis is on withdrawal, on not following natural inclinations, on not exercising power everywhere one is able to.[18] Here, it is both the result of going beyond perspective, and part of the decreation process itself. This perhaps goes some way towards answering criticisms of Simone Weil on the grounds that she deals inadequately with specific loving relationships between individuals: it is not possible to exclude all such relationships from any part in the concept of love, otherwise we would never learn the meaning of the word at all, a meaning which is conveyed only through instances of where it does and does not apply.[19] My 'education' in love is governed by my capacity to withdraw for a critical moment, to look rather than eat. A child will see something desirable, though dangerous, and before its parent has time to realise what is happening, the hand has gone out to grab the prize, sometimes with disastrous results. We must learn, says Simone Weil, not to act in this way, the 'natural' way. We must nurture the 'eternal part of the soul', that part which 'feeds on hunger'. She continues:

When we do not eat, our organism consumes its own flesh and transforms it into energy. It is the same with the soul. The soul which does not eat consumes itself. The eternal part consumes the mortal part of the soul and transforms it.

...

To make the perishable part of the soul die of hunger while the body is still alive. In this way a body of flesh passes directly into God's service. (*FLN*286)

In another passage she suggests that this use of the body as a physical object in which the autonomous self is destroyed is a kind of sacrament. Making the parallel with Christ who in the Host becomes an object to be eaten, she proposes this as a model through which we may desire to be only a thing, like Christ (*FLN* 261). As an extension to this, giving bread to the hungry can also be a kind of sacrament, provided it is done in perfect purity. She cites the instance of an afflicted individual, who has been practically des-

---

Simone Weil's: 'One of the birds is the eternally silent, unbound Self or Purusha by whom all this is extended and he regards the cosmos he has extended, but is aloof from it; the other is the Purusha involved in Prakriti.' *Essays on the Gita*, New York, 1950, p. 71.

[18] Cf. Thucydides, 'Through a natural necessity, every creature whatsoever, as far as it is able, exercises all the power at its disposal', a passage from *The Peloponnesian War* (v, lxxxix) often referred to by Simone Weil (e.g. *N*, 163, 190).

[19] See Rowan Williams, 'The Necessary Non-Existence of God', in the present volume, below.

troyed against his will by circumstances. If such an individual is the beneficiary of an act of love, however brief, he may revive for just long enough to consent to decreation. In such circumstances, the giving of bread can be equivalent to giving eternal life (*FLN* 261). In any case, the imitation of Christ demands that we serve others in their material needs: as Christ fed the hungry, so must we. 'It is not for a created being to induce them to renounce their created existence' (*FLN* 213). Elsewhere, she suggests that our conduct towards others partakes of the same paradox as creation itself. When we have recognised that we are nothing, she says, we pass over 'to God's side' (*FLN* 218). But far from trying to teach others that they are nothing, we must treat them according to the fiction that they are something – a parallel to the fiction already referred to that God maintains on our behalf in creation.

At first sight, it would seem shocking on Simone Weil's part to suggest that treating people as if they were 'something' is based on a 'fiction', a lie, a pretence. It would seem oddly out of step with some of her major insights into social responsibility and its basic principles. In *The Need for Roots*, she is quite clear as to the extent of an individual's obligations towards another human being. 'There exists an obligation towards every human being for the sole reason that he or she is a human being' (*NR* 4–5). This obligation is eternal and unconditional, and is related to the desire for pure good which exists in every individual, and which is the foundation for the respect due to him by every other individual (*SE* 220). This respect can only be exercised in terms of people's earthly needs, from the most obvious physical ones of food and shelter, to their moral needs, such as order, liberty, obedience, responsibility etc. (*NR* 6 *et seq.*). The contradiction implied with the insights revealed by non-perspective is perhaps only apparent: social organisation necessarily involves treating others from the outside, as 'the other', having in common only that desire for pure goodness found in every individual. Decreation, on the other hand, is a strictly personal matter: as we have already seen, one does not decreate others, it is an affair between the solitary soul and the source of all goodness, and so it is impossible to treat others as one must treat oneself. It is again a question of perspective.

In practical terms, one may well ask what a society of decreated beings would be like. Simone Weil clearly saw little hope for her own times. But there is a suggestion that something that was at least going in the right direction had existed in the past, and that was in the Languedoc civilisation of the twelfth century, a subject to which she devotes two essays, 'The Romanesque Renaissance' and 'A Medieval Epic Poem' (*SE* 44–54, 35–43). It is not the place to go into detail concerning this civilisation, which she admired intensely, except to point to some of its characteristics which indicate for Simone Weil that this society operated in a state of grace. Most importantly, as in the best of Greek civilisation, it was a society based on the knowledge and refusal of force (*SL* 48), that is to say, a recognition that force rules virtually everywhere, and a refusal to regard it as good. This rejection, accompanied by 'loathing and contempt', is 'the other face of the compassion which goes out to everything that is exposed to the ravages of force' (*SL* 48–9). In a note in the American notebooks, a clear relationship is established between this compassion and the process of decreation:

Compassion is the recognition of one's own misery in another. Recognition of one's own misery in the affliction of someone else.

. . .

Compassion is natural to man if the obstacle of the feeling of the 'I' is removed. It is not compassion that is supernatural, but the removal of that obstacle. (*FLN* 209–10)

In relationships between individuals, the same note is struck. The Languedoc civilisation was the one in which courtly love flourished, which, in her interpretation, has as its object a human being, but is not covetous. 'It is simply a patient attention towards the loved person and an appeal for that person's consent' (*SL* 50). It does seem therefore that Simone Weil envisaged the possibility of decreation playing a role in a viable society. It was imperative for her, in fact, to see how these ideas could be worked out in practical terms, that they should find their incarnation in matter. It was perhaps inevitable, however, that this civilisation should perish when confronted with the superior armed forces of the crusade under Simon de Montfort.

This inevitability is a perspective through which one should raise, if not answer, the question of the worldly 'viability' of the decreated individual, again one who refuses force. An individual who illustrates admirably the problem is the character Jaffier in Simone Weil's play, *Venice Preserved*. Jaffier, it will be recalled, is the mercenary sent with his fellow-mercenaries to destroy Venice, but who, when he suddenly realises the beauty of what he is about to destroy, reveals the conspiracy, having obtained a safe passage for his companions. The promise is not kept, the others are captured and tortured, and Jaffier, in a state of extreme affliction, leaves the city for exile and certain death. Jaffier is used by Simone Weil as a kind of Christ-figure, a perfectly pure being whose sufferings are redemptive. Unlike Christ, however, Jaffier does not start perfectly pure: at the beginning of the play he is a normal, active human being, excited by the prospect of the conflict to come and the spoils that will certainly be his. The transformation in this case comes through the vision of beauty, which brings him up short, stops the forward movement of his projects and desires, and allows the entry of the supernatural. Certain actions then become impossible to him, and his sufferings become redemptive by a process described in the Marseilles *Notebooks*: if a human being who is in a state of perfection, his autonomous self completely destroyed, falls into the state of affliction equivalent to that which would bring about the exterior destruction of his autonomous self if it was still intact, then there is the 'plenitude of the Cross', absence of God, redemptive suffering (N 342). It is the dark night of the soul signalled by St John of the Cross, but, because totally consented to, having the power to stop the evil which would have resulted in destruction. The role of beauty here is a double and a paradoxical one, and forms a parallel to the contemplation/eating sequence outlined above: it is the trigger to a higher awareness, part of the decreation process, but at the same time a perspective beyond perspective is necessary to perceive true beauty. Beauty is something which is for contemplation, not for consumption, and demands a withdrawal of the self for its true appreciation. It is also clear that it is not simply an aesthetic category but, because in true Platonic fashion it is a reflection of the good, the tangible form of the good, it has precise moral implications. Because Jaffier does not reject the vision, he becomes literally incapable of destruction. This moral quality to the perception of beauty is not surprising when one realises that, for Simone Weil, love of beauty and love of one's neighbour were simply different forms of a single, decreated love (*FLN* 87), even when these loves remain implicit (cf. also *FLN* 81, *IC* 175).

Ultimately, then, in Simone Weil's vision of the decreated being, there is only God as a willing being, and matter which is entirely docile to his law. The creature when decreated is merely the passage of the love of God for the Son which passes through creation (*FLN* 102). There is then no autonomous self set up in opposition to

God's will. It is clear that Simone Weil was not unaware of the problems posed by the realisation in practical terms of many of these ideas. The problem lies partly in a tendency, already noted in her early years by her teacher Alain, to push ideas to their logical conclusion, resulting in much that is unsettling, and indeed revolutionary, in her thinking. The absolute nature of her thought also produces difficulties: convinced that only absolute good has the power to produce a lesser good, she saw her vocation as an attending on that good, while paradoxically knowing that it could never be translated into material terms, indeed that it should not, or else it could not be absolute good. Towards the end of her life, in London, she comments poignantly in a letter to Maurice Schumann on her inability to reconcile 'the affliction of men, the perfection of God, and the link between the two' (*SL* 178).

In the same way, she knew that although, again paradoxically, the perfection of God's perspective was what the creature must aim at, it was impossible to ask for it, since it inevitably demanded a passage through affliction. Privations, she says, are useless if they are generated by the autonomous 'I'. They have value only in the form of obedience (*FLN* 127). This is one of the difficulties in the interpretation of the 'Example of Prayer' which figures in the American *Notebooks* (*FLN* 243–5), and which is problematical on several levels. Its air of cold detachment, its anonymity, which allow the 'I' to be interpreted as both Simone Weil herself and another first-person subject is only one of the barriers to an unambiguous reading of the text.[20] It is, indeed, one of those passages which most frequently bring down the charge of masochism upon Simone Weil. One of the most balanced, and also most professionally competent, analyses of this charge relating to Simone Weil as a whole has been made by Marie-Annette Fourneyron, herself a psychiatrist, in a paper published in the *Cahiers Simone Weil*.[21] Following a detailed consideration of the theses and practice of Masoch, she concludes that the inspiration in the two cases was entirely different: that whereas Masoch sought suffering as an end in itself, to be enjoyed *per se*, for Simone Weil, suffering rightly understood was a passage to a higher

[20] See for an illuminating sylistic discussion of the 'exemple de prière' Joan Dargan, 'Form and Ardor: a stylistic Comparison of Prayers by Simone Weil and Pascal', unpublished paper given at the American Weil Society Annual Conference, Wooster, Ohio, May 1991.

[21] M.-A. Fourneyron, 'Pour en finir avec le masochisme de Simone Weil', *CSW*, 11:1 (March 1988), pp. 57–64, and 11:2 (June 1988), pp. 155–64. See also G. Raimbault and C. Eliacheff, *Les Indomptables: figures de l'anorexie*, Paris: Seuil, 1989.

reality. Fourneyron points to a passage in the *Notebooks*, indeed, where Simone Weil suggests that there are two kinds of physical pain, one (for example going to the dentist) which tends to make the sufferer 'lose' the feeling of reality, while the other (she gives the example of gathering up sheaves full of thorns with one's bare arms) constitutes a contact with reality (N 4). Fourneyron also emphasises the distinction made by Simone Weil between suffering and punishment. Suffering, in her view, has no meaning, and to see it as a punishment is to interpret it as a consolation, in other words, an escape from reality (cf. N 484). The human void resulting from the destruction of the self referred to in the 'Example of Prayer' is therefore more akin to the passive night of the senses evoked by St John of the Cross (referred to by Simone Weil in the passage immediately preceding the 'Example of Prayer'), than to the perverted quest for suffering on which Masoch was bent.

To turn to the prayer itself, and to some of the problems it poses, in its first phase Simone Weil asks that she be deprived of all her natural faculties, be reduced entirely to the level of an idiot, unable to think, string two words together, or even move. The second phase asks that all her natural faculties be entirely obedient to God's will, so that every movement, every thought, is a kind of microcosm of creation at its most perfect, but then that all this should be torn away from her, transformed into the substance of Christ, and given as food to the afflicted, who lack every nourishment of body and soul. And that she should be paralysed, reduced to the level of an idiot, etc.

The first and key observation to make about this prayer is Simone Weil's own: that it is impossible to ask such things. They are accomplished in spite of oneself, although with one's consent. This is coherent with Simone Weil's insistence, which we have noted at several points in this essay, that if we appear to seek affliction, it is not really affliction. A further point concerning the difficulties surrounding its interpretation is made also by Simone Weil, in her despairing cry that all these spiritual phenomena are totally outside her competence, and that she doesn't really know what she's talking about. Furthermore, she adds, she is incapable even of telling herself honestly that she doesn't know what she's talking about. This provides a further key to the passage, in the sense that the division of the soul at this point is stark: the natural part of the soul (the 'I' of 'I know nothing about it' (*FLN*245)) is incapable of comprehending

that to which the uncreated part of the soul aspires – and we as
readers 'read' with that same 'natural' part. There is the further
problem of the relationship between the two parts: it is not clear
whether they refer to a temporal sequence, or a change in perspective, or what exactly their relationship is. Nevertheless, taking the
prayer as a whole, it conforms closely to the decreative process as we
have been following it. The natural part of the soul must disappear,
to leave only that part which is in total conformity with God's will.
The natural capacities of the human being – the senses, the intelligence, and so on – are of value only in so far as they are used as food
for the deprived. This is, however, not at all the same as saying that
they are valueless; it is the difference, in Simone Weil's view,
between the work of art that is dictated by genius, and that dictated
by talent: in the former, the personality of the author does not come
into it, he or she is a mere channel for truth, food for the spiritually
hungry, whereas in the latter, however brilliant, there is only the
author's personality. The harsh vision of the 'Example of Prayer' is
perhaps no more than an uncompromising statement of this same
perception: the abandonment of the autonomous perspective is the
only path to truth, and the only basis for the moral life. In fact, is she
not simply spelling out the implications, with characteristic consistency and honesty, of 'Thy will be done'?

For an understanding of the context in which Simone Weil could
wrestle with such ideas, and to get some sort of perspective on them,
it is important, however, to realise the extent to which her reflections
prolong a well-documented and comprehensive mystical tradition.
We could begin perhaps with that classic of mystical thought,
Meister Eckhart,[22] called by Simone Weil a 'genuine friend of God'
(*WG* 79), whose doctrine of *Abgeschiedenheit*, usually translated
'detachment', is in many respects similar to Simone Weil's 'decreation'. As for Simone Weil, so for Eckhart human beings are, in their
natural state, so totally self-oriented that it is necessary for all
earthly things to be stripped away until nothing remains on any
level of the natural individual. Like Simone Weil, he knows that 'to
be empty of all things is to be full of God, and to be full of all
creatures is to be empty of God'.[23] This is why he sets detachment

[22] I am grateful here to Terry Tastard, author of *The Spark in the Soul*, London: Darton,
Longman and Todd, 1989; Mahwah NJ: Paulist Press, 1990, for indications of parallels
between Eckhart and Simone Weil.
[23] Eckhart, 'On detachment', in *Sermons and Treatises*, trans. and ed. M. O'C. Walshe,
Shaftesbury: Longmans, 1987, III, p. 121.

higher than love or humility, both of which are creature-regarding. The emphasis is no doubt different here, in that Simone Weil would lay greater stress on love, but she, like Eckhart, would argue that a loving disposition towards one's fellow-beings is only possible for the decreated soul. The resulting 'no-thingness' to which the self is reduced in both Simone Weil and Eckhart is not so much a destruction of something real, as a revelation of the true void of the human 'I'. 'All creatures are pure nothing', as Eckhart says.[24] (It is interesting to note in passing that this is one of the Propositions for which Eckhart was condemned by Pope John XXII.)

For both Eckhart and Simone Weil, the stripping process involves not only the abandonment of what is obviously material and carnal, but of those aspects of human beings that make them most fully human: as Simone Weil prays that she might lose her mental faculties to the point where she is reduced to idiocy, so Eckhart claims that 'Memory, understanding and will, they all diversify you, and therefore you must leave them all: sense perceptions, imagination, or whatever it may be that in which you find or seek to find yourself'.[25] The soul is to be detached even from the idea of God, since any ideas regarding the divine are brought in 'from without through the senses',[26] affirms Eckhart, recalling Simone Weil's 'purifying atheism'. He likewise holds that 'For you to know God in God's way, your knowing must be a pure unknowing, and a forgetting of yourself and all creatures'.[27] The resulting 'darkness and ... unknowing' has clear affinities with the teachings of St John of the Cross (whom, as we have noted, she seems to have been reading at this time), who was influenced by Eckhart on this as on other points. It also recalls the anonymous author of the fourteenth-century *Cloud of Unknowing*, roughly contemporary therefore with Eckhart, who enjoins the soul to 'crush all knowledge and experience of all forms of created things, and of yourself above all'.[28]

Another parallel, with a figure less well known than Eckhart, can be seen with the eighteenth-century Jesuit philosopher Jean-Pierre de Caussade, whose book *Self-Abandonment to Divine Providence* was compiled over a century after his death from letters and notes.[29]

---

[24] Walshe, I, p. I.   [25] Sermon 2, Walshe, I, p. 39.   [26] Walshe, I, p. 40.

[27] Walshe, I. See also Tastard, *The Spark*, p. 44.

[28] *The Cloud of Unknowing*, trans. and introd. C. Wolters, Harmondsworth: Penguin Books, 1961, ch. 43, p. 103.

[29] Jean-Pierre de Caussade, *The Sacrament of the Present Moment*, trans. Kitty Muggeridge from the original text of the treatise on *Self-Abandonment to Divine Providence*, London: Collins,

Central to his mysticism is the idea of 'self-surrender', whereby the soul rejects progressively all earthly considerations, until it is entirely in conformity with the will of God, a concept which has obvious affinities with Simone Weil's decreation, and with the 'Example of Prayer' referred to above. For de Caussade, happiness is the fulfilment of divine purpose, and that is revealed in everything without exception that occurs in the world. 'Therefore', he says, 'whether or not souls are deprived of thought, speech, books, nourishment, companionship, health or even of life itself, does not matter.'[30] Conforming to the divine image is thus brought about not by cleverness, intelligence, or subtlety of mind, but rather by a 'passive acceptance and yielding'.[31] This emphasis on the passiveness of the receptive soul occurs throughout the volume: he speaks of 'waiting on the good pleasure of God', in a 'continuing state of passivity',[32] of 'passive surrender to [the will of God]',[33] and of the importance of 'self-surrender and complete passivity',[34] recalling both Simone Weil's idea of 'attente', and her commitment to Stoic ideas on loving acceptance of the world order. Images of destruction also abound in de Caussade: the body and the soul do not reveal their true brilliance until they are 'reshaped, melted, broken up and shrunk',[35] God is seen as a sculptor fashioning a work by means of cutting-away, and by repeated blows on the 'cruel chisel'. 'I suffer each cut of the chisel as though it were the best thing for me, even though, to tell the truth, each one is my idea of ruin, destruction and defacement.'[36] Faith is 'death and destruction to the senses for they worship creatures, whereas faith worships the divine will of God',[37] although, with a sense of paradox that reflects Simone Weil's own, and that tends to run throughout mystical thinking, he maintains that 'divine purpose both kills and quickens with one stroke: the closer to death the more it seems to bring life'.[38] However, it is clearly a transfigured life, since 'the point must be reached when the

1981. I am indebted to Martin Andic of the University of Massachusetts for bringing de Caussade to my attention.

[30] *The Sacrament of the Present Moment*, p. 98.
[31] *The Sacrament of the Present Moment*, p. 96.
[32] *The Sacrament of the Present Moment*, p. 22.
[33] *The Sacrament of the Present Moment*, p. 26.
[34] *The Sacrament of the Present Moment*, p. 78.
[35] *The Sacrament of the Present Moment*, p. 43.
[36] *The Sacrament of the Present Moment*, p. 75.
[37] *The Sacrament of the Present Moment*, p. 83.
[38] *The Sacrament of the Present Moment*, p. 105.

whole of creation counts for nothing and God for everything'.[39] As here, so in Simone Weil's vision, ultimately there is only God, and what is in conformity with God's will, and the supreme function of creation and created beings is to reveal a divinely ordained world order.

To make these parallels is not necessarily to suggest that Simone Weil had a close knowledge of the writings of other mystics. She knew the work of St John of the Cross intimately, that of Eckhart at least in part, whereas there is no documentary evidence of her having come across that of de Caussade. Many similarities can be attributed to a vision and an expression common to mystical thought. Simone Weil had, in any case, her own very individual contribution to make to that tradition, notably in her acute sensitivity to the affliction that was so often a part of the decreative process, and her consequent conviction that it could not be sought, only consented to. There is no martyr-complex in Simone Weil. If, in spite of the clear evidence that her perceptions continue a long tradition extolling the *via negativa*, the suspicion remains that Simone Weil over-emphasised the negative in her search for spiritual perfection, and that her condemnation of the autonomous 'I' is too absolute, she might well claim in her own defence that something akin to the doctrine of decreation is absolutely necessary to correct the natural tendency of all human creatures to see the universe from the I-perspective. The autonomous 'I' has no need of anyone to boost its claim to existence: it makes its own point noisily and incessantly, and, because it is common to every one of us, each individual feels threatened by any doctrine that would seek to challenge its hold on power. The universe, on the other hand, has no one to represent it, and neither have all those countless powerless individuals and forgotten minorities who, by definition, cannot bring themselves to my attention. The more I say 'I', the less they truly exist. And so we kill and maim, and hurt and humiliate our neighbour, and despoil this planet of ours – because it is natural to do so. Simone Weil's doctrine of decreation reminds us, at the very least, that there is another, less destructive way of perceiving the universe, and hence of interacting lovingly with all that it contains.

[39] *The Sacrament of the Present Moment*, p. 69.

CHAPTER 2

The necessary non-existence of God

Rowan Williams

> Of two men who have no experience of God, he who denies him is perhaps nearer to him than the other.
>
> The false God who is like the true one in everything, except that we do not touch him, prevents us from ever coming to the true one.
>
> The 100 possible thalers in Kant. The same applies to God.
>
> We have to believe in a God who is like the true God in everything, except that he does not exist, for we have not reached the point where God exists.   (N 151)

These observations from Simone Weil's Marseilles notebooks are her most concise crystallisation of a theme which evidently preoccupied her a great deal in her last years; echoes are found throughout both the Marseilles and the New York notebooks, and – less clearly – in some of the published essays. It has not, to my knowledge, been systematically traced and discussed, and it presents all kinds of problems to the would-be interpreter. What follows is not the exhaustive treatment that this motif deserves, but an attempt to locate Weil's gnomic remarks on the non-existence of God in relation to other and better-known themes, and to suggest how the idea throws into sharp relief some of the central strengths and weaknesses of Simone Weil's vision – most particularly, her understanding of love, divine and human.

This essay is in no sense an attempt to reduce Simone Weil's vision to a cluster of contradictory and questionable principles. But I believe that, in her account of the grammar of the words 'God' and 'love', there are troubling points of tension. It is possible to read *Waiting for God* and *The Need for Roots* and to emerge with a very positive sense of her love for the world in its resistance to the desires and projects of the ego, a love both committed and purged from self-regard. This is not a mistaken reading, and other essays in this book rightly draw attention to the moral and social resourcefulness of such a vision. Yet, even in these works, the vision is shadowed by other elements, which need to be brought into focus if this resourcefulness is to be properly apprehended. Not to weigh these elements means not being able to understand why Weil's legacy is still so widely seen as morally problematic. If the present essay seeks to do something of this job, it is not with the aim of derogating from Weil's seriousness and significance: quite the contrary. Her thinking is neither merely edifying nor merely 'occasional'; it is a powerfully comprehensive vision, none the less compelling for its strains and its moral ambivalences. Depth is not coterminous with consistency, in Weil any more than in Plato or Hegel.

I

The issue arises in the *Notebooks* in connection with the question of what she calls 'concordant composition'. Human contact is fraught with danger (moral danger) in that need and willingness to respond appropriately to need seem to be systematically uncoordinated: one person's need threatens the other and drives them away. There is no time for the relationship to establish itself. 'Concordant composition' seems to be a way of designating how circumstances might develop so as to allow such need to be met; but, as we know, such a development is not to be seen in the world we inhabit. Because human need is real and urgent, our inclination is to *manufacture* a meeting of our needs, reordering circumstances through our imagination; and this, Weil claims, is an infallible way of blocking access to the true 'composition' in which needs are truthfully or accurately met. From our necessarily limited standpoint, it is impossible to know what such true concordance between the time in which I am aware of my need and the time of the world's process would look like; so my only choices are to accept discordance, unfulfilled need, in the present, or to lie. To accept discordance is thus to accept that I cannot imagine the good (and must not try). In the language she uses elsewhere, it is to accept 'the void' (cf. N 148, 153, 198, 204, 410–11, 431, 491, 545, etc.) to face the contradictoriness of our desires (we cannot realise simultaneously the conditions for attaining all that we desire as good). And this indefinite deferral of a good that can be seen or imagined or understood is a moment of contact with the 'supernatural', in the sense that it steps aside from the realm

of motivations determined by specific goals, particular states of
affairs: it is a wanting of nothing in particular – or, to put it more
provocatively, it is a wanting of *everything*, a consent to the ensemble
of things. It is union with 'the will of God': 'A plurality of distinct
and convergent motives places the will [presumably by means of the
acceptance of the necessary collisions between the plurality of goals]
in contact with what is above the sphere of particular motives'
(N 239).

Thus the determination of desire by a specific state of affairs,
wanting this rather than that, is a barrier to the 'supernatural', the
realm in which alone desire is truly and truthfully met. For desire to
open itself to a non-illusory fulfilment is for it to refuse to *imagine*
fulfilment. The desiring or needy human subject must learn to
conceive fulfilment, the 'concordance' of need and circumstance or
time, as 'non-existent', at least at the level at which the mind
normally perceives. 'Before placing oneself in the position where
[concordant composition] may be felt, not by the sensibility, but by
the higher part of one's being, one must have felt to what extent it is
non-existent' (N 151). These are the words immediately preceding
the observations on God's existence with which we began, and the
connection of thought is clear. To imagine God is, Weil implies, to
conceive a state of affairs, a determination of circumstances, which
will inevitably be conditioned by my needs, and will be a falsehood.
Even if I imagine *as an object in my mental world* the God who is
characterised by the selfless abandonment, the creative letting-go of
reality which is, for Weil, the crucial element in truthful speech
about God, I am thereby kept away from the God who can be truly
talked about precisely because God has been brought into my
mental world, in which all objects are – so to speak – tainted by the
particularised wants of the unredeemed subject. So to 'believe' in
God, if it is not to be the manufacture of a 'false concordant
composition', becomes an intensely paradoxical affair: if God is in
our minds, God must be 'imagined' as not existing, not involved in
any real or imaginary circumstances. The *grammar* of our talk of God
can appropriately be refined, so that we know what we are talking
about – that is to say, there is a proper place for objecting, 'You
can't say *that* about God', when faced with models of a vindictive or
arbitrary divine power (such as Simone Weil identified in the Jewish
Scriptures and in much of the rhetoric of the Catholic Church). But
the assertion of God's existence cannot be part of this grammatical

exercise – hence the allusion to Kant's dismissal of the ontological argument on the grounds that object and concept do not differ in *content* according to whether the object is real or possible ('The real contains no more than the merely possible. A hundred real thalers do not contain the least coin more than a hundred possible thalers', *Critique of Pure Reason*, trans. Kemp Smith, p. 505). We are thus able to sort out what we must say about God in order to be talking about God at all; but we cannot affirm that this God exists over against us, an agent within the system of agencies, a subject with whom I can converse, a particular determination of my own existence in the world.

'We have not reached the point where God exists.' The denial that God exists as a particular determination of the way the (my) world goes is itself a strategy that only makes sense in the context of a process not yet completed. We are to 'believe in', to put our trust or hope in, a God who, while not a particular determination of the world, represents that relation to the world towards which I aspire if I am at all interested in truthfulness – that is, if I am at all human. Weil believes that we are constituted as human by our hunger for the good as such, that hunger which prevents us from being content with the satisfaction of this or that specific need by a specific good and thus – if we let it – warns us that the search for specific goods will turn our desire back towards the ego and thus foster the manufacturing of illusory final fulfilments (e.g., N 487–94; cf. *SNLG* 159). We want the good, and want it so badly that, on the one hand, we are unhappy with the specific goods we attain, and, on the other, we long to be able to tell ourselves that this or that good adequately meets our needs as we understand them; our temptation is therefore to reshape in our speech and thought what the world provides for us into a form acceptable to our account of our needs – and so to cut ourselves off from the good as such, which we reach only by recognising that our needs are not met in the terms we prescribe. There *is* (if our human being is not simply condemned to utter futility, if our deepest desire is not a misapprehension) a correct, an undistorting vision of, and relation to, the world, a way of receiving the good-as-such; and to speak of God is to speak of that possible relation to the world as real.

I am absolutely certain that there is a God, in the sense that I am absolutely certain that my love is not illusory. I am absolutely certain that there is not a God, in the sense that I am absolutely certain that there is nothing real which bears a resemblance to what I am able to conceive when I pronounce that name, since I am unable to conceive God – But that thing, which I am unable to conceive, is not an illusion. (*N* 127)

And

If God should be an illusion from the point of view of existence, He is the sole reality from the point of view of the good . . . God exists because I desire Him; that is as certain as my existence. (*FLN* 157)

My desire for the good-as-such, which, to be fulfilled, must be, and can only be, an acceptance of the world as such, is – if it is not 'illusory' – the desire to occupy that 'place' where the creator stands in respect of creation. This is not a place *in* the world (let alone at the centre of the world; see, for example, *WG* 158–60). If my love or desire, my longing to receive the good-as-such, is somehow 'grounded', not a self-serving fantasy, then there is such a 'place'; there is God. The rigorous purgation of our desire for this or that outcome, this or that determination of circumstances, is not asceticism for its own sake, but the sole possible means of testing whether desire can survive in the absence of specific objects; if it can, it cannot be self-serving, a matter of fantasy under the control of the needy ego. And to know this, presumably, is to know 'that my love is not illusory'. 'God exists because I desire Him' must mean something like,

The desire for the good is utterly independent of any particular story of need and gratification; it is our *fundamental* relationship to what is not ourselves; we cannot *not* orient ourselves – once we have stopped lying about need and fulfillment – towards such a relationship, testing ourselves against what that relationship entails; but that relationship is not an 'ideal' towards which we strive or struggle, as if it needed to be brought into being; it is there *before* our wills get involved in anything.

The reality of God is the truth that the world can be, and in some sense already is, seen and affirmed, loved, as a whole; that it is possible to say yes to all that is or has been in the world, and that this possibility is entirely independent of what I or any other individual as a matter of fact can or does achieve. If the world may be seen as 'let' to exist, precisely as it is, God is what lets it be, and so is appropriately talked about in the kenotic mythology Weil habitually employs ('God renounces . . . being everything . . . to the extent of being nailed to the cross', *N* 193, among many other instances). For me to love the world as it should be loved, unconditionally, requires me to see the world as an object of unconditional love *prior* to my own hoped-for growth towards love; and that is to see the world as loved from beyond the world, loved by a God who can be characterised as 'attention without distraction' (*FLN* 141).

I do not want at this stage to comment on the connections of argument here, but it may be helpful to note a couple of possible misinterpretations of what Weil is saying. First, and most obviously, the divine 'position', the point at which 'concordant composition' is discernible, can sound like a position from which the world can literally be seen as a whole, and all its chains of circumstances traced and understood. This is clearly not what Weil means; such a position could only be a fantastic projection of our need to grasp patterns and explanations, precisely the kind of need which the ascesis of accept-ance is meant to suppress. 'Composition', she says, is 'felt ... by the higher part of one's being' – an unhelpful turn of phrase, but designed to separate out the sense of composition, the accepting love of the world, from the ego and its imaginings and demands for graspable satisfaction. The position of divine love is not one of total comprehension, but of total openness to reality beyond the self. Second, there are the apparent contradictions between Weil's differ-ent remarks about conceiving God. I must believe in a God who can be spoken of, who has the qualities of the true God and so can be the subject of, at least, 'grammatical' discussion; yet 'there is nothing real which bears a resemblance to what I am able to conceive when I pronounce that name'. The key, I think, is in the word 'nothing real'. What I am able to conceive in saying 'God', what I may conceive more or less accurately, intelligibly and consistently, depending on how carefully I do my grammatical work, is some-thing that *cannot* be an object among others in the world inhabited by the needy ego. There is no thing in the world's reality to which the name 'God' applies. I cannot but conceive God as some sort of object, because I cannot (logically) conceive what is not in the world; the paradox is that the more faithfully I purify my concep-tion, the clearer it should be that what I am talking about cannot 'exist' in worldly reality. The experience of faith is, as Weil says, the confidence that, in spite of this, my talking about God is not idle or vacuous – though it must be absolutely minimal if it is not to become so ('Not to speak about God ... not to pronounce this word, *except when one is not able to do otherwise*', *N* 234, and cf. *N* 326). But such confidence depends on the conviction that the world can be loved unconditionally, it depends on the possibility of the purification of my love – which has not yet happened ('We have not reached the point where God exists'). So: God is 'there' before us, in that the possibility of pure love is 'there', whatever happens to me, and God is not 'there', because the possibility has yet to be realised in me, the one who is trying to talk about God.

It seems, then, that while I am still on the way to learning love, I can only properly speak of the true God by refusing to recognise anything *in* the world as divine presence – i.e. as claiming our unconditional desire. No item or episode or person in the world, no determination of circumstances, can be the end of our desiring. But if I *had* reached the 'place' of unconditional love, I should not need to speak of God and indeed *could* not do so, since I should stand in God's place ('we have passed to the side where God is', *IP* 153). Thus there is never a moment when I can legitimately or intelligibly speak of God as 'existing', as a concrete reality over against me. But the last thing this means is that God is a fiction or a projection, or a tool to purify my spiritual consciousness. It is I who must become a 'tool', a passive instrument in the hands of love (*FLN* 132, 243–4, etc.); I must enter the process of 'decreation' so that between the world and unconditional love no barrier is set up in the shape of an ego with plural and specific needs or projects. If God is to be real, to 'exist' in a sense other than that in which determinations of the world exist, I must *cease* to exist – that is, I must cease to be an object to myself, a self-conscious reflector on my needs and projects. 'To say "I" is to lie' (*FLN* 132; cf. *FLN* 337–8 on the difference between the 'I' being destroyed from without, by force, and the 'I' being eroded from within, by attention). 'All the things that I see, hear, breathe, touch, eat, all the beings that I meet – I deprive all these of contact with God and I deprive God of contact with them to the extent to which something in me says "I"' (*N* 378f; cf., for example, *N* 364 and 404). So long as I have before my mind *images* of want and fulfilment, I am failing to see the whole, to love unconditionally: I distinguish between what I want and what I don't, and so fail to reflect the absolute impartiality of God in letting be a world which is absolutely silent about God, which allows no conclusions to be drawn about the divine nature from the way it goes (only from its bare existence). 'The image of the indifferent power of God is the passive obedience of the creature' (*FLN* 130). The acting, choosing, ordering ego cannot be united with God, cannot love unconditionally. As long as it is in operation, it is necessary to deny God's existence as an item in the subject's consciousness; and when it has ceased to operate, God's existence does not need to be affirmed – it is simply the point from which I see. Not that it then becomes *manifest*: 'God is always absent from our love, as he is from the world; but he is secretly present in pure love. When the presence of God is visible in love, then it is the presence of something other than God' (*FLN* 275). In other words, if I am a 'pure' or unconditional lover of the world, if God is present in my 'supernatural' virtue (*FLN* 111, 145, 339, etc. and *WG* 149–50, etc.), this does not mean that I become for some other hungry ego a sign of God, a determination of the world that speaks of God, my virtue is not an explanatory problem, a miraculous hiatus in the world. I am simply a means whereby love is made present. That this should be so requires, if it is to be properly interpreted (not explained) that we have to hand a language about unconditional love, about God, about the death of the ego and the reality of God's love in that 'moral space'; but having this language is itself part of the process of life in faith (it has no meaning otherwise), and so has nothing to do with any thing in the world that might be triumphantly pointed to as an epiphany of the divine.

Thus the *content* of the world, in an important sense, is not *changed* by love – that is, no new occult force is introduced into it as an extra item or datum for the mind. Grace is what happens when a self is entirely freed from self-assertion and the quest for gratification of needs, and this *makes a difference* to the world because it interrupts the transmission of violence from self to self which Weil sees as endemic in unredeemed creation (see the essay on the *Iliad*, for her finest treatment of this). It does not bring in some specific 'power' not present before. If love sought to change the world in the sense of bending circumstances to the preferences and plans of a self, it would not be unconditional. Real love does what *must* be done, what circumstances impose (*N* 29–30, 57, cf. the remarks in *N* on the *Bhagavad-Gita*, especially 80–94, and the notes on war, pp. 32–5; how are we to 'obey' the need to take up arms in defence of human freedoms and yet show in our conduct of war that desire for unconditional acceptance that alone can preserve peace? How do we fight not for power, but in order to change the mind of the enemy towards the possibility of – powerless – acceptance as a goal for both sides?) Real love is therefore not bound by goals, since obedience is nothing to do with setting goals. It transforms by obeying the impersonal requirement of truthful seeing.

This brings us to a final set of ideas connected with the non-existence of God which I want to examine before attempting any assessment or development of the themes so far discussed. Real love is not love of anything in particular – or rather not of anything *as* particular.

> We cannot stop ourselves from loving. But we can choose what it is we love.
> We ought to love what is absolutely worthy of love, not what is worthy of it in certain respects, unworthy of it in others (Plato).
> Nothing which exists is absolutely worthy of love.
> We must therefore love that which does not exist.
> But this object of love which does not exist is not devoid of reality, is not a fiction. For our fictions cannot be more worthy of love than we are ourselves, who are not.
>   (*N* 220)

Compare:

God alone is worthy of interest. (*FLN* 126)

And:

There are two objects for us to love. First, that which is worthy of love but which in our sense of the word existence, does not exist. And second, that which exists, but in which there is nothing it is possible to love. That is necessity. We must love both. (*FLN* 324)

And:

The appropriate object for love is God, and *every man who loves something other than God is deceived, mistaken.* (*SNLG* 104)

Love finds no object that has an unconditional claim upon it; yet – Weil seems to assume – the grammar of love is such that uncon-ditionality is part of authentic love (could we say that this is so because ove is not something exhausted by the gratification of any specific desire? because it is 'underdetermined' by objects?). Love must therefore direct itself at what is not – at the reality of unconditional love itself, at the position of total acceptance 'outside' the world. 'If love finds no object, the lover must love his love itself, perceived as something external. Then one has found God' (*FLN* 260–1; the reference to Augustine, *Confessions* 3.1, substantially misunderstands the import of that text – though Weil might have found grist to this particular mill in the *de Trinitate*). But if love loves the possibility/ reality of unconditional love for the world, it is thereby returned to love of the world, to the love of 'necessity'. 'Necessity, in so far as it is absolutely other than Good, is Good itself' (*N* 424): if the good-as-such is unconditional love, it is the love of everything that is *not* the good-as-such; in loving itself, it loves its opposite, necessity, the God-forsaken world. The world is loveable through the medium of the good; indeed, there is a kind of to and fro movement between the necessary and the good which will (once again, if we *let* it) purify our love. Objects and goals in the world 'refuse' to be a final good for us, they retain their irreducible otherness, and so frustrate the will which wants to absorb them: this is the experience of evil and the root of our 'affliction', *misère*; but it is also 'the form which God's mercy takes in this world' (*N* 495), in that it can save us from the ultimate lie of believing ourselves satisfied. We must learn to love what will not, and cannot, be absorbed into ourselves. This is why, in Weil's justly famous essays, 'Forms of the Implicit Love of God' and 'Reflections on the Right Use of School Studies', so much stress is laid on the training of the spirit by submission to, and acceptance of, the specific structures of the world, the density of other persons, the given shape of intellectual disciplines: encounter with the given, the non-negotiable, is the painful defeat of the self, and therefore is grace. It instructs us that what can be given to us by the world is not what we want for our gratification. Our initial efforts at, and fantasies of, love (search and gratification, itch and scratch) are brought to nothing, and we are challenged to love not what we want but the sheer otherness of what is there – almost (in principle at least) an *undifferentiated* otherness, in the sense that it is indifferent with respect to my specific wants or articulated needs.

We can only be at home in the world when we have given up the search for that thing, that person, that set of circumstances that will secure our existence, guarantee our being at home (*N* 469). To know that the world as necessity, as utterly and finally other than my will, is incapable of sustaining my love (in the form towards which my love aspires, the form of unconditionality) is the necessary condition of loving the world. I love the world properly only when I have found 'evil', resistance to my gratification, in every determination of the world. As Weil repeats so many times, God is found only in the experience and the understanding of divine absence, which is also the experience of the impossibility of love *in* the world.

'The appropriate object for love' is the sole *subject* of love – that which is not the world, which is not 'there', God.

II

So far, I have done no more than attempt to read and unravel Simone Weil's thoughts on God's existence and non-existence (well aware of the Weilian ambiguity of 'reading'). In the second part of this essay, I want to ask how far all this hangs together in Weil's own terms and in the light of some wider considerations, and what sort of things are being taken for granted in her vision. First, however, we should register the extreme importance for the philosopher of religion of Weil's pivotal observation that the more carefully you examine the grammar of 'God' in its traditional uses (God as creator, as 'last end' of creation, as Trinity, as source of unconstrained grace and mercy), the more it should be clear that we are not talking about an item in any possible list of objects, but about what is other than the world as such. And – a subsidiary point to this – the kind of reality appropriately ascribed to such a God is not an issue to be settled by attempts to prove that there is some determinate subject properly called 'God', but is only appropriately dealt with by way of a much more taxing set of questions. These questions have to do with the evaluation of lives purporting to be lived 'before' God: Are their goals and desires 'illusory' or not? Does the language of the divine serve self-oriented purposes or not? Are the changes or 'conversions' involved in such lives adequately characterised in terms of an immanent psychological economics or not?

Like all questions dealing with adequate interpretation rather than adequate explanation, they are incapable of definitive answers accessible to universally agreed methods of inquiry. To borrow an idiom not particularly at home with Weil's normal discourse, they are irremediably 'conversational' issues – matters in which interpretative talk and exchange will simply continue. If – for the interpreter of religious language – the possibility of God is bound up with the possibility of an undeceived life lived 'before' God, a life that can be argued to have integrity and not to be governed by fantasy, then – for the religious believer – the exposition and 'defence' of religious language will be bound up with the effort to provide expositions of what holiness might humanly entail.

So much, I believe, stands from Weil's argument, and it imposes a proper austerity on theological utterance, certainly in so far as it might presume to elucidate how divine action might proceed, as if we were dealing with a subject possessed of determinate goals and choices such as we have. But it is precisely this consideration about the necessary distance between what can be said of finite subject, and what could be said of God, that prompts unease with Weil's analysis of love. She moves very rapidly from the facts of the mobility, fluidity, and discontent of human love to the conclusion that there is an *essence* of love that is unconditional. I want certain specific goods, and my ordinary living has in it a substantial amount of self-regard in that it looks for these goods to be provided, these needs to be fulfilled. If these needs *are* met, we are able to go on existing; but that is not enough, we did not want simply to go on, but to find rest or fulfilment (N 494–5). Love is not satisfied by the meeting of needs, but goes on expanding. If our needs are *not* met, we are tempted to manufacture goods or to pretend that the goods we have attained are an adequate answer to our desires. This cuts us off from reality and so again has the effect of actually increasing our hunger. And if love is thus unsatisfiable, whether or not it achieves any specific goals it sets itself, it is oriented towards unconditionality.

The trouble with this analysis is that, like all essentialist accounts, it is damagingly abstract. It elides things that are habitually and reasonably distinguished in speech. I may have specific goals and desires of which I can intelligibly say that I shall know when they have been satisfied. Of many of these (feeling hungry at a particular moment, wanting to get on with writing a letter, and so on) I can say that, when satisfied, they have no further significance. There are circumstances in which 'ordinary' desires may take on a massive importance and fill our horizons. Normally, however, I know that not *everything* depends on this being fulfilled in some exactly specified way, and that there will be other things I shall need or want in much the same way at a future date. This level of desiring is properly irrelevant, I think, to Weil's argument. We should not – except very loosely ('I'd love a biscuit') – talk of love here as a rule. But the cases of ordinary wants taking on extra significance open the door to something closer to what Weil is interested in. To a starving person, the thought of food has ceased to be a casual or 'routine' desire: survival depends on it. And, more generally in human experience, people may come to believe that their survival – or at least their survival as self-respecting persons – depends on attaining some particular goal which to an observer looks trivial or dispensable. This binding of one's inner security or sense of identity to some external object or person or state of affairs normally indicates a profound affective disorder – so that success in gaining one's goal will by no means allay the underlying fear, need, and vulnerability. This is much more what Weil takes as her starting-point; and if she says, in effect, that this condition is far more pervasive than we might like to think, we ought to take her seriously. After all, the state of the human world does not suggest that human beings have sorted out their desires and their sense of identity or security particularly well – René Girard's account of the fundamental role of 'mimetic rivalry' in socialisation and social relation might be adduced here.

Now there are certainly circumstances in which another person may be entangled in this binding of the self to something external; my value and security may come to depend entirely on my needs and wants being met by a particular kind of human relationship – by a variety of what we usually call human love. In pursuance of my interests (as I imagine them), I may manipulate or tyrannise over someone else, deny their right to be themselves or to have interests other than my supposed interests, and so do profound injury to them. In Weilian terms, I reduce them to something like the condition of an inanimate object in respect of my desires. Weil's claim is that this is endemic in ordinary human relations. If I love someone as a particular individual, this means that their particularity is attractive to me. *These* features of their reality meet or gratify my expectations, they are pleasing by my standards; my selection of them as objects of love means that I have found reason to ignore or discount other aspects of their reality and to withhold love from other individuals not possessed of the relevant desirable features. Thus my love of the individual as individual is *necessarily* an attempt to 'cannibalise' them, to bring them into *my* world on *my* terms. This is not, we should realise, meant to be an empirical observation about the prevalence of distorted or selfish motivations in human relations; it is designed to show what must be involved in 'loving' the particular and the temporal. And, because love has been defined as essentially unconditional, it is also meant to show that love of the individual as such is not really love at all. To think that it is is, as Weil says, a 'mistake' – not a sin, but a plain error, a misuse of words, a conceptual, and not just a moral, solecism.

Because this is the nature of the argument, it cannot be met simply by saying that not all relations are corrupt and self-serving in this way – though I believe it is legitimate to object to the characterisation of inadequate love as a 'mistake'. To say that *all* specific uses of the word 'love' to refer to human relations are misplaced, in the light of a highly controversial prescriptive redefinition of love as essentially unconditional, is to do a rather futile violence to language. If a word is *never* rightly applied in a specific instance, we could never actually learn how to use it, because learning to use a word involves learning to recognise *instances* where it does and does not, apply. We could not learn how to use 'love' from a transcendental argument of the kind Weil presents. But if this is so, we do not and cannot begin with or argue from an 'essence' of love. Love is a word we are taught to apply to certain sorts of relationship, fraught with all the ambiguities characteristic of human relationships as such, relationships vulnerable to time, chance, forgetfulness, and corruption. Certainly we learn how to distinguish between kinds or even degrees of love, we develop ways of identifying, in ourselves and others, levels of self-interest or moral self-referentiality in love that are destructive; we learn, perhaps, how potent in human relations is the desire to be in control, to write scripts for others to perform. But the point is that we learn to distinguish more and less corrupt and damaging kinds of love precisely in the process of particular relationships; we learn about the way in which hidden or tacit, unacknowledged needs dictate our loves only if failure or impasse force us to reflection. And this means that a substantial part of what I learn about love is bound up with a growing clarity about my needs, a reduction in the number of illusions I nurture about myself. I become more capable of distinguishing between the reality of other people and the projections of my buried needs. This means that I am free to enter relationships knowing better what I am asking of another, and better able to see clearly what another person is in him or herself, not only as they relate to what I want. In short, I may learn how to engage with another person in both the respects in which they meet my needs, *and* the respects in which they do not. *Both* are inseparable from engagement with the particularities of an individual life; the alternatives are not the de-realising of another by reducing them to what serves my need, and the loving of the other as an impersonal 'given'. And understanding love in such terms is not separable from reflecting on, and learning from, my own affective history: exploring the development of my 'standpoint'.

Love as something learned from the constant and critical reappropriation of the history of my relationships is not imaginable as independent of a point of view, a place in the world. This should not, however, be taken to mean that we learn love from introspective recollection, or that love is a calculated 'plotting' of the ego on the world's territory, a highly self-conscious strategy. The recognition that it is bound up with a point of view (and thus a subject's and a body's history) is a recognition that what we call 'love' is tied to contingency, to the unpredictable convergences of my self-understanding, my language for and about myself, and the alien depths of other human beings. To purify love is to learn how egotistic fear and fiction work to smooth out the particular otherness of another person, so that my language remains uninterrupted, my control unchallenged, my involvement in time and chance unacknowledged. And to know this contingency in the event of love is precisely to retain and nurture an apprehension of the *difference* of this or that 'other', their own contingency; to be surprised, delighted, puzzled, hurt by them in a way which witnesses to their unassimilated reality, an independent hinterland to their side of the conversation (it is worth comparing Weil here with Levinas on the human face as the 'trace' of the transcendent, that which utterly resists mastering). At its most serious, when love involves a real and costly appropriation in imagination of another's standpoint – what we should call compassionate love – it involves a kind of 'analogical' skill, reading the history of another person through the medium of the possibilities of which my own contingent history has made me aware. If we can make observations about the grammar, rather than the essence, of love, they would have to include reference to a point of view, evolved in time: the 'place' of divine love, outside the world, is unimaginable, not because we are unmitigatedly sinful, or mistaken about the definition of love, but because we are finite, and our love is therefore necessarily temporal and positional. If, by grace or hard work or both, we manage to broaden the scope of our love so that we are able to give patient attention, to respond joyfully and generously, to the presence of a wide variety of others, this suggests not that we have abandoned a point of view, but that we have learned not to let our responses be totally dictated by what we believe to be our needs, and to accept, or even celebrate as a gift, what in another person is irrelevant to my imagined need or expectation.

Further: love is not, as we ordinarily understand it, a matter of attitude in the sense of a modification of our interiority. The 'responses' just mentioned are to do with behaviour. In that sense, we are right to be wary and rather sceptical about claims to universal love; we want to see what a pompous moraliser like Leigh Hunt's Abou ben Adhem actually *does* with particular people in particular circumstances. Weil is inclined to identify particularised love with particularised projects; but, in fact, when she writes about obedience to circumstances, she is effectively making the connection between love and response to specific needs in others. And that alertness to the specific – which saves her notion of love from the reproach of absolute quietism often levelled against it – is rather inadequately catered for by the definition of love as essentially non-positional and devoid of specific direction. There is certainly a tension here in her thinking. Love must be directed to the *whole* system of necessity; but necessity is, of course, precisely what is experienced in this or that encounter, precisely the raw otherness and resistance of this or that piece of the world's process. It is not simply 'otherness as such', not *simply* the generalised absence of God. Or again: a human being can only be loved unconditionally 'if one loves an attribute of him which is indestructible' (*FLN* 282–3); yet unconditional love does not love *any* attribute, any feature which is deemed deserving of love (*N* 220). What is to be loved is surely the absolute contingency, the mortality, of a person: the object freed from the future that our egotistical imagination longs to project (*N* 553), the object or person as radically vulnerable to destruction by time and chance (*N* 218–19; and cf. *N* 483 on God's 'infinite love for finite things as such').

The nature of the tension in Weil's thinking arises, I believe, from an awkward duality in her understanding of 'submission to time' ('Renunciation is submission to time. Suffering causes time and space to enter into the body ... The mortal soul is subject to necessity'; *N* 221). On the one hand, she insists that we have no alternative to loving necessity – the world of limits and particularities – if we are to love truly at all (*N* 492); and this means renouncing the power we should love to have over the future and coping with the limit imposed by a present situation, task or person. In this sense, submission to time suggests an acceptance of the temporally conditioned character of my response, as well as of the object (task, person ...), because I could not truthfully or appropriately respond to a temporal object without letting its temporality shape my own part in the relation. On the other hand, we have seen that Weil can speak as if the temporal conditioning of love were a matter of error and corruption, an obstacle to unconditional love. It seems as if we can only properly love the particular by having no *attitude* to it in its particularity whatsoever. Such a love is safe from the corruptions of the particular: it is a 'submission' to the fact that detached love for the particular is impossible in the world, and thus an acceptance of death. 'One must place one's life in something one cannot touch on any account. It is impossible. It is a death. It means no longer being alive. And that is exactly what is wanted' (N 484). Thus the love for which we aim should be invulnerable, indestructible; such love is only possible in the attitude-less relation to the world of a dead consciousness, a non-consciousness. Death is the ultimate submission to time.

The paradox here is that the dead consciousness is, *as such*, no longer submissive to time, but free of temporality; it is not simply a pure passivity of awareness (whatever exactly that would mean), receiving without judgment or projection what the world proffers, but beyond both action and passion. Or, to put it another way, the problem is that the 'dead' consciousness only does the work Weil wants it to do if its deadness is some sort of willed strategy on the part of a living consciousness; otherwise, there is a hopeless contradictoriness in speaking of deadness as the paradigm for love of, and submission to, the temporal. But this suggests a 'death' which is precisely a work of the imagination, a seizing of the future: suicide is an assertion, an act of *force* (compare Weil's rather startling paragraphs in N 428–6, on the will as a 'principle of violence; which must be made to do violence to itself' – a model which she is obviously aware of as being in tension with the bare acceptance of 'desires and aversions, pleasures and pains' that she has just commended). She has rightly grasped that love from no point of view is not a possible position for a finite subject. She has attempted to surmount the impossibility by – effectively – identifying loving consciousness with no consciousness at all. And I cannot see how this can conceivably be a way of talking about an ideally receptive mode of consciousness – quite apart from the moral ambiguity of the 'strategy of suicide' on Weil's own principles. These tensions are very suggestively and sympathetically explored in J. P. Little's essay in this volume; but I should like to look a little beyond the 'presenting' points of strain to some possible sources for them.

Let me propose, tentatively, that there are at least two rather wider problems in Weil's thought and idiom which intensify her difficulties over the love of particulars. The first is discussed by Peter Winch in his recent book, *Simone Weil: 'The Just Balance'*. He argues, correctly, I believe, that Weil's account of the relation between work and thought is askew in its insistence (at least in some texts) that the paradigm of successful work is something like the solution of a mathematical problem. Such a process is totally free of the 'accidental', it cannot be interrupted by the unpredictable history of the world. Now, as Winch points out,[1] this works as a *grammatical* observation about what counts as a mathematical problem and its solution, but not as a description of what it is like for a specific person to solve a problem at a specific point in time: 'while geometrical figures are independent of contingencies, the mind that thinks about them is not'.[2] The action of the mind in working on a mathematical problem is not, in fact, all that different from the action of the mind in working on any kind of problem: it belongs to all our discourse about the mind's action to involve reference to the struggle with historical and material circumstance, with the uncontrollable. Weil herself is clear enough about this in certain contexts.[3] But her language repeatedly slips towards the notion that the interruptions of circumstance somehow *corrupt* or *distort* the mind's conceptions and purposes.[4] It is not simply that we are always enmeshed in the business of overcoming obstacles; the world of contingency is, as such, an obstacle, over against the freedom of the mind, a freedom shown in our capacity to form 'pure' mathematical conceptions.

My suggestion is that what Simone Weil has to say about the love of particulars and the imperative towards 'purity' of response reproduces the difficulties she runs into with her account of the mind's work. The subject is, in both cases, conceived as fundamentally beyond *conditions*: seeing the forms of geometry of the structures of mathematical proof is, *more Platonico*, bound up with seeing the form of the good (unconditional letting-be), since both can be said to

---

[1] Winch, *The Just Balance*, pp. 96–7.   [2] Winch, p. 98.   [3] Winch, ch. 6.

[4] See Winch's remarks, pp. 73ff., on the curious idea that any geometrical figure constructed in the world involves a *mistake* when compared with the ideal form.

survive unscathed whatever in particular may happen in the world. Furthermore, in both cases, the mind or subject as pure or unconditioned, and thus supremely active and free, is, in concrete terms, powerless; it cannot form the world to its conceptions, and falls into error if it mistakes any worldly outcome for its eternal object. In the activity of mathematics, this error is unavoidable once particular figures are constructed (as they must be – cf. N 237 on 'error as a source of energy'). In the moral life, however, as we have seen, there *is* the possibility of escaping error, by a mode of response to the world from which the ego, the will oriented to temporal ends, is absent ('We are not defiled by actions from which we are absent'; N 57). When this occurs, the relation between situation and response is simply one of congruence. What needs to be done is done – just as in the case of the mathematical operation. When the body in the world can perform only one action in response to a situation, we have 'equilibrium', 'true balance' (N 57, and many other instances) – at least when that 'inevitable' response is the fruit of a conscious policy of withdrawing from the situation the force of the ego, a fully willed submission.

If we reflect a little further on the implications of Weil's understanding of the willing self as both unconditioned and powerless, we come to the second source of her difficulties. This is, admittedly, a more speculative suggestion. Recent discussion of the post-Cartesian development of epistemology (and I think particularly of Stanley Cavell's work) has characterised this history as the quest for a place where no 'claims' are made, no *interest* is involved. It should be possible to identify the pure case of knowing, where the cognitive subject registers a state of affairs without distorting mediation: hence the significance of self-presence as a paradigm of knowledge in this tradition, from Descartes' *cogito* to Moore's 'This is a hand'. Is it possible to see Weil's language here as a kind of ethical and spiritual transcription of this canonisation of cognitive disinterest? Truth is attained only in a position devoid of particularised interest, self-serving or self-reflecting perspectives, mediation through the minds and words of others. Weil's moral truthfulness, her encounter with the reality determinative for the life of the spirit, likewise pulls towards a suspicion of mediation's capacity to block vision, and a search for a position without location in respect of affective relations. Mediation is wholly central to her characterisation of being in the world, yet it is also the source of 'infinite error'. The moral and spiritual task is so to live with mediations that they become the means of eradicating the errors inseparable from being in a position in the world. The subject's position is irretrievably tragic.

If it is true that the Cartesian and post-Cartesian subject is meant to stand to the world in the relation of an effectively absent God, as the vantage-point of freedom from particular determination which only that which is quite other than creation can enjoy, we have a further elucidation of Weil's understanding of the non-existence of God. The same holds for the reverse – that is, if the God of modern abstract theism is conceived as doing the job of the Cartesian ego. The epistemological claim is that, even without God, there is the possibility of a point from which things may be seen truly or justly. Weil accepts the 'modern' conclusion of God's absence from the world, and claims that there is still the possibility of a point from which things may be *loved* justly. But for her the establishing of that possibility is a genuine re-establishing of God, since we must love what is not the world before we can rightly love the world, and we cannot love what is only the creation of our minds. Thus the transcription of the 'view from nowhere' aspiration from the episte-mological to the spiritual sphere has the effect of overcoming atheism without reinstating a divine object: modernity overcome by modernity, perhaps. Whether or not anything like this is part of Weil's *conscious* project, this particular philosophical problematic may be worth considering as a possible locus for her subtle discussion of God's 'existence'. Indeed, the profoundly Kantian nature of her delineation of God's reality shows quite plainly where she is most at home: as in the second Critique, God is the 'invisible' condition for the possibility and intelligibility of our moral aspiration being realised. The logic of our moral life is such that what we hope for must be conceived as capable of actualisation. To conceive our hope in this way, not as an account of what any individual may hope to attain, but as a standing reality beyond the history of phenomena, *is* to conceive of God, God 'on the side of the subject and not on that of the object' (*N* 358).

We are left with a tantalisingly uneven and paradoxical picture. So much of the energy and resourcefulness of Weil's thought, especially in the published essays in *Waiting for God* and *Science Necessity and the Love of God*, comes from a sense of the positive value of the finite – the good life as the fruit of contemplative attention directed to the otherness and uncontrollability of the world, free from the urge to coerce the world into patterns the ego can cope with. This side of her vision assumes that to be human is not to be an absolute initiator or an independent and self-regulating mental substance. The positive contribution of this valuation of uncontrollable otherness is admirably developed by the essays of Richard Bell and Eric Springsted in this collection. Yet her speculation is haunted, most clearly in the late notebooks, by the sense that the necessarily frustrated subject, the limited point of view, is somehow the source of error, a corruption of some potentially divine subjectivity only thinkable for us in terms of negation, passivity, absence, death.

Thinking (or acting) in the first person, that is, out of our finite point of view, is slavery (*IP* 153); liberty is when the 'I' is not there, and God loves God, me and the world in one single unconditioned, unspecific, eternal, indiscernible action (or non-action, perhaps). There is no truth or value in the particular point of view I have as observer, or in the position or stance of what is observed: 'In the universe as seen from a point of view there can only be imaginary forms of balance and plenitude, and thanks to an unlimited exercise of the imagination' (*N* 146). Hence, too, we cannot and must not love ourselves except 'because God loves us' (*N* 278) – and thus, presumably, *as* God loves us, that is, unconditionally and impersonally, as part of the whole fabric of the necessary. God loves that particular perspective of creation which can only be had from the spot where I am; but only when I am absent from it – i.e., not really as a *subject's* perspective. Any other love of God for me as an individual is not conceivable, especially when 'I feel so clearly that even the affection which human beings evince for me can only be a *mistake* on their part' (*N* 364, my italics). But perhaps the most revealing remark on this side of the balance is in the New York notebook (*FLN* 218): 'creation is a fiction of God's'. The otherness of creation to God is reduced to a kind of divine play, in which the *purpose* of creation is decreation: God 'cannot create anything which is God, and ... cannot be loved by anything which is not God' (*N* 330); God is loved to the extent to which creation is destroyed (as subject). Our acceptance of this condition for loving God is our absolution of God for the 'crime' of creation (*FLN* 94–5; cf. 140 and 263), for letting-be a world destined for dissolution, and working towards that dissolution in the process prodigal of terror and pain.

As suggested already, the problem here may be that, in her

interest in the uncontrollable otherness of world and context, the specificity of that otherness, so superbly evoked in *Waiting for God* and *The Need for Roots*, slips away into concern with otherness-as-such – a 'resistance' to the ego which can be abstracted from the labour of working with this or that bit of unyielding environment. A profoundly suggestive philosophy of work (again, lucidly set out in Winch's study and discussed by Clare Fischer in this volume) is entangled with a rather different project – alterity overcome by the dissolving of the positional subject, so that otherness is no longer to be *negotiated* (the term is meant to recall Levinas once again).

When she writes in this vein, it is certainly a dissolution she envisages, not some kind of *Aufhebung*. She echoes Hegel to the extent of envisaging the 'essential' position of finite spirit as identical with that of infinite spirit; but is about as far removed from Hegel as possible in absolutising the alienation of subject and world (there can never, in Weil, be an identity between the process of the world and the activity of the spiritual subject). And the paradoxical effect of remaining at the stage of the 'unhappy consciousness' is that there is no positive evaluation of what consciousness is conscious of, no story of spirit becoming itself in material encounters. Yet something like this would certainly be a possible way forward from the more constructive elements in the Weilian analysis, once something like the Hegelian dissolution of the individual mental substance has been digested. This is simply to put in the terms of her own philosophical formation what can be more adequately pursued in terms of the Wittgensteinian critique of the privileges of mental privacy. But the mention of Hegel is also meant to draw attention to the possibility of talking about the overcoming of the individual perspective, not by the denial or dissolution of points of view, but by a consistently relational and dialogical account of the shaping of human awareness – which would also take seriously the formation of any particular awareness by history, that dimension so often elusive in Simone Weil's thinking. Pursuing this further would lead us into the intriguing area of Weil's aesthetics. Consider for example her insistence that the beautiful in verbal art must be like the visually beautiful, a wholly *contained* movement, a point in space rather than a duration in time, let alone an indeterminate duration in time (i.e. something leaving emotional or interpretative 'loose ends', something with imperfect formal closure), or a set of non-contingent relations, as in music (*N* 4–5; cf. she remarks on tragedy, *N* 620 – 'Shakespeare's tragedies are second-class with the exception of *Lear*', because *Lear* alone succeeds in containing its dramatic movement in a formal way, being a play essentially about power, death, and justice). But this would take us too far afield for the present.

It is hard to attempt any conclusion. Weil's analysis of how God is to be spoken of remains one of the most difficult and challenging of this century, and for that very reason it is important not to canonise it or domesticate it. I have tried to show that, as she presents it, it collapses under a weight of contradictory pressures. How much it helps to propose psychological or sociological explanations for the enormous problems she has with the possibilities of self-love or love of the particular I am not sure, though the questions are worth posing. What, as a woman, is she culturally 'allowed' to think about her body? What on earth is going on in her extraordinarily vitriolic and silly comments on Judaism – a real demonisation of her own heritage? These issues are mercilessly raised by unsympathetic readers like Giniewski';[5] and those convinced (as I am) of Weil's significance and seriousness should not be allowed to brush them aside. However, I have not attempted to tackle them directly in these pages.

If there is a general observation to be made, perhaps it is this: the identification of an imperative to love (as a finite being) with an imperative to take the stance of the creator towards the world is a sure way of undermining the intelligibility of what we can say about love itself (certainly in a religious context; but not exclusively). It is also, theologically speaking, a misunderstanding of the logic of creation. For thinkers like Augustine and Aquinas, the relation of the world to the agency on which it depends, considered in the light of the whole context of revelation, tells us that God wills that there be goods, interest, goals, not identical -- even formally – with the good of self-contemplation that God as God enjoys. God wills what is not God, and so wills a world in which creatures are called to move towards their own immanent goals – certainly within an ordered system in which the highest good is the creature's conscious or 'rational' relation with the creator (so that the interests of self-aware beings are more significant and comprehensive than others), but not in such a way that any specific interest, any legitimate 'natural' need, is dispensable or negligible. The good of the self-

---

[5] P. Giniewski, *Simone Weil ou la haine du soi*, Paris, 1978.

aware creature is union in love and knowledge with God, but within the limits imposed by the nature of creaturehood – temporality, changeability: the complete grammatical break between what is properly said of God and what is said of the creature means that union with God is intelligible only as a *process* of transformation within the order of creation, and never (even 'in heaven') amounts to an identity of subject. Hence the love appropriately given to the self and to objects in the world is (for Augustine at least) a quite complex affair, the struggle so to understand the interests of self and others that they may be woven in to the fundamental and decisive interest of the reasonable subject – the need to be moving further into that trust in God which enables the particular human subject to become a sign of divine trustworthiness to others, and thus to be at one with God's love towards the world. This model is no less serious than Weil's about the impossibility of identifying God or grace as a determinate item for consciousness.

The exposition of this doctrine, of course, raises problems of its own; but what it does succeed in doing is establishing the reality and legitimacy of interests other than God's 'interest'. In simpler terms: to reflect upon and assess the particular needs of myself or anyone else is not a moral catastrophe so long as it is done within the framework of a synoptic sense of the good of creatures made for the love of God. Thus, such reflection and assessment may lead to all sorts of re-visioning of what we think are needs and goods, but will *not* attempt to discard entirely the significance of the variety of personal goods. Because of this, it will be painfully vulnerable to the tragic collision of interest, to the destructive misconceiving of needs, and so on. But this 'fragility of goodness', to borrow the title of Martha Nussbaum's profoundly perceptive and imaginative study, is not a matter of global moral failure, not a *mistake*, not a humiliatingly wrong place for the moral consciousness to be. This is what moral and spiritual life *is* – just as mental life *is* the negotiation of unforeseen (historical) circumstance.

Simone Weil often writes as if she so believed, and yet repeatedly reintroduces the spectre of the 'pure' subject, free from place and time; she thus makes it increasingly hard for herself (the last notebooks contain some of her harshest observations on this) to give an intelligible account of loving what is transitory in its own terms. The only valid interest is eternal – the paradoxical interest of securing a non-position in the world, so that even action apparently directed towards the need of another is really an allowing of the balance of things to remain in position, rather than the fruit of reflective (and fallible) assessment of needs. If we are to take seriously those ways in which Weil helps us to grasp and reflect on the necessarily finite and vulnerable standpoint of moral thought and action, we need to understand also as fully as possible what it is that pushes her argument in the direction of what I think is a morally and intellectually ambiguous, if not unsustainably paradoxical, account of what it is to love God and the world. Without disputing most of her observations on the grammar of 'God', on the existence of God as something other than a particular determination of circumstances in the universe, it is, I think, possible to challenge the assimilation of this grammar to that of the finite moral subject in a state of grace. This also suggests that what Weil implicitly proposes as the controls for our language about God might also need to be challenged. As noted earlier, Weil effectively argues that the ungraced soul *cannot* truthfully speak of God, since it will inevitably conceive God as object, while the graced soul will not speak of God because it has no position over against God's. Words about God can only legitimately be uttered in the process of clarifying what is involved in the difference between the soul's state with and without 'grace' (the acceptance of death for the ego). But if the intelligibility of moral finitude is better preserved by a rather more densely textured account of creation and the relationship between infinite and finite, then the systematic prohibition against saying 'I' to God (N 173) can properly be broken in a language both of praise and of repentance – the acknowledgement of creation as the establishing and sustaining of a non-divine point of view precisely in its vulnerability and unfinishedness.

CHAPTER 3

God and concept-formation in Simone Weil

D. Z. Phillips

My aim in this essay is to do no more than to *indicate the direction* in which we have to look, according to Simone Weil, if we want to appreciate the forms concept-formation takes where the notion of God is concerned. In her work there are, of course, detailed explorations of what it may mean to come into contact with God. My remarks, in that context, amount to no more than scratchings of the surface, and other essays in this volume go into greater detail. At first, my more limited objective may seem to have little to do with the observations we find in *Gravity and Grace*. In his introduction to the work, Gustav Thibon says, more than once, 'Simone Weil speaks as a mystic and not as a metaphysician' (*GG* xxxi). Certainly anyone who has attempted to study her work at all seriously, will have experienced the difficulty in distinguishing between her philosophical and religious observations. Language which may be acceptable as part of a religious meditation, may raise all sorts of difficulties if offered as part of a philosophical analysis. Nevertheless, care must be taken in drawing the distinction between mysticism and metaphysics. It may be drawn in a way which blunts the specifically *philosophical* challenge in Simone Weil's work. This has happened, it seems to me, in the following remarks by Thibon:

I shall be particularly careful not to pick a quarrel with Simone Weil about words. Her vocabulary is that of the mystics and not of the speculative theologians: it does not seek to express the eternal order of being but the actual journey of the soul in search of God. This is the case with all spiritual writers. When in the *Dialogue* of Saint Catherine of Siena Christ says to her: 'I am that which is, thou art that which is not', this formula which reduces the creature to pure nothingness cannot be accepted on the plane of ontological knowledge. It is the same with expressions used by so many mystics who speak of the poverty of God, of his dependence in relation to the creature, etc: they are true in the order of love and false in the order of being. Jacques Maritain was the first to show, with perfect metaphysical precision, that these two vocabularies do not contradict each other, for one is related to speculative and the other to practical and affective knowledge. (*GG* xxx–xxxi)

It is odd to make this sharp distinction between speculative and practical knowledge with respect to Simone Weil. She argues, as did Kierkegaard and Wittgenstein, that speculative systems often contradict what is evident in practical and affective knowledge. For example, some speculative philosophical systems have denied that we can be certain of the existence of physical objects, while our everyday dealings with them belie this claim. Such systems have also claimed that the existence of human beings, other than oneself, is a matter of inference and conjecture, based on analogical reasoning from one's own case. But, in our daily dealings with other people, the question of whether they are human beings simply does not arise.

For Simone Weil, it is not enough simply to note these tensions. We must explore the tendencies in us which give rise to them. The result of becoming clear about them is not the devising of better speculative systems, but a questioning of the need for them. Simone Weil wants to bring us back from metaphysical words to real words. Instead of drawing a sharp distinction between speculative and practical knowledge, she urges us to give practice, human action, a central place in our speculations. Unless we do this, Simone Weil argues, we cannot account for concept-formation in any context, whether, for example, that context concerns perception or religion.

These conclusions can be illustrated by a familiar philosophical puzzle which she faced early in her work: How can we be sure that the experiences we have when we seem to confront the world, actually reflect the order of that world? She noted that in the expression of this question, experiences are thought of as passive. As a result, an unbridgeable gap seems to be opened up between the experiences and the world, and between one experience and another. Simone Weil argues that one reason we have this problem is because we ignore the centrality of *action* in our experience of the world. In his introduction to her *Lectures on Philosophy* Peter Winch says:

Action is conceived, in the first instance, as a series of bodily movements having a certain determinate temporal order. In its primitive form action is quite unreflective. Human beings, and other animate creatures, naturally react in characteristic ways to objects in their environments. They salivate in the presence of food and eat it; this already effects a rudimentary classification (which doesn't have to be based on any reflection) between 'food' and 'not food'. Our eyes scan objects and connect with other characteristic movements of our bodies, we sniff things or sometimes hold our noses), we exhibit subtly different reactions to things we put into our mouths – corresponding to such classifications of tastes as 'sour', 'sweet', 'salty', etc. – and so on. These reactions are refined and developed as we mature; and some of these refinements and developments are responses to training by other human beings around us, A staircase is something to be climbed, a chair is something to be sat in: compare Wittgenstein's remark: 'It is part of the grammar of the word 'chair' that this is what we call "to sit on a chair".'[1] As Simone Weil expresses it: 'Everything that we see suggests some kind of movement, however imperceptible. (A chair suggests sitting down, stairs climbing up, etc.). (*LP* 31)

Winch continues:

Our recognition of the qualities of things, in its most primitive form, is itself expressed in characteristic reactions; reflective action – action based on a prior recognition – is a subsequent, more sophisticated stage, presupposing the prior formation of appropriate concepts. (*LP* 11–12)

Here we do not have a sharp break between the conceptual and the practical. On the contrary, the primitive reactions of which Simone Weil speaks are central in what is meant by concept-formation. It is in these reactions that we are, from the outset, part of, and linked with, the world. In relation to perception, Simone Weil sums up these conclusions in a striking way:

The very nature of the relationship between ourselves and what is external to us, a relationship which consists in a reaction, a reflex, is our perception of the external world. Perception of nature, pure and simple, is a sort of dance; it is this dance that makes perception possible for us. (*LP* 52)

Simone Weil insists that when we reflect on religion, here too, as in the case of perception, we need to take account of the centrality of human reactions in concept-formation. Yet, when this suggestion is made, it meets strong resistance in contemporary philosophy of religion. It is as though some kind of exception is being sought for religion. Some say that an expressive, rather than a cognitive, view of religion is being advanced (as though *that* distinction clarified anything). But we might as well say that Simone Weil is advancing an expressive, rather than cognitive, account of perception. What Simone Weil is concerned to explore, in fact, is the forms concept-

[1] Ludwig Wittgenstein, *The Blue and Brown Books*, Oxford: Blackwell, 1958, p. 24.

formation take in religion. In making human reactions central in her account, she is not adopting a defensive strategy for religion for apologetic purposes. As we have seen, the centrality of human reactions is equally essential in an account of how our notions of physical objects, tastes, smells, colour, etc. are formed. Simone Weil is not advancing *hypotheses* about concept-formation, but rather exploring the contexts in which concepts have their meaning. As Simone Weil says: 'We do not have to understand new things, but by dint of patience, effort and method to come to understand with our whole self the truths which are evident' (*GG* 105).

But, if the truths are evident, why do we need patience, effort, and method to be clear about them? One reason is that when we philosophise we ignore the surroundings in which concepts have their sense. We think we know their grammar *prior* to looking at their actual application. As we saw, by treating perceptual experiences as passive, Simone Weil shows how an unbridgeable gap is created between perceptions and their object. Similarly, by treating religious experience as passive, an unbridgeable gap is created between the experience and the reality of God. In both cases, the formative role of human reactions is ignored. Of course, that formative role is not the same in the two contexts.

As a result of ignoring this formative role in religion, the surface grammar of religious belief misleads us. We ask whether the word 'God' refers to anything, or worse, whether it 'stands for' anything. Once we do so, we become embroiled in grammatical confusions. We treat the word 'God' as a name and ask whether there is an object which corresponds to the name. We do this, Simone Weil says, despite the fact that the surroundings of belief in God show that we did not acquire the concept in this way at all. If we paid attention to the actual surroundings, Simone Weil tells us, we would find that belief in God is formed via a hunger for an absolute goodness and love which cannot be satisfied by any object, by anything that exists. (Cf. Rowan Williams' essay, p. 56f., above). The irony is that while the sceptic asks for the object, the existent, which is the bearer of the name 'God', Simone Weil is insisting that any object one discovered, of necessity, could not be God. No object can be worthy of the worship due to God. Of course, for the sceptic, this is equivalent to saying that 'God' is a fiction. But this conclusion, according to Simone Weil, can only be drawn by ignoring the actual use of the word 'God'. She insists: 'This non-existent object of love is not a fiction, however, for our fictions cannot be any more worthy of love than we are ourselves, and we are not worthy of it' (*GG* 100). Seeing that 'God' is not an object, an existent among existents, is a necessary precondition for freeing ourselves from confusions concerning the concept. Simone Weil insists: 'Nothing which exists is absolutely worthy of love. We must therefore love that which does not exist' (*GG* 99).

Simone Weil marks out the context in which concept-formation concerning the notion of God has to be explored in the following striking remarks:

A case of contradictories which are true. God exists: God does not exist. Where is the problem? I am quite sure there is a God in the sense that I am quite sure my love is not illusory. I am quite sure that there is not a God in the sense that I am quite sure nothing real can be anything like what I am able to conceive when I pronounce this word. But that which I cannot conceive is not an illusion. (*GG* 103).

Simone Weil is not saying, as some have thought, that we can have no conception of God. What is she doing if not attempting to clarify that conception? She is saying, it seems to me, that if we want to understand what is meant by the reality of God, we should look at what it means to love God. If, on the other hand, we treat 'God' as a name and look for the bearer of the name, we will find nothing. Whatever you think you can conceive *in that context* nothing real corresponds to it. The notion of God, properly understood, cannot be conceived in this way. But, Simone Weil concludes, it does not follow from the fact that God cannot be conceived of in *this* way, that God is an illusion.

If we want to see how the word 'God' is used, instead of emphasising that it is a substantive, we would do well to see how the word concerns the reality of a certain kind of love. Simone Weil is saying with John, in his First Epistle, 'He that loveth not knoweth not God; for God is love' (1 John 4:8). For her, the 'is' in 'God is love' is not an 'is' of predication. Rather, we are being given a grammatical rule for one use of the word 'God'. This being so, it is not a rule which needs an underpinning by reference to some kind of object, thought of as the bearer of the love in question. To use Wittgenstein's terms, the language-game involving the word 'love', in this context, is in no way incomplete. To think otherwise, Simone Weil insists, is to be guilty of misunderstanding. In this respect, in the search for an object-like referent, atheism, she says is quite right in its denials. She says, 'Of two men who have no experience of God, he who denies him is perhaps nearer to him than the other' (*GG* 103). Such atheism, Simone Weil argues, may be used as a form of purification. Denying that God exists, in one context, may at least prepare the way for an appreciation of the context in which talk of God has its sense. Thus, when Simone Weil asks us to consider the sense in which God is love, she is not considering some practical aspect of the matter which needs supplementing by a speculative aspect. She is saying that if our speculations are to concern real words, this is the context to which we must pay attention. She is not saying, as Thibon would have us believe, something which is false in 'the order of being', but true 'in the order of love'. If we want to use such language at all, a language which may obscure more than it illuminates, Simone Weil may be said to insist that, where the reality of God is concerned, the only 'order of being' *is* 'the order of love'.

Those who trade on distinctions between the cognitive and the expressive, will say that this conclusion sacrifices all considerations of truth where God's reality is concerned. But is this so? Certainly not as far as Simone Weil is concerned. She asks, 'How can we distinguish the imaginary from the real in the spiritual realm?' (*GG* 47). Is that a question by someone with no concern for truth?

Simone Weil wrestles with the question of truth in the spiritual realm in two contexts. In the first, she argues that whereas love of God is real, the other loves which possess us are not. For me, this claim raises a number of difficulties; difficulties also discussed in Rowan Williams' essay (see pp. 62–8). She seems to suggest that we do not find sufficient that which we say we love: wealth, power, consideration, friends, the love of those we love, the well-being of those we love, etc. By contrast, love of God is not an illusion. According to Simone Weil, we deny these matters only because we lie to ourselves. She claims: 'it is only necessary to be honest with oneself to realize that there is nothing in this world to live for' (*SNLG* 148). What does saying this amount to? Her answer is found in a further claim:

... all the goods of this world, past, present or future, real or imaginary, are finite and limited and radically incapable of satisfying the desire which burns perpetually within us for an infinite and perfect good. All men know this, and more than once in their lives they recognize it for a moment, but then they immediately begin deceiving themselves again so as not to know it any longer, because they feel that if they know it they could not go on living. (*SNLG* 158)

These remarks make a love of finite things look like a product of self-deception. But there is no reason for saying that a desire for an infinite and perfect good can be found in every man, or any reason for saying that the desires men do have are strategies of self-deception to hide this fact from themselves.

In some ways, Simone Weil's remarks remind one of Socrates' discussion with Polus in the *Gorgias* concerning the tyrant Archelaus. Sometimes, at least, Socrates, when he says that Archelaus is not really happy, seems to be suggesting that Archelaus does not really want what he says he wants. Of course, this might have been the case. For all its outward show, his boastings at his unscrupulousness could have hidden a terrible hunger in his heart. But, from what Polus tells us, this does not seem to have been the case. Of course, Socrates would not have been satisfied to live like Archelaus. He may have found it difficult to believe that anyone could be satisfied with such a life, although I doubt that. In any case, Polus certainly would not be satisfied to live the life Socrates lived, and he did find it hard to believe that anyone would want to live in that way. But that gave him no reason for saying as he did, that Socrates really wanted to live like Archelaus, if he would only admit it. Equally, however, I see no reason why Socrates or Simone Weil should say that Archelaus, if only he were honest with himself, really hungers for an infinite and perfect good, and does not really want what he says he wants.

Simone Weil offers a further consideration which is meant to show that men are not really satisfied with finite things, which creates for me further difficulties. She says that, in order to see that there is nothing in this world to live for, 'We have only to imagine all our desires satisfied; after a time we should become discontented. We should want something else and we should be miserable through not knowing what to want' (*SNLG* 148). Now, it is true that utopias which seek to give a picture of human life free of all limitations present a horrific or banal prospect, depending on the details of the picture. What is problematic is the bearing such unreal depictions is supposed to have on life as it actually is. It is entirely unclear how they are supposed to show that I do not really think worth desiring that which I desire *in my actual situation*.

It should not be thought that Simone Weil always came to the conclusions I have criticised. Elsewhere, instead of saying that the desire for a perfect and infinite good burns in every human being, Simone Weil says that the possibility of awakening such a desire cannot be ruled out in any man, a somewhat different claim (*SE* 219). Also, instead of the general thesis that there is nothing in the world worth living for, elsewhere what Simone Weil says is that what love of God amounts to is found in turning one's attention away from finite things. This does not involve her in the claim that we do not really desire and find satisfaction in finite things when we say we do.

But what kind of attention is involved in love of God? This brings us to the second context in which Simone Weil says it is essential to distinguish between the imaginary and the real in the spiritual realm. How is this to be done? For her, much of the answer depends on what reactions are called forth by the limits of human existence: birth, death, the presence of unavoidable suffering, the arbitrariness of fate, the contingencies of time and place. Concept-formation in religion may go in a number of different directions in face of these limits. Sometimes, the directions taken involve fantasies. For example, faced with the question of why one should heed moral considerations, some people invent a policeman in the sky, an infantile morality, for which religion has so often been criticised. Simone Weil thinks such criticism is justified: '... what do you tell a child if you want to explain to him that he should never tell lies? If the family is a religious one, one will explain to the child that God knows everything. This answer to the child's question makes a policeman of God. Obedience which is understood in this way is not a virtue' (*LP* 171).

But, faced with the limitations of human existence, obedience to God is often thought of as justified prudence. Simone Weil says that, when the world does not smile on us, we invent a God who does. She would not deny, therefore, that there is a great deal of truth in Feuerbach's claim that were there no wishes there would be no gods. Such gods are the result of thwarted attachments. We hope that disappointments in this life will be compensated in the next life. Theodicies try to spell out why the disappointments have to be suffered in the first place. Others, appalled at the vulgarity of the explanations theodicies offer, still want compensations for life's disappointments. They say that reasons for our predicament do exist, but that they are too deep to fathom at the moment. Sooner or later, however, God or the gods will have to justify themselves. They, too, will not accept what Simone Weil calls 'the silence of god'. Instead, they attempt to transcend the limitations of human existence by offering a compensatory future state of affairs which may, or may not, be the case. One set of contingencies is met by the promise of another set of contingencies. Although the second set is supposed to be transcendent, what we have, Simone Weil says, is an attempt to meet the finite in terms of the finite. She warns: 'We have to be careful about the level on which we place the infinite. If we put it on the level which is only suitable for the finite it does not much matter what name we give it' (*GG* 48–9).

The reason we have to be careful is because we make 'God' the mere product of imaginary consolations. Such a god is man writ large, conceived as an extension of human powers. Such an extension is often found, Simone Weil claims, in the God of the early Hebrews and the gods of Roman religion. She regarded these deifications of human power as idolatrous, and stated baldly that the promise of compensation offered is simply a lie. Such promises do not amount to real words; they do not really sustain us when we are faced with suffering: 'As a rule our imagination puts words into sounds in the same way as we idly play at making out shapes in wreaths of smoke; but when we are too exhausted, when we no longer have the courage to play, then we must have real words' (*GG* 102). But we will not arrive at real words in religion unless we put fantasy aside. Simone Weil says, 'We must prefer real hell to an imaginary paradise' (*GG* 47). The imaginary paradise is a sign of our continuing attachments; the futile attempt to make the temporal permanent. For Simone Weil, a precondition of distinguishing between the real and the imaginary in the spiritual realm is a readiness to face real loss without false consolations. She says, 'Attachment is a manufacturer of illusions and whoever wants reality ought to be detached' (*GG* 14).

For Simone Weil, the notion of God's will is formed through the practice of detachment. Detachment involves acceptance of the limitations of human life, and a recognition that they cannot be denied. Simone Weil says:

The beings I love are creatures. They were born by chance. My meeting with them was also chance. They will die. What they think, do and say is limited and is a mixture of good and evil. I have to know this with all my

soul and not love them the less. I have to imitate God who infinitely loves
finite things in that they are finite things. (*GG* 97)

The supernatural is contacted in a certain relation to the natural, a
relation in which a distinctive attention is given to the limitations of
human existence. Necessities are accepted as such. This much is
sometimes recognised in colloquial speech when something is said to
be in the lap of the gods. But the attention Simone Weil is speaking
of is a form of love in which necessities become vehicles of grace.
Such love says that nothing is ours by right and that we should not
make ourselves the centre of things. Other human beings and the
natural world are seen under the aspect of a gift. Simone Weil calls
this love, love of the beauty of the world. She says it is an implicit
form of the love of God. It is what enables her to say, 'Limitation is
the evidence that God loves us' (*GG* 95). Simone Weil gives the
following example of how reflecting on the limitations and contingencies involved in the meeting of her parents leads her to think
of God:

We want everything which has a value to be eternal. Now everything
which has a value is the product of a meeting, lasts through this meeting
and ceases when those things which met are separated. That is the central
idea of Buddhism (the thought of Heraclitus). It leads straight to God.
    Meditation on chance which led to the meeting of my father and mother
is even more salutary than meditation on death.
    Is there a single thing in me of which the origin is not to be found in that
meeting? Only God. And yet again, *my* thought of God had its origin in
that meeting. (*GG* 87)

It is important to remember, however, that Simone Weil's notion
of love of the beauty of the world involves trials and tribulations as
much as blessings. This should be sufficient to show that the love she
is talking about is not an aesthetic response to an object. The love is
said to be love of the beauty of *the world*, and 'the world' is no more
an object than God is. She, as always, insists on distinguishing
between the imaginary and the real. We must avoid false consolations. For her, the notion of God's will is expressed in unavoidable sufferings. The concept is not given prior to such occurrences.
She says: 'God sends affliction without distinction to the wicked and
to the good, just as he sends the rain and the sunlight. He did not
reserve the cross for Christ ... No event is a favour on the part of
God – only grace is that' (*GG* 101). That grace, contact with God,

occurs, according to Simone Weil, as a response to a gaze turned in that direction from the midst of suffering. Here is what that gaze involved for her:

If I thought that God sent me suffering by an act of his will and for my good, I should think that I was something, and I should miss the chief use of suffering which is to teach me that I am nothing. It is therefore essential to avoid all such thoughts, but it is necessary to love God through the suffering.

I must love being nothing. How horrible it would be if I were something! I must love my nothingness, love being a nothingness. I must love with that part of the soul which is on the other side of the curtain, for the part of the soul which is perceptible to consciousness cannot love nothingness. It has a horror of it. Though it may think it loves nothingness, what it really loves is something other than nothingness. (*GG* 101)

Some have seen in remarks such as these a denial of human dignity. Nothing could be further from her intention. For her, dying to the self, to being a somebody, is to see all human beings as children of God. They are seen as such, however, only to the extent that they are loved as human beings. Only in the context of such love and respect, Simone Weil says, can someone help the sufferer without thinking that he is something, and the sufferer can receive charity without feeling bought. This is a religion of real words, instead of false consolations. She insists: 'A test of what is real is hard and rough. Joys are found in it, not pleasure. What is pleasant belongs to dreams' (*GG* 47).

For Simone Weil, the test of what is real in the spiritual realm is determined by the illumination given to earthly things. She says: 'Earthly things are the criterion of spiritual things . . . Only spiritual things are of value, but only physical things have a verifiable existence. Therefore, the value of the former can only be verified as an illumination projected on to the latter' (*FLN* 147). As we have seen, Simone Weil says that the spirit of the attention found in love of the beauty of the world constitutes contact with God. The sense arrived at in such attention does not depend on one event occurring rather than another. That is why she says, 'The only good which is not subject to chance is that which is outside the world' (*GG* 98). For her, this good is God. It can never be, however, an additional object, not even an additional super-object, to all those objects which come to be and pass away. No such object could fill the grammatical role Simone Weil has elucidated. God is not an additional existent, but the Spirit in which all existing things are seen. Simone Weil says, 'The object of the search should not be the supernatural, but the world. The supernatural is light itself: if we make an object of it we lower it' (*GG* 118). Thus, for Simone Weil, God is more real than anything that exists. God does not belong to the world of finite things, but gives sense to it. In saying this, she is not turning away from the supernatural, but locating its grammatical context. The concept of God is mediated through the necessities and limitations of human life. Simone Weil concludes: 'It is precisely by this antithesis, this rending of our souls between the effects of grace within us and the beauty of the world around us, on the one hand, and the implacable necessity which rules the universe on the other, that we discern God as both present to man and as absolutely beyond all human measurement' (*GG* 101 fn).

Further difficulties can be raised beyond those I have discussed in this essay concerning *the kind* of illimination 'the eternal' brings to earthly things. Certainly, there are tensions in what Simone Weil says, and Rowan Williams, in his essay, is correct in drawing attention to them. There are those moments when her remarks shock us by their unattractive austerity: 'I feel so clearly that even the affection which human beings evince for me can only be a *mistake* on their part' (*N* 364. Rowan Williams' italics; see p. 72). Rowan Williams is absolutely right in claiming that her analysis of 'unconditional love', 'like all essentialist accounts ... is damagingly abstract' (p. 63). There *are* times when she does violence to the character of *particular* relationships and particular loves.

On the other hand, in seeking to trace the source of this tendency in her thought, there is a danger that Rowan Williams succumbs to the same essentialism. I do not think there is much to be gained from the suggestion that Simone Weil's views can be appreciated in terms of post-Cartesian developments in epistemology, 'the quest for a place where no "claims" are made, no *interest* is involved ... the pure case of knowing, where the cognitive subject registers a state of affairs without distorting mediation: hence the significance of self-presence as paradigm of knowledge in this tradition, from Descartes' *cogito* to Moore's "This is a Hand"' (Williams, p. 70). He asks: 'Is it possible to see Weil's language ... as a kind of ethical and spiritual transcription of this canonisation of cognitive disinterest?' I think the answer must be, 'No'. Accepting such a view would do violence to too much of what Simone Weil has to say about the importance of mediation; an importance which Rowan Williams recognises. Indeed, the suggestion would deny all the central contentions I have tried to outline in this essay concerning Simone Weil's insights about concept-formation in religious belief.

In doing justice to the vulnerability of human life, to its inevitable conflicts and contradictions, Rowan Williams is attracted by Martha Nussbaum's notion of the 'fragility of goodness'. He finds it 'profoundly perceptive and imaginative'. He goes as far as to say that this 'is what moral and spiritual life *is* ... the negotiation of unforeseen (historical) circumstance' (p. 75). Here we can begin to do violence to the grammar of 'the divine'. It is the very sense of the vulnerability to which Rowan Williams refers which can give rise to the sense of God's unchanging reality, the sense of a love with which there is no variableness or shadow of turning. No doubt, human beings do stumble to realise such love in their lives. In giving an account of this, what is ragged must be left ragged. It would be a major mistake, however, to incorporate the vulnerability of *our relation* to divine love, *into the grammar of that divine love itself.* If that is done, we shall fail to see how that love can give a sense to the vulnerability which it could not have otherwise. There may be tensions in Simone Weil's attempts to elucidate what that sense comes to, but what she is struggling to grasp must not be modified for that reason.

In trying to convey, as best one can, the grammatical insights of Simone Weil, in contemporary philosophy of religion, one is faced with a number of formidable difficulties. First, as we have seen, it is not enough to note a tension between our practice, what we do, and our speculative systems. We must unravel the tendencies which lead us astray. We have seen what happens when we treat 'God' as a name and look for the bearer of the name. To appreciate this, however, we have to show philosophical patience in paying attention to what lies before us; to what Simone Weil calls 'evident truths'. But this is where the difficulty resides. Even when these 'truths' are evident in people's lives, they may still give confused philosophical accounts of them. This happens in the case of tables, chairs, tastes, and smells, so it is hardly surprising that it should happen where the use of the word 'God' is concerned. How easy it is to think that if 'God' does not refer to an object or, as philosophers sometimes prefer to say, an entity, the word 'God' can simply indicate, at best, a useful fiction. The philosopher's task is to uncover the source of these temptations.

At this point, we are faced with a second difficulty. Speculative systems have denied that we can be sure of the existence of physical objects. We are not being dogmatic in rejecting this claim. There is nothing corresponding to atheism where belief in the existence of physical objects is concerned. Attention to practice, to what people do, reveals the unreality of the philosophical denials. The denials reveal a misunderstanding of the logic of the language concerning physical objects which people use when not philosophising. The same cannot be said of the use of the word 'God'. Here, atheism amounts to saying that belief in God is meaningless to the atheist. Does the atheist misunderstand? Not if this means misunderstanding the logic of the language, since he has no use for this language. It does not get off the ground for him. Nevertheless, despite this additional difficulty, the philosophical task remains unchanged, namely, to become clear about the grammar of religious concepts when they *are* used in people's lives. This is no more than an elementary requirement in understanding any human activity. The achievement of clarity need not lead one to embrace what one becomes clear about, or rule out even active hostility towards it.

In the appeal to the use of religious concepts in people's lives, a third difficulty arises. That use is mixed. William James spoke of the variety of religious experience. He refers to Isaiah's great vision of God in the temple, but he also refers to the lady who was comforted by the thought that she could always cuddle up to God. Simone Weil was certainly aware of this variety. As we have seen, she notes that, for some, God is a policeman in the sky. Her vital distinction between supernatural and natural religion marked, for her, the difference between an acknowledgement of grace and the deification of human power. In her work, she explored the different hopes and expectations which surround these different conceptions of religion. It must be admitted, therefore, that Simone Weil, in this comparison, gives priority to certain religious possibilities to the detriment of others. It is also important to remember, however, that she thought the possibilities she emphasises are central to Christianity and to most of the major religions of the world.

Yet, even in the case of the religion she regards as idolatrous, there are active religious responses in the lives of the people concerned, even if they are not particularly admirable. What are worse, in some ways, are the debates of philosophers, *pro* or *contra*, where the words are unreal words, having little connection with what is really at issue. As we have seen, Simone Weil says, 'I am quite sure that there is a God in the sense that I am quite sure that my love is not illusory' (*GG* 103). Philosophers have said that love of God presupposes belief in the existence of God. Simone Weil thinks such talk is idle as a characterisation of what she means by contact with God, since she insists, 'There is no other relation between man and God except love' (*SNLG* 157). The route to God is via hunger, not via an assessment of belief of the kind which preoccupies so much of the epistemology of religion. Simone Weil says:

We must only wait and call out. Not call upon someone, while we still do not know if there *is* anyone; but cry out that we are hungry and want bread. Whether we cry for a long time or a short time, in the end we shall be fed, and then we shall not believe but we shall *know* that there really is bread. What surer proof could one ask for than to have eaten it? But before one has eaten, it is neither needful nor particularly useful to believe in bread. What is essential is to know that one is hungry; and this is not belief, it is absolutely certain knowledge which can only be obscured by lies. (*SNLG* 159)

The philosophical doubts seem unreal in this context. Simone Weil does not deny that these doubts arise. She is certainly not saying that they should not. But, for someone who has come into contact with God, Simone Weil says, 'the doubt concerning the reality of God is purely abstract and verbal, much more abstract and verbal than the doubt concerning the reality of the things of sense. When such a doubt presents itself one has only to entertain it unreservedly to discover how abstract and verbal it is' (*SNLG* 158). Should not this also be the case for a philosopher who, even if he does not embrace religion, pays attention to the grammar of the religious commitment Simone Weil is talking about? Philosophers' words become unreal when they are not mediated through the realities of human life she draws to our attention. For her, many speculative systems fail this vital test:

The limitless is the *test* of the one: time, of eternity: the possible, of necessity: variety, of the unvarying.
   The value of a system of knowledge, a work of art, a moral code or a soul is measured by the degree of its resistance to this test. (*GG* 96)

Simone Weil applied this test rigorously in her own work. She would not lie against religion, but she would not lie for it either. In her intellectual work, as elsewhere, she strove for real words. One of her former pupils says of her:

Her whole life was an illustration of the words of Goethe which she loved to quote and which we once used as a conclusion of some piece of work: 'Action is easy, thought is difficult; to reconcile action and thought is the most difficult of all.' She was not afraid of difficult tasks, and did not realise that she was accomplishing them. (*LP* 26)

CHAPTER 4

The concept of reading and the 'Book of Nature'

Diogenes Allen

This essay has two principal concerns. First, it seeks to examine Simone Weil's concept of reading (or *lecture*) from the point of view of its interconnections with other concepts in her thought, namely, necessity, order, suffering, work, and decreation. This will help show how her thoughts are organised, which for the study of Simone Weil should be of particular concern, since she so prized order.

The second concern is with the natural world. From the earliest writings and practices of the Eastern Christian Churches, it was believed that God could be known from two principle sources: the 'Book of Scripture' and the 'Book of Nature'. The visible things of nature were thought to be an adumbration of the invisible God, and it was thought possible 'to discern, in and through each created reality, the divine presence that is within and at the same time beyond it. It is to treat each thing as a sacrament, to view the whole of nature as God's book.'[1]

We hear more than an echo of this tradition in Weil's remark,

As one has to learn to read, or to practise a trade, so one must learn to feel in all things, first and almost solely, the obedience of the universe to God . . . For us, this obedience of things in relation to God is what the transparency of a window pane is in relation to light. As soon as we feel this obedience with our whole being, we see God. (*SNLG* 180, 179)

According to Weil, we are always reading events and people, since all that we are aware of is invested with meaning. We shall find that for Weil the *meaning* of some thoughts, such as a letter to a mother announcing the death of her son, can have the same effect or

---

[1] Kallistos Ware, 'Ways of Prayer and Contemplation', in *Christian Spirituality*, edited by Bernard McGinn and John Meyendorff, New York: Crossroad, 1985, p. 398.

93

impact as a physical sensation caused by a fist blow to the stomach. So, too, can an adequate reading of nature cause a person to be powerfully but joyfully gripped by God's loving presence.

The conviction that nature mediates the divine presence virtually disappeared in Western civilisation with the rise of classical physics in the early modern period. First, nature was viewed as a machine and God's existence was posited to account for the apparent design in nature (Deism). Later, nature widely came to be viewed as the ultimate reality. Today, even believing academic theologians have little to say about nature mediating God's presence. In Protestant Christianity, nature as a source of knowledge of God and as part of the exercise of a spirituality that leads to intimate contact with God largely disappeared with the collapse of Hegel's philosophy of nature in Germany, and with the rise of Darwinism in the English-speaking world.

My concerns in this paper with the concept of 'reading', and with the idea that nature manifests God, come together in an examination of how Simone Weil attempts to restore, or make plausible for us today, a supernatural reading of nature. These two concerns are clearly connected in Weil's thought. For example, in the passage just quoted, in which Weil points out that when nature's obedience is fully felt, we see God, she refers immediately to some of the same images – a blind man's stick, and a penholder – that she uses in her 'Essay on the Notion of Reading', to explain what she means by the concept of reading.

A major concern of Simone Weil's life after she had a visitation by Christ was to experience the presence of God in all things. For example, she desires: 'a life in which the supernatural truths would be read in every kind of work, in every act of labour, in all festivals, in all hierarchical social relation, in all art, in all science, in all philosophy' (*FLN* 173).

At the core of the realisation of this ambition is the development of the concept of reading, and in particular learning to read nature's operations religiously. This involves a recognition that many readings are debased readings, as the following passage indicates:

... contemplation of eternal truths in the symbols offered by the stars and the combination of substances. Astronomy and chemistry are degradations of them. When astrology and alchemy become forms of magic they are still lower degradations of them. Attention only reaches its true dimensions when it is religious. (*GG* 120)

THE CONCEPT OF READING

The concept of reading can be found throughout Weil's writings, but only one short essay of a few pages is devoted exclusively to it, namely the 'Essay on the Notion of Reading'. In this essay, she takes it that we are already language users and literate. She seeks to define a notion which she calls 'reading' because it is analogous to actual reading. When we read a book or a newspaper, we have black marks on white paper. But these marks are hardly, if at all, noticed, and if they are, their intrinsic features, such as the colour of the ink and paper, are usually a matter of indifference to us. What matters is the meaning that we read. Furthermore, the meaning seems to be given directly: 'We are not given sensations and meanings; only what we read is given; we do not see the letters' (*ER* 298).[2] Weil notes in passing that this is why proofreading is difficult.

Simone Weil claims that the example of the blind man's stick, as found in Descartes, in which a blind man knows through a stick what is beyond his body, is 'analogous to reading' (*ER* 298). She writes (switching to the example of a penholder to make the same point),

Everyone can convince himself in handling a penholder that to use it is as if one is carried to the end of the pen. If the pen runs into some unevenness in the paper, the skip of the pen is immediately given, and the sensations of the fingers and hand across which we read it never even appear. And yet the skip of the pen is only something that we read. (*ER* 298)

The sensations in the fingers and hand, like the black marks on white paper, are hardly, if at all, noticed. It is as if we are *directly* in contact with what is at the end of the pen, namely, the unevenness of the surface of the paper on which we are writing. The unevenness is what we 'read', just as the meaning of the shapes is what we read when we look at black marks on white paper. Meaning is not an intrinsic feature of signs or words; this is why the black marks on white paper are barely noticed.

We are not, of course, actually reading with a pen in precisely the same sense that we read a book or a newspaper. But it is analogous to actual reading, as the black marks on white paper in one case, and

---

[2] I am using a translation of this essay done by Martin Andic. The citations in the text are to the published translation noted in the list of abbreviations.

feelings in the fingers and hand in the other, are not attended to; and something else is attended to as if it is directly given (meaning, in the one case, and the unevenness of the paper's surface, in the other).

Simone Weil shows that the analogy is so strong that the name reading is suitable for every moment of our awareness. She does this by comparing the effects of actual reading to the effects of physical causes, and shows that every moment of awareness exhibits the same effects. Although black marks on white paper are themselves often not noticed, or are matters of indifference when we are reading a book or newspaper, they may have the power to affect us in the same way as a fist blow to the stomach or touching something hot with our hand.

A man receives, without being ready for it, a fist blow to the stomach; everything changes for him before he knows what has happened to him. I touch a burning object; I feel myself jumping before knowing I am burnt. Something takes hold of me. It is in this way, that the universe treats me and I know it by this treatment. (*ER* 297)

Actual reading has some similarities to the reflex action of doubling up when unexpectedly hit in the stomach or jumping when burnt by a hot object. It is involuntary; and it is immediate. For a moment, what is real takes the whole person over; it grips one.

One is not surprised by the power of blows, burns, and sudden noise to grip us; for we know or believe ourselves to know that comes from without, from matter, and the mind has no part in it, except to submit to it. The thoughts that form us impose emotions on us, but do not grip us so. (*ER* 297)

Weil stresses that our thoughts can cause us to feel emotions, but such emotions do not grip us as do the feelings that come from blows and burns. We are not surprised that the feelings caused by blows and burns grip us, because we are aware that they are caused by something outside us. But reading, in contrast to mere thinking, can have effects that are comparable to being hit by a fist in the stomach or touching a hot object.

Some black strokes on white paper, that is very different from a fist blow in the stomach. But sometimes the effect is the same. Everyone has more or less experienced the effect of bad news that one receives in reading a letter or newspaper, one feels gripped, upset, as by a blow. (*ER* 297)

In addition, it is as if the pain dwelt in the bit of paper itself, just as the burning dwells in a hot object.

Sometimes when time has lulled the pain a little, if the letter suddenly appears among the papers one is handling, a more vivid pain surges, also gripping as if it came from without, as if it dwelt in this bit of paper in the way burning dwells in the fire. (*ER* 197)

Weill claims that black strokes on a page may effect us in the same way as physical causes because of their meaning.

Two women each receive a letter announcing to each that her son is dead; the one faints at her first glance at the paper, and never again until she dies will her eyes, her mouth, her movements, be as they were. The second remains the same, her look, her bearing does not change; she does not know how to read. (*ER* 297f)

Weil draws the following moral.

It is not the sensation [black strokes on white paper], it is the meaning that has gripped the first woman, in attacking the mind immediately, brutally, without her taking part, in the way that sensations [resulting from a fist blow or hot object] grip. All happens as if the pain dwelt in the letter, and leaped from the letter to the face of her who reads it. (*ER* 298)

Yet the pain does not reside in the black marks on white paper. And as far as the visual sensations themselves are concerned – the blackness of the ink and the whiteness of the paper – they are not even noticed. 'What is given to sight is pain' (*ER* 298). All the examples Weil gives in the *Essay* tend to evoke strong emotions: pain, hatred, fear, a sense of being menaced, but reading is not limited to strong emotions, since we are always reading, and we of course do not always feel strong emotions. None the less, we constantly feel ourselves gripped by reality.

'It is in this way that at every instant of our life we are gripped as if from without by the meanings that we ourselves read in appearances' (*ER* 298). It is not as if there is 'an appearance and an interpretation' (*ER* 299). What is given to us is meaning, and we are *always* reading. It is as if the entire world is like the contents of a book. 'The sky, the sea, the sun, the stars, human beings, all that surrounds us is in the same way something that we read' (*ER* 298f.). What is given to us is like what is given when we read from a newspaper or from a book.

Even should we misread, we simply replace a misreading by a more adequate one. What is called a corrected illusion of the senses is a modified reading. If in an empty road at night I believe I see not a tree but a man in ambush, a human and menacing presence imposes itself on me and, as in the case of the letter, makes me tremble before I even know what is the matter; I go nearer and suddenly all is different, I no longer tremble, I read a tree and not a man. There was not an appearance and an interpretation, a human presence had penetrated by my eyes into my soul, and now suddenly the presence of a tree. (*ER* 299)

Weil stresses not only that we are always reading but also that the readings are involuntary and imposed on us:

... the meanings that considered abstractly seem to be simple thoughts spring up on all sides around me, take hold of my soul and change it from moment to moment in such a way that, to translate a familiar English expression, I cannot say that my soul is my own. I believe what I read, how could I do otherwise? If in a noise I read honor to be won, I run toward this noise; if I read danger and nothing else, I run away from it. In the two cases, the necessity of acting like this, even if I feel regret, imposes itself on me in an evident and manifest way, like the noise, with the noise; I read it in the noise. (*ER* 300)

We are gripped as if from without by the meanings that we ourselves read in appearances. 'So one can debate endlessly the reality of the external world' (*ER* 298). Weil says that this points to a contradiction. '*For what we call the world, that is the meanings we read; this is therefore not real. However this grips us as if from without; this is therefore real*' (*ER* 298, my own translation, her emphasis).

The suggestion that the world is the meaning we read and therefore not real is misleading. We are not to think of Kantian categories or schemata which render the world phenomenal and utterly block access to noumenal reality. Nor are we to think that Weil means to imply a relativism, in which social and cultural forces lead to a variety of readings and a variety of worlds, with no way to adjudicate between various socially determined readings or worlds. Her remark must be read in conjunction with her claim that we are *gripped* by meaning, and what grips us is real. We see here the importance of what she chose to compare to reading. The parallel she draws between reading the unevenness of a piece of paper with the tip of a pen and reading black marks on white paper indicates that, just as the former is contact with what is real, so too is the latter. The contrast between mere thinking and reading makes the same point. Mere thinking can arouse feelings, but they do not grip us as does reading. Finally, reading is compared to the sensations caused by an unexpected blow to the stomach, and indicates that reading too is a contact with what is outside ourselves. Our world is the meaning we read; that we are gripped indicates that we are in contact with reality.

Both of these facts are important. Taken together they indicate that we usually read from a perspective. The meanings we receive are not false. Given a perspective, what we read is indeed what ought to be read from that perspective. Painful and pleasurable sensations as such, for example, are not illusions. But, because they are read from a limited perspective, they are not an adequate reading of reality. None the less, we are gripped by reality.

The apparent contradiction between meaning not being real and the fact that in reading we are gripped by what is real is, therefore, resolved by the recognition that our sensations are readings from a limited perspective. But we must take this contradiction into account because it impels us towards a more comprehensive perspective whereby we may, on the one hand, read more adequately, and, on the other hand, understand why readings from a limited perspective are indeed legitimate readings. This is what lies behind Weil's rhetorical question, 'Why wish to resolve this contradiction, when the highest task of thought on this earth is to define and to contemplate the insoluble contradictions that, as Plato says, draws us upward?' (*ER* 298). To be drawn upward is to be drawn to a more comprehensive perspective. What are needed are more adequate readings of that with which we are in contact, not an abolition of meanings, so that we have things-in-themselves, apart from meanings.[3]

But how are we drawn upward? By an apprenticeship that

---

[3] We are reminded here of Plato's *Republic* in which all things have a degree of reality. The visible things of the universe are an adumbration of those which are invisible. According to the allegory of the cave, a conversion from visible things is needed to begin the ascent. According to the divided line, the progression is from reflection of sensible things, to generalisations concerning sensible things, to the foundation of sensible things in intelligible ones, especially mathematical ratios, and finally to the form of the Good which is the source of the ratios that act as limits and so render sensible things into an ordered, harmonious, beautiful whole. Weil seems to offer an updated version of this Platonic vision by stressing the role of the body, and in particular the role of manual work in the ascent.

The passage in *First and Last Notebooks* on page 131 is particularly instructive for understanding the role of contradiction in leading one to ascend to the supernatural. Eric Springsted's, *Christus Mediator: Platonic Mediation in the Thought of Simone Weil*, pp. 85–9 is an especially valuable account, as is the essay by André Devaux in this volume.

modifies our readings. When our apprenticeship is complete, we not only read differently, but we can understand how less comprehensive, or inadequate readings come to be made.

I have also perhaps a power to change the meanings that I read in appearances and that impose themselves on me; but this power is also limited, indirect and exercised by work. Work in the ordinary sense of the term is an example of it, for each tool is a blind man's stick, an instrument for reading, and each apprenticeship is an apprenticeship in reading. When an apprenticeship is complete, meanings appear at the end of my pen, or a phrase in printed characters. For the sailor, the experienced captain, whose boat has become a sense to him like an extension of his body, the boat is an instrument for reading the storm and he reads it quite otherwise than the passenger does. Where the passenger reads chaos, limitless danger, fear, the captain reads necessities, limited dangers, resources for escaping them, and obligation of courage and honor. (*ER* 301f.)

The captain, because he has gone through an apprenticeship, is able to read more adequately than the passenger; for though there is danger, and fear in the face of danger is appropriate, the danger is not limitless, because the captain knows what can be done to avert it. The captain is able to give a more adequate reading of the reality that grips both passenger and captain. Though our world is the meaning we read, what is important is to rise to a higher perspective that enables us to make more adequate readings, i.e. to receive other and more adequate meanings.

There are even higher perspectives than that occupied by an experienced captain, whose perspective enables him to make a more adequate reading of a storm than a passenger can. The higher perspectives reveal different, and progressively more sophisticated, meanings concerning the natural world; and these meanings are superimposed on each other. We are able 'to read necessity behind sensation, to read order behind necessity, to read God beyond order' (*GG* 123).

Crucial to the highest reading is the ability to read nature's order as obedience to God. When we see the order of nature as obedience to God, then the natural world becomes *transparent*, as is a window pane, and we see God.

One of the greatest obstacles to this reading is the suffering caused by the operations of the natural world. Suffering seems to contradict, or at least count against, the idea that the source of the universe is the Christian God. It is here that Weil stresses that in reading, the medium through which we read is itself hardly, if at all noticed, and, if it is, we are indifferent to it. The sensations of pain, as well as of pleasure, are the result of the obedience of the natural world to the will of God. Painful sensations caused by untoward events can be a barrier between us and the love of God. But if we learn to read our sensation otherwise, the natural world's operations, which because they cause us pain act as a barrier between us and the love of God, actually become a passage way.

In the essay, 'The Love of God and Affliction', immediately after Weil speaks of nature becoming transparent to God as a window pane is to light, she says that we have to learn how to read before black strokes on white paper have meaning. Likewise, a captain must learn to read the swell of waves for them to have a different meaning for him than they do for a passenger. She then applies this to learning to read God through the sensations of pain.

As one has to learn to read, or to practice a trade, so one must learn to feel in all things, first and almost solely, the obedience of the universe to God. It is truly an apprenticeship; and like every apprenticeship it calls for time and effort. For the man who has finished his training the differences between things or between events are no more important than those perceived by someone who knows how to read when he has before him the same sentence repeated several times, in red ink and blue, and printed in this, that, and the other kind of type. The man who cannot read sees only the differences. For the man who can read it all comes to the same thing, because the sentence is the same. Whoever has finished his apprenticeship recognizes things and events, everywhere and always, as vibrations of the same divine and infinitely sweet word. Which is not to say he will not suffer. Pain is the colour of certain events. When a man who can and a man who cannot read look at a sentence written in red ink they both see something red; but the red colour is not so important for the one as the other. (*SNLG* 180)

In the opening of *Waiting for God*, Weil says we must love absolutely the entire universe as a whole and in each detail, including evil in all its form, and she uses her frequent image of a penholder to explain in what sense she intends this astounding claim to be understood: 'In other words, we must feel the reality and presence of God through all external things, without exception, as clearly as our hand feels the substance of paper through the penholder and the nib' (*WG* 44).

In *The Need for Roots*, Weil uses as an example the meeting of two dear friends after a long separation. The friends embrace each other so hard that it hurts them. But the pain is a mark of their love for each other. So too God sometimes embraces us through the grip of the universe very hard, causing pain, but those who have completed their apprenticeship know that it is love that grips them through the universe and, because of their detachment, they are indifferent to the pain they feel, and attend only to the love of God (*NR* 289).

She makes the same point with her example of a beloved waiting for a message from a lover. It does not matter whether the message when it comes is gruff; it is still treasured because it is a message from a lover. To one who has completed an apprenticeship, the pain that results from the medium of God's presence is a matter of indifference, or is discounted, because there is indirect contact with divine love.

The mystery of reading is that meaning is *given* to us, by all that surrounds us. We do not create these readings; they are involuntary and are imposed on us. And they are not present in the media which convey them to us (anymore than they are in the penholder, or in the sensations in the fingers of the hands). We are not really, for example, at the far end of the penholder, yet we are in contact with what is there. Even should we not read fully or adequately what is there, we are always gripped by reality. Our task is to undergo various apprenticeships so that we are capable of receiving more comprehensive readings. And we can rise to higher perspectives so that more adequate and more comprehensive readings replace limited ones. To read from the point of view of our sensations, as does a passenger, is a much more limited perspective than to read necessity behind sensations, as does a captain. Ultimately, when we read order behind necessity and God behind order, nature becomes transparent to the presence of God.

In the 'Essay on the Notion of Reading', Weil says she sought 'to define a notion that has not received a suitable name, and to which the name reading may be fitting' (*ER* 297). She raises several questions which she does not there resolve. Perhaps the most important is the nature of the apprenticeship that enables us to rise to higher perspectives so as both to receive more adequate readings and to be able to distinguish more adequate readings from less adequate ones. We will describe this apprenticeship by an examination of how we can learn to read nature as obedience to God's will or, in other words, see how we modify our readings and in particular how we achieve a supernatural reading of the world.

A SUPERNATURAL READING OF THE NATURAL WORLD

We will describe the apprenticeship that leads to higher perspectives and more adequate readings by explicating Weil's remarks that we are:

> to read necessity behind sensations,
> to read order behind necessity,
> to read God behind order.

Weil is concerned with the way truths from different levels make their way into our awareness. In the 'Essay on the Notion of Reading' the effects of the ego on reading are ignored. But Weil believes that most of our thoughts and actions are self-centred. We stand at the centre with all other people and events in orbit around ourselves. Everything is seen from our perspective and evaluated, understood, and thought about in such a way as to enhance, comfort, or protect ourselves. We do this as automatically as matter and energy perform their operations. This self-centredness causes us to read people, events, and nature incorrectly (*WG* 158–60; *GG* 122).

One way in which self-centredness can be punctured is by the operations of the natural world. Its reality impinges on our bodies. We are material beings, and as material beings we are subject to wear and tear, accidents, illness, aging, and death. When one of these impinges on us, our usual way of responding is egocentric. We say or think, 'Why did this happen to me?' 'What did I ever do wrong?' This is often said with a sense of indignation, outrage, offence, self-pity. These are just a sample of a host of quite automatic and normal reactions to adversity.

These automatic responses can be the occasion for *reflection*. They can be the occasion to ask oneself: 'Why did I think I was immune to such misfortune?' 'Why did I think that pleasant and unpleasant things are parcelled out according to some scheme of merit?' Such reflections can lead us to recognise more fully something we already know: we are material, and, as pieces of matter, we are vulnerable to injury, illness, and decay. To realise this is to realise our status, our place, to realise what we are. It is to come to terms with a hard fact. Indeed, to come to terms with necessity.

Adverse contact with matters helps free us from the false readings caused by our egocentricity. It brings us closer to reality. To recognise that we are vulnerable pieces of matter, and that this is an inescapable fact about us, is to read *necessity* behind our sensations. It is to perceive the operations of the natural world as indifferent to our welfare. 'The absence of finality is the reign of necessity. Things have causes not ends' (*WG* 176–7).

Simone Weil's understanding of the necessity of nature is not equivalent to the way present-day scientific laws are understood. Descartes argued that matter consists of extension, and that its motions are describable by the necessary relations of geometry. Matter is completely transparent to thought. For Weil it is not. She uses the ancient Greek distinction between the unlimited and limit. The unlimited is brute force, the stuff of nature. Limits are geometric ratios and proportions. The natural world is a cosmos, that is, an ordered and beautiful whole because of geometric ratios and proportions. The mind can grasp ratios; nature apart from ratios is not capable of being grasped by the mind. This means that the stuff of brute material force, the unlimited, is unthinkable. In addition, the ratios or limits that enable the universe to be a cosmos, orderly as a whole and in its parts, are themselves immaterial. This ought to be evident in present day science.

The operations of the intellect in scientific study makes sovereign necessity over matter appear to the mind as a network of relations which are immaterial and without force. Necessity can only be perfectly conceived so long as such relations appear as absolutely immaterial. (*NR* 290)

This analysis of the natural world in terms of the unlimited and limit enable Weil to make a transition to the world's operations as exhibiting obedience to God.

Forces in this world are supremely determined by necessity; necessity is made up of relations which are thoughts; consequently, the force that is supreme in the world is under the supreme domination of thought. (*NR* 191).

One of the controversial issues of the modern world has been the question whether we need to make reference to an intelligent source of the order of the universe, or whether the laws of nature, which science discovers, account for the operations of the natural world without any need to infer an intelligent source. In this dispute most attention has been devoted to the argument from design.

According to the argument from design, the order of the universe so strongly resembles artifacts designed by human beings that it is probable that the universe has been designed. Now and again, in the discoveries of science, some arrangement is discovered for which no scientific explanation is available. The only options seem to be that the arrangement is the result either of chance, or of superhuman design. But, when a scientific explanation for the arrangement is eventually found, both chance and design are dropped. Scientific explanations of natural phenomena seem to eliminate the grounds for inferring superhuman intelligence to account for them.

To claim, as Weil does, that nature consists of a network of necessary relations also seems to eliminate the possibility of a supreme intelligence as the source of nature's order. For, to show that the relations are necessary seems to have reached a terminus of explanations. If the relations are necessary, in the sense that they could not be other than they are, then the reason they are as they are is because there is no alternative.

But Simone Weil does not rely on the argument from design, nor does she use the term 'necessity' in the sense that the relations between members of the universe (the laws of nature) logically cannot be other than they are. They are necessary in the sense that human beings are subject to them, and human beings are not their source and cannot alter them. But this does not mean that the natural world is the ultimate or final reality. The crucial point for Weil is that the necessary relations we grasp with our minds in our study of nature are *immaterial*.

This is easier to see if we think in terms of pure mathematics, and in particular pure geometry. A line in pure geometry is without any physical force, and unlike any line we draw, it has no width. It cannot be sensed; it is conceivable only in thought. The immaterial relations described in pure geometry are necessary relations, and only in thought do we have the relations of logical necessity. Yet it is by means of geometric relations that we grasp the natural world and understand its operations. The pure relations themselves have no force, yet the material forces of the world are subject to them.

Simone Weil's reasoning, therefore, seems to be as follows. Matter as such is unthinkable. What makes nature thinkable is the logically necessary relations of mathematics, especially geometry. But logically necessary relations are the product of thought, not matter. This means that matter, which is unlimited or indeterminate, is encountered as formed in a harmonious and orderly cosmos because it is governed by relations which are themselves immaterial and the product of intelligence. The brute force of nature is under the supreme direction of thought or mind:

Brute force is not sovereign in this world. It is by nature blind and indeterminate. What is sovereign in this world is determinateness, limit. Eternal Wisdom imprisons this universe in a network, a web of determinations. The universe accepts passively. The brute force of matter, which appears to us sovereign, is nothing else in reality but perfect obedience ... That is the truth which bites at our hearts every time we are penetrated by the beauty of the world. That is the truth which bursts forth in matchless accents of joy in the beautiful parts of the Old Testament, in Greece among the Pythagoreans and all the sages, in China with Lao-tse, in the Hindu scriptures, in Egyptian remains. (*NR* 285)

The necessary relations that produce a cosmos, that is, a harmonious, balanced set of relations, are evident to our senses in the beauty or splendour of the universe. When the operations of nature hurt us, we are aware of nature's brute force. When the operations are pleasant to us, we do not notice its brute force. But if nature were nothing but brute necessity, and not beautiful and obedient to God, we could not love it as a totality. We would hate nature when it hurt us. But we are able to modify this reading by changing perspectives. From the perspective of our minds, it is a balance of necessary relations. With respect to our affections, it is loved because it is beautiful.

When our thoughts are not dominated by our desires and needs, we may see nature as perfectly obedient to God, and its operations as the results of eternal wisdom. Brute force is ordered by thought, but clearly not by human thought. We are subject to nature's force, and we can modify it to achieve our ends to a very limited degree, as does a ship's captain. But, as thinking beings, we are on the same side as that which dominates nature's force. This happens when we detach ourselves sufficiently from our egocentrism to see nature as a network of necessary relations. The human mind is then not a subject to force: to being driven by lower readings of its pleasure and pains, desires, and wants. The human mind is functioning so that it is subject only to truth. It is then that the human mind is grasped by eternal wisdom; eternal wisdom is perceived in the universe as the balance of necessary relations, and enjoyed in the beauty of the universe. Beauty is the radiance of truth.

Weil writes:

So long as man submits to having his soul taken up with his own thoughts, his personal thoughts, he remains entirely subjected, even in his most secret thoughts, to the compulsion exercised by needs and to the mechanical play of forces. If he thinks otherwise, he is mistaken. But everything changes as soon as, by virtue of a positive act of concentration, he empties his soul so as to allow the conceptions of eternal Wisdom to enter into it. He then carries within himself the very conception to which force is subjected ... He is certainly not lord and master of creation ... but he is the master's son, and the child of the house ... A little child belonging to a wealthy home is in many respects under control of servants; but when he is sitting on his father's knees and identifies himself with him through love, he has a share in the father's authority. (*NR* 291)

MEANINGS SUPPLIED BY THE SOCIAL ORDER

Egocentrism and the suffering caused by the operations of the natural world are not the only reasons we do not read as accurately as we might. We must also rise above those meanings supplied by the social order, especially those meanings supplied by the social groups to which we belong, such as a Marxist trade union that invests events with revolutionary significance, or a fascist political party that invests a leader with messianic powers. As Rolf Kühn puts it, 'There has to be a *deconstruction* of all the received and elaborated meanings of the collective.'[4]

Kühn rightly places Weil in the tradition of Kantian critical philosophy. He cites Alain's comment on Weil's early essay, 'Reflections on the Causes of Social Liberty and Oppression', that her work is 'Kant continued'. Kühn reminds us that according to this tradition:

any perceived reality, including those of the historical and social fields, is based on constructed representations and that criticism of this power [faculty] requires a demonstration of a symbolizing 'mechanism' which explains the signifying origin of what seems natural to immediate consciousness and ruling institutions.[5]

Simone Weil stresses the *constructed* nature of readings supplied by the collective in the social order, and exhibits the forces of egotism and 'gravity' that produces these constructed representations, but

---

[4] 'Le mond comme texte – Perspectives herméneutiques chez Simone Weil', *Revue des Sciences Philosophiques et Theologiques*, October, 1980, pp. 509–30.
[5] Kühn, 'Le mond comme texte', p. 510.

she does not share Kant's view that appearances are phenomena that block access to a noumenal reality, as we mentioned earlier.

To approach social institutions from the perspective of critical philosophy is indeed to continue Kant. But Weil is not unique in this. It has been done, and continues to be done, in various ways by different thinkers, most of whom are influenced by Hegel, Marx, and Nietzsche. Where Weil exhibits distinctiveness, perhaps, is that there is no demarkation of reason into 'speculative' and 'practical', with the passions essentially separated from both, as in Kant. This is perhaps most evident in concrete cases of perception, as in Weil's telling example of a French person who sees a Nazi soldier after the fall of France. What is read is not a soldier *and* hate; what is read is hate.[6]

Simone Weil may also be said to represent an advance on Kant, because it is from an analysis of some concrete situations that she gains access to what is not constructed by us. It is precisely the emotional effects produced by representations that enable us to realise that we are gripped by reality, even when our reading is inadequate.

Above all, by criticism we can find more adequate representations to give us more adequate readings. This is the basis of her objection to algebra. Algebra consists of a set of signs which are unsuitable for contact with reality. The signs and their transformations may give us accurate results, but the connections in reality between the operations of the signs and the results of the operations are not apparent to our minds. We do not have contact with reality through the signs used in the operations: 'algebra: the method is in the signs, not in the mind . . . these automatic applications of method lead, of themselves to something new; so one invents without thinking – that is what is so bad (*FLN* 27).

Simone Weil, therefore, preferred geometry to algebra, because it is conducive to readings which give us contact with the notion that nature consists of a tissue of limits and ratios, ideas which we have already seen are so rich in aesthetic and religious significance. She claims that it is the use of geometry by the ancient Greeks in their science that largely accounts for the intimations of Christianity among the Greeks.[7]

---

[6] *The Notebooks of Simone Weil*, trans. Arthur Willis, London: Routledge and Kegan Paul, I, p. I has a variant of this passage whose original I cannot presently find.

[7] See, *IC* especially the essay, 'The Pythagorean Doctrine'. One is here reminded of Newman's famous distinction between notional and real apprehension, the manipulation of terms without an actual apprehension of the reality they concern.

It is the same with our work in a complex economic system. We are paid for performing tasks, but the money we receive does not enable us to read the relations between our work and what our money can buy. Money is analogous to magic: money provides us with goods as an incantation executes a magician's wishes.

> We must accept that our actions shall be only *indirectly* connected with the satisfaction of needs; but let the intermediate stages be sufficiently few for the relation between cause and effect to be perceptible, although indirect. Aim: that the conditions of existence should be such that AS MUCH AS POSSIBLE IS PERCEIVED.
>
> People used to sacrifice to the gods, and the wheat grew. Today, one works at a machine and one gets bread from the baker's. The relation between the act and its results is no clearer than before.
>
> That is why the will plays so small a part in life today. We spend our time in *wishing*. (*FLN* 19)

Machines can also destroy thought, or take the place of thought. Instrumental machines, because they are adaptable for all sorts of tasks, are analogous to a sailor with his ship. But automatic machines leave a person nothing to do but to tend them. The thought it took to *design* the machine is now built into the machine so that to *operate* it requires no understanding of it and so no genuine thinking. A machine, like algebra and money, is not conducive to more adequate readings of reality. 'Money, mechanization, algebra. Three monsters of contemporary civilization' (*GG* 139).

GRASPING AND BEING GRASPED

The 'Essay on the Notion of Reading' is a late one. But we find Weil wrestling with the same problem of our knowledge of reality in her very early work on Descartes, *Science and Perception in Descartes*. In that diploma essay, Weil started from the side of thought or mind and progressed to knowledge of external reality through directed action. Four years later, in her *Lectures on Philosophy*, she began at the opposite end. She tried to interpret all reality from a materialist point of view, until thought or mind becomes evident from directed bodily movement or action. In the *Lectures*, she pointed out that it is *concepts* which are used in a fashion analogous to a blind man's stick to give us a grip of the world. Concepts or thoughts employed by the body in manual work put one into contact with reality just as a blind man's stick enables him to touch and feel, as if directly, the contours of the world. In manual work we use our minds and our thoughts to gain contact with what is not our minds and thoughts. In this fashion, although the contact is mediated contact, it is experienced as direct contact.

Personal or direct contact with reality took on a new dimension in the late 'Essay on the Notion of Reading.' Here it is not we who grasp reality, but reality which impinges on us and grips us. In the earlier writings that we have mentioned, freedom was understood primarily in terms of having an understanding of the operations needed to overcome some obstacle and to achieve some goal, and selecting the means to the goal, even if one did not have a say in the setting of the goal. This was before her experience of factory work, in which she learned that such limited freedom was impossible under the prevailing working conditions, especially with fragmentation of the work process and machine minding. Her experience with affliction led her to abandon her previous Kantian position that one could keep one's moral personality intact even in impossibly oppressive external conditions. One can be reduced to the point where one does not think that one has a right to any consideration (*WG* 66–7).

This was also before her religious conversion. One indication of the effects of that conversion is the way it modified her view of how reality is to be known – by being gripped – and her view of how individual human value can be sustained. Weil's religious conversion introduced her to a kind of force that elevates us, even though we are utterly subordinate to it. It modified her ideal of freedom. No longer is it modelled exclusively on the craftsperson. Now freedom is consent to being integrated into the flow of the created order. She cites the utter obedience of brute matter to the divine will as the image of perfect obedience. Manual work (along with death) are seen as the best ways of re-entry into the flow of matter.

In *Waiting For God*, Weil tells us that she had three vital contacts with Christianity. The first was in Portugal where she witnessed a religious procession in a very poor fishing village. It made her realise that Christianity is a religion of slaves. The second event took place in Italy at the church in Assisi devoted to St Francis. She felt herself forced to her knees. The third was at Solemes during holy week, while reciting George Herbert's poem, 'Love', which led to a visitation by Christ.

This visitation only half convinced her mind, but the experience of a force she henceforth referred to as grace or love completely won her heart. It motivated her search for a religious understanding of reality, which would finally convince her mind. A way to deal with the question of God, which previously she considered to be an insoluble problem, eventually became evident. It was a matter of receiving or waiting, not of grasping but of being grasped.

Waiting, however, is not utter passivity. It involves the activity of an apprenticeship, of which suffering and manual work are a major part, and which modifies our readings:

Man places himself outside the current of obedience. God chose as his punishments labor and death. Consequently, labor and death, if Man undergoes them in a spirit of willingness, constitute a transference back into the current of supreme Good, which is obedience to God.

Death and labor are things of necessity and not of choice. The world only gives itself to Man in the form of food and warmth if Man gives himself to the world in the form of labor. But death and labor can be submitted to either in an attitude of revolt or in one of consent. They can be submitted to either in their naked truth or else wrapped around with lies. (*NR* 300–1)

Our apprenticeship has as its result what Weil calls 'decreation'. Decreation is a rich notion with several aspects. The one which is particularly relevant to our concern with reading is that in decreation it is not we who do the reading. Rather, we ourselves become like a pencil, or a stick, or like marks on paper so that God can perceive the created universe through us. Rather than God's streaming through the natural order to us as light through a window pane, now it is we who become transparent as a window pane for God's love to pass through us to other creatures:

To be what the pencil is for me when, blindfold, I feel the table by means of its point – to be that for Christ. It is possible for us to be mediators between God and the part of creation which is confined to us. Our consent is necessary in order that he may perceive his own creation through us. With our consent he performs this marvel. If I knew how to withdraw from my own soul it would be enough to enable this table in front of me to have the incomparable good fortune of being seen by God. God can love in us only this consent to withdraw in order to make way for him, just as he himself, our creator, withdrew in order that we might come into being. This double operation has no other meaning than love, it is like a father giving his child something which will enable the child to give a present on his father's birthday. God who is no other thing but love has not created anything other than love. (*GG* 35–6)[8]

---

[8] For a more complete discussion of 'decreation', see J. P. Little's essay, above. Richard H. Bell's essay, below, discusses how God's love as characterized in this quote is linked with justice and thus to human practices.

Weil is not speaking of our annihilation. Rather, it is that we are creatures of God, yet we live as though we are unrelated to God. 'God allows me to exist outside himself. It is for me to refuse this authorization. Humility is the refusal to exist outside of God' (*GG* 35). God loves this acceptance or consent to our non-being, since this is the acceptance of ourselves as God's creatures, dependent for our being on God's own. We refuse to live outside of God.

We also think of ourselves as the prime value around which to judge the value of everything else, as it gratifies our wishes and desires. 'The self is only the shadow of sin and error cast by stopping the light of God, and I take this shadow for a being' (*GG* 35).

It is this shadow that is to disappear in order that through our love for God, God's love may pass through us unhindered to all of his creatures, both human and nonhuman, in our vicinity.

As Creator, God is present in everything which exists as soon as it exists. The presence for which God needs the co-operation of the creature is the presence of God, not as Creator but as Spirit. The first presence is the presence of creation. The second is the presence of decreation. (*GG* 33)

Paradoxically, the problem of individual worth finds its resolution here. We have such a limited perspective, responding to the universe in terms of our sensations of pain and pleasure, and to all things from ourselves as beings independent of God. We seek to elevate ourselves and thereby suffer debasement, by occupying too limited a perspective.

A woman looking at herself in a mirror and adorning herself does not feel the shame of reducing the self, that infinite being which surveys all things, to a small space. In the same way every time that we raise the *ego* (the social *ego*, the psychological ego etc.) as high as we raise it, we degrade ourselves to an infinite degree by confining ourselves to being no more than that. When the *ego* is abased (unless energy tends to raise it by desire), we know we are not that.

A beautiful woman who looks at her reflection in the mirror can very well believe that she is that. An ugly woman knows that she is not that. (*GG* 29)

It is only by consenting to allow a universe to exist without oneself that one can live in God and know God as Spirit, loved by God, and loving the universe as God does. 'I do not in the least wish that this created world should fade from my view, but that it should no longer be to me personally that it shows itself' (*GG* 37).

It is in *The Need for Roots*, in particular, that Weil develops the concept of this essential identity all of us share as the foundation for her social and political philosophy. It is because we have been made to receive God's presence as Spirit that we have absolute value, and this is also the reason we are all worthy of respect.

Prior to her conversion Weil had only known forces that restrict human freedom. Even on such an abstract philosophic topic as our knowledge of the external world, Weil reads Descartes with an eye on the social oppression inherent in a division between the class of people who have the capacity and opportunity to know in terms of the dominant model of science, and those who are debarred from such knowledge because of the lack of capacity or opportunity. A different conception of science, one modelled on that of the thought and perception of a craftsperson, would enable all manual workers to have a degree of freedom from the social oppression of the savant, if they themselves were allowed to organise their work.

But, after her religious experience of a force that is gracious, nourishing, and uplifting, Weil came to see the network of relations that made up the universe as a symbol of divine love. Earlier we saw that, according to Weil, brute force is not sovereign in this world. Rather, the necessities of the universe are the result of limits imposed by an eternal wisdom. Brute force that is supreme *within* the world is *under* the supreme domination of thought. We can come to realise that nature is obedient to God when we empty ourselves of all personal thoughts, and thereby come to be obedient to eternal wisdom ourselves.

Decreation involves a non-reading. That is, as we become transparent to the divine love, we achieve such detachment that we notice only the divine love, paying no regard to all the readings from lower and less comprehensive perspectives, to which we could attend if we wished:

We also find here the reason for the paradox that a perfect reading is impossible. To think of a reader of a true text that I do not read, that I have never read, is to think of a reader of this true text, that is to say God; but at once there appears a contradiction, for I cannot apply this notion of reading to the being that I conceive when I speak of God. (*ER* 302)

God does not read because God does not have a perspective. When we, by our consent, become transparent to the divine love, our perspective does not vanish. Because our reading is always from some perspective, and God, who does not read, knows reality perfectly, we have the paradox that a perfect reading is impossible.[9]

Finally, there is also a non-reading to be sought in relation to people. We are not to use people as extensions of ourselves to read the rest of the universe. 'The relationship between me and another man can never be analogous to the relationship between a blind man and his stick, nor to the inverse relationship either' (*NB* 24).

This is because another person is 'another point of view under which all things appear' (*N* 24). Another person is capable of giving his or her consent to God. We may not, therefore, seek to change their readings by force, whose extreme form is war, but only by education (*N* 23–5; *ER* 302). To love another person is to feel with one's whole self the existence of another point of view able to consent to God. One does not read another in terms of accidents, for example in terms of their appearance and their status in the social order, any more than we notice the colour of ink in which a message is written.

SYMBOLS

According to Weil, there is another proof that nature's necessity is in actual fact obedience to God.

[The proof] consisted in the symbols attached to the relations themselves, as the signature of the painter is affixed to a picture. (*NR* 291)

Geometry thus becomes a double language, which at the same time provides information concerning the forces that are in action in matter, and talks about the supernatural relations between God and his creatures. It is like those ciphered letters which appear equally coherent before as after deciphering. (*NR* 292)

Today, science, history, politics, the organization of labor, religion even, in so far as it is marked by the Roman defilement, offer nothing to men's minds except brute force. Such is our civilization. (*NR* 295)

Similar remarks are to be found throughout Weil's writings, especially after her conversion. They are indeed very alien to our civilisation today, and impossible to evaluate here. They call for a specific study in their own right. But at the very least they suggest a deeper way to study ancient Greek civilisation, and, indeed, the

---

[9] The issue of perspective or point of view is discussed further in both Rowan Williams' essay, above, and Martin Andic's essay, following.

fables and myths of ancient cultures which she took so seriously, because she believed that they showed that ancient peoples regarded the universe as mediating a reality not contained by it.

Simone Weil's more fundamental argument that nature's necessities are actually obedience to God which we have considered, is less foreign and clearly quite plausible. We do see nature as a tissue of necessary relations, save on the quantum level, and mathematical relations are immaterial on all levels. Weil gives a religious reading of these facts by pointing out that, since we are not masters of the universe, nature's necessities are not *our* thoughts, and the beauty that is a result of necessity calls forth our love. This line of reasoning enabled Weil to claim that, given the point of view from which they are made, various readings are accurate. Thus we may say:

It is one and the same thing, which with respect to God is eternal Wisdom; with respect to the universe, perfect obedience; with respect to our love, beauty; with respect to our intelligence, balance of necessary relations; with respect to our flesh, brute force. (*NR* 295)

And given a person who can move successively from sensations to necessity, from necessity to order, from order to God, we have:

A life in which the supernatural truths would be read in every kind of work, in every act of labor, in all festivals, in all hierarchical social relations, in all art, in all science, in all philosophy. (*FLN* 173)

CHAPTER 5

Discernment and the imagination

Martin Andic

Simone Weil was one of the most discerning political minds of the twentieth century,[1] and she was concerned all her life to learn how to discern truth from illusion, reality from appearance. Her friend and biographer, Simone Pétrement, commenting on a personal text of 1934, remarks that it reveals Weil's supreme goal at that time to have been 'not to live in a dream, [but] to live in the truth, to be in the world'; she intends, that is, to be tied to people by what is true and real in her emotions and not marred by illusion or dream; she means to love not in imagination, but in truth, and to live in friendships that are not imaginary, but real; and she reproaches herself for having failed in this so far.[2] Pétrement shows how in her early epistemological writings Weil emphasises the importance of controlling the imagination, and in her political ones the need to discriminate imaginary words and things that serve injustice and violence from real ones that do not. Weil herself outgrew her early attachment to Marxism as a comprehensive ideology, while preserving to the end her active love of justice; and she came to accuse herself of criminal negligence towards France in failing to discern the treasonable tendency of pacifists.[3]

When religion became more important to her she resisted baptism partly because, as she tells Father Perrin, she fears the Church as a

[1] Thus David McLellan, *Simone Weil, Utopian Pessimist*, London: Macmillan, 1989, p. 2: 'Whether it was Berlin, Barcelona, Billancourt [the Carnaud factory], or London she had an instinct for being in the right place at the right time and for discerning by a supreme effort of unprejudiced attention, and her unique blend of Plato and Marx, the underlying reality of what was happening.'

[2] Simone Pétrement, *Simone Weil, A Life*, trans. Raymond Rosenthal, New York, Pantheon 1976, pp. 219–24, at 222f. This is parallel at many points to the pre-war notebook: see *FLN*, e.g., at 4f, 6 'Not to be an accomplice. Not to lie – not to stay blind,' 12, 37, 41, 43.

[3] Pétrement, *A Life*, 65f, 279f; *OL* esp. 1 (quoting Sophocles' *Ajax* 477 'I would not give a cent for the mortal whom empty hopes can set afire', 23, 123, 169–95; *FLN* 345f. Simone Weil was certainly one of those who hunger and thirst for righteousness, and she studied with all her soul how to discern it and realise it. See Pétrement, *A Life*, 5, 576, and *N* 466f.

social structure and suspects herself of being too ready to join col-
lectives (*WG* 52–5, 77f), and even after her many conversations with
him, and following her deep studies of Greek philosophy and literature, the *Bhagavad-Gita*, and the Bible, she says, she was so much
afraid of the power of suggestion that is in prayer, and in friendship
with religious people such as he, that she would not pray to the God
whom she loves and to whose truth she adheres; and in her notebooks she continually asks herself how to distinguish the real from
the imaginary in the spiritual domain, a question that became
pressing to her after her own mystical experiences.[4] Moreover, she
constantly suffered from her own imagination of the suffering of
others in which she had no share: the affliction of others afflicted her
until she could do something to help. Thus she tells her brother
André that reading the newspaper stories about famines distresses
her terribly; she writes to Maurice Schumann and others that the
suffering all over the world obsesses her and devastates her with
grief, and only by sharing the hardship and danger can she find
relief; she informs Dr Broderick at the sanatorium where she died
that she cannot eat when she thinks of the starvation in France. Not
only the suffering of human beings, but the destruction of culture
overwhelms her imagination. In New York, says André:

I brought her a newspaper to look at. There was a huge ad by the
department store, Macy's; it took up a whole page. They were selling, for
sixteen thousand dollars, a Spanish cloister of the twelfth century. The
stones of the building were in the store's warehouse and were numbered
accurately, one after another. I believed that this would amuse her; she had
a capacity for black humor. Instead, this news threw her into a violent bout
of fever. She experienced a kind of horror I had not expected. She was no
longer herself; with time, her sensibility had gone beyond the limits of the
normal.

This story appears in the biography by Gabriella Fiori, who comments 'Simone was living the "dark night" of the world in her own
body.'[5]

---

[4] *WG* 70f, 62, *N* 320f, 325f; *WG* 68f, 71f, *SL* 136–42, *N* 311 'Analogy between mysticism and
   mental pathology ... (Ought [the study of mental pathology] be regarded exclusively as a
   study of the imagination?'); *FLN* 65f, 195, 198 'The whole problem of mysticism ... is that of
   the degree of value of sensations of presence.' See further *N* 472, we love God with our sexual
   energy (what else?), yet 530f carnal love is, as Plato says, a debasement of divine love (cf.
   WG 171f), and the modern idea of sublimation is foolish, since the better cannot come from
   the worse; and *FLN* 127, 325, 351; *EL* 48f divine love looks *mad*.

[5] Pétrement *A Life*, 386, 397, 482f, 516f, 536; cf. 51, 371, 469f, 477; and Gabriella Fiori, *Simone
   Weil, An Intellectual Biography*, trans. Joseph Berrigan, Athens, GA: University of Georgia

Thus the problem of disciplining the imagination and discerning reality was not merely a theoretical matter of interest for her, but a practical matter of life and death.

In my essay I will try to show how she addresses both the theoretical and the practical sides of the problem together. First I will explain how, in her earlier writings, Weil generally treats the imagination as deceptive and dangerous, occasioning as it does merely carnal and self-centred perspectives and points of view. The key to reading correctly is, she thinks, a negative effort of detachment and 'decreation' that makes us impersonal mediating instruments of the divine vision and love that is our highest and inmost identity. And second, I will argue that in her later writings especially she relies also on a positive notion of imagination, according to which it serves this highest part of us as an element of identification and analogy, justice and love, faith and genius, and thus of supernatural knowledge and poetry, so that at their highest level imagination and discernment are one. In concluding I will accent the practical dimension for Simone Weil of discernment and of imagination in this positive mediating role, linking her views with those of several other twentieth century writers.

I

Weil's earliest notions of imagination are on the face of it, drawn from her teacher Alain and from Descartes. In her first topical essay for Alain in 1925 on 'Imagination and perception', she defends his thesis, with his own examples, that mental images of something are not pictures, but bodily movements that make us feel or imagine that we are seeing it when it is not actually there, a view that invites comparison with Gilbert Ryle's contention that visualising is not seeing likenesses of what we imagine but 'seeing' it.[6] Again in her diploma dissertation for Brunschvig in 1930 on 'Science and Perception in Descartes' (*FW* 31–88), she develops Alain's reading of

---

Press, 1989, pages 241f; cf. 71, 132, 141, 211, 215, 304f. See also *SE* 48f, and 172, 182 where, writing to Georges Bernanos, she remarks that she does not love war, but most horrible is not to be in the front line, and she quotes the Persian in Herodotus 9.16 'the worse human pain is to understand much and be able to do nothing'.

[6] *Oeuvres Complètes*, I, Gallimard, 1988, 297f; cf. Pétrement, *A Life*, 32, 35f, Gilbert Ryle, *The Concept of Mind*, Hutchinson 1949, ch. 8. Sartre's writings on imagination seem to owe much to Alain: see *Imagination*, 1936, trans. Forrest Williams, Michigan, 1962, especially pp. 120–5 the 'Theory of Alain', and *The Psychology of Imagination* (1940, trans. Philosophical Library 1948).

Descartes as at once opposing imagination to understanding, and uniting them as servant and master. Being pictorial, imagination is a bodily power, like sensation, but it is an indispensable instrument in the exploration of the mathematics of the world in which we live: for geometry is itself a physics, and perception, which has a natural geometry, is an exercise of understanding and imagination together. Imagination is my *grasp* of the world, but if I merely yield to it then I am delivered over to the world through the blind and capricious passions to which it subjects me, and I grasp nothing and accomplish nothing in it; whereas if I control my imagination through work, then I am active and free and I perceive what is real. This is the goal of science, to make the mind master of the imagination, and thereby of the world (*FW* 41, 50–4, 71–9, 84f).

In her class on imagination at Le Puy in 1931–2 (see *CSW* 8 (1985) 121–6), she again begins from Descartes' double view of it as the body's response to sensation, and the mind's turning to the body to control such responses. She argues that 'Man must regulate his imagination', by directing the movements that make him perceive. An artist saves himself from unruly imagination by objectifying it and by following a fixed form when he writes poetry, or the veins in marble when he sculpts forms; a scientist saves himself by measurements and verification, and in ordinary perception we do it by attention to the pure appearance, recorded without interpretation, dispassionately, and by suspecting our beliefs and going to see for ourselves: 'Every time we become aware that imagination is imaginary, we are saved' (cf. Socrates in the *Protagoras* 356d–357b, and *Republic* 10.602c–3b). We can analyse our spontaneous bodily reactions, our impressions, by geometry, which she calls a 'gymnastic' revealing the necessity that is what is real in our experience: by geometry we resolve movements into simpler ones, figures into straight lines, as Descartes and Archimedes did; we can thus make mechanical models of natural phenomena; or we can simply reduce them to algebraic formulae. But algebra, she remarks, 'offers no difficulty to the imagination for the salvation of one's soul. He who does algebra loses time.' She means, I think, that it offers no difficulty to be overcome by moving to a higher level, so that who ever does algebra loses his labour if he wants to learn to think dialectically and on several levels. (See again *Republic* 7.521d, 523–525a.) But it seems that it is not imagination itself that moves us to a higher level, although it occasions this move. She admits that it is the source of grand hypotheses and analogies, but appears to say that we can find real analogies in relationships only by ignoring imagined resemblances, and thus by submitting imagination to understanding, so that its role in science is to be overcome. Many of these thoughts are taken further in her year course in philosophy at Roanne in 1933–4. Imagination plays a role in the perception of shape, depth, and space; in illusions, comparisons, and habits such as cycling; in science and the formation of hypotheses based on analogies, though once again the scientist must look for identity of relationships and set aside mere similarities found by imagination: he must purify his thought from it, because he loves truth (*LP* 49–51, 47f, 40; 81, 87, cf. 42; 85, 209, 122, 128, 194f).

Likewise, in the pre-war notebook imagination is generally something negative: in dramatic literature, she writes, the imagination is 'a third fatality' or destiny that drives men mad, along with war and passion (*FLN* 47f); she tells herself to 'cut away ruthlessly everything that is imaginary in your feelings . . . You live in a dream. You are waiting to begin to live' (4, 11, cf. 55); and she complains that society makes an imaginary screen between nature and man, though 'Lack of flexibility of imagination . . . [is] the second screen' (20, 11). This last remark is suggestive, and, in fact, we see her noting once again Descartes' idea that there must be a discipline of imagination if science is to become a genuine *art* of thinking: a truly scientific education will include the teaching of a 'gymnastic' of the imagination along with method, criticism, and verification, as well as dance, song, and drawing, in order to give the imagination enough 'flexibility' to support the mind (11, 46). The goal is to *perceive* as much as possible, she says (9, 19), and so through work, science, and art, to become fully conscious of the conditions of knowledge and action, which is to say fully conscious of the *necessity* to be handled in effective action, and so to recreate or redefine and understand our life (18, 22, 44). This implies a positive role for controlled imagination, for example in 'envisaging concretely the relation between effort and the results of effort', in the explorations through art of 'the pact between the mind and the world', namely that nature to be commanded must be obeyed (22, 30, 44f); in the use of tools that transform our motions and extend our body, like a blind man's stick, a lever, or a sail, and in the formation of habits presupposed by genius (20ff, 36f); and in the development of analogies (11, 38f, 46).

Finally, in her 'Reflections on the Causes of Liberty and Social Oppression' of 1934 (*OL* 37–121) – which she jokingly called her

'Magnum Opus' and her 'Testament', because it was a farewell, not just to syndicalist politics, but to all her old life on entering the factory work – she remarks that 'mental confusion and passivity leave free scope to the imagination' so that our political life is filled with idols and monsters like capitalists and agitators within and evil empires without, the nightmare object of 'that dizzy fear which results from loss of contact with reality' (*OL* 118; cf. the shadows in the Cave of *Republic* 7.514ff). She gives more examples of these lies and imaginary objects in an essay of 1937 on 'The Power of Words', or 'Let Us Not Start The Trojan War All Over Again' (*SE* 154–71): *national interest, democracy, corporate greed, security, order, peace*, these are phrases with 'lethal absurdity' over which men fight as bitterly as the Trojans and Greeks fought over Helen; the vacuity of such words obscures reality and stupefies the mind, and makes men willing to die and even to forget what life is worth (*SE* 170, cf. Pétrement 262, 297–9): 'To clarify thought, to discredit the intrinsically meaningless words, and to define the use of others by precise analysis – to do this, strange as it may appear, might be a way of saving human lives' (*SE* 156).

It is a way of saving us from imagination or delusion, a way of saving our humanity. We must learn to use instead such words as *limit, proportion, balance, condition, interdependence, with respect to, in so far as, in the measure that*; and to criticise in detail the lazy abstractions and false absolutes of *nation, security, capitalism*, and the rest; we must hunt down these shadows that incite imaginary conflicts and stifle genuine ones: 'What is required is discrimination between the imaginary and the real, so as to diminish the risks of war, without interfering with the struggle between forces [sc. the struggle for justice] which, according to Heraclitus, is the condition of life itself' (*SE* 171, cf. *OL* 130f, 146). Weil does not suggest here, as she does for example in 'A Note on Social Democracy' in 1937, that imagination in a good sense may itself be an element of this struggle against injustice and oppression;[7] imagination is still something to be overcome.

[7] *SE* 150–3:

> Imagination is always the fabric of social life and the dynamic of history ... imagination remains and will remain a factor in human affairs whose real importance it is almost impossible to exaggerate ... It may happen that the state of the imagination would allow a government to take a certain measure three months before it becomes necessary, while at the moment when it is necessary the imagination cannot be persuaded to accept it ... it is essential for a politician to resist the influence of collective imagination, standing coolly apart and tapping it as a motive force for his political purpose ... If anyone lacks this art of seizing the right moment, his good intentions only pave the road to hell ... The material of the political art is the double perspective, ever shifting between the real conditions of social equilibrium and the movements of collective imagination.

II

In the Marseilles notebooks of 1940–2 we find more detailed reasons why uncontrolled imagination is bad. Generally, it is bad in so far as what is imaginary is unreal, non-existent, ineffective (N 134, 142, 416, cf. 97, SL 139); it blocks out the truth and prevents contact with reality (N 326, 150f, cf. 313, FLN 288), in a sense takes reality from it (N 28, 553, cf. 8, 563), and so is *degrading* because falsehood is (N 79f, 136, 221f, 556).

More particularly, as she remarks in an early entry, we can always imagine or read our situation so as to seem to justify *any* action, so that; 'Without control over the imagination, one can do anything whatever . . . Later on, one reads differently, but the action has been accomplished . . . The fault does not lie in the action, it lies in the reading' (N 36, cf. 196, 275, 294). This passage implies that *reading* is an act of imagination (cf. N 24, 53, 221, 316); and the implication is confirmed in her important 'Essay on the Notion of Reading', dating apparently from about this time, where she emphasises that the imagination in reading is involuntary belief. The opening paragraph of the essay includes these striking words: 'There is a mystery in reading, a mystery the contemplation of which can doubtless help, not to explain, but to understand other mysteries in men's lives'. (ER 297, cf. N 482). I shall say more about this mystery later, but simply note here that the mystery that she actually mentions is that our sensations grasp us as if they themselves *were* what we read through them, for example the bad news that we read in a letter. What we call reality is the meanings that we read and not reality itself, and yet in and through these meanings reality grasps us as if from outside us.[8] Sky and sea, sun and stars, men and nature, all that is reading material, and our whole life is a texture of meanings. Work is reading, and tools are instruments of reading, like a blind man's stick (see Descartes, *Optics* 1, 6 and *FW* 53, 79); and learning to use them is learning to read, an apprenticeship:

When an apprenticeship is complete, meanings appear at the end of my pen, or a phrase in the printed characters. For the sailor, the experienced captain, whose ship has in a sense become like an extension of his body, the

---

[8] It is not the other way around, that *we* grasp reality, as in Weil's earlier writings: see *FW* 78 'It is through work that reason grasps the world itself and masters the uncontrolled imagination,' and Diogenes Allen, 'The Concept of Reading and The Book of Nature', this volume, pp. 109–14. Notice, however, her remark, just quoted, that the contemplation of the mystery in reading can help us 'to grasp [*saisir*] other mysteries in human life'. See further

ship is an instrument for reading the storm, and he reads it quite otherwise than the passenger does. Where the passenger reads chaos, limitless danger, fear, the captain reads necessities, limited danger, a duty to act with courage and honor.

Acting on oneself or others consists in transforming meanings ... War, politics, persuasion, art, teaching, all action on others consists essentially in changing what men read. (See *ER* 301f, cf. *IC* 45, *N* 24, 30)

We read something differently when we look at it from different points of view; for example, we may read money as a convenient solution to our problems or as a deposit to be returned to its owner; we may see a man led to Rome in triumph, as just another defeated barbarian chief or as our king (*N* 23, 39). We may be compelled to particular readings by war or led by education or inspired by beauty and example (*N* 24f); but, left to ourselves, we read mechanically and following gravity (*N* 41f, 160), the moral gravity that draws us away from our highest and towards our lowest desires (*N* 71ff, 138, 218); we seldom realise it when we are reading what passion suggests, and we read for the easiest form of equilibrium (*N* 195), or to maintain our standing and defend our pride. Our life is more than three-fourths *imaginary* and fictitious (*N* 355, cf. *SNLG* 161; *WG* 170; *IC* 100): war, crime, revenge, extreme affliction (*N* 160, cf. 140, 153, 483f), killing and suicide (*N* 277, 498), riches and power (*N* 221),[9] ineffective goodness (*N* 416), spiritual progress, salvation and paradise (*N* 320f), and even the love of God (*N* 437, 492, 586), all of these are, or can be, imaginary. For 'the imagination (when uncontrolled) is a producer of a balanced state, a restorer of balances and filler up of voids' (*N* 139).

We imagine counterweights for defeats (*N* 166), consolations for sufferings and losses (*N* 149), elevations to compensate humiliations (*N* 244); we protect weakness and sweeten bitterness (*N* 424, 484): in effect, we *lie* in order to avoid admitting the misery and dependence, the nothingness, that seems to us impossible to bear otherwise (*N* 79f, 153, 198), for it would mean the death of the self that we tell ourselves we are, though it would open the way to grace (*N* 44, 135f).

N 23, 84, 526: through reading reality appears, but it *is* not the appearance; it is present but not contained therein.

9 See *Venise Sauvée*, 77: Jaffier: 'When I see this city, so beautiful, so powerful and so peaceful, and I think that in just one night we, a few obscure men, will be masters of it, I feel as if I were dreaming.' Renaud: 'Yes, we are dreaming. Men of action and enterprise are dreamers; they prefer dreams to reality. But by force they compel others to dream their dreams. The conqueror dreams his own dream, the conquered dreams another's dream.'

Men exercise their imaginations in order to stop the holes through which
grace might pass, and for this purpose, and at the cost of a lie, they make for
themselves idols, that is to say, relative forms of good conceived as being
totally unrelated forms of good ...

Idolatry is, therefore, a vital necessity [in the Cave]. To think on
relationships is to accept death. (N 145, cf. 150)

The imagination, filler of the void, is essentially a liar. It does away with
the third dimension, for it is only real objects that are in three dimensions.
It does away with multiple relationships. (N 160).

These idols are false absolutes, such as work, money, and property
(N 144), or royalty and the honours it bestows regarded as good in
themselves, when they are good only by convention and as means
(N 593, 563, cf. 124, 149f); as Plato points out in *Republic* 7, these
social institutions are artificial things, while the goods – that is, the
prestige, power, and wealth – that we imagine we will find in them
are only shadows of true good (N 551, *IC* 136): to us they are good
when really they have only become necessary (N 49, cf. *WG* 200f).
In fact it is the force of the social, the pressure of public opinion, that
makes us do this; and in this sense it is the social itself that is the
object of every idolatry, and the source of the prestige that it projects
(N 197, 618, 592, cf. 311 'Perhaps every attachment is of a social
kind?'); for the 'We' so transcends, constrains, and intoxicates the 'I'
as to become nearly indiscernible from the divine, whereas in fact it
is the domain of the devil, the Great Beast of *Republic* 6.492f and
Revelation 13.11.

The Devil is the collective. [Which in Durkheim is the divinity.] This is
clearly indicated in the Apocalypse by that Beast which is so obviously the
Great Beast of Plato.

Pride is the devil's characteristic attribute. And pride is a social thing ...
the instinct of social conservation ...

The Devil is the father of all prestige, and prestige is social. 'Opinion,
queen of the world.' Therefore opinion is the devil. 'Prince of the world'.

If two or three of you are gathered together in my name, I shall be there
with you.

But suppose there are four? Would it be the devil who was among
them?[10]

---

[10] *FLN* 304f. Pascal, *Pensées* (trans. Krailsheimer, Penguin 1966) no. 44: 'Imagination decides
everything; it creates beauty, justice, and happiness, which is the world's supreme good. I
should dearly like to see the Italian book, of which I know only the title, worth many books
in itself, *Dell' opinione regina del mondo*. Without knowing the book, I support its views, apart

'You shall be as Gods.' The sin in desiring to be as gods otherwise than through participation in God's divinity. We are born with this sin. It is Lucifier's. (*N* 216)

What comes to us from Satan is the imagination ... What Satan offered was imaginary. Riches and power are imaginary. (*N* 218, 221)

The devil in us is the 'We,' or rather the 'I' with a halo or 'We' about it (*N* 308), for it is the imagination that makes us want to be like God without God, like him in his power not his love (*N* 235, 539), and that bestows upon us a fictitious divinity by putting us at the centre of the universe in space and time, values and being (*WG* 158f). The carnal, self-centred imagination subjects us to, and makes us idolise, the social, and the prestige and power that it loves as absolute goods to be piled up for ourselves. Moreover, the idols with which the imagination responds to affliction, and to the fatigue and disgust produced by work that destroy our ability to conceive relationships, do seem to provide for a time the energy we need to go on (*WG* 221, *SNLG* 124); yet these idols stop the holes through which supernatural energy might descend if only we emptied ourselves of them; such absolutes seem to us vitally necessary, while to think of relationships dissolving them is dying to all that we live for (*N* 150, 145). We can do it only by withdrawing in thought from social life:

Relationship breaks violently with the social. It is the monopoly of the individual ...
    The faculty of relating belongs to the solitary spirit. No crowd can conceive relationships. [That] a certain thing is good or bad with respect to ... insofar as ... that escapes the crowd. A crowd cannot add things together. The way out is solitude. (*N* 592f, cf. *OL* 82)

In so far as the idol is some future good that will balance present evil and that we feel *must* come because the evil is impossible to bear, or belongs to us as our *due* and our right (*N* 153, 211; *FLN* 101; *WG* 222–5); Weil also says that escaping the Cave is turning from the future, that '*Time* is the Cave', or more particularly 'The chain in the Cave is *time*,' and the remedy is 'To look at one thing at a time' (*N* 618, 551, 37).

Now looking at one thing only at a time seems contrary at first to

from any evil it may contain.' Cf. Pascal, no. 665 'An empire based on opinion and imagination ... is mild and voluntary ... Thus opinion is like the queen of the world, but force is its tyrant', and 554 'Power rules the world ... but it is opinion that exploits power'; John 12:31, 14:30; Matthew 18:20.

looking at one thing in relation to other things; but the point is, I think, simply that we turn our desire for good, absolute unqualified good, from the future, and endeavour to find it, not in the present which is by hypothesis unendurable fatigue and affliction, but in the eternal within the present (N 618, 212), by accepting whatever must come as the will and love of God (N 259, 583, cf. WG 43f, 89, 131, 157). 'That also is a "death"' (N 551); a death to all that we live for in our imagination.

Seeing relationships, Weil says, is seeing 'the third dimension' of things; but to understand this we must return to reading. The first step in reading well is to notice the fact that we *are* reading, and the mechanism of our reading, and also to notice the possibility of other equivalent readings and of the falsehood, or at least the incompleteness, of our own (N 36, 41f, 39; cf. 121 'Method of investigation: as soon as one has thought upon a certain matter, to discover in what sense the contrary is true'). This is justice and wakefulness (N 43, 87), and the condition of real goodness and forgiveness (N 108, 196). This awareness of multiple readings or perspectives detaches us from, and lifts us above, them, and as it were transports us to a centre from which we behold disinterestedly 'the different possible readings – and their relationship – and our own only as one among them' (N 47).[11] This is in itself 'not to read' partially, and 'to read the non-reading' that is impartial (N 42, 63); it is the *Tharpa* of Tibetan Buddhism (N 316), the *satori* and the pure perception of Zen (N 396f), the non-judging judgment of the New Testament Christianity (N 201, 316), the equal, indifferent, vision and love of God (N 146, 276, 224, 289, cf. WG 97, 209). As we must move around a body in order to learn to perceive its reality, so we must read in order to get beyond reading (N 319, 334); but this non-reading is another *kind* or level of reading (for we must read it), a detached, impersonal, corrected kind (N 39, 40, 44f, 197) that is the perception (or as we shall say, the discernment) of the reality of what is present to us. God loves this perspective of creation from where I am, but 'I' (my lower, carnal self) must withdraw so that he can see it, which is to say I see it truly only when I see it as *he* does, as one of infinitely many perspectives that he also sees (N 464, 302), so that I see it as it were universally (N 280f, 284), from the

---

[11] Also N 45 and 48. Cf. Chuang Tzu 2.3 'When the wise man grasps this pivot [of Tao], he is at the center of the circle, and there he stands while "Yes" and "No" pursue each other around the circumference.' (trans. Thomas Merton.)

true centre of all.[12] Now this is an equality of acceptability, not validity: for as Weil remarks in another connection: 'There has not to be any choice made from among the opinions (except in certain cases); they should all be entertained, but arranged and lodged at suitable levels (*N* 139).

There is thus a vertical hierarchy of readings, and of opinions or beliefs generally (*N* 141, 144, 152), as it were an architecture in depth (*FLN* 122, 208f), a composition on several planes, that is a criterion of reality and truth (*N* 8, 87, 160). This is to grasp the *third dimension* of things, by rising to a higher level from which one sees simultaneously what on a lower level is seen only successively:

It is always a question of rising above perspectives through the composition of perspectives, of placing oneself in the *third dimension*. (*N* 239)

The gradation of the correlations of contraries is the third dimension, height, the one from which we are excluded by gravity. (*N* 458; cf. 71, 81, 84, 233, cf. 361, 485 the cubes.)

This is what mere imagination cannot do:

Free oneself from the effects of unreality: *in the imaginary world, one single set of relationships*. (*N* 30, her emphasis.)

The imagination . . . is a liar. It does away with the third dimension, for it is only real objects that are in three dimensions. It does away with multiple relationships. (*N* 160)

The Cave. The third dimension is lacking. Paul . . . (*N* 319)

The reference to Paul is, I take it, an allusion to Ephesians 3.17–19, understood as linking the dimensions of the love of Christ to the distance between God and the creature (*N* 239, 380, 400), and again to:

---

[12] This centre is not *a* perspective or point of view, in so far as these are by definition partial, that is, it is 'a point outside space, which is not a point of view, which has no perspective, but from which the world is seen as it is, unconfused by perspective' (*SL* 136; see also *N* 19, 46, 146, 191, 224, 234, 239; *FLN* 70, 84f; 87, 270; *WG* 72, 159f). But it is reached by a *composition* of perspectives, a detached 'reading of non-reading' that metaxically draws us up to the infinite vision of God. (*N* 47, 63, 221f, 239, 275, 369). In such a Taoistic reading without reading, 'it is not we who do the reading', rather we let God see through us, as Diogenes Allen remarks: see this volume, above, and *N* 364, 401, and 422 on Racine, Giotto, and Cézanne, with *ER* 302 God does not (merely) read. See also *IC* 48–9, 133–4, 186–7, *WG* 97–8, 128; *SN* 197 and page 135, note 17, below.

Evil. Third dimension of the divine. (N 260)

Evil is the shadow of good. All real good, endowed with solidity and density, projects evil. It is only imaginary good which does not project any. (N 414)

When the Cave-dwelling imagination fills voids and restores balances, then, it lies to us by hiding the *evil* that is not only the inescapable cost of good in this world – the good that is relative and opposed to evil, arbitrary, and subject to necessity – but also the distance that our love and desire has to cross, the *reality* of real things, through which we may read God. If love prefers a real hell to an imaginary paradise (N 321), imagination would prefer it the other way, pursuing a good that is not there and ignoring the good that is there. But the relationships that it does not see are not only horizontal, as it were, but vertical, stretching not only across and within the manifest world, but above and beyond it as well.

III

We can see more clearly why imagination is degrading if we consider the *detachment* required for deliverance from it:

The reality of the world is made up for us of our attachment. It is the reality of the 'I' which is transferred by us into material objects. It is in no wise *external reality*. The latter only becomes perceivable through total detachment ...
  Beauty: reality [seen] without attachment. (N 318f, cf. 365)

Perfect detachment alone makes it possible to see things in their nakedness. (N 533)

This detachment that lets us perceive reality and feel its beauty is also *renunciation* (N 297, 335), *nakedness* (N 120, 213, 282), and *death* (N 61, 261, 411, 554). This death is not destruction or suicide, but *decreation* (N 247, 258, 262, 342), not absence of being, but another kind of being: a self-effacement that makes us an organ of God's vision and creative love (N 344, 364, 401, 297, 309, 616 – see further J. P. Little's essay in this volume). It is a *humility* that consents to being nothing apart from God (N 123, 485; *FLN* 97, 353), that knows we have no rights over the future and do not possess it, and that submits to being nothing but what we are in the present and so accepts the void of all personal good (*FLN* 101f). Humility knows and consents to our subjection to time, change, and the destruction, if God wills it, of everything in us, including the supernatural part that is his presence in us (*WG* 225f); it is an attentive patience that accepts everything that he may chance to send us in time, and thus consents 'to being a creature and nothing else' (*FLN* 217). That is to say, by causing us against gravity to descend in the scale of force without being compelled to, humility acknowledges that we can be compelled to, and by renouncing prestige it agrees to our nakedness of any permanent good of our own, and by accepting time it accepts our *incarnation* as dependent creatures.[13]

Whosoever humbleth himself shall be exalted. We must therefore humble ourselves to the ground ... We have to discard the illusion of being in possession of time; to become incarnate.

Man has got to make an act of self-incarnation, for he is disincarnated by the imagination. What comes to us from Satan is the imagination. (*N* 217f, cf. 221f)

Incarnation means obedience to God, who commands us to love our neighbour, and who himself became incarnate in order to teach us to serve men in their flesh (*FLN* 150; *N* 280, cf. 222, 297). It is assimilation to God's love for God across the greatest distance of affliction (*WG* 123f), by accepting all suffering as our own, given to us by God in creating us, and so as *human* suffering to which any of us is subject (*N* 281f, 285) even God as the Son who suffers in us and with us yet loves the Father through and beyond it (*N* 263). Incarnation means acquiring a 'universal sensibility' related to beauty (*N* 284), whereby we feel all affliction as human affliction belonging not only to us, but also to 'God captive in the flesh' (*N* 281), who suffers as we can or do suffer and yet loves as we should love (*N* 191, 213, 564), namely by accepting this suffering because it exists, and loving God from whom it comes (*N* 288, 305, 340, 342). This is making the 'I' *universal* (*N* 293), or releasing the universal 'I' and its compassionate love that is usually blocked by imaginary barriers between ourselves and others (*N* 288f, 295, 284; *FLN* 210, 327, 318). It is in fact, according to Weil, uniting ourselves to the Soul of the World (*N* 75,

---

[13] Cf. *WG* 170; Pétrement, *A Life*, pp. 44, 462; Gustave Thibon, *Simone Weil as We knew Her*, trans. Emma Craufurd, Routledge, 1952, p. 115; and McLellan, *Utopian Pessimist*, p. 181. See further Vincent van Gogh, *Letters*, (1958), 2.234, no. 347; Thoreau, *Journal*, 20.x.1855, 28,viii.1851, *Walden*, 2.22.

178f; *FLN* 296), to the divine *Atman* within (*N* 19, 123, 126ff, 197; *FLN* 322), the Supreme Identity co-ordinating all readings from the true centre above and beyond them all (*N* 99, cf. 39, 43, 45, 47f).

To explain this more fully we must take a closer look at detachment. Only perfect detachment, says Weil, lets us view things naked, without the fog of false values read into them by imagination, which always reads in goods to come that will restore balances and fill voids (*N* 533, 139, both quoted above).

The imagination is always linked with desire, that is to say, with value. It is only desire without an object that is empty of imagination, God's real presence is in everything that is unshrouded by imagination. (*N* 533)

Desires become reality when we remove from them the cloak of imaginary satisfaction. (*N* 175, her emphasis)

To try to love without imagining. To love appearance in its nakedness, devoid of interpretation. What one then loves is truly God. (*N* 273, her emphasis)

To love God through and beyond a certain thing is to love that thing in purity; the two sentiments are identical (*N* 283)

To restrict one's love to the pure object is the same thing as to extend it to the whole universe. (*N* 21, her emphasis)

Supernatural love is the organ by which we adhere to Beauty, and the sense of the reality of the universe is identical in use with that of its beauty ... the only organ of contact with existence is acceptance, [or] love. That is why Beauty and Reality are identical ... why pure joy and the feeling of reality are identical (*N* 308f, cf. 288)

What is the connection between desires without an object, love, and the perception of reality and its beauty? To love is to look with detachment from any desire to possess the object, and to consent that it should *be*. But why is this to desire it 'without an object?' Isn't the beloved, the object or our desires, even if we desire it without any further objectives, such as to acquire it and use it? Of course it is; but Weil means, I think, that we desire it because it exists and is presented by God, and we love it because we desire what we have, not the other way, because we have what we desire. Our desire and love, in other words, should have no particular object, but simply an orientation to the reality of whatever in general is present, and to God within and beyond it (*N* 202f, 593). Desire is, or proceeds from, our 'supplementary energy', supplementing what we need barely to live: it is free floating and, when directed to objects, it makes them loved (*N* 45, 100f, 421); imagination is, or is made up of, or supplies or steals, this energy by providing objects and satisfaction (N 124, 221, 284). As energy, all desires are precious, and they become real when we remove imaginary satisfaction, in the sense that as energy they are true when torn from their objects, and 'This wrenching apart is the condition of truth' (N 204, cf. 213 renunciation puts us 'in possession of the truth of the world'). Now this truth is not, or is not only, perception, but possession and enjoyment. Its condition is not lack of desires but lack of an object to our desires: in other words, we have what we desire when we desire it purely, or with detachment (N 15) and so universally (N 21, 279, 49).[14] For:

So long as we are alive, we continue to feel desire; and this very desire is the fullest possible good if we prevent it from focusing itself in a particular direction, from subordinating itself to a particular object that is only feebly representative of the good. (N 493)

Our very being itself is nothing else than this need for the good. The absolute good lies wholly in this need. (N 491, cf. 489)

This desire for absolute good constitutes the foundation of my being (N 562).

We possess this absolute good as soon as we wholly detach our desires from all other things in order to desire it absolutely, in fact as soon as we wholly desire to desire it, since this pure desire is itself the good, the divine love itself. Hence we have only to desire that what is, should be, as God wills, and we have it, as God does (FLN 143f, 157ff, 307, 310, 317 'When desire is reality it is possession.'). It is a universal love, directed to particulars: something supernatural (N 123, 93, 285, 318; cf. 95, 'Love men as the sun would if it could see us', (N 129), God is an impersonal Person who 'loves ... as an emerald is green. He *is* "I love".')

Thus the detachment that universalises our sensibility and makes us see truly, also, and more deeply, universalises our desire and makes us love and even possess truly, because it unites us with God, the *Atman* within, the Soul of the World.[15] We *see* truly because we

---

[14] Cf. N 216, 218, 366, 422, 461 quoting *Isa* Upanishad 1, 'enjoy through detachment'; and 19f quoting *Chandogya* Upanishad 8.2f.

[15] Cf. Fiori, pp. 41 'Simone Weil wanted an identity that coincided with the universe. For her, being herself meant freedom from all belonging', 52, 133 'Simone was intrinsically repelled by the idea of becoming a "persona", a mask. She wanted to bring to realization her very *substance* and to offer it to everyone upon the earth through the attentiveness of impersonal love', 215 our 'adherence to reality consists in our expansion in the universe, to love it and to recognize it as our homeland'.

desire and *love* truly. This is the sense in which love is the vision of reality (see *N* 288, 292, 295.)

Now this vision is discernment, and consequently we can say that discernment is not so much the solution to the problem of imagination as it is itself the problem. The problem is how to discipline the imagination and discriminate reality; the solution is this pure universal desire, and the detachment and faith presupposed by it and realised in it. We can also see now why it is that imagination *degrades* us:

Every time we raise the 'I' ... we degrade ourselves to an infinite degree by reducing the self ... that infinite being which beholds all things ... to being no more than that. (*N* 244)

I have got to be nothing; for all that I am is infinitely less than God. If I take away from myself all that I am, there remains ... [only God]. (*N* 120, cf. 23, 48, 150, 159, 213)

In so far as we are other than God, however, renouncing everything that we finitely were and will be in the imaginations of others and ourselves is becoming nothing but creatures who can mediate between God and one another (*N* 126; *FLN* 132, 244, 312). But we must not *know* too much about it, or the imagination will once again degrade both God and ourselves (*N* 20f, 323, 174, 283f); this is why *obedience* and *humility* are supreme virtues (*N* 327, 275, *WG* 57, 225f): our highest action is to desire to obey, to empty ourselves of all imaginary good and to value in ourselves only what is beyond ourselves (*FLN* 136; *WG* 338, 274).

How do we *know* what the obedient action is? We may be mistaken; and yet we can be sure that God wants us to do what we believe to be his will when we have thought of him with detachment, attention, and love: 'For if we ask him for bread he will not give us a stone' (*N* 233; *FLN* 150). We recognise his will for us by a sense of *necessity*, the irresistible feeling that this is what we *must* do, and the only thing that we *can* rightly do in love of him (*N* 96, 214, 256). We therefore purify ourselves from imagination, that is to say, we purify our obedience from pride, and our love of God from idolatry, by doing nothing, beyond our clear duty, but what we feel compelled to do when we think of him with love and the desire to obey him (*N* 150, 239, 303), while at the same time we desire that this shall become all our action:

Nothing is easier than to fall into an imaginary love of God. True love does not shield one from imaginary love so long as true love does not occupy the entire soul, for imaginary love can be added on to true love. Imaginary love occupies a place, which is [then] not an empty one, where true love cannot enter.

We should give God the strict minimum of place in our lives, that which it is absolutely impossible for us to refuse Him – and earnestly desire that one day, and as soon as possible, that strict minimum may become all. (*N* 326, cf. 296)

This is why atheism can be a *purification* of our understanding of God, by admitting that he is greater than anything that we conceive or imagine, and so a purification of our love for him, by detaching our desires from anything that consoles or elevates us (*N* 126f, 238, 242). Let us tell ourselves (our lower part) that he does not exist, and let us never the less love him and desire to obey him as the only good, and he will surely manifest himself to us in this desire; for he is only present to pure attention and love.[16] He will exist in us and for us when this loving attention has drawn all our soul into it. It grows in us exponentially, and is our whole and only freedom. (*N* 205, 463f, 500; *IC* 186 'to be free, for us, is to desire to obey God. All other liberty is false', cf. *WG* 124f, 129f, 133, 188f, 214.)

IV

We come now to discernment. To discern is literally to sift apart (from Latin *dis* + *cernere*, cf. concern, certain, secret, discretion; and Greek *diakrinein*, to separate), and thus to detect, distinguish, or discriminate, for example, what is right or true or real, or right from wrong, true from false, real from imaginary. We can thus discern something absolutely, so to say, to discern it *from* or *in* another, and so perceive it precisely or distinctly. Discernment, for Simone Weil, evidently amounts to perceiving without imagination, reading truly, and attending purely. It is an achievement, or, rather, as we shall later say, a grace: we can read badly and attend impurely and without discipline, but our discernment is true or it is not true discernment. What are its objects? Let us review briefly Weil's explicit uses of this concept.

[16] *N* 142, 151, 421, 489; *FLN* 157f, 292, 317ff, *WG* 210–13, *IC* 17, 76, 199. *N* 515, 527 'Absolutely pure attention . . . is attention directed toward God; for he is only present to the extent to which such attention exists', cf. Kierkegaard, *Postscript* (trans. Swenson and Lowrie 1941), page 178 'God is a subject, and therefore exists only for subjectivity in inwardness.'

In mathematics we discern levels or planes at which terms are linked that we cannot link on lower levels (see *N* 548–9). We discern *Providence* in events, even if not special plans that are not each of them only one of infinitely many plans of Providence in those events (*WG* 177; *NR* 281, *N* 302, *FLN* 72). Through renunciation we discern *reality* and the true centre of all beyond all (*WG* 159f; cf. *N*318), and thereby the mechanism of necessity everywhere and the rule of force (*WG* 159f, *SNLG* 80, *IC* 24, cf. 178). We discern true *beauty* (*WG* 165; cf. *GG* 135) and purity (*NR* 235, cf. 234, 236), the justice and love that reveal the truth about necessity and force (*IC* 48), and the beauty of silent affliction and truth as opposed to the devil's imitation of beauty (*FLN* 341). We discern falsehood and cruelty (*WG* 112, *NR* 229) and crimes and the cry of injustice (*NR* 38, *EL* 44, *SE* 12), and souls in affliction if Christ looks through our eyes (*WG* 119, *N* 338). We discern what to say, feel, and do about *precious* things (*N* 141), for example what to think and do about faith, dogma, and sacraments (*WG* 74; cf. *PSO* 133, and *PSO* 151 the motives for honesty), and what must be done because it can be (*N* 224 we find this by analogy), what will be good or bad for us (*GG* xiii), ends (*N* 617), and appropriate laws (*NR* 211). With trained attention we discern the very *soul* of people behind their words and silences (*WG* 108 the Curé d'Ars), their real motives and the value of these, though perhaps only God knows them fully (*NR* 207, 251, see also 199 secret thoughts and needs, *FLN* 345 the propensity to treason in pacifism. Compassion discerns the *virtues* of other (*NR* 173), and lends them an objective existence, so that the loss of a friend who saw the good in us is to us a loss of being (*N* 219). With 'Faith, a gift of reading', we discern the value of words such as 'I love you' (*N* 220). Again, if we see others and ourselves 'in a three-dimensional space' we can discern our own *faults* and can ask and obtain forgiveness (*N* 196, cf. *PSO* 78), but generally we cannot see them (*NR* 21, *SE* 162); for we lose discernment as we grow indifferent to justice (see *NR* 244, cf. 259; *EL* 142, *FLN* 351). We can discern and join the side of least injustice, though really to fight for justice we must love to the point of madness, humanly speaking; and only the 'madness of love' draws us to discern and cherish equally every earthly possibility of beauty and happiness and fulfilment (*SJ* 5, 9, *N* 466f; also see the essay by Richard Bell in this volume on justice and madness). Similarly, we discern *truth* only if we love truth unto death, and are ready to give up all reason to live rather than lie (*NR* 250; cf. *N* 160f, 195 no love of justice guarantees truth of reading). We discern the value of fruits, and so of the tree, for example of intuitions by that of the discursive thoughts that follow upon them (*N* 43), and the way contradictories are both true, or both false (*N* 637). As Plato says, only those directly trained by God discern the good, and thus true greatness (*NR* 227; cf. *SNLG* 98, *Republic* 6.492; *PSO* 53). It takes a supernatural discernment to tell the truly *religious* from the merely social (*N* 270; *WG* 46, 198, cf. *OL* 174), the difference in weight between true gods and false ones (*N* 482). It is difficult to discern the relative truth of religions, which is known only from inside them, or their hidden equivalents, and perhaps only God really knows the truth of each (*WG* 183, 185). We discern *holy* things, or God in the words of Christ, or the meaning and truth of words such as 'A man has no greater love than to lay down his life for his friends' (*N* 245f, 283f). We discern the presence of Christ and the love of God in a man by his compassion, the true sign and consequence of the love of God in him (*WG* 93f, 119).[17] We discern the *divine*, not indeed in itself, but in ourselves, in divine inspirations, and in everything around us, through faith, which is a gift and requires purity of heart and rejection of everything manifest, that is to say, everything merely relative, imaginary, or idolatrous, to which our desire might be attached (*N* 219, cf. 318; *WG* 96f).

To be able to study [the supernatural as such], one must first of all be able to discern it. Faith is therefore necessary, in the true sense of the word. (*N* 226, cf. Heraclitus D18, 86)

Faith. It is for the intelligence to discern what forms the object of supernatural love. For it must perfectly discern all that which is at the level of intelligible truth and all that which is below it. All that which is neither the one not the other is the object of supernatural love. Discrimination on the

---

[17] See also *FLN* 146f:

Iliad. Only the love of God can enable a soul to discern the horror of human misery so lucidly and so coolly without losing either tenderness or serenity ...

According to the conception of human life expressed in the acts and words of a man I know (I mean I would know if I possessed discernment) whether he sees life from a point [of view] in this world or from above in heaven.

On the other hand, when he talks about God I cannot discern (and yet sometimes I can ...) whether he is speaking from within or externally.

It seems to follow that we know the love of God in another by that which is in ourselves, so that our love is discerned by our discerning another's, like known by like. Cf. Kierkegaard, *Works of Love* (trans. Hong 1964), p. 33: the best proof of love is 'love itself, which is known and recognized by the love in another. Like is known only by like. Only he abides in love can recognize love, and in the same way his love is to be known.'

part of intelligence is essential in order to separate supernatural love from attachment ... to something which we name God.

Love (*agapē*) is a disposition of the supernatural parts of the soul. Faith is a disposition of all the parts of the soul – and of the body as well – each one assuming with regard to the object of love the attitude suitable to its nature. Justice, according to Plato. (*N* 241; cf. *FLN* 131; *Republic* 4.443c–4a).

In other words, with faith we actively adhere with all our soul to what we love, even as we discern it to lie above and beyond what we can fully understand. Intelligence thus discerns the divine *mysteries* that imply the truths that we recognise to be truths. It cannot penetrate them, but only locate them precisely, or distinctly: that is to say, it cannot fully explain why they are true or even what they mean, but only what they are (cf. *N* 238, 336; *FLN* 262; cf. Kierkegaard, *Postscript* 438), although love can illuminate them and active faith can make us experience their truth:

Faith is the experience that the intelligence is lighted up by love. (*N* 240)

Faith creates the truth to which it adheres ... The domain of truth is the domain of truths created by certainty ... A virtue created by faith. It is necessary to [determine] this domain. (*FLN* 291, cf. 132, 207; *WG* 107, 209)

A mystery is thus more than a symbol, for it cannot fully be understood and it really transforms us when we contemplate it, metaxically drawing us up into itself. (*N* 238, 325, 400f, 434). The mysteries include not only the Trinity of God (*N* 336, 403) and his incarnation and grace, and his presence in the Eucharist and the Cross (*N* 341, 221, 238, 308, 315); they also include beauty, suffering, compassion, justice, gratitude, truth, and obedience in their interrelation or identity (*IC* 190, 196; *N* 281; *FLN* 91, 292, 150; *NR* 234), the unity of love of God and the love of neighbour (*N* 281, cf. 274), the unity of necessity and the good (*SNLG* 174), as well as possibility, time, and perception (*N* 240, 273, 482, cf. *ER* 297).

Now if it is only by love that we touch the reality of the world and feel its beauty (*N* 308f), and if it is intelligence lit by love that discerns it and faith that so actively and entirely adheres to it that we experience it and thereby come to know it, then it follows that discernment of reality is itself a work of love. Thus,

Faith is the experience that the intelligence is lighted up by love. Truth as the light coming from good – the good that lies above essences. The organ in us through which we see truth is the intelligence; the organ in us through which we see God is love (*N* 240).

Love is the soul's looking. (*WG* 212, cf. 170)

Discernment of the mysteries of God and, in the light of these, the reality of the world in which we live is *supernatural knowledge*, the true reading of God in every appearance as its higher dimension (see *FLN* 109f, 92; *IC* 176f, 199f).

Weil seems to compare it to Spinoza's knowledge of the third kind.[18] Now Spinoza is a naturalist and rationalist, and Weil would more likely than not say that he makes the intelligence too active and not receptive enough (let us remember that he was driven out of the synagogue); but we can see what she means by this comparison if we consider that the three kinds of knowledge – perception, discursive thought, and intuition or contemplation, correspond to three levels of reading – of things, relationships, and God:

Superposed readings: we should read necessity behind sensation, order behind necessity, and God behind order.

We must love all facts, not for their consequences, but because in each fact God is there present. But that is tautological. To love all facts is nothing else than to read God in them (*N* 267)

When we read God in everything as the cause by which it exists, we unite ourselves to the Son who loves unconditionally and equally in all things; when we unite ourselves to the Father and see them as he does, with his unconditional love accepting each thing equally, we see its order as obedience to him and as beauty, in effect as the Word or Son (*WG* 97f, 123f, 130, 145, 158, 164f, 175; *NR* 285–95). This is a double vision like that of Janus, who looks with one gaze in two directions; or, as Weil says, with superposed readings. It is such universal love and vision of particulars beyond all private partial perspectives or points of view that Weil calls 'non-reading' (*N* 41 'not to read is better', 63 'read the non-reading'): for God does not read, or see from any point of view (*ER* 302; *N* 146). But we do look at particulars one at a time, each as it is presented, so that reading

---

18 *N* 22 'knowledge of the third kind = reading', 35, 37, 145, 189 'Reading and knowledge of the third kind', 239, 334, 512. See further 40 'To read in all outward aspects – God', 220 'To read God in every manifestation ... To know in what way each appearance is not God', 267 'To love all facts is to read God in them', 194, 275, 281, 512, 535. Spinoza, *Ethics* 2.40–2, 5.25–36.

God in it (as the Father who loves us), and beauty and obedience (of the Son who loves him), could be called *true reading* as well as non-reading. True reading is divine non-reading, seen from below. This is why 'There is a mystery in reading, a mystery the contemplation of which can doubtless help, not to explain, but to grasp other mysteries in human life.'

Reading in the highest and fullest sense, therefore, is discernment of the mysterious reality of the supernatural in all things (*WG* 137, 175; *FLN* 72, 91, 123), so that we truly discern them *from* illusion, when we discern God *in* them. It is this reality that becomes for us not less, but more, when we know the reality of God (*WG* 215; *IC* 188; *SNLG* 112). We read and discern it only by attention made pure of everything imaginary, and illuminated by love and desire of the true.

We do not, let it be emphasised, discern God or read him, absolutely; we only read and discern his reality through appearance, when we love these in their nakedness and purity, reading in them nothing but God who presents them to us (*N* 267, 273, 283). Our discernment, therefore, is not a grasping activity, but a gracious receiving and detached adherence with love and faith. It is a gift of the spirit, as Paul says (I Cor. 12.1–11, cf. *N* 220).

It is received, however, only by those who seek it. This means that discernment is irreducible to the pure direct seeing without looking of Zen noted by Weil. We may think that pure seeing is a better and fuller grace and blessing, because less human and more divine, more like the eternal sight of the Father. Nevertheless, it is Christ, the perfectly just man, who is our model, longing and praying through the dark night (*IC* 138–43, *N* 263, 374, 376); and Christ tells us to ask and seek and knock, and that the lost who return are a greater joy to their Father (Luke 11:5–13, 15:3–32). So Weil writes, that God gives his bread to whoever asks for it, but only to him who asks, and only his bread (*FLN* 120) and that truth, beauty, and goodness are revealed only to the purest and fullest attention (*N* 449, 527). We are to seek grace, though without desiring it with the lower part of our soul, possessively. We are to wait *en hupomenē*, in patience, setting aside everything that is not the good, attentive in silence, immobility, and love, and God descends with truth lighting our intelligence. Attention is the task, discernment is the reward.[19]

---

[19] Thus *N* 583 'Everything that is contained in the present moment is a gift', but *WG* 112 'We do not obtain the most precious gifts by going in search of them but by waiting for them',

If discernment thus presupposes active attention, it is also oriented to, and realised in, action, that is, action mediating the divine love and vision. This is suggested by the verbal link, noted earlier, between 'discernment' and 'discretion': we attend or bend ourselves towards something in order to discern what we are to do or say or think about it (see, *N* 141, 224, 338, 617), just as it may be left to our own discretion what is to be said or done. I will return to this point in my conclusion.

V

We have seen only the detached, decreated, incarnate, universalised soul lit by supernatural love can discern reality from illusion, read justly, and attend purely. We shall understand this better if we recognise now how imagination in a positive sense is constantly implied in Weil's treatment of discernment, reading, and attention.

To imagine is literally to *picture*, or make or perceive a likeness (from Latin *imago*, copy, cf. *imitari*, and Greek *mimeomai*, to mimic), and *not* to perceive that of which (or in that aspect in which) this is a picture or likeness. We speak of imagination in order to point out a contrast with actual present perception, and as often to speak of a failure or success as to speak of some present performance. To imagine may be to have made a mistake that is due to ourselves and not our outward circumstances, or again to pretend to ourselves what is not so in order to consider how things would be or look if it were, and thus to think of it, or suppose it, or visualise it, sometimes correctly (see *IC* 51, 142, 153, 201), when it is not actually presented; or it may be to daydream about it, not necessarily to settle any question about it. What is *imagined* is not perceived, but made up or invented, and what is *imaginary* is unreal and only in our imagination, perhaps false and unreasonable (thus Weil's word *l'imaginaire* at *N* 320, 325); but what is *imaginative* is commendably inventive or formulated with imagination: it differs from perception,

that is, we cannot discover them by our own unaided powers, but only desire them with selfless attention and love; 197 'we should do nothing but wait for the good and keep evil away ... This waiting for goodness and truth is, however, something more intense than any searching', cf. 111 'Attention is an effort, the greatest of all efforts perhaps, but it is a negative effort', 110–14, 133, 193–7, 210–13 we turn *from* falsehood and let God turn us *toward* him.

Discernment of reality from mere appearance thus involves an attentive, negative operation of questioning and exclusion, literally a sifting, as in the 'Not this, not that' of the Upanishads, e.g., *Brhad-Aranyaka* 4.4.22.

and goes beyond what most of us most of the time would notice or think or conclude; it is fresh, original, spontaneous, not ruled by the merely obvious or conventional, but free of it, and free to grasp a deeper truth or reality. It may be, for example, a sympathetic grasp of the reality and need of another creature, the other's pain or joy, fear or desire; and it need not be pictorial or visual. Thus to imagine is sometimes to fail, but often it is to succeed.

Simone Weil has this positive notion of imagination, as well as the negative one. As we have seen, she would say that to read is to imagine, and, while this can be false, delusive, and degrading, when merely self-justifying or excusing, consoling or inflating, there is also a selfless or impersonal reading and imagination that is controlled by intelligence illuminated by love, beholding the supernatural truth and reality that is the mysterious presence of God in the world, the truth providentially inscribed, as she likes to put it, so that we can read it everywhere (N 36, 40, 99, 220, 515, 596; FLN 337; $SNLG$ 150f).

Again, she says 'it is necessary *really* to transform the imagination within oneself' so that we are able to *act*, not for a personal reward, but because we cannot help doing what it is right to do: this is 'non-active action' and 'what the saints understand by obedience', of which the subordination practiced in religious orders is the image. We have to make systematic use of 'the imagination, supplier, or stealer of energy', in order to bring ourselves to do what we want to: it is a matter of 'transferring energy' by reading, attention, and analogy (N 124f, 174f, 177, 249f).

This transference of energy can constitute a transference of identity, in that we *identify* ourselves with what we desire and love. Thus we transfer ourselves into our neighbour when we feel his suffering as our own, because it is human suffering, and even the suffering of God within us; this universal sensibility, or self-transference, as she notes in many passages, is an imaginative act (N 154, 177, 282, 284f; FLN 97, 135).[20] But then so, therefore, is our self-identification with the universe, or with God, or with the love of God in us, the highest part of ourselves; and so again is the self-effacement, self-renunciation, and *decreation* that is its condition (N

[20] See also the 'performative' transference in Weil's remarkable words to Antonio Atarés from Casablanca, cited in Fiori *Intellectual Biography*, p. 229: 'I charge the stars, the moon, the sun, the blue of the sky, the wind, the birds, the light, the boundlessness of space, I charge all that is forever near you, with my thoughts for you and with the joy that I desire for you and that you so richly deserve.'

19, 21, 323, 483, 637; 253, 291, 401). We discover the *Atman* within us by limiting ourselves to what we are now and here: 'The imagination ... must be cut off from all objects in order that it may be caught up by the infinite' (*N* 221f, cf. 212f, 313).

Our love is real when directed to particulars, and becomes universal by 'analogy and transference', although it is by love that we learn what analogy and transference really are. Like transference, analogy seems to be an act of non-pictorial imagination, and so in a way is *mediation*. When we say, for example, that 1 is to 3 as 3 is to 9, 1 is 'transferred into' 3 and 3 is transferred into 9, but also 3 'becomes' 1 and 9 'becomes' 3; in this continued proportion or analogy, 3 'is' both 1 and 9, and mediates 9 and 1; a just man is like a square number between whom and divine unity mediation is possible, for he has made himself to be to the mediator what the mediator is to God, an active instrument of the divine love (*N* 603; cf. *FLN* 132, 250, 312, 352; *IC* 159 'Whoever is just becomes to the Son of God as the Son is to his Father', *IC* 170 'By assimilation with the Christ, who is one with God, the human being lying in the depths of his misery attains a sort of equality with God, an equality which is love'). Thus imagination is an element in *justice* and *love*, in so far as justice is establishing an analogy, or discerning and acknowledging an identity of relations (*N* 349, 346), and in so far as love *is* justice (*IC* 175f; *WG* 139f). Imagination is likewise a part of *faith*, inasmuch as faith is 'a gift of reading' and 'a conjecture by analogy' (*N* 220, 438; *WG* 148), and so also of the discernment of the *metaxu* or middle terms by which we ascend to God and descend with him to the world, inasmuch as these are not to be invented, but found in the nature of things, written there for us to read (*N* 596, 448f, 616; *SE* 219f).

Imagination was an instrument of *science* for the Greeks (*N* 27), whereby they saw in the geometrical mean, or mean proportional, an image of the mediator and his incarnation, and in the circle, wherein a right-angled triangle giving the mean proportional can be inscribed, an image of God, indeed considered as a self-contained movement in which beginning and end are one, an image of the Trinity (*N* 439, 512, 528; *IC* 191f; *NR* 291f). Seeing in one thing the *image* of another, is *reading* the other in the one:

If, indeed, [the Greeks] read the Incarnation in the proportional mean, the Unity and Trinity of God in the pole and the rotation of the celestial equator, the Cross in the relationship between the celestial equator and the

ecliptic, and again in integration, in the balance ... what a marvelous
existence was theirs! ... [they] saw in geometry the image of the Incarnation (divine images, reflections of reality). (N 441, cf. 406).

Weil herself proposes to look for images and analogies of human
experience in the world, for example falling and rising as debasement and purification (N 71ff, 81, 84), water as decreation and
obedience, fire as change and new life (N 330, 124f, 117, 120), light
and shadow as good and evil (N 78, 81), chlorophyll in plants
enabling them to feed on light and raise their leaves to it as the grace
of God enabling us to rise out of ourselves into his life (N 223, 367f,
517, 535, 543f). Analogies enable us to express otherwise inexpressible realities and relations (N 69, 72). She remarks that 'The
ancients had a way of employing the same words at different levels
by analogical transposition, which confuses everything if we fail to
recognize it' (N 370), for examples, *pneuma*, breath or spirit (N 337,
367), or suffering and joy, human and divine (N 507); and she
quotes Eusebius on 'the transpositive way of the Greek mysteries'
and mentions the non-canonical saying of Christ, 'Become good
change makers' (*FLN* 180). She argues that the cube in relation to
its perspectives, and the stem of the sundial in relation to its
shadows, can, either of them, 'by an analogical transposition furnish
the key to the whole of human knowledge': the key, namely, that
each, though never really seen in its appearances, never the less
determines their variations and is therefore to be read in them as
their third dimension (*IC* 179). It is evidently an act of imagination,
non-pictorial and yet constructive, to transpose analogically, and to
assign words and beliefs to their proper levels, in other words, to
compose or superpose perspectives or readings, so as to understand
paradoxes and contradictions, and to build the vertical hierarchy or
architecture in the soul.[21]

It is thus imagination that recovers the poetry of the world and
recognises it in a particular human being, the divine symbolism and
metaphor throughout of which Christ is the key (*FLN* 191, 98).
Simone Weil writes:

[21] N 8 'the non-hierarchical representation of the world (science) and the hierarchical
representation are combined in the great works of the painters ... Whence the need for
composition on several planes (which is perhaps the key to all the arts)', 63 'Highest art,
order without form ... The presentation of several forms in the same object lifts the
spectator (the reader) above form', 98f, 139, 160, 163, 486, 530f; *FLN* 122, 179, 206, 208f,
270 'it is an indispensable purification of thought to set out the subject on one plane, thus

... the splendor of the heavens, the plains, the sea, and the mountains ... the silence of which is borne in upon us by thousands of tiny sounds ... the breath of the winds or the warmth of the sun ... beauty in a human being enables the imagination to see in him something like an equivalent of the beauty of the world. (*WG*171, see also 160, *SNLG* 151f. and Patrick Sherry's essay below)

Art, or rather a work of art, revealing the beauty of the world, especially if inspired by a transcendent model, is clearly an exercise of the higher imagination; for art is based on 'transfers of imagination' and the perception of beauty on 'a transposition of sensibility' (*WG* 168f, *N* 412, *IC* 89f; *N* 419; *FLN* 75); Weil speaks of reading a melody as our model for reading every part of the world, and says that such aesthetic contemplation is 'the key to supernatural truths' (*N* 260, 627, cf. 254; *FLN* 361). She writes that 'The way of ascent, in the *Republic*, is that of degrees of attention' (*N* 627); but for Socrates this movement begins with, and returns to, picturing, *eikasia* or imagination, as the philosopher returns to the world in order to turn others to the light, and so in the *Republic* Socrates composes the simile of the sun, the divided line, the allegory of the cave, not to mention the ship of state, the great beast, the dragon in the lion in the man within the man, the judgment in the great meadow, and the choice of lives by the spindle of necessity. Likewise Simone Weil assists us with her imagery of gravity and light, beggars and parents, doors and gates, prisoners and pregnancies, sun and emerald. She constructs a long list of images of Christ the mediator in religion and literature (*FLN* 321f); and she knows that images can be a protection against certain forms of idolatry: for example, we can address the collective soul that we do not see as creator of heaven and earth, but not the piece of carved wood that we do not see (*N* 214); in other words, the higher imagination can help us to *purify* ourselves of the lower.

True literature, for example, can deliver us from fiction: for fictional writing presents good and evil in an imaginary or fictitious way, making evil seem interesting and good boring, by ignoring the difficulty of good and its cost to the ego, and the destructiveness of evil and its cost to the heart. Fiction, in other words, ignores moral gravity, and the density or third dimension of reality, the way good and evil are mixed together in this world. The literature of genius,

eliminating any point of view about it ... But several cross-sections have to be taken, as in a mechanical drawing. A single cross-section leads to error.'

however, tells the truth about them: it shows evil as our boring pursuit of our personal advantage, and good as our heart's desire realised in impersonal joy and even intoxication. The two forms of writing exercise and nourish two different levels of imagination, as we might say: our mechanical materialistic egoistic fantasy and our free moral visionary imagination (*N* 143f, 154, 180, 160–9). *Genius* is evidently the imagination controlled by intelligence lit by love: it shows the world as it is for divine love, to be accepted (where we cannot now change it for the better) because it exists and is beautiful despite, and even because of, its bitterness and misery.[22]

Evidently it takes genius to inspire a people, the task Simone Weil addresses in the closing section of *The Need for Roots*: it is a matter of striking the imagination, as she says in her unsuccessful 'Proposal for a Project of Front-Line Nurses' (*SL* 149f, 157; cf. *SE* 150–3). It means in part using words like *God, truth, justice, love*, and *good*, that give light and lift us towards a perfection that we cannot adequately conceive: these words are dangerous to use and are like an ordeal, for they are false, absurd, and even defiling to those who speak or hear or write or read them unworthily.[23] Only genius, which is to say the highest imagination and saintly humility, can use them well, so as 'to make us grow wings to overcome gravity'. (*SE* 24; *SNLG* 160–5; *WG* 99; *NR* 224–6, 422: Weil's examples of genius seem always to be poets, painters, and musicians, such as Homer, Aeschylus, Sophocles, Shakespeare (*Lear*), Racine (*Phèdre*), Giotto, Velazquez, Bach, Mozart.)[24]

The truths presented thereby, when united to the love of truth, become what Weil calls 'active truth' in us, destroying error: in other words, they become supernatural reason, and discernment, the spirit of truth that is love (*FLN* 353, 110 'But supernatural reason only exists in souls which burn with [sc. which desire and possess] the supernatural love of God,' *FLN* 349f, cf. 253, 267).

---

[22] *N* 255, 258 'It is through its bitterness that the *Iliad* is beautiful. There is no first-class art without this core of bitterness', *N* 261 'By the perfectly pure contemplation of human misery we are caught up to heaven', *N* 285, *FLN* 144–8, 260 'Believe that reality is love, while still seeing it exactly as it is', 336 'Only a just man made perfect could have written the *Iliad*.'

[23] *N* 193f, *SE* 33f, *N* 486f good things, such as communion, are good for the good and evil for the evil, 508 for the evil they are 'an incitement to crime', 540 for them holy things become demoniacal, cf. *IC* 171. Thus Rabbi Akiba (*c.* AD 100) speaks of writings that 'defile the hands of the impure'. The writings of Simone Weil belong, I imagine, to this category.

[24] On the 'right' use of supernatural concepts to 'overcome gravity', see the essay by Eric Springsted in this volume.)

The coincidence at the highest level of imagination and discernment is shown by two further passages. The first is actually Weil's last entry in her journal: 'The most important part of teaching = to teach what it is to *know* (in the scientific sense). Nurses' (*FLN* 364, cf. *SL* 149–53). Nurses who really know *read* the pain of their patients as human suffering, *feel* it as their own, and therefore *act*, to relieve it, according to their training: each of these three exercises the imagination (*N* 36, 124, 177, 280–5). More generally, the best action follows on the reading of our situation in the light of supernatural truth, and that reading is discernment and yet imagination as well (*N* 219f, 224, 283, 480, 535).

The second passage comes at the close of her draft on 'The Pythagorean Doctrine'. Learning to know God in everything, like learning to recognise geometrical solids or to use tools or to read writing, is undergoing an apprenticeship involving transference and a change of sensibility, and God helps us by giving us sacraments and beauty everywhere:

All human life, the most common life, the most natural, is made thus. As soon as we analyse it, we find a tissue of mysteries completely impenetrable to the intelligence.

Human thought and the universe constitute the books of revelation *par excellence*, if the attention, lighted by love and faith, knows how to decipher them. The reading of them is a proof, and indeed the only certain proof. After having read the *Iliad* in Greek, no one would dream of wondering whether the professor who taught him the Greek alphabet had deceived him. (*IC* 201)

The upshot of my argument is this. Even if Simone Weil usually regards imagination as an act of the mediocre, merely natural part of us, like the will, she often requires it to serve our highest, supernatural part; but then she calls it not imagination, but genius, just as she calls will that consents to pure good, not will, but spirit, attention, and love (*N* 527, 627f; *FLN* 219f, 283; *WG* 43–5, 220f). Genius entails humility, like everything that serves supernatural love, and Weil so strongly links imagination with pride that it would not be easy for her to say that imagination can ever be genius, or divine; never the less both possibilities are clearly implied in her thought, as when she writes:

The imagination is given to us so as to make it descend.
The imagination is the supplementary form of energy. In so far as it clings to a part of the world, it lies (false readings). It must be cut off

[sc. detached in desire] from all objects in order that it may be caught up by the infinite. (*N* 221; cf. 215 n. 1 quoting John of the Cross)

Those poets had genius, and it was a genius oriented towards the good ... The works of authentic genius remain, and are available to us. Their contemplation is the ever-flowing source of an inspiration which may legitimately guide us. For this inspiration, if we know how to receive it, tends – as Plato said – to make us grow wings to overcome gravity. (*SNLG* 162, 165, cf. *N* 155, 440)

God is the supreme poet. (*FLN* 194; cf. *WG* 160f., 164f; 180)

VI

For Simone Weil, reality is discerned only by the eye of *love*.[25] As she lay dying so Pétrement relates, 'She told [Dr. Broderick] that she was a philosopher and interested in humanity' (Pétrement, p. 537). Her philosophy is, as I should like to put it, a contemplation with a view to discernment, and a practice inspired by love:

The proper method of philosophy consists in clearly conceiving the insoluble problems in all their insolubility and then in simply contemplating them, fixedly and tirelessly, year after year, without any hope, patiently waiting ...
There is no entry into the transcendent until the same faculties – intelligence, will, human love – have come up against a limit, and the human being waits at this threshold, which he can make no move to cross, without turning away and without knowing what he wants, in fixed, unwavering attention.
It is a state of extreme humiliation, and it is impossible for anyone who cannot accept humiliation.
Genius is the supernatural virtue of humility in the domain of thought. (*FLN* 335)

Philosophy (including problems of knowledge, etc.) is *exclusively* an affair of action and practice. That is why it is so difficult to write about it. Difficult in the same way as a treatise on tennis or running, but much more so.
Subjectivist theories of cognition are a perfectly correct description of those who lack the faculty which is extremely rare, of coming out of themselves. A supernatural faculty. Charity. (*FLN* 362)[26]

25 *WG* 158–60, *N* 240, 288, 209, 308; *FLN* 362. Cf. *Bhagavad-Gita* 4.31, 40 there is no *world* or *joy* for him who does not *give* and *believe*.
26 Cf. also Pétrement, *A Life*, viii, 44, 403–6, Fiori, *Intellectual Biography*, 21, 31, 33f (quoting Alain). See further McLellan, *Utopian Pessimist*, 272: 'for her, contemplation was not a means of stopping a nauseating world and getting off, but of seeing the world in a different and truer perspective and, above all, of developing a sharp eye and ear for the traces of God in all human activity and experience'.

Weil's thought that philosophy consists in clearly conceiving and contemplating its insoluble problems and requires fixed, unwavering attention, humility, and practice, brings to mind a number of contemporary writers not known to her, but whose views are strikingly similar to hers. I will mention here three such writers, the second and third of whom have, in fact, drawn upon her work.

First, there is Ludwig Wittgenstein, who gives a careful account of reading in his *Philosophical Investigations* (drafted between 1932 and 1949), and a discussion of physiognomic seeing that resembles Simone Weil's treatment of discernment and pure attention to the naked appearances: like her he emphasises that there actually *are* for us only appearances, with higher dimensions to be read; but this is not ontology so much as phenomenology, a call for further description rather than explanation.[27]

Second is Iris Murdoch, who has done so much to make the thoughts of Simone Weil available to her readers in English. For Murdoch, goodness is connected with knowledge, with what she calls: 'a refined and honest perception of what is really the case, a patient and just discernment and exploration of what confronts one which is the result not simply of opening one's eyes but of a certainly perfectly familiar kind of moral discipline.'

The discipline she mentions here is that of detaching ourselves from our selfish sensual fantasy, and exercising our imagination in such a way that we attend to people with faith and love, wishing to see them as they are and not merely as we wish to see them (or even as they see themselves, for that may be fantastic too). If fantasy is mechanical and passive like an avalanche or river, imagination is free and active, as a great artist is free. 'To be free is something like this: to exist sanely without fear and to perceive what is real.' Such

---

[27] *Philosophical Investigations*, Part I sections 156–71, and Part II section xi, especially pp. 194–216, *Zettel*, sections 220–6; *Investigations*, section 126 'Philosophy simply puts everything before us, and neither explains nor deduces anything – Since everything lies open to view there is nothing to explain. For what is hidden, for example, is of no interest to us'; *Philosophical Remarks*, p. 283 'A phenomenon isn't a symptom of something else; it is the reality'; *Zettel* section 614 'Why don't we just leave explaining alone?' See H. L. Finch, *Wittgenstein: The Later Philosophy*, Humanities, 1977, ch. 11, for a discussion of Wittgenstein's non-ontological physiognomic phenomenalism with 'a Machian (not to say Goethean) respect for appearances', the phenomena of everyday life, the *face* the world presents to humans. Finch quotes Goethe 'Do not look for anything behind the phenomena; they are themselves their own lesson', Hoffmansthal 'Depth is hidden. Where? On the surface', and the *Togan Koji*, a Noh play 'What is there to explain? All things are just the realm that is before one's eyes.' Cf. Simone Weil, *N* 283 'To love God through and beyond a certain thing is to love that thing in purity; the two sentiments are identical.'

sanity and perception is a discernment by imagination of truth from fantasy, moved by love. This could be said to be the central theme of Murdoch's writing as a whole.[28]

The third is the German theologian Dorothee Soelle, who reverses this terminology of mere fantasy and true imagination, and emphasises the '*Phantasie*' of Jesus: this bursting of conventional boundaries, his openness and freedom that seek the fulfilment and wholeness of human beings. It is 'the "know how" of love', she says, that makes real obedience and discernment possible, inexhaustible in finding new and better ways, ceaselessly working for the true good of others. 'Its whole aim is to discover, to make visible, and to disclose that which is invisible', the more abundant, fully human life of God.[29]

Let us now return to the passage from the London notebook in which Weil defines philosophy in terms of contemplation, practice, and love; and let us note well that the love that accomplishes this contemplation and practice, and unites her to human beings, also *separates* her from them,[30] and even for a time from God: for as her imagination of the affliction of other binds her to them and causes her to doubt for a time even the goodness of God, so her struggle to see how the love of God can allow the sufferings of others leads her to join herself (as it were in the imaginative act of them all) to the redemptive suffering of Christ. This is the dark night of the soul: it is isolation, nakedness, and silence.[31]

---

[28] *The Sovereignty of Good*, Routledge, 1970, page 38; 'The Darkness of Practical Reason', *Encounter* (July 1966), pp. 46–50, at p. 50. Compare, e.g., Jane Austen, *Pride and Prejudice*, edited by Tony Tanner, Penguin, 1972, pp. 234, 236 'the affair ... was capable of a turn which must make him entirely blameless throughout the whole ... I who have prided myself on my discernment ... Vanity, not love, has been my folly', and George Eliot, *Middlemarch* edited by W. J. Harvey, Penguin, 1965, pp. 845f. 'She began now to live through that yesterday morning deliberately again, forcing herself to dwell on every detail and its possible meaning. Was she alone in that scene? Was it her event only? She forced herself to think of it as bound up with another woman's life ... that base prompting which makes a woman more cruel to a rival than to a faithless lover, could have no strength of recurrence in Dorothea when the dominant spirit of justice within her had once overcome the tumult and had once shown her the truer measure of things.'

[29] *Beyond Mere Obedience* (1968, trans. Lawrence Denef, Augsburg 1970), especially chs. 9–11. Soelle discusses Simone Weil in *Suffering* (trans. Everett Kalin, Fortress 1975), ch. 6.

[30] *WG* 48f, 54f; cf. Thoreau, *Walden* 5.11 'A man thinking or working is always alone, let him be where he will', and Kierkegaard, *Postscript* (trans. Swenson and Lowrie, Princeton 1941), page 68 the subjective thinker 'thinks the universal, but as existing in this thought and as assimilating it in his inwardness, he becomes more and more subjectively isolated', also Søren Kierkegaard, *Journal and Papers*, trans. and ed. Howard and Edna Hong, Bloomington: Indiana University Press, 1967–78, sections 114, 1825, 4050, and *Works of Love* 64, 80, 351f.

[31] *SL* 178, *WG* 91, *N* 255, *FLN* 94f; *WG* 119f, 123f, 126, 132: *N* 26, 213, 260, 513, *SE* 17, *SNLG* 196–8.

In his introduction to *The Simone Weil Reader*, George Panichas mentions some words in Italian inscribed on a small plaque attached to Weil's gravestone by an unnamed donor: '*La mia solitudine l'altrui dolore ghermiva fino alla morte*'. Panichas renders the words, 'My solitude held in its grasp the grief of others until my death'.[32] Juana Rosa Pita tells me that the Italian here is flexible enough to allow a reversal of subject and object, and further that *ghermiva* is related to *germinare*, to grow, suggesting the reading: 'The suffering of other fed my solitude unto death.'[33]

I think that we should accept both of these readings, setting the first below the second as presupposing it. For Simone Weil's compassion for and imaginative discernment of human affliction *divided* her from God as well as from human beings, in order finally to identify her with them in redemptive love. But, as she would say, this was only for the highest part of the soul, with which the natural part as such, the fantasy as we can call it, had nothing to do; although it too, so it would seem, was finally drawn up with the whole soul into this love.[34]

---

[32] *The Simone Weil Reader*, page xviii; spelling corrected from Cabaud, *Simone Weil à New York et à Londres* (Plon 1967, p. 94, and Fiori, *Intellectual Biography*, p. 322. The plaque was no longer there when I visited Ashford in March 1990.

[33] Cf. Cabaud's French version 'ma solitude la douleur d'autrui l'a tormentée jusqu'à la mort'. Fiori's reading, making *la mia solitudine* the subject but *ghermiva* passive, comes to the same as Panichas'. If *ghermiva* really is related to *germinare*, then perhaps the inscription can be linked, by way of Psalms 80.5 'the bread of tears' (cf. 42.4, 102.9) and Isaiah 30.20 'the bread of adversity and the water of affliction', to George Herbert's 'you must sit down, says Love, and taste my meat. So I did sit and eat.'

[34] I thank John Hellman for a remark at a meeting at Notre Dame in April 1984 about the discernment of Simone Weil which suggested to me the idea for this essay; and Richard Bell, André Devaux, Pat Little, Kathleen Sands, Miklos Vetö, and especially Roy Finch, for comments that led to improvements in it.

CHAPTER 6

On the right use of contradiction according to Simone Weil

André A. Devaux
Translated by J. P. Little

To Richard Bell, in great esteem, gratitude and friendship.

Reality represents essentially contradiction. For reality is the obstacle, and the obstacle for a thinking being is contradiction.
Simone Weil, *N* 387

In her article in the May 1941 number of the *Cahiers du Sud*, published in Marseilles where she was staying, Simone Weil contrasts two kinds of philosopher: those who, applying the Socratic method, reflect on nature and on the meaning of their thoughts, and those who 'construct a representation of the universe according to their own fancy'. Only the former, she says, are 'true masters of thought', and she singles out among them Plato, Descartes, Kant, and Husserl. She thereby remains faithful to a well-established French academic tradition. Among the second 'type of philosophers' are, in her view, builders of systems, and she sees in Aristotle and Hegel the highest representatives of that family. She recognises in their theses 'a certain poetic beauty', and praises 'the marvellously penetrating formulae' sometimes present in their work, but she, for her part, adheres resolutely to the first line of reflection, which is that of true philosophy, 'as eternal as art'.[1]

Now, for those who claim to be faithful to the inspiration of philosophy as methodical research, the experience of contradiction is fundamental. Simone Weil gives herself the explicit task of 'taking the human condition as it is',[2] and also of describing it as it is. This faithful description starts from the idea that the human condition is defined by an essential contradiction, that is, that man, 'with a straining after the good constituting his very being, is at the same

[1] *Cahiers Inédits*, I (Marseilles, late 1940–early 1941). (Fonds Simone Weil at the Bibliothèque Nationale in Paris.) Her essay on 'Philosophy' from the *Cahiers du Sud*, May 1941, can also be found in *FW* 283–9.
[2] *Cahiers Inédits*.

time subject in his entire being, both in mind and in flesh, to a blind force, to a necessity completely indifferent to the good' (*OL* 173). Such is Simone Weil's claim in her essay in *Oppression and Liberty*, 'Is there a Marxist doctrine?' 'So it is', she adds, not otherwise, 'and that is why no human thinking can escape from contradiction'. Our destiny is to live in the uncomfortably 'double' situation which is our lot, and with the sense of being torn apart which results from it: 'contradiction is that which our mind tries to get rid of and is unable to' (*N* 387).

Simone Weil had been made aware of the importance of contradiction from her youth, through the teaching of René Le Senne (1882–1954), who was her first philosophy teacher, during the year 1924–5, at the Lycée Victor-Duruy in Paris. One of Le Senne's principal theses is that contradiction is a fortunate obstacle, which comes and interrupts the spontaneous flight of consciousness and makes it alert. When it meets contradiction, the mind is diverted from abandoning itself lazily to the given. Contradiction is indeed real, but it only exists, according to Le Senne, for an active consciousness, seeking unity. Hence the danger is that one makes oneself at home in contradiction and finds a resting-place there, whereas a human being's vocation is to confront it and try to get out of it by an effort of personal creation. In a formula which clearly recalls Le Senne's line of argument, Simone Weil writes in *La Source Grecque*: 'In matters of the intellect, what calls thought [towards being] is what contains contradictions. In other words, relationship'.[3] But whereas Le Senne emphasises the duty of inventing a resolution to contradiction, Simone Weil insists more on the idea that people must allow themselves to be carried away beyond themselves in an act of obedience to which they have consented.

Contradiction can indeed be the sign of a logical error which an undemanding mind accepts complacently, but it can also, in certain cases, be 'a sign of truth' by the way it conforms to the very essence of humanity. Simone Weil invites us, therefore, to be discerning when confronted with contradictions: there are true and authentic ones, but there are also false and artificial ones which we ourselves fabricate. If the contradiction is only apparent, there is in fact only a simple correlation of opposites. For example, between manual and

---

[3] *La Source Grecque*, Paris: Gallimard, Coll. *Espoir*, 1979, p. 106.

intellectual work, it is easy to posit a relationship capable of dissolving the contradiction by insisting upon the notion of co-operation between the two kinds of work. But there are cases where the contradiction cannot be eliminated. We are then dealing with what Simone Weil calls 'essential contradictions'.

The most fundamental of all contradictions is that which opposes good and necessity, or again, justice and force, since the terms which compose them are radically distinct but none the less experienced by consciousness: people desire justice but, at the same time, cannot avoid being subject to force. Nothing therefore is more important, for the sake of mental hygiene, than to place 'clearly before oneself the essential contradictions of human thought',[4] failing which, one runs up against them unexpectedly and falls into a state of confusion.

Faced with the real contradictions from which our intelligence cannot escape, we are then going to be obliged to reflect on the use we can make of them, for 'there is a legitimate and an illegitimate use of contradiction' (*OL* 173). The latter consists in 'coupling together incompatible thoughts as if they were compatible' (*OL* 173), or making the union of opposites too rapidly, by remaining on the level at which those opposites are manifest. Thus, 'when one extols the opposite of a certain evil, one remains at the level of that evil', instead of raising oneself to the level of the good (*N* 447). Between the *ancien régime* and the revolution of 1789, in France, Simone Weil sees an alternation without progression, since, if domination passes from the oppressors to the oppressed, or if we pass from the imperialism of the bosses to that of the workers, we have not taken one single step towards the good, and disorder continues to reign. The wrong use of contradiction, therefore, lies in the combination of two incompatible affirmations as if they were compatible, on the level on which they are opposed.

Diametrically opposite, the legitimate use of contradiction supposes first of all an attentive examination of the apparent incompatibility between two thoughts, so as to see whether that incompatibility resists all attempt to abolish it. It may be that on reflection one of the terms judged incompatible disappears and, with it, the supposed contradiction itself. That is the case of numerous inconsistencies in

---

[4] *Cahiers Inédits*, I.

society which can be abolished thanks to a programme of intelligent reform.

On the other hand, if the two incompatible thoughts continue to present themselves together to the mind, the contradiction itself must be recognised as a fact. Once convinced of this fact, the mind must 'conceive of a relationship which transforms contradiction into correlation'.[5] The soul is then 'pulled upwards'. To reach this stage, the mind must learn to use the two terms of the contradiction like 'a two-limbed tool, like a pair of pincers, so that through it direct contact may be made with the transcendent sphere of truth beyond the range of the human faculties' (*OL* 173) – that sphere which, as an adolescent, Simone Weil had despaired of ever entering, as she wrote to Father Perrin (*WG* 30).

Contradiction conceived in this way becomes, then, an intermediary between the world of the senses and the intelligible world, and the contact with the latter is none the less direct as a revelation of the supernatural. There is legitimate use of contradiction when the suffering it imposes impels the soul to go higher than the original plane where the opposites were perceived, but to go higher 'one must be pulled'. For Simone Weil, 'what the relation of contraries can do so as to touch the natural being, contradictories conceived together (really conceived together) can do so as to touch God' (*N* 363).[6] She has given many illustrations in various domains, notably in that of mathematics, of this right use of contradiction. But it is in the realm of the religious life that the fruitfulness of the idea of contradiction asserts itself most convincingly. In this domain, contradiction is seen at one and the same time as a criterion of truth, and as the hold gained by transcendence over the human intelligence, when the latter allows itself to be raised to a higher level where the incomprehensible unity of the opposing terms becomes an inescapable reality.

In God, good and necessity are one: that is the mystery capable of illuminating the believer, as we see in the varied religious traditions which are authentic, that is to say, those that are founded on the assurance that God is good rather than powerful – in particular in the Christian dogmas of the Incarnation and the Trinity. Christ, fully God and fully man, is living contradiction and, at the same

---

[5] *La Source Grecque*, p. 106.
[6] Cf. *N* 341: 'Two truths conceived simultaneously through the link supplied by relation enable us to seize hold, as with two sticks, of a point that is situated outside our direct range.'

time, mediating Saviour who allows contradiction to be overcome, just as the circulation of love among the three divine persons creates harmony in the Pythagorean sense, as 'a common thought of separated thinkers'.[7]

The problem of the existence of God illustrates a very clear case of contradictions which are also true: God exists and God does not exist. For, writes Simone Weil, 'I am absolutely certain that there is a God, in the sense that I am absolutely certain that my love is not illusory.' But she adds immediately: 'I am absolutely certain that there is no God, in the sense that I am absolutely certain that there is nothing real which bears a resemblance to what I am able to conceive when I pronounce that name, since I am unable to conceive God' (*N* 127). By conceiving the union of two antagonistic thoughts concerning the existence of God, I am able to practise the art which Simone Weil recommended, the art of 'superimposed readings' which allow me to recognise necessity behind and through sensations, order behind necessity and, behind necessity, God who gives order to the world, creator of all the beauty in the world. It is by a strategy analogous to 'reading' that we are enabled to love the 'impersonal God' through the 'personal' and reciprocally. Such is the 'harmony of opposites' which was an inspiration to the Greeks – the harmony which consists in 'the simultaneous grasping of different things' (*N* 409).

These examples work together to prove that contradiction is indeed 'our path leading towards God because we are creatures, and because creation itself is contradiction' (*N* 386), contradiction between the Creator, who is infinite good, and the creature, who is limited. Indeed, according to Simone Weil, 'the supreme contradiction is the creator–creature contradiction, and it is Christ who represents the union of these contradictories' (*N* 386). He is thus essentially passion. Simone Weil says that sanctity, which is imitation of Christ, or order of the world, is 'the simultaneous existence, in the comportment of the soul, of incompatible elements' and, as such, comparable to a balance 'which leans to either side at once', like the Cross (*N* 391). The simultaneous existence of contrary virtues in the soul transforms these virtues into 'pincers for reaching up to God' (*N* 394), or, according to another image which Simone Weil is fond of, into a lever which transports the soul 'to the other

---

[7] *Intuitions pré-chrétiennes*, Paris: Fayard, 1951, p. 127.

side of the unopenable door' (*FLN* 131). Thus the simultaneous thinking of contradictory truths, and the simultaneous exercise of contrary virtues, lead to one and the same threshold, where 'the persistence and humble spirit of waiting' makes the host within open that door which our own strength cannot even get ajar.

If the use of contradiction as a means to pass to the transcendent realm allows a contact with supernatural reality, it is clear that its negation will prevent any right use of essential contradiction. This is the origin of Simone Weil's main objection to Marxism, when it ceases to be a fruitful method for analysing social reality to become materialist doctrine. This doctrine, indeed, 'attributes to matter the automatic manufacture of the good' (*OL* 174), forgetting the infinite distance separating good from necessity. Any systematic materialism, therefore, can only be an inauthentic form of religious life, a lie and an imposture, since the resolution of contradictions that is claimed leaves us on the worldly plane of history. In Simone Weil's eyes, it is a typical example of the false union of opposites, which consists in 'seeking harmony in Becoming, in what is the exact opposite of the eternal' (*N* 616). Marxism gave in to the illusion of 'believing that by walking straight in front of one, one necessarily rises up into the air' (*N* 447), that force is of its own accord oriented towards the good, an assumption that is totally false.

Regarding essential contradictions, Simone Weil says that philosophers are wrong to try and resolve them, 'instead of destroying them', and she gives as a prime example the contradiction between the world and God. For dialectic, challenged because it remains 'horizontal', Simone Weil wants to substitute vertical composition, on several planes in hierarchical order. At the back of her mind there is a meditation on the notion of value – another central theme of René Le Senne's philosophy, whose major work, published in 1934, is entitled *Obstacle and Value*. Simone Weil also defines philosophy as 'a reflexion on values': therein lies its particular vocation, compared with science and art which assume the existence of values without having to reflect precisely on them. Values indeed have reality as object only for the mind that thinks them, but that reality as object of thought cannot be denied: 'every person is interested in value above everything else, or rather the more or less confused feeling of value is what we call interest',[8] that interest which determines feelings and actions. By permitting a hierarchical description of planes of reality, axiology promotes the right use of contradiction, showing that it is universal values – the true, the beautiful, the good – which draw us upward.

Simone Weil notes, in the article on 'Philosophy' evoked at the beginning of these remarks, that those philosophies which follow the interrogative method of Socrates are 'all oriented towards salvation' – an intellectual salvation which can be seen as a prelude to spiritual salvation. This is because these philosophies, essentially reflexive, apply the Platonic precept which calls on one to 'turn towards the truth with the whole soul', that is, with all the parts of the soul, each part being assigned to a specific object. This movement of conversion of the spiritual faculty of looking remains unchanging throughout time, but embraces a particular cultural context according to the epoch. This is why Simone Weil wrote to the philosopher Jean Wahl in 1942, while they were both guests of the United States of America: '[truth] requires to be expressed through the only approximately good thing we can call our own, namely science' (*SL* 159). Science, rendered pure once more, is all the more appropriate to this task in that it issues from religious thought, as is indicated, according to Simone Weil, by Greek geometry, the inspiration of which we have to rediscover. Truth is eternal, but it has to be 'transposed' and translated, generation after generation.

In her aim to make the Socratic approach relevant for the modern world, Simone Weil emphasised the value and the efficacy of attentive contemplation. The last notebook which she had the time and the spirit to fill with personal notes, in London, in 1943, opens with this definition: 'The proper method of philosophy consists in clearly conceiving the insoluble problems in all their insolubility and then in simply contemplating them, fixedly and tirelessly, year after year, without any hope, patiently waiting' (*FLN* 335). In this manner she was to make of humility the specific virtue of the intelligence confronted with metaphysical problems. It is the same attitude that she counselled for the analysis of the treasures preserved in universal folklore, to which she devoted herself passionately in her last years: 'Method is necessary for the understanding of images, symbols etc. One should not try to interpret them, but contemplate them until their significance flashes upon one' (*N* 334). Patient waiting and the

---

[8] *Cahiers Inédits*, 1.

right orientation of the soul's gaze are the two ways of philosophical salvation, which is 'transformation of being' gained as a result of effort expended upon oneself.

Simone Weil was convinced that this method of abolishing contradiction by discovering the unity of opposites implicit within it was within the reach of every mind, provided that the disorder of social injustice had not extinguished that innate capacity to 'drink the light, whatever it may be, that bursts forth from every kind of contemplation' (*ibid.*),[9] as a spring bursts forth from a rock. Thus conceived as a search for wisdom, as its very etymology suggests, philosophy is a 'virtue', declares Simone Weil, encompassing in this beautiful word both interior strength and exterior courage. Joy, true joy, is the reward for this effort of discipline upon the understanding and the will – the joy which is one with the feeling of 'the fulness of the sentiment of the real' (*N* 222), 'in the thought that God is' (*N* 291), the joy which can be communicated among minds when there reigns a climate of mutual confidence, such as that which brought us together at Cambridge, and then at Wooster.

[9] Cf. *FLN* pp. 130–1: 'God has placed in every thinking being the necessary capacity of light for controlling the truth of every thought.'

PART II

Readings toward a divine humanity

CHAPTER 7

Rootedness: culture and value

Eric O. Springsted

Simone Weil once noted that the slogan-like quality of capitalised value-words creates an effective smoke-screen that keeps us from seeing what is really behind them. Each age has its own set of such words. Ours has introduced 'Pluralisms'. Far from signifying one thing at all, 'Pluralism' has at least four different meanings. It can refer:

1 to the fact that people think differently;
2 to the fact that groups differ on what they hold valuable;
3 to the idea that our differences over what is good and valuable is not always a strict matter of right or wrong, but of differing cultural histories;
4 to the liberal notion that what is good and valuable is essentially a matter of individual choice.

Because of this plurality of meanings, calls for 'Pluralism' run the gamut from recommending that we be tolerant of others and humble about our own opinions to a rather dogmatic insistence that there are no goods other than those we choose, and no ultimate, universal good to choose.

Important differences are concealed by the single term. One who believed that either 3 or 4 is true would see the relation between culture and values very differently than a medieval crusader, although a crusader would have been well aware of cultural differences, and could have made use of them intellectually and economically whenever his sword was sheathed. But a common difference does not entail a common meaning. While the liberal view, 4, may rest on, and incorporate a recognition of, 3, to believe that our values are historically and culturally contingent does not necessarily imply that what is good only extends as far as human will. In so far as it does not, thereon hang two very different alternatives of how we view our values, our history and world, and ultimately to how we shall live.

I

Why are values now often regarded as culturally and historically contingent? The explanation itself is historical. Once we assumed the existence of clear and distinct ideas and believed our ideas clearly mirrored nature. The success of science seemed to prove it. However, once we began to engage in philosophy of science, once we began to reflect on what we were doing as thinkers, the older picture appeared a fantasy. Since the Enlightenment Karl Marx has taught us about ideology, the presentation of ideas as objective when they are merely reflections of contingent social and material conditions. Wittgenstein has taught us that our words, without which we cannot say anything about anything, have their validity within a cultural context, and that none are universally privileged. Thomas Kuhn has taught us that science is not, as Bacon suggested, induction from hard facts, but the result of historically contingent research paradigms.

Nowhere has all this been quite so clearly recognised as in social, political, and moral philosophy. While attempting since Kant, if not before, to find hard-and-fast primary moral principles, philosophers have always recognised that such principles are established on shakier ground than scientific ones. Contemporary disavowals of essentialism and epistemological foundationalism have nearly completely undermined that ground for many.

Thus moral philosophy has now tried to stress, as Bernard Williams and Martha Nussbaum have done,[1] that there is no single answer to the question: 'What should I do?'; it, rather, provokes a futile effort with which we have lived since Plato. It has discovered, in Charles Larmore's words, 'patterns of moral complexity,'[2] declaring our seemingly transcendent values to be cultural and historical, contingent and not universal as Kant thought. Undisturbed by this turn of thought, contemporary moral philosophy has felt a certain

---

[1] Bernard Williams, *Ethics and the Limits of Philosophy*, Cambridge: Harvard University Press, 1985; Martha Nussbaum, *The Fragility of Goodness*, Cambridge: Cambridge University Press, 1986.

[2] Charles Larmore, *Patterns of Moral Complexity*, Cambridge: Cambridge University Press, 1987.

degree of liberation, and tried to teach us to enjoy the rich fruits of diversity in lieu of transcendent certainty.

Indeed, much contemporary moral philosophy has tried to teach us that commitment to unimpeachable, transcendent values is not only philosophically indefensible, but also unwise. While few philosophers would agree with Arthur Schlesinger jun.'s sophomoric remarks crediting all wars to non-pluralists,[3] they have become increasingly suspicious of single principle moralities – with good reason. Not only do such moralities cause us to miss the rich diversity of moral experience, they are positively misleading. Sometimes they even create fanatics. The notion of freedom which Enlightenment liberalism considered an absolute moral principle is an example. Broadly construed, it is hardly absolute; instead, as Marx suggested, 'freedom' is too often simply a justification for the socially strong. But that is not always recognised. Philosophies of freedom quickly become ideologies of freedom used to dominate others, rather than to liberate them. As Nicholas Lash observes, what happens is that not only has appearance been confused with what is really going on, but it is assumed that what goes on here, today, ought to go on everywhere and at all times, and further that it necessarily goes on.[4] Thus appearances taken to be necessary moral principles are easily used to justify, and even create and demand, some very bad behaviour.

The call to recognise values as contingent and historical has not been greeted with unmixed enthusiasm. Many defenders of absolute principles have complained that all this contingency entails moral relativism. While we may dismiss at the onset objections based on *passé* metaphysics and absolutism,[5] at least two important questions need to be considered carefully. First, is there any binding quality to morals which we believe to be contingent and related only by historical and cultural accident? Second, how, when values and morals are only accidentally related to human life, can a moral agent find, or make, any sort of coherent moral life, any sort of life with deep meaning?

In response to the first question, we may simply note the degree to which it is question-begging. Why is it that only necessary and

[3] *The New York Times Review of Books*, July 23, 1989.

[4] Nicholas Lash, *A Matter of Hope*, Notre Dame: University of Notre Dame Press, 1982, p. 59.

[5] As Richard Rorty has argued (*Philosophy and the Mirror of Nature*, Princeton: Princeton University Press, 1979), a full-blooded relativism is the alternative to absolutism, and to find absolutism meaningless similarly empties relativism of meaning.

universal principles can bind us morally? Why, we may ask, should we assume this at all?

Ironically, the reason why it is assumed turns out to be itself historical, involving as it does a concept of the person that began in Renaissance humanism. It was then that we began to look into ourselves to find a world of meaning, instead of looking outwardly towards some universal principle on a macrocosmic scale. This budding inward reliance then found full bloom in Kant, who posited an ideal inner autonomous self that chooses the good and is radically prior to all social and historical determination. Within Kant's philosophy, this concept of the self does not undermine moral commitment for a very good reason. For Kant the transcendental subject maintains its radical freedom precisely by generating moral principles on which to act, and, since Kant believed that rationality was universal and necessary, it meant that all subjects could, and would, if rational, generate the same principles. This allows for a society which is a kingdom of ends and of perfect, procedural justice. When we realise, however, that there are no universal principles, a problem does arise, at least as long as we maintain the same view of the self. The self, still thought capable of unconditionally choosing its own good, yet no longer operating under a universal rationality, is thought to be cut loose from any shared values, other than a respect for the right to choose. In short, it easily becomes what Alasdair MacIntyre calls the 'emotivist self',[6] exactly the democratic man whom Plato feared.

Yet what reason is there to think that we are autonomous in quite that way, *other* than our supposed ability to generate universal principles? There is little. In a masterful critique of John Rawls' attempt to reinterpret the Kantian transcendental ego, and thereby to establish a rational system of pure procedural justice, Michael Sandel has argued that the problem with Kantian liberalism is precisely its improbable view of the person, and that *it*, and not a lack of universal principles, is what is damaging morally, for who we are is constituted to a very great extent by our social relations and allegiances. Sandel writes:

But we cannot regard ourselves as independent in this way without great cost to those loyalties and convictions whose moral force consists partly in the fact that living by them is inseparable from understanding ourselves as

[6] Alasdair MacIntyre, *After Virtue*, Notre Dame: University of Notre Dame Press, 1981, chs. 2, 3.

the particular persons we are – as members of this family or community or nation or people ... Allegiances such as these are more than values I happen to have or aims I 'espouse at any given time' ... They allow that to some I owe more than justice requires or even permits, not by reason of agreements I have made but instead in virtue of those more or less enduring attachments and commitments which taken together partly define the person I am.[7]

If Sandel is right that ourselves are, in fact, to an important degree social, then having numerous, contingent moral allegiances is neither surprising nor troublesome. We can no more avoid some degree of social solidarity and shared social values than our limbs can live on their own without being connected to the rest of our body. Thus what most liberal societies need to worry about when faced with anarchy in cultural values is not a lack of universal principles, but about having historical values, such as individualism, which have come to override all other competing values and which are more the result of economic factors[8] than metaphysical insight. So the problem involved in our fear of moral anarchy is not one of having no shared principles but of having ones that do not allow us to flourish. As Stanley Hauerwas ironically remarks, when Western liberal society keeps telling itself that human beings are autonomous and selfish, it is no surprise that people become that way.[9]

So having contingent values *per se* need *not* entail cultural and moral relativism; indeed, by recognising that values are primarily cultural products, we may simply dismiss 'cultural relativism' as a contradiction in terms, since any value is necessarily something that is shared. Our cultural values have, in Simone Weil's phrase, 'gravity', a certain weightiness all their own which is extremely difficult to overthrow in fact, if not in fancy.

The real problem is not having values that will give our lives weight, it is finding meaning and coherence in the values that bind us, a sort of 'grace', or lightness. Socially imposed duties that bind us to others can become onerous unless we can make sense of those duties in a way that we can personally commit ourselves to them. The pressure of social duty, for example, may keep a teacher

---

[7] Michael Sandel, *Liberalism and the Limits of Justice*, Cambridge: Cambridge University Press, 1982, p. 179.

[8] Cf. C. B. MacPherson, *The Political Theory of Possessive Individualism: Hobbes to Locke*, Oxford: Oxford University Press, 1962.

[9] Stanley Hauerwas, *A Community of Character*, Notre Dame: University of Notre Dame Press, 1981, p. 79.

faithfully correcting papers and advising students. It does not keep him from *ennui* or despair. Also, not all our duties cohere, nor are they commensurate. The histories that have brought Western culture to where it is today, and that impinge on us, do not form a seamless garment. On the contrary; they often present us, their heirs, with competing and incommensurate demands. How then do we put a meaningful moral life together?

One of the best liberal attempts at an answer without recourse to absolute principles comes from Richard Rorty. Arguing that we need to accept the contingency of our selves and our languages, he has suggested that culturally we should employ a nominalist and historicist rhetoric, instead of the rhetoric of absolute philosophical principles. This nominalist rhetoric, he argues, should help us understand that what binds cultures together are 'common vocabularies and common hopes', with the former dependent on the latter 'in the sense that the principal function of the vocabularies is to tell stories about future outcomes which compensate for present sacrifices'.[10] We need to be aware that our values are not based on absolute principles, and we need culturally and personally continually to weave together and balance what values we do have in such a way that they present concrete alternatives and scenarios. Not that we ought to be, or can be, sceptical when doing so; Rorty 'cannot imagine a culture which socialized its youth in such a way as to make them continually dubious about their process of socialization.'[11] Rather, he suggests, that while socially bound, we ought at the same time to engage in private, ironical projects of self-creation and redescription, which cannot, because of our social nature, destroy the public vocabulary. 'Ironists have to have something to have doubts about, something from which to be alienated', he notes.[12]

Rorty's use of 'irony' is not, as I understand it, a call for anything like Cartesian scepticism. Rather, it seems far closer to what is often called self-knowledge, if by the term we do not redevelop mistaken notions about the self. It may even be a call for wisdom in the sense that the book of Ecclesiastes used the term. Irony involves a deep personal recognition of contingency in our cultural values, a recognition that 'man cannot find out what God has done from the

---

[10] Richard Rorty, *Contingency, Irony, and Solidarity*, Cambridge: Cambridge University Press, 1989, p. 86.
[11] *Contingency, Irony, and Solidarity*, p. 87.　　[12] *Contingency, Irony, and Solidarity*, p. 88.

beginning to the end' (3:11). Yet it also calls us not to doubt those values, but to imagine new uses for them; if wisdom is not absolute, 'it excels folly as light excels darkness' (2:13). Far from distancing us from others, this irony is precisely what allows us to see others as people, as individuals, and not simply as examples of a category. By understanding that our categories and values are limited, our actions cease to be limited by them. In this sense, Rorty's irony can even be a principle of reformation. Deliberately anti-utopian, it is the sort of thing that may save us from utopias.

To summarise the above arguments briefly, I claim that the recognition that our values are cultural products, plural in form and radically historical, does not entail, or even imply, moral anarchy or relativism between persons in a culture. The very fact that we are historical, socially conditioned beings, and not ahistorical egos, that we speak a common language already infused thoroughly with values, argues that what values we have are no less binding on us for being cultural than they would be if they were thought to come from God himself. Furthermore, such recognition may even be morally good for us to the degree that it keeps us from absolutising the values peculiar to our own history, and thus making us insensitive to others. It keeps us from absolutising ourselves. In this sense, it even allows for a certain degree of moral change, or dare we say, moral improvement? But, we must ask, does it involve denial of an overarching good?

II

Surprising as it may be to do so, I want now to argue, that Simone Weil in her last writings advanced similar 'pluralist' views, at least in so far as she argued not only that cultural values are historical, but that they ought to be positively valued as such.

It is, of course, surprising to say this given Simone Weil's own harsh criticism of social institutions as the 'Great Beast' of Plato, or as belonging to the prince of this world. It is equally surprising, considering how often she makes remarks to the effect that true morality has always been the same everywhere and at all times, that divergences from that morality are perversions or simply false. However, I shall argue that, if we take her latest writings, those composed in London during 1943 shortly before her death, we shall find a far more nuanced view than her dogmatic, undialectical words would suggest. These writings are not piecemeal observations, but part of a much larger synthesis she was making of her religious and social ideas, a synthesis of which she was conscious and to which she refers in one of her last letters to her parents 'as a deposit of pure gold ... indivisible ... [and] more compact.'[13]

I shall contend that, while Weil did indeed continue to talk of the Great Beast, and inveigh against what might be called 'moralities of gravity', she began to discover that the necessity, the gravity, under which social life operates is not antithetical to an absolute good but a 'metaxu' to transmit that good. She recognised that the values we hold are initially a function of our culture, and we as social and material beings do not exist outside culture. As such they are contingent. But, if we can get the right sort of perspective on cultural values and learn how to balance them and make them cohere, they may point to something more ultimate. For Weil the solution hinges on seeing our history as a matter of being rooted.

To a degree there are similarities here with Rorty's liberal humanist position. There is also a decided alternative to that position. For within these late writings she also insists that the point of balance around which cultural values needs to be centred is divine and supernatural, and not simply the product of human imagination. But, in saying so, she is not interested in this supernatural centre to justify cultural values as such; rather she offers it as an alternative to a humanistic vision which makes us rely purely on our own imaginative, rational, and historical resources which taken alone add only further chapters to a genealogy of power. Her alternative is one of hope in a world which can genuinely be tragic.

III

In order to present Weil's position I shall proceed by partially reconstructing her writings from the London Period. Three of the most important ones, 'Human Personality', *The Need for Roots*, and the misleadingly titled 'Draft for a Statement of Human Obligations' can be put in just that order. This order, I argue, reflects a development of her most mature thought on culture and values, as she moves from a critique of cultural values in 'Human Personality' which sets up the problem in a way with which she is satisfied

---

[13] I take this to refer particularly to what she was writing in London.

through her insights in *Need for Roots*, to her succinct answer in the 'Draft'.

On the proposed reading, 'Human Personality' is the earliest of these essays. On the surface it is also here where there is the most evidence *against* the claim that Weil smiled upon historically contingent social values. It is this essay that claims 'the collectivity is not only alien to the sacred, but deludes us with a false imitation of it' (*SE* 14). It also contains her attack on Personalism as she claims that personality is nothing but a social creation which entitles us to no natural rights. This, along with her seemingly sarcastic remarks about important cultural values such as rights, personality, equality, and democracy as being mediocre and belonging to a realm of 'middle values', lends supposed evidence to the position that Weil was on a precipice overlooking Manichaean political acosmism, if not over it. Her tone, if not her language, seems an outright attack on 'moralities of gravity' as if there were an either/or decision to be made between them and 'moralities of grace'.

The tone of voice, however, hides the very positive achievements of this essay. Yet that tone is necessary, because the first achievement of the essay is Weil's reaching a point of great personal clarity on where she disagrees with the assumptions of mainline liberal and humanist political philosophy, the particular object of her criticism. Once this is clear her project will not be confused with another's, once she has washed the terms clean, she is able to use them in a new and far more positive way.

Let us first consider the specific, named object of Weil's attack, the movement known as Personalism. If unaware of what exactly this movement involved, based on Weil's portrait of it, we might assume it to be a movement that celebrated individualism and egotism. This is far from the case. In many ways Personalism represented simply a focused liberal view of the person. It stressed that persons are not only individuals, but that they possess both an intrinsic dignity and basic rights that are best respected in a free and responsible democratic society. While Personalism is normally associated with Emmanuel Mounier, it seems evident that Weil had Jacques Maritain in mind.[14] For Maritain personality is a 'metaphysical centre', referring 'to the highest and deepest dimensions of our being'.

---

[14] On Weil's relation to Personalism, and evidence that it is Maritain to whom she is referring, see Simone Fraisse, 'Simone Weil, la personne et les droits de l'homme', *CSW*, 7:2, June 1984, pp. 120–32.

Personality is what enables 'one freely to perfect and freely to give this substance'.[15] It is 'interiority to oneself'. Personality is also the bearer of inalienable rights which Maritain believed were best respected in a democratic society where each individual is duly respected.

How could Weil possibly object to this highly moral position? There are two reasons. First, partly by virtue of her early studies of Marx, she simply did not believe that there was a metaphysical self or that there are universal and inalienable rights. Personality for her is but a function of what she calls 'social matter', analogous to physical matter, operating with its own quasi-mechanical laws. As she argues in another of her last essays, 'Is There a Marxist Doctrine?', not only is there this social matter, but also 'psychological matter', and that 'under all the phenomena of a moral order, whether collective or individual, there is something analogous to matter properly so-called' (*OL* 177–8). Thus for Weil the philosophical problem with Personalism specifically, and classical liberalism more generally, is that it fails to see that its notion of the essentially free inner person, and the inalienable rights he supposedly enjoys, are but historically and socially contingent outworkings of social forces that have been reified. It is an ideology.

Weil's second reason for objecting to Personalism is deeper. Not only is Personalism philosophically uncritical, it also fails to do what it set out to do – to protect the dignity of human beings. By locating human dignity in a metaphysical inner core, believing that their analysis is universally and necessarily applicable, the Personalists fail to see the very real possibility that human beings can be crushed and destroyed. They thus fail to see the real nature and depth of human suffering, convincing themselves that destruction cannot really happen; it is a metaphysical impossibility. Weil, however, having discovered 'affliction' in the factories several years before, knew differently. Human beings can be destroyed. As she put it in the essay on the *Iliad*,

[Might] when exercised to the full ... makes a thing of man in the most literal sense, for it makes him a corpse ... [But] from the power to transform him into a thing by killing him there proceeds another power,

---

[15] Jacques Maritain, *Scholasticism and Politics*, New York: The MacMillan Co., 1941, pp. 62, 63.

and much more prodigious, that which makes a thing of him while he still lives. (*IC* 24, 26)[16]

By mislocating it, Personalism and liberalism thus fail to understand what is really sacred about a human being, and thus ultimately fail to allow for a really deep sense of justice in dealing with other human beings. Borrowing the phrase, 'pulling one's self up by one's own bootstraps', one can see what has gone wrong. Believing that there is always an essential person inside, liberalism thus believes that there is always somebody inside who can do the pulling up, who can overcome circumstances, no matter how bad they are. Weil, however, tries to get us to see that there may be nobody left inside at all.

This view is often troubling to anybody who wants to be uncompromising in her respect for persons. How can we respect one who is no person at all? This obviously troubled Weil for, she asks, if we are but concatenations and wielders of social forces, what makes us sacred and the object of moral respect?

The answer she gives is that it is simply nothing more than our inchoate striving after good. Minimal in form, that is a supremely important answer. One does not respect others because of something they are or have, which, after all, may be quite accidental. Rather, true respect means respecting them as a whole, and for whatever keeps them whole. Their attempt, their need to unify life is, for Weil, exactly what this inchoate striving after good is. To be cruel to a person in any way thwarts that striving, for he would receive evil when he hoped for good. What then damages the people we hurt is rarely the specific injury, but the thwarting of their aspiration for a whole life, body and soul.

In traditional philosophical terms, Weil's location of the sacredness of a human being owes little to either metaphysics or essentialist thinking. Instead it rests in a primitive human hope. If Weil then calls this sacredness 'impersonal', it is not because she wants it to be abstract; it is because she wants it to be less abstract. And what is abstraction but what Personalism has done in emphasising a single, albeit important, feature of the human person, placing it beyond the play of contingent forces, the realm of the personal?

But why is liberalism, particularly in its notion of rights, inadequate for recognising that hope and dealing with it? For Weil, the

[16] Cf. also my *Simone Weil and the Suffering of Love*, Cambridge, MA: Cowley, 1986.

answer simply is that that aspiration is for a good that is, in Plato's words, 'perfect, adequate and desirable'.[17] And the reason she thinks that the aspiration is so high is precisely because notions such as inalienable rights, crucial to the Personalist picture of the person, fail to be of much help when dealing with the afflicted. Through numerous observations made in the factory and in watching court cases being tried in Marseilles, she realised that there was something profoundly unsatisfactory in the way that the poor and disenfranchised left these institutions. Pure procedural justice, even when followed scrupulously, simply was not enough. Their suffering simply was not being heard, even though they had had their day in court. Something was continually being left unsaid. What was left unsaid, was what is, in fact, unsayable. What is spoken, on the other hand, in procedural justice are the words that make up social personality. Thus she concluded that even the notion of rights, supposedly eternal and universal, is a matter of the contingent play of social forces, incapable of satisfying our deepest hopes. It is not hard, then, to conclude, as she did, that a democracy, even one where procedural justice is never perverted, also does not enjoy a necessary and unassailable status.

The essay 'Human Personality' is, to be sure, a critique of collectivities and the false absoluteness they give to a supposed inner person. But, on the reading I have given it, its focus is not really collectivities as such; the essay is most fundamentally a highly pointed and focused criticism of certain notions of persons and moral principles that can make collectivities oppressive. Even liberalism simply does not do enough for people, nor, for that matter, does it let us do enough, because it keeps us from seeing a much deeper problem of justice.

This critique of liberal doctrine has an important positive side, though. It allows Weil to make a crucial distinction between two senses of justice. First there is a social conception of justice embodied in the notion of rights, making it a contingent, historical matter. But there is also a second, more vital sense of justice to which we ought to pay closer attention if we are ever going to do anything for those who do not share, for whatever reason, in the distribution of social power. That is, she says, a 'supernatural' sense of justice. This justice operates when an individual hears something more than he has been

---

[17] *Philebus*, 22b.

culturally conditioned to hear, when he hears the silent word of affliction which the language of rights cannot speak. This point has been taken up at greater length in the essay by Richard Bell in this volume.

The distinction, however, appears to leave Weil with exactly the sort of problem we suggested above that she might have. Namely, it appears that societies and cultures are irredeemably trapped in the realm of necessity, unable, by their very collective nature, to express and appreciate what is essentially only heard by individuals. They appear to be all gravity, and no grace. This distinction, important as it is, seems to undermine radically the importance of social and cultural activity. To be sure, Weil says, the words that express collective, cultural values are 'valid in their own region, which is that of ordinary institutions' (*SE* 33). Still, they are quite distant from what Weil is calling 'real justice'. That, at least, would be the impression with which we are left were it not for some hints that she leaves at the end of the essay, hints which she later will develop in such a way as to reorient cultural values.

The first hint comes in her suggestion that there are certain words such as God, truth, justice, love, and good which have a power in themselves to illumine and lift the soul towards the good, a power which is realised when we 'do not try to make them fit any conception ... [for] what they express is beyond our conception' (*SE* 33). What exactly could Weil mean here? That certain words, like sacraments, confer grace *ex opere operantis*?

What is meant by this suggestion is obscure, but not particularly mysterious or occult. Weil simply means that, in order to break out of our linguistic and cultural moral cocoons, we need some kind of public expression of the fact that we are in such cocoons. People need o be made aware of the limited nature of their cultural morality, at least so that they might become aware of another sort of morality. At this point it seems that Weil had in mind that these 'big' words would function in the public realm, not so much as real lingustic operators, than as icons whose purpose is to remind us of the less than absolute nature of our public morality, and to draw our attention morally upwards. They do not negate the force of cultural conventions and morality, nor condemn them, they simply put them in perspective. These words indicate an object of striving that words such as 'rights' and 'personality' otherwise terminate too quickly.

Weil's suggestion bears a certain analogy to Rorty's use of 'irony' in so far as both writers, while believing that reason is inescapably public, also want to find a way to appreciate, and go beyond, any sort of moral conceptual determinism and its illusory claims to absoluteness. If Weil is not exactly calling for a nominalist rhetoric, she is looking at least for a way to use language that will demystify most moral terms by standing them against some real absolutes. Weil and Rorty differ, though, on two important points. The first is that Rorty's irony is formally aimless, aimless in the sense that the individual alone remains in control of his choice. Thus his irony remains wedded to certain liberal notions (such as pluralism 4) as he freely admits. Weil, though, thinks there is an aim. Yet she is wise enough not to place its domain unwittingly back in the public realm.

The second difference is that Weil thinks that there can be a public expression of this contingency other than a 'historicist rhetoric', and that there can be a public expression which will help serve as a positive reorientation of cultural values *vis-à-vis* supernatural justice. Hardly believing that cultural values are essentially opposed to justice, she thinks that if they are oriented correctly, if they are balanced around a supernatural centre, and inspiration, they can serve a higher purpose.

IV

The views laid out in 'Human Personality' are not without their difficulties. While refusing to fit words such as 'God', 'good', 'justice' etc. to limited conceptions might give a better perspective on our other value words, one may very well ask whether it is possible to avoid giving them a limited conception. The temptation seems almost irresistible. For example few thinkers have ever had such a deep sense of the transcendence of God as Augustine. Think how in the *Confessions* he found God nowhere in the mountains, the air, nowhere but in his own breast. Yet he was quite willing not long afterwards to identify the bloody suppression of the Donatists with God's will. It was not until the *City of God* that he truly realised his inconsistency.[18]

Weil was not unaware of the problem as an examination of the writings following 'Human Personality' will show. It is in those

[18] Cf. R. A. Markus, *Saeculum: History and Society in the Theology of St Augustine*, Cambridge: Cambridge University Press, 1970, on this recognition of Augustine.

writings that she tries to find a way in which the transcendent nature of 'God', 'truth', and 'good' are not degraded, but which can never the less be thought by limited, historical human beings.

The writing known as 'A Draft for a Statement of Human Obligations' is an important case in point. In fact, if its original intended usage is kept in mind, its very existence and Weil's constant reworking of it indicates the degree to which she believed that there needed to be a public profession of ultimate, supernatural justice so that the word would not be just left hanging. That intended usage was as a 'proposed examination of Resistance groups',[19] a sort of public credo, undoubtedly meant to replace Enlightenment slogans such as 'Liberté, Egalité, Fraternité', and even Maritain's preferred 'International Declaration of the Rights of Man'.

The intended replacement is canny. Despite sounding dogmatically descriptive, closer examination shows that it is no *quicumque vult*. Its initial central features are, to be sure, seemingly descriptive, including a profession that there is a reality outside the world which is the sole realm of good; that this good corresponds to the human longing for absolute good; and that it is only through individual persons that this good 'descends and comes among men' (*SE* 219). On the face of things it seems that she says little more than she did in 'Human Personality'. It may even appear that her position is inconsistent in so far as public profession of good with specifications is an attempt to make 'good' fit some conceptuality.

A fragment from the London period outlines her motives for proposing such a credo and clarifies her project. She writes:

Sketch of the foundation of a doctrine (chiefly for the use of study groups in France): A doctrine is quite insufficient, but it is indispensable to have one, if only to avoid being deceived by false doctrines. The sight of the pole star never tells the fisherman where he ought to go, but he will never make his way in the night unless he knows how to recognize it. (*EL* 151)

This credo was, therefore, never meant as a metaphysical description or explanation; it was meant to give orientation – a pole star for navigation. She adds, 'for when a man wants something that he

---

[19] Simone Pétrement, *Simone Weil, A Life*, New York: Pantheon, 1976, p. 493. It is quite clear that this profession of faith was important to Weil. Her manuscripts include at least three drafts of it, with the one now printed being the second. She further condensed it in the last, apparently so that it could be used as a sort of creed. It is also clearly later than the opening sections of *The Need for Roots*, since all three versions contain truth as a need of the soul, whereas truth appears in the *Roots* manuscript as a later insertion. In this respect, *Roots*

cannot name, one can easily make him believe that he wants some other thing, and turn the treasure of his energy away toward something indifferent or evil' (*EL* 151).

But how does one avoid vacuity while still trying to give orientation? First, as part of giving this orientation, Weil notes, it is necessary to clear away inadequate doctrines. That is, I have suggested, part of the aim of 'Human Personality'. Second, in order not to be misunderstood, she adds to this doctrine in the 'Draft' the intended *effects* of this credo, namely: (1) that the recognition of this supernatural good carries an obligation to act on it, to bring its light into play in the natural world; (2) that a society is good or evil, is a legitimate society, in proportion both to the degree that there is within it a consent to this good and to the degree of the 'distribution of power between those who consent and those who refuse' (*SE* 222). She also states that, to be just, a state must ensure that 'all forms of power are entrusted, as far as possible, to men who effectively consent to be bound by the obligation to all human beings ... and who understand the obligation' (*SE* 223).

Now what does it mean to make a profession like this? To say that it involves subscription to a systematic and descriptive utopian orthodoxy would be a wooden reading, indeed, especially since she has explicitly called it simply a 'pole star', and has said that simple 'belief' or subscription is not enough. Rather, the profession has illocutionary force, above all making action primary. It is in this way that supernatural justice is not simply an empty phrase, but a definite way of acting. It is a commitment to playing out that justice in life of the one making the profession. These additions, therefore, suggest that Simone Weil's supernatural justice must be played out socially, and that she hardly believed that the social world is entirely alien to justice.

Therefore, whereas 'Human Personality' sought to distinguish the social world from that of transcendent good, and social justice from supernatural justice, the 'Draft' assumes a link between the two, a link in human action. It is in this link between the necessary and the good, established through the consent and action of individuals, that Weil wants to find the balancing point around which cultural values can be centred, reformed, and thus used as means of contact with a higher sense of justice.

contains the discovery of her problems in 'Human Personality' and the 'Draft' is a formulaic creed based on it.

It is fairly clear, if we again consider the full range of Weil's London writings, that she was intensely interested in this problem of links and balances, particularly in light of the fact that a war, a struggle of natural forces, was going on. Not only was she interested in raising the question of what kind of justice it was for which the Allies were fighting,[20] she was also interested in seeing how cultures and nations, by the way they actively orient themselves to the good, are essentially religious and can be evaluated as such.[21] They may, for example, with what she calls 'only an infinitely small difference' in their values at the strictly verbal level, either be idolatrous by putting those values in service of something finite such as national sovereignty and prestige, or be mediators of the good. A similar concern for the individual's consent to the good also led her to call both for a repression of political parties, which she thought coerced souls by propaganda, and for an end to colonialism. Until such things occur she believed that society could not be renewed, and higher justice could not be incarnated in it, since the violence of propaganda and the hegemony of the national state over the lives of its citizens effectively denies and dissolves the essential link to the good, no matter what they claim they believe.

It is this link above all with which Weil is concerned in these last writings. She did not want to revise and undo a culture's values, but she did want to reorient them so that they provide, and make apparent, that link. Thus the word 'culture' for Weil carries the sense of the verb 'to culture', for she envisions culture as a vital medium in which human beings grow and which nourishes them.[22] Weil's concern, then, is not to replace culture as if it were faulty because it did not have full-grown plants, but of making sure it is nourishing.

Yet this still is quite abstract. What possible means exist to do all this? What are the resources and how are they tapped? For Weil, what is required is a way by which a culture, which through its history is rooted in something more ultimate than itself, can provide nourishment for the people who comprise it.

[20] Cf. the essay, *'Luttons-nous pour la justice?'* in *EL* but also 'Is There a Marxist Doctrine?' in *OL*.

[21] Cf. particularly, 'A War of Religions', in *Selected Essays* as well as *The Need for Roots*. Cf. also E. Springsted, 'The Religious Basis of Culture: T. S. Eliot and Simone Weil', in *Religious Studies*, March, 1989.

[22] Cf. Mary Deitz, *Between the Human and the Divine: The Political Thought of Simone Weil*, Ottowa: Rowman and Littlefield, 1988, ch. 8.

V

It is in the beginning of *The Need for Roots*, when she discusses the relation of rights and obligations and the 'needs of the soul', that she discovers and specifies this link. It is here that she finds the key to answer the sorts of questions with which she was left at the end of 'Human Personality', and where we find the transition to the subtle formulations of the 'Draft,' allowing them to be read in the way I have suggested.

The question left by 'Human Personality' was, we may recall, how natural justice, exemplified by the notion of rights, can be reconciled and linked with supernatural justice, exemplified by the eternal obligation to respect what is sacred in human beings. The problem is that rights belong within the entirely contingent realm of necessity, and are not *pace* the 'men of 1789', either universal or necessary features of moral thinking. Since they are also rooted in social power, not only do they provoke and justify moral contentiousness, they are incapable of teaching us how to hear or deal with powerlessness. Thus there is a problem, not because the notion of rights is worthless, but because the supernatural justice which can hear and respond to the hurt of the afflicted itself cannot be so neatly defined in such concrete terms. Its seeming resistance to concretion would make it appear impossible to institute within the concrete world.

The solution proposed in *The Need for Roots* comes in its opening pages where Weil gives a distinctive analysis of rights, at once denying them absolute status since they are cultural products, and yet at the same time making them a link to supernatural justice. She does this by proposing that we, indeed, see rights as specific cultural values, but as having a legitimacy, i.e. a fundamental concern for the person, that ultimately derives from supernatural justice via an obligation each human being has towards others. Rights are then simply the specific historical and cultural specifications of this obligation which actualise it, but never exhaust it. Thus rights (but not obligations) are mutable in changing historical circumstances. But even if rights are thus historically contingent, when they are the result of obligation meeting need they are also historical witnesses to specific acts of recognition of the sacredness of human beings, to the descent of good 'among men'.

The point of this proposal is to solve the problem of respecting the sacredness of human beings when that sacredness does not rest in any one thing, including personality, and when we cannot concretely pay supernatural respect to persons without trying to make the universal reside completely in a contingent act directed towards a contingent self. Therefore, taking up a suggestion made in 'Human Personality', Weil proposes that since what is sacred in a person, her concern for ultimate good, is affected by what happens to her in the world of concreteness, we can at least respect her indirectly by dealing with what Weil calls the 'needs of the soul'.[23] These needs, analogous to bodily needs, if not met, would cause her to despair of good. It is by paying attention to these needs that we can, and indeed must, concretise our obligations in such ways that aspiration for good continues to live in her.

How this solves the problem left behind by 'Human Personality' is that by dealing with the 'needs of the soul' one does not leave 'God', 'truth', and 'justice' as empty conceptions. They have meaning in how we recognise and treat others. But such words also can never become conceptually determinate for they indicate a 'something more' that we can never exactly capture conceptually.

Simone Weil thus gives a way of approaching morality that is distinct from the classical liberalism of universal and inalienable rights. For Weil, rights do involve morality, but they neither define or limit it. Like personality itself, which rights has traditionally protected, rights must be understood in the context of a larger whole, and have validity only within it. It is important to understand here that, by claiming that each specific right owes its real moral force to an external obligation, Weil is *not* trying to legitimate each contingent right directly at all. Neither obligations nor rights can be thought of as principles, and there is no sort of calculus for each possible circumstance which entails a specific right by deriving it from the eternal obligation for respect. Simone Weil's approach is far more organic, and far more 'personal'. The importance of recognising obligations is to give a historical moral sense that balances specific rights as a whole within a society.

An example will help us to see the distinction. For Simone Weil a democratic society may feed, or even satiate, a person's need to

---

[23] Weil lists as the 'needs of the soul': order, liberty, obedience, responsibility, equality, hierarchism, honor, punishment, freedom of opinion, security, risk, private property, collective property, truth, and the need for roots. Except for order and the last two, these needs are listed as pairs to be *balanced*.

believe herself an equal to others, yet still fail to really provide respect for her. For example, it may ignore a concomitant need for a hierarchy of values and purposes that she can respect. The better society balances the two. Within a morality of principles, however, any right to equality tends to be absolute, regardless of what else is the case. Even on Rawls' nuanced view, which allows for the tailoring of equality in the original position, there is no tailoring of it afterwards for historical contingencies. The principles are absolute, even if they contain an empirical twist. What is the key for Weil, on the other hand, is the eternal obligation we have to the whole person which insists that not only must any right be tailored continually, it must be tailored within a specific cultural whole. It is, of course, precisely for this reason that she declares the need for order, that is to say, 'a texture of social relationships such that no one is compelled to violate imperative obligations in order to carry out other ones' (*NR* 10), as the first of the soul's needs, the one most nearly touching on the soul's eternal destiny.

It is clear that Weil has broken with a Kantian rationalism that seeks to extend the reign of law over the whole world. Her claim is that individual cultures should continue their own traditions and remain bound to them, since both cultural and personal identity is bound up inextricably within that unique history. What needs changing in any culture, then, is rarely institutional forms, but how those forms are balanced against each other by relation to a centre, a centre represented by the notion of supernatural obligation. We need to worry less about actual institutions, than how they work as a whole upon individuals.

VI

Not surprisingly, Weil's attempt to find meaning for supernatural justice in a world of gravity has attracted liberal criticisms as being ultimately apolitical. Mary Dietz has sought to show,

just how bereft of political possibility – of action (individual or collective), social transformation, emancipation, even the mere betterment of everyday life – her mysticism is ... [H]er mysticism grants no value or meaning to either individual autonomy or collective political action.[24]

With more self-awareness of his own liberalism, Michael Ignatieff has argued that:

[24] *Between the Human and the Divine*, p. 124.

[Simone Weil] didn't like rights because they were specific, precise, and enforceable by law, and as such truncated the full compass of the human good ... But surely it is an illusion, a dangerous illusion, to suppose that a politics can be based on supposedly indubitable facts of human nature. The human good is conflictual; moral conflict is real, and a regular feature of the social world; people disagree about what people need. That is where politics comes in. The language of rights represents the extent of our agreement about human ends ... To denounce the language of rights as Weil did ... it is ... also to deny politics its vocation, which is the adjudication of irreconcilable conflict between competing ends ... In denying that human ends were in conflict, Weil was wishing away politics altogether.[25]

The point appears to be well taken. But one may well ask what exactly is meant by talking about 'irreconcilable conflict between human ends'? For, while contemporary social life may show conflict (pluralisms 1–3), too often that fact of social life slides over into a theory about ends (pluralism 4). For example Charles Larmore in his *Patterns of Moral Complexity*, after lucidly arguing for a liberal ideal of political neutrality towards differing ideals of the good life, goes on to state: 'Thus, if we detach morality from religion, we must reckon with a fundamental *heterogeneity* of morality ... The *ultimate* sources of moral value are not one but many.'[26] A fact of social life has just become a theological dogma.

If Weil does not worry about individual autonomy or collective political action, it is precisely because there is an issue deeper than the continuation of present politics, an issue on which she thinks thinking has gone wrong in Western moral and political philosophy. It is because we have seen individuals as ahistorical and autonomous, capable of, and entitled to, decide on issues of good that the purely procedural justice necessary for collective action becomes the sole issue of justice. For the same reason modern Western culture shows a certain hatred of the past which in turn makes collective action necessary to establish a just society in the future. Weil, however, is not interested in defining a single just political form, as Marx *and* liberals do; she doesn't even believe there is such a thing. She is less interested in changing what we are doing than in changing the way we do it. Otherwise, to force change is to remain within the realm of necessity.

Thus Weil's political and cultural philosophy tries to find hope by

---

[25] Michael Ignatieff, 'The Limits of Sainthood', *The New Republic*, 18 June 1990, p. 44.
[26] *Patterns of Moral Complexity*, p. 138, emphasis mine.

discovering a way that the limited world of necessity might have meaning, and it does so by trying to reduce human alienation from the natural order by relating that order to the deepest human aspirations.

This is nowhere seen quite as clearly as in the longest part of *The Need for Roots*, where Weil unravels the metaphor of rootedness. What is at stake in that metaphor is no less than the belief that human beings subject to material and historical conditions must be able to find some way to use those conditions to recognise supernatural good and the obligations to people that that recognition implies. For Weil, it is the idea of roots that finally bridges the cleavage between the limited values of social necessity and the undefinable values of supernatural justice.

What is ultimately implied in the idea of humans having a natural need of the soul for roots is that it is by the natural need of feeling a part of a larger historical social whole one may come to finally identify with the centre around which all necessity is balanced. Despite her oft expressed reservations about particular natural loves, I do think that Weil, like Plato in the *Phaedrus*, recognised that love and justice begin, not impersonally and universally, but within particular communities and with particular people. The problem then is how to metamorphosise this particular love, born out of natural need for others, into one of universal concern, both for all people and for the whole of the particular persons whom one loves, even when they have unattractive aspects.[27]

There is an important sense in which the historical communities in which we find ourselves play a role analogous to natural love. We are originally bound to them by very natural reason; if not by personal preference, then at least by virtue of the fact that they give us our sense of personal and moral identity. They do so not simply by moulding us, but because they are that with which we identify and thus individuate ourselves. As John Dewey argued, 'Stability of individuality is dependent upon stable objects to which allegiance firmly attaches itself ... Assured and integrated individuality is the product of social relationships and publicly acknowledged functions.'[28] Thus, communities are not imperious creators of our

[27] Cf. my *Christus Mediator: Platonic Mediation in the Thought of Simone Weil*, Chico, CA: Scholars Press, 1983, pp. 205–7.
[28] John Dewey, *Individualism: Old and New*, New York: Capricorn Books, 1962, p. 52.

persons, but creators because they allow us our ability for self-creation – or decreation.

For Simone Weil, where our relation to historical communities is disanalogous to personal loves is that communities are simply not persons. But, if they proceed by an inexorable gravity, never the less, they can at least be organised in their parts around a supernatural centre. They are not that centre, and that above all has to be recognised. But they can witness to the centre, and can be so organised by men and women who do recognise it. If as natural they cannot force consent to a centre or make anyone recognise it against their consent, they can at least dispose persons to recognise that centre. In this sense, while they provide us with limited values which naturally bind us, they, if read properly, may allow us to understand the fulcrum on which those values are balanced. They allow us to see beyond their limited nature, to invite us to criticise them as limited, and can therefore become transparent.

It is on this line of reasoning that a peculiar idea that Weil had about cultures beginning in an original divine revelation, and which she was developing at the same time she was writing *The Need for Roots*, begins to make some sense. It is the idea that cultural and social activity, while certainly the outworking of nature and necessity, is actually the historical response to whatever value a culture holds as ultimate: ultimate not simply in conception, but in act.[29] Thus limited cultural values can actually serve a non-natural purpose by being a response to that revelation, which in its cultural forms invites further response. Cultures become in this sense, she says, 'the formation of attention' (*EL* 160).

We can now see quite clearly what exactly the idea of rootedness itself is meant to convey. It is not simply by having 'roots' in the most general sense in a community that we are nourished, but by that community itself having roots that draw upon the supernatural.[30]

[29] This idea of a culture being a balanced reaction to revelation may have been part of Weil's inspiration for her project for a front-line nursing corps. It was just that sort of act of selfless heroism that could reorient and rebalance a culture's values. How significant Weil thought this would be can only be guessed at. The point, though, is that this sort of act is precisely what she had in mind when she talked about a culture being a reaction to an original inspiration.

[30] The prime example of what this notion of balance might mean within a culture can be seen in two earlier essays Weil wrote on the culture of Languedoc in the twelfth century, which flourished as a balance between the neo-Manichaean sect known as the Cathars and the Catholics. Weil suggests that neither possessed the truth, but by virtue of balancing their otherwise incompatible viewpoints, achieved a great culture where human beings were truly respected.

So Weil is far from dismissing cultural values, the values of the middle realm, as having no worth. They have great importance in so far as they can be related to something more fixed. So said, we can also understand why Weil spends so little time trying to emphasise politics, as Dietz would have her do, as the result of human action and creation.[31] As creatures of necessity we inevitably do act and create; but that is not what is problematic for Weil. It is how we see and describe our activities as related to some higher purpose.

Not to see this is to seriously misread fully the last 90 per cent of *The Need for Roots*. For, in the sections on how France came to be uprooted and how it might re-root itself, Weil is concerned above all with showing how the centre became perverted in French history, thus altering the moral and spiritual balance of activity. What that history of uprootedness is meant to show is that the state itself gradually became the centre of all obligation, commanding all affection and duty. This is what allows her to claim that not only is the state a perverse centre because it is finite itself and the wielder of finite forces, but also that it maintains itself as the centre at the cost of failing to allow its citizens recognition of values other than those which brought it into power. For example, in her discussion of false greatness, Weil not only criticises an unfortunate conception of greatness as being responsible for the rise of truly evil people such as Hitler, but also argues that we have little defence against similar future excesses as long as our actions are motivated by the same idea of greatness that inspired him. The centre in this sense, whatever it is, affects the outcome of all our actions; until it is located in what is truly good, our actions will tend to our own moral destruction.

Therefore the goal of rootedness is much less a matter of changing our specific, cultural values – that may be asking the leopard to change his spots – as it is a matter of changing how we read those values and orient them. The point, for example, of her criticism of modern science is not to get rid of science, but to look at it differently, especially in its relation to an ultimate goal for which we hope. Or, similarly, in suggesting that labour ought to be the spiritual centre of any culture the point is not to send everybody back to work on a farm for re-education, it is to put something other than the foolish Marxist and liberal hope for freedom from necessity at the centre. Our actions so understood, cannot help but change

---

[31] *Between the Human and the Divine*, p. 185.

according to what Martin Andic has called a sort of 'spiritual mechanics'.[32]

VII

In an earlier section of this essay I suggested that Simone Weil's position bears certain similarities to Richard Rorty's in so far as both admit cultural values as binding upon us, not for metaphysical, foundationalist reasons, but purely and simply for social ones, while at the same time seeking a way to add some sort of insight into their limited nature which allows us to redescribe them in such a way that we can find a deeper, more personal morality. By such a means both Rorty and Weil go beyond classical Enlightenment liberalism. But here, of course, the similarity stops. Rorty obviously is not interested in finding a supernatural centre to contingent social values, other than perhaps as an outmoded way of talking about how to make personal sense of them. Simone Weil, on the other hand, quite clearly wants to call this centre supernatural. Rorty's 'irony' is indeed a long way from Weil's 'consent to a reality outside time and space', even if both tend to be related in similar formal aspects to cultural values.

What exactly is the difference? It can be seen in a question Peter Winch raises about Weil's use of the supernatural. Noting accurately that she does use the term as a way of countering an all too common morality of shallow concern for others, he asks, nevertheless, what real sense there is to the term since: '[O]ur reactions to beauty, and to each other, are as much a part of human nature as our other reactions. Even if it could be shown that these reactions are comparatively rare in relation to other opposing reactions, we should be a long way from considering them as supernatural'.[33] But the point is not to give the supernatural as an explanation for morality; rather, Winch continues,

I believe the point of this sort of language is to provide a way of expressing the connections between various attitudes, interests, strivings, aspirations, which are all part of our 'natural history'. It is only because

---

[32] Martin Andic, 'Spiritual Mechanics', unpublished essay delivered to the American Weil Society, 1989.
[33] Peter Winch, *Simone Weil: The Just Balance*, Cambridge: Cambridge University Press, 1989, p. 197.

they are part of our natural history that we have any chance of making sense of the notion of the 'supernatural'.[34]

What Winch is subtly pointing out is that philosophically Weil's 'supernaturalism' is not an explanation intended to defeat 'naturalism', but that it speaks more of a type of life to be lived. In this sense, there is a similarity with Rorty to the degree that both are looking for something that makes a difference to our natural history and is locatable in it. Both are hoping to find a way to achieve the rare, beautiful moral action.

I think that Winch's analysis is essentially correct and that Weil recognised the problems of a purely conceptual approach in her later writings. As she notes, if words such as 'God', 'just', 'good', and 'love' are to be effective they have to operate within the public sphere, and have to be linked to our history. Embedded within this history, their real function is to provide and show an alternative to an all too dreary and mediocre moral vision. But that does not mean that the difference between her and Rorty is simply one of terms. There is still a substantial difference implied in that term 'supernatural'.

Where that difference lies is in the hope it implies. The issue at stake is one that is raised by Simone Weil in the essay, 'East and West: Thoughts on the Colonial Problem' (in *SE*). Arguing that natives in French colonies need to be rooted in their own cultural traditions, she raises the question of why it is important for any group to maintain its past. The reason has to do with the question of whether or not we are self-sufficient in the world. If we are not, and cannot gain a sufficient perspective on the world to live by building rational systems from ground zero out of our native capacities, then our cultures and the treasures of the past they embody become an essential means of help. They, above all, give us the alternatives we need when present imagination fails. Thus far she is perhaps not very different from Rorty, other than in laying greater emphasis on the need for a tradition. Her question about self-reliance, though, can be taken at a deeper level as well, a level at which she is asking whether or not human capacities are sufficient for life that hopes for good.

The issue can be enjoined by comparing Rorty's treatment of George Orwell's *1984* with Weil's analysis of what she called afflic-

---

[34] *The Just Balance*, p. 211.

tion. In discussing O'Brien's treatment of Winston, Rorty notes that what Orwell has shown us about cruelty is not so much that O'Brien can force Winston to admit that $2 + 2 = 5$, but that he puts Winston in a position where he actually wants Julia, whom he loves, to be tortured instead of himself. The result? Winston can no longer weave a coherent story about himself as a moral agent. He can no longer identify with himself.

[T]he belief that he once wanted them to *do it to Julia* is not one he can weave a story around. That was why O'Brien saved the rats for the best part, the part in which Winston had to watch himself go to pieces and simultaneously know that he could never pick up those pieces again.[35]

Simone Weil, in a similar way, after her factory experience notes that one of the chief characteristics of affliction is not just having to operate in an irrational system, but that in time the agent becomes both alienated from the larger world and directs that alienation towards herself. She finds nothing to love, and nothing in herself with which to love. Winston, in this regard, may be a prime example of what Simone Weil means by affliction.

Now in such cases what are the human alternatives? Rorty, since he is considering Orwell's value as a writer, does not really address the question other than arguing that Orwell, by imagining O'Brien's awesome cruelty and its effect on Winston, shows us something about the nature of cruelty and thus teaches us to avoid it. But what of someone who is genuinely in this position? Of someone who, in Nussbaum's sense of tragedy, has to choose between incompatible values, knowing that his choice will destroy him? If he cannot escape, in any sense, total and utter personal destruction, not only is his outcome tragic, the universe itself will be read as tragic. Weil, on the other hand, while fully admitting the existence of tragedy, lives destroyed, by virtue of her super-naturalism suggests that the loss need not be ultimate, and that one may hope even in such circumstances.[36] For her, what supernatural means, I suggest, is seen in our reading possibility in impossibility, in reading love and goodness behind every event. It is a life of hope.

Simone Weil, unlike orthodox Christian theologians, of course does not place that hope in a realm of future rewards. And for that reason what her supernaturalism amounts to is a bare, undefinable

---

[35] *Contingency, Irony, and Solidarity*, p. 178.
[36] Cf. my *Simone Weil and the Suffering of Love* on this point.

hope, a faith in a goodness that transcends the human attempt to imagine – and limit – goodness and the human capacity to despair.

That hope is, as Weil suggests, something undefinable, for in the words of the Letter to the Hebrews, it itself is the evidence of what is unseen. But, as the Letter to the Hebrews makes plain, that is already quite a bit of evidence for there is an entire 'cloud of witnesses', an entire history that makes it plausible. To be rooted in that story makes, as Weil says, only an infinitely small difference. But it may be a difference around which we can balance all other values, and a difference which keeps us from lying to ourselves and falling back into a false absolutism. Thus, if there is no proof for choosing her supernatural vision to a humanistic one, there is at least a choice and a real alternative.

CHAPTER 8

Simone Weil and the civilisation of work

Clare B. Fischer

> Our age has its own particular mission, or vocation – the creation of a civilization founded upon the spiritual nature of work. (*NR* 96)

The claim placed upon us by Simone Weil's call for a new civilisation is not remarkable. Other prophetic figures throughout history have made such demands for a revitalised order, and some, including Gandhi and Marx, have understood the centrality of work in this transformative process. Weil is asking, however, that revitalisation be tied to an understanding of work which is spiritual. Unique in her call and relentless in her belief that civilisation could be bettered, in spite of her ambivalence about the extent, and efficacy, of social change, Weil provides an important message to those struggling with work's meaning.[1] It is the challenge of her vision which gives shape to this essay, particularly in its applicability to a global world at the end of the twentieth century.

The reference to 'our age', of course, refers to a period fifty years past. I do not regard the passage of years as particularly significant with respect to Weil's meaning for the contemporary reader. Although technological advances have substantially changed the appearance of the workplace, most of Weil's criticisms of organisation and process remain salient. Her powerful analysis of work's centrality and its place in the disarray of modern civilisation continues to apply, perhaps with even greater force, when we look to the post World War II developments of both service sector work and multinational manufacture. I contend that both features of the

---

[1] Although Weil's 1934 essay on work seems pessimistic, she did provide a sketch for an ideal society (*OL*). Her last essay (*NR*) offers a programmatic vision which, by contrast, is more constructive and optimistic in tone, in spite of the fact that she wrote this in the middle of the war.

current economy demonstrate how the assembly-line of Weil's analysis has been adapted to non-manufacture and exported to the Third World.[2]

Weil maintained a steady interest in work as a central feature of culture throughout her intellectual life. Her earlier reflections dating back to her student days reveal concern for the relationship between thought and action, and the vulnerable position of workers denied their ability to think or integrate themselves as problem solvers and doers. She observed that the division of labour based upon manual skill and intellectual activity was an appalling basis for work's organisation, and she remained a vigilant critic, throughout her days, of practices of divisive labour. As her thinking matured, the implications of its consequences for civilisation sharpened. Her relentless outcry against indignity and diminution of the worker's full personhood grew to a piercing lament in her last writings. In these Weil rejects the societal denial of spiritual yearning of the worker, and advances a sense of human fullness that encompasses the needs of the soul. She observed in her late writings that even the labourer could not identify these aspirations because the civilisation had displaced meaning with illusory ends. The worker's quest for meaning had been detoured even by labour-oriented associations. Clearly, the demands of worker associations did not, nor do they presently, address the state of the worker's soul; the dimension most precious to Weil is ignored. In Weil's restorative treatment, however, fullness of the worker enlarges and deepens human presence. She offers a spiritual theology of work which denies the hidden, silenced realm of the spirit and calls it forward as central and essential to any proposal for work's reform. Integrity is to be comprehended, then, as a reconciliation of all human facilities and aspirations.

Two questions absorb my attention in this essay, each related to the spiritual labour of the postmodern worker. The first probes the relationship between worldly reform effort and the discipline of spiritual labour. I inquire into this relationship in the pages to follow by asking how labour's disorders connect the worker to transcendent truths, and suggest that Weil offers a multi-transformational and interrelated vision. My second inquiry seeks to understand why Weil privileges the manual efforts of the worker in her image of a restored

<hr />

[2] See my forthcoming study of Weil's work theory and its relationship to contemporary feminist theory in *Our Mother Country is Hope*.

civilisation. Following her lead that 'physical labour' should occupy a central place, serve as its 'spiritual core', I ask what it is in the nature of such physical effort that inspires this elevation. As much as I believe all of Weil's reflections on work to be relevant, I focus, in this essay, on her later contributions, notably her essay on factory work and *The Need for Roots*. It should be mentioned that her continued ruminations about Marx's approach to labour and human justice are pivotal to her critique of civilisation but are not discussed here.[3]

In assessing Weil's notion of transformed work I have incorporated aspects of another critic of Marx who, like Weil, struggles with his insights regarding emancipated labour. Agnes Heller, a contemporary moral philosopher, provides significant analysis of social and political trends in the 'postmodern' world.[4] She has long been associated with the critical thought of such luminaries as Lukács, Arendt, and Habermas, and currently holds the Arendt Chair at the New School of Social Research in New York. Her insistence upon rational values and the role of citizens in choosing and discerning bears resemblance to Weil's early formulation about the integrity of thought and action. However, I have found Heller to be particularly helpful in continuing the critique of civilisation that Weil initiates. She provides a rigorous analysis of post-World War II culture and argues persuasively that our reluctance to claim public responsibility may lead to global disaster. Heller's background includes years of education in her native Hungary, and a considered reception of classical Marx, as well as of the later Marxists interpreters. She, like Weil, appropriates the author of *Capital* with a distinct commitment to human freedom and non-alienated work.

Theorists have been suspicious of the term 'civilisation' of late, recognising that it either includes too much or too little. On the one hand, it serves as an abstraction which assumes cultural identity without reference to the particularities of history and geography. On the other hand, it suggests an elite or exclusive clustering of cultural characteristics which seem to privilege the Western world. Heller writes that civilisation is a constructed notion which was

---

[3] An excellent source for this is Lawrence Blum and Victor Seidler, *A Truer Liberty, Simone Weil and Marxism*, London: Routledge, 1989.
[4] Among Agnes Heller's works cited here are *A Radical Philosophy*, Oxford: Basil Blackwell, 1984, hereafter cited as *RP; A Philosophy of Morals*, Oxford: Basil Blackwell, 1990, hereafter cited as *PM*; and written with her husband, the political philosopher Ferenc Fehér, *The Postmodern Political Condition*, Oxford: Polity Press, 1988, hereafter cited as *PPC*.

'invented in the west as one universal among many' (*PPC* 133). The realisation that this construct is deeply imbued with an ethnocentric bias, a European privilege, has been the source of much controversy in recent years. It is probably correct to conclude that Weil's concept of civilisation cannot be reduced to an ethnocentric understanding which obliterates all trace of cultural tradition. Although there is a good deal of ambiguity in her notion of civilisation, it is fair to say that she perceived it both as transcendent, and as historically particular. In *The Need for Roots*, where civilisation and its transformation is the subject of her reflections, both the destiny of the human soul participating in cosmic reality and the destiny of the French post-war occupation is combined in her analysis. It is probable that the prescriptive dimensions of her analysis, regarding French polity and education, really refers to French circumstances. On the other hand, the list of human needs – physical and spiritual – transcend history and geography, and partake of humankind in its relationship to the divine.[5]

It is notable that this ambiguity is echoed by the former rector of the United Nations University in his efforts to reconcile universalising and specifying trends within the global context. Soedjatmoko, in his remarks before a conference on 'The Transformation of the World', spoke of the need for redefinition of cultural constructs such that they would incorporate both the cultures within and without.[6] Even as these meetings entertained discussions relevant to the matter of a transformed world, little was said about the place of work and values attached thereto. It is therefore essential that consideration be given to those like Weil and Heller who have attempted to throw light on the condition of ordinary people in the context of a shifting civilisation. Both women seek redress of the imbalances which militate against justice.

Both Weil and Heller discern that there are deep troubling trends within a civilisation that must be addressed in order to assure life and its continuation. They provide a diagnostic analysis of the diseased civilisation, and suggest that a fast fix cannot touch the depth of the problem. For Weil, the problem is attached to the deprivation of the human soul which, in large measure, has been

[5] Eric Springsted in his essay, above, has suggested Simone Weil's embrace of 'pluralism' without relativism, and certainly shows how particular cultures relate to the transcendent – or the 'supernatural' in Weil's term.

[6] In Anisuzzaman and Anonar Abdel-Maleh, eds., *Culture and Thought*, London: Macmillan, 1983.

brutalised by bad work and demeaning incentives. Although Heller's language is not spiritual, her depiction of a value confused populace adds to Weil's rather grim account. Her analysis focuses upon the restless and ceaselessly dissatisfied postmodern who finds no completion in the work done, or meaning of the energy released. Not unlike Weil's uprooted workers who find no solace in the real possibilities for betterment, Heller's subject is a citizenry which cannot engage in practical reasoning or render vital decisions. Yet it must. We live in an age when critical decisions about our resources and the status of the nation-state ought not be left to a privileged few. Weil also knew this danger and believed that her rootless citizen opted for escapism rather than responsible engagement. It should be added that neither Weil nor Heller blame the victim as such. Rootless and restless persons have emerged because the civilisation has long evaded primary concerns. For Heller the misleading seductions of wealth, power, and success obstruct the path to an enlightened engagement. For Weil the illusory offers of better pay or more time for leisure cannot equip the worker to take on the cloak of leadership.

The consequences of the abandonment of public responsibility are harsh. Technological advances, while advantageous for some, can lead to catastrophes which will end life in this universe. According to Weil, the modern worker is a homeless person, even though there is a place of residence. The lack of belonging promises to produce apathy and withdrawal from social responsibility. Where workers are 'homeless in their own places of work', she warns, 'they will never truly feel at home in their country, never be responsible members of society' (*FWK* 64). The dispossessed are, in fact, detached from any meaningful association, and work requirements encourage this attitude for sheer survival. Heller, by contrast, does not implicate the work world as such as the source of a disengaged citizenry, nor does she designate any specific institution as most culpable in the damaging effects upon modern persons. Rather she invites her reader to take hold and work towards a world of habitable institutions which encourages full participation in all activities that belong to a well-conceived life. She joins Weil in rejecting the dependence upon a rights orientation, and argues that needs are central to human fulfilment. I will explore how Weil and Heller understand needs in the context of their respective approaches to a transformed civilisation in a later section of this essay. For the time being it is important to note that Weil and Heller appreciate the reality of needs, and recommend certain of these as essential to their vision of a life relieved of hazardous and demeaning choices.

THE DISORDER OF CIVILISATION

Nine years before her death in 1943, Weil wrote the long essay on oppression and liberty which she referred to as her 'testament'. In her systematic effort to grasp the obstacles to free and fulfilling labour, Weil dismissed the expectations of ideologues and the polemical arguments for revolutionary change. Liberated work had much to do with the status of the manual labourer, in this classic essay, and the possibilities of integrating thought and action which would fortify the working class in their struggle for authentic participation. Her essay advances an image of the primacy of this form of labour over supervisory or intellectual work, and signifies an early indication of Weil's partiality to manual labour. It is only in her later writing that this partiality assumes spiritual significance and becomes the basis for her appeal to a restored social order of spiritual labourers.

There is no lack of irony in Weil's focus upon the manual worker, given that this effort is most likely to incur the greatest distress and displacement. Shortly after writing the 'testament', Weil experienced something of the hardships of the workroom, and came to know concretely how her hunches and insights measured up in light of everyday physical labour. As a consequence of this factory experience, Weil was able to record impressions and evaluate conditions, permitting her voice to speak for the many labourers whose voices are muted by the cultural arrangements which offer few opportunities for open communication.[7]

Weil reveals that the question of who speaks for whom is an essential one, leading directly to the matter of how the worker is spiritually affected by mean labours. The hidden character of factory life has much to do with misleading accounts either by those who have not directly experienced daily life in the workroom, or by those who speak in deceptive ways. In the opening pages of her essay on 'Factory Work', Weil remarks that the factory is mysterious, a place unspoken because it is the site of relentless suffering. The

[7] See 'Factory Journal,' in *FW* 149–226.

worker is either silenced by evasiveness or a habit of muted acceptance. In this numbed and silenced stance, the worker appears
unbelievable and perhaps absurd. Noise invades the workroom and
prohibits ordinary talk; illusion pervades the culture and narrows
communications about how the factory worker experiences the daily
routine of assignments. The worker creates 'forbidden zones where
thought may not venture and which are shrouded by silence and
illusion' (*FWK* 64).

Thus Weil breaks the silence in her testimony, labelling her
account as one of impression. She presents us with an account of
suffering laid bare and unmediated by explanation. She is witness,
speaking for those who cannot, and yet must, be heard. In risking
such impressions Weil throws light upon the dark corners of our
working world, and invites us to glimpse the debilitating details of
paid labour. Her description should not be dismissed as pertaining
to factory life in a time now long past. While conditions in Europe
and in the United States may have improved for many workers,
much of the manufacturing world (especially in the Third-World
countries) might be characterised as Weil did fifty years ago. Thus,
her representation of voices within those dreary rooms continues to
be critical for our understanding of demeaning labour.

Only two decades ago, Studs Terkel sought out testimonies from
American workers which he edited and published in a volume
appropriately entitled *Working*.[8] In the voices of our contemporaries
one hears the violence to body and soul which Weil decries in her
essay. Even so-called white-collar workers express their unhappiness
with work, and question how life has come to such an impasse. Nora
Watson, an editor and one of Terkel's subjects, speaks of this
narrowing of possibility: 'Most of us have jobs that are too small for
our spirit. Jobs are not big enough for people.'[9] The anxiety of
contemporaries reveals some consciousness of dissatisfaction. Weil's
experience suggests that the pressures of the job produce an over-
riding sense of disgust. Anxiety is not even attached to a recognition
of loss. 'The pervasive anxiety – the anxiety of not working fast
enough – that is diffused through every working moment becomes
concentrated ...' (*FWK* 58).

It is time and space that represent the pivotal measures of worth,
the basis of every worker's engagement with work. In the creation of

[8] Studs Terkel, *Working*, New York: Pantheon, 1972.   [9] Terkel, *Working*, p. xxiv.

a part, rates are established and payment calculated. Time functions as limit, and is perceived in terms of the sovereign time-clock: 'Piece-work provides a personal end. But how heart-breaking, how degrading it is, when you put everything you have in you into something, to have as the end in view a few extra pence!' (*N* 596).

The indignity of reducing oneself to an automaton controlled by clock and machine and rewarded with minimal wage! Weil's sense of the twisting of means and ends is clear enough, suggesting that the worker comes to internalise false purposes, and to have no comprehension of how labour could be other than a daily routine of suffering, a limited exertion for money. She writes of the 'minds nailed down to a point in time', identifying the totalising impact of human beings transformed into day labourers.

In her later writing negative transformation will prove to be the ground upon which she constructs a positive notion of spiritual labour, a transformation which brings true meaning to the effort. Just as time enters the body and mind of the disheartened and over-taxed labourer, it becomes a wondrous connection with the universe in spiritual terms. Thus, also, her observation about work and its demand for concentration which is mindless. In the barren setting of a work site deprived of meaning, the mindless manipulation of objects provides the labourer with no sense of thought's presence; only an alert state is required, particularly in order to avoid accident. In her later reflections, this concerted effort is related to Weil's notion of attention, a disciplined, detached way of looking that leads the practitioner closer to the truth.

The essential difference between the spiritual labourer and the person working within the factory is that the former consents to the rigorous demands, while the latter consents only to brute force. There is no opportunity for the worker to exercise control over any facet of the work to be performed, and circumstances within the site assure inconstancy of the flow of activity, and uncertainty about how the job is to be completed. Supervisors act capriciously, arbitrarily shifting workers to and fro, machines break down, material is inaccessible – all these factors and more disabuse the worker from any thought about initiative or contribution. There is no trace of the worker upon the work, only the physicality that becomes symbolically attached to the products.

These experiences of disempowerment cannot yield strong citizens. Weil is all too aware of how the factory job erodes both energy and a sense of worth. Only fear of job loss and the assurance of the paycheck keep the worker engaged. This motivation destroys sociability at the work site and produces a docile labour force that finds daily living intolerable, relieved only by the promise of increased wage or time off. The consequences of such debilitated people within the civilisation which proclaims equality and democracy are incalculable. 'No society', Weil warns, 'can be stable in which a whole stratum of the population labors daily with a heart-felt loathing' (*FWK* 71).

The population, then, of the civilisation Weil seeks to change is heavy with failed lives. Illusion, violence, dispirited people shape the moral cloth of mid-century Europe. Work is emptied of meaning and attachments to 'false greatness' undergird policy. A renewed civilisation cannot depend upon the past or dreams of a future concocted out of ideological rhetoric – a point often made by Weil and which deals not only with work, but ideological rhetoric linked to all of our human social, political, and economic life. This Weil asserts in assessing how such vast change might be accomplished. In her expression of next steps woven through the text of *The Need for Roots*, obstacles to revitalisation are named and referred to as powerful barriers to change. The list is short, but Weil makes clear that each of the obstacles is pervasive and tenacious; they are: false greatness, degradation of justice, idolisation of money, and the absence of religious inspiration, (*NR* 219). Every obstacle is relevant to the discussion of work in our civilisation and, I contend, provides the starting place for Weil's reform proposal and her vision of spiritual labour. In short, the obstacles represent illusory ends, and her effort is designed to disperse falsity and construct a scheme which opens to the real.

Weil does not picture herself, as such, as one of the analysts who will endeavour to bring about a renewed social order. She writes, in *The Need for Roots*, that inquiry must be undertaken before action, and investigators must be equipped to approach the questions in an entirely unprecedented way. The inquiry is both of scientific and religious substance, and the two methods must be held together. The investigator is like an anatomist who grasps the shape of the 'enormous animal'. But the anatomy must be grasped as of supernatural importance, and considerations of the healthy soul are to be incorporated into the full report of essential changes.

Agnes Heller would probably not qualify as one of Weil's

unprecedented anatomists. Her writing does not explicitly refer to the supernatural realm which Weil insists upon. None the less, her descriptive efforts do qualify her to be an important contributor. She offers an exacting account of the status of our civilisation, suggesting that moral discourse is a critical dimension of renewal. The precision which Weil requires for civilisation's understanding is yielded in Heller's efforts to locate the character of dissatisfaction in our age. This experience of restless non-fulfilment has its basis in modernity, and has developed into a deeply dangerous expression of value irrationality. It is to Heller's analysis of our condition that I now turn in order to examine how civilisation is understood in contemporary moral philosophical terms.

According to Heller (and her collaborator Fehér in the study of postmodern culture), modernity remains the pervasive culture upon which postmodernity is 'parasitic'. What characterises the development of postmodernity, which followed waves of existentialism and alienation, is its wide embrace of pluralism and its refusal to accept utopian or messianic projections. This movement fosters two dangerous qualities that the authors identify: moral relativism and boundless pluralism, the latter being best exemplified as an attitude that 'anything goes'. Worrisome in its expansiveness and value instability, the authors suggest that in our climate of flux and fragmentation the universalisms of modernity might be re-examined. This endeavour would permit them to discover the 'ties which still hold our world together'.

Turning to their pivotal construct, dissatisfaction, the authors alert us to the fact that this idea and experience has served modernity well. Within the three 'logics' of modernity: capitalism, industrialisation, and democracy, constant movement beyond what is already at hand sparks activity and assures a state of dynamic progress. Thus, dissatisfaction works, but it has unsupportable consequences which Fehér and Heller are prepared to indict: 'For the ideology and practice of universal dissatisfaction is fuelled by, and in turn fuels, a cycle of unstoppable growth which is increasingly disruptive of the conditions of modern life' (*PPC* 12).

Dissatisfaction is associated with needs which can not be absolutely satisfied no matter how industrious the actor. This brings about a state of disquiet and yearning for more. Weil's discussion of unfilfilled workers could be congenial to this analysis and she would conceivably assert that false greatness has something to do with unstoppable growth. Although the language of false greatness is not represented in Heller's position, the fragility of motivation is clearly recognised.

Dissatisfaction is tied to both material and subjective conditions, the latter representing a person's understanding of self as contingent. Heller and Fehér develop a careful account of the transition of the self, from traditional understandings to a modern sense of self-choosing, suggesting that this reality has much to do with the condition of satisfaction and its unfulfilled status. They point to the shift from a traditional division of labour, where expectations were defined by the past, to the modern functional division of labour that opens possibility to workers. Thus, a self-choosing of occupation with a recognition of limit introduces the tension of freedom and contingency into the world of work and culture in general. The crisis that develops is one in which a self perceives enormous distance between expectations and experience, between contingency and destiny.

There is no remedy for this recognition of the gap, according to Fehér and Heller, and dissatisfaction with its restless momentum will prevail. However, there need be no sense of captivity to this round of getting and not getting enough. The authors assert that dissatisfaction must be assessed in terms of the distinction between choosing needs and satisfying wants, the latter being a form of need which originates in, and is satisfied from, the outside. Wants are contingent, then, upon sociopolitical circumstances and technological development and accessibility. The former sense of need attaches to the idea of destiny and self-determination. 'A want-oriented person seeks self-determination', according to the authors, 'in subjecting himself or herself to a kind of determination which does not stem the Self's own choice' (*PCC* 28). The *Self* chooses with recognition of ability and others' needs. Satisfaction in a dissatisfied world can be experienced to the extent in which rational discourse and social exchange emerge and encourage a 'heightened sense of responsibility'. However, our contemporary 'want-oriented' culture is not a hospitable climate for conviviality. It enjoys ever-expanding consumption, but the sense of nihilism and the values of egoism and individual satisfaction contribute to the loss of sociability and political engagement so necessary to a thriving democratic civilisation.

We discover in this assessment qualities that Weil discovered to be pervasive fifty years earlier. Both women recognise that civilisation cannot promise good life, or life for that matter. Heller remarks that the discussion of end – as in the end of the self, the end of philosophy – which typifies postmodern discourse reveals a type of 'death wish', a mood that detracts from life-commitment. She writes that 'it indicates the needs which are met and satisfied by self-hate and self-abasement'. Her vocation as a 'radical philosopher' directs her towards a life-affirming approach. She begins to suggest this in the notion of 'universal gesture', defined as doing as 'human beings as such' with others 'in sympathetic reciprocity, solidarity, friendship.' (*PPC* 58).

THE TRANSFORMATION OF CIVILISATION

No image conveys Weil's distinction between unfree labour in a flawed civilisation and free labour in a redeemed civilisation better than the following:

A happy young woman, expecting her first child, and busy sewing a layette, thinks about sewing it properly. But she never forgets for an instant the child she is carrying inside her. At precisely the same moment, somewhere in a prison workshop, a female convict is also sewing, thinking, too, about sewing properly, for she is afraid of being punished. One might imagine both women to be doing the same work at the same time, and having their attention absorbed by the same technical difficulties. And yet a gulf of difference lies between one occupation and the other. The whole social problem consists in making the worker pass from one to the other of these occupational extremes. (*NR* 95)

This passage from prison to new life follows no straight line, nor is it divided by earthly spiritual concerns. In Weil's understanding of the transformative, labour reform and the identification of spiritual labour share the same pathway, but it is a somewhat circuitous one. The principal guide post is consent which allows no violence; obedience is another beacon which allows no subjugation along the way.

The uprootedness of our civilisation, which Weil describes as fragmentation and nihilism, can only be addressed by constructing institutions and work sites that are authentically places of home. Similarly, Heller identifies home as a high value. In Weil's experience one of the rare moments of solidarity and true expression of workers' proprietary feeling (i.e., a sense of being at home) occurred during the strike of 1936. She remembered how joyous the former work-mates she knew were as they occupied the factory and brought their families into the workrooms. It is this memory which infuses Weil's proposal for factory reform. For joy must be integrated into the work progress, and exhibited in every facet of the work day. How can the fleeting memory of 1936, or those equally elusive moments on the factory floor when one comrade smiled at another, be transformed into a revitalised work organisation?

In the final section of her essay on 'Factory Work', and in the exposition of uprootedness in *The Need for Roots*, Weil provides a thorough account of the positive transformation of the urban and agrarian work world. In this effort, and in her discussion of spiritual transformation, Weil displays an economy or ecological sensibility about her observations and experiences in the factory and the field. No detail is lost or unattended in the light of her effort to redeem the terrible negations of civilisation. In a notebook comment the possibility of 'lost suffering' is encountered, and Weil writes that if this is not used for detachment it will culminate in a 'warped soul'. Her own experience of suffering invites a point of entry into the soul's requirements.

The transformative task turns such demeaning life experiences as submission, mindless concentration, clock-bound attention, sheer fatigue, and physical pain into positive visions. Concretely, the worker's motivation would depose the sovereignty of money and fear, and install interest and meaning in the work done. This activity would not overcome toil, but toil would make sense in terms of the worker's genuine knowing of what had to be done, what purposes were being achieved, how effectively skill and intelligence entered into the process and the product. In the free work site, where workers experienced themselves in the fullness of their capacities, significance would be defined by operatives not managers. Moreover, the social utility of effort would be grasped. In other words, 'through all their travail they are creating objects called up by the needs of society, and that they have a real if finite right to be proud of them' (*FWK* 68).

In order to achieve this transformation, structural changes in the workplace and in the larger society would have to be undertaken. Boredom would be reduced by ridding most manufacture of human manipulation, installing automation, and developing schemes of variation on the assembly line. It is obvious to us in the late twentieth century that this has been achieved in many factories, but not even the most efficiently run plant has secured a system which is totally without repetitious and demanding manual acts. Weil knew that her reform would not displace some monotony, and prescribes this as a useful technique for the spiritual labourer.

The sense of belonging is closely associated with accessibility of information and fuller engagement in the planning of work tasks. Weil emphasises the function of education in the workplace, in both urban and agrarian settings, asserting that there are concrete actions which follow from trust.

Historically, workers have distrusted management, and for good reason. Management has assumed its charges to be pliable, unintelligent objects without the capacity for development. These stereotypes and antipathies stand in the way of genuine transformation. Personal and organizational changes demand a new way of looking at the 'other', the manager who must now perceive the worker as intelligent and capable of learning; the worker who must accept some discipline and control. In lieu, however, of the former insistence upon a division that held knowledge to be the office resource, and workroom to be pure physicality, the body and mind will be reconciled within the labour process. This can be enhanced by the factory policy of explaining the entire production process and goal-setting arrangement to the worker. In a period of learning time the operative will soon know much and feel confident to educate the foremen and manager about the best procedures. In other words, collaboration will substitute for authoritarian orders and ceaseless competition.

The relief from pressure stimulated by machines that are designed for the product and not the producer, by closely supervised activity, by impatient and infantilising 'bosses', should create a more joyous atmosphere and prepare the worker to 'own' the work, if not the plant. In part, this sense of ownership will be encouraged through tours of the whole operation, and instruction not only in how the process is conceived, but also in what the product is used for.

The labour associations of France came in for a great deal of criticism from Weil because she believed them to be negligent of the country's youth and inattentive to real reform. How could an adjustment to wage or hours worked be a satisfactory solution to such deep systemic problems, Weil inquires. She answers crisply that a shortened day still requires that hardship be incurred by some for a more compacted period, and an increased wage could never assuage the ill-will founded upon evil relationships and demeaning tasks.

The vision of dignity that must be realised in genuine reform requires large-scale change in society as well as in the factory. Weil demands a decentralisation of industry, private ownership of homes and tools, worker education, and youth programmes designed to prepare the next worker generation to approach labour with interest and confidence.

Returning to the image of two women engaged in a sewing task, it will be recalled that the prisoner toiled without benefit of motivation other than fear. She symbolises the civilisation that Weil regards as irretrievable without radical renewal. Surface remedy or cosmetic modification will only encourage illusion among workers and contribute to greater despair. As a piece-worker without compensation, veritably 'doing time', the imprisoned garment worker remains an emblem of rootless, meaningless gesture.

By contrast, the pregnant seamstress could be the worker of Weil's renewed civilisation, who sews because she loves. In some ways the expectant mother is every worker awaiting something better than unfree labour. She is half-way between reform and spiritual labour in Weil's double sense of transformation. Creating her layette with complete knowledge of what that requires (supplies, energy, numbers of articles, etc.), the free seamstress controls her process and brings all of her faculties to the task. Her attention is associated with the end process, not only the product constructed by her effort, but the eventual use by her child. Her joy is what the joy of liberated workers might be: a sense of right engagement and for good purpose.

As a spiritual worker, the pregnant seamstress represents the worker who loves in her expectation. She awaits birth, patiently accepting that her body embraces another. In this case, not the divine, but a growing foetus. In her serene acceptance she knows a gentleness that is far removed from the force which subordinates her sister in the prison. They are removed from one another, but remain two women engaged in a similar task. One attests to the need for large-scale social change, the other to the ever-possible reality of spiritual labour.

In the positive transformation of the labourer who is spiritually inspired, matter and object return as critical experiences. For the enslaved, submissive factory hand, matter dominates and turns a person into an object which serves other objects – product and machine. Weil's reform programme would lift this yoke and invite the worker to resume personhood. If we were to stop short of Weil's vision and not incorporate her grasp of a labour defined by spiritual meaning, we would lose the full sense of her notion of plenitude. It is a fullness that is experienced by the spiritual worker who comes to know labour as the Passion. It is an experience of inner illumination which eliminates the need to answer to the question of work's meaning.

The theological importance of Weil's embrace of the Passion can only be measured in terms of the prevailing view of work as penitential or as co-creative. In this latter sense, human labour is justified in all its hardship as a partnership with the Creator.[10] To grasp that suffering has a spiritual utility which can lift the worker to a higher plane is a difficult message, but one which lies at the core of Weil's embrace of the crucified labourer.

Work, as such, is not imitation of Creation, but of the Passion. It is as toil that it partakes of an inspiration. For anyone who was so strong that he never was tired and never suffered in any way, work could not possibly represent a point of leverage. (N 372)

Toil will not be reduced no matter how extensive a social reconstruction of production there may be. It is a condition that is familiar to the peasant who bends over the crop and, fatigued at day's end, knows throughout the body what toil has meant. Time and space have pierced the skin and allowed contact between this world and the universe to be made. And through this penetration a person glimpses beauty as the order of the world.

At first reading, the acceptance of transformation experienced as the conversion of body into matter, 'some wooden instrument', does not seem to be consonant with the vision of social reform Weil advances.[11] Surely the factory or agrarian labour does not want to be objectified and subject to another's use as a tool. Weil is not proposing this, nor is she offering a contradictory programme of work. She is locating human work in a context that is larger than our earthbound reality, and colours the sense of work's dignity with supernatural significance. The scale of human activity had long engaged Weil's attention, from her student essays to her disputations with Marx's revolutionary call for radical social and economic change. Neither a romanticised ennobling of labour for the sake of

[10] See the papal encyclical *Laboram Exercens*, 1982; also, M. D. Chenu, *The Theology of Work*, (Chicago: Henry Regenery Co., 1963).

[11] J. P. Little's essay, above, explores Simone Weil's notion of 'decreation' as spiritual transformation. This is what Weil is getting at here.

nation-building, nor a historical critique of emancipation which dismisses necessity, suffice for her understanding of free labour. She notes that she will write an essay on 'the dispersion of labour' which will 'result in the good'. This good integrates a profound respect for labour and purpose, a respect which demands the 'plenitude' not possible where supernatural truth has been cast aside.

Weil's expansive vision seemingly answers to the woman Studs Terkel cited earlier, who reported that jobs are too small for the spirit. Weil's reform project and vision of a new civilisation insist upon space for the soul or spirit which requires both radically improved work conditions and a grasp of work's meaning in its most 'rooted' sense. Not only does she prescribe that the poetry which lifts the head and the spirit be brought to the factory floor and infused in the peasant's life, but she supplants illusory greatness with the simplicity of cosmic citizenship. Every human belongs to creation, and every gesture redeemed serves as an intermediary between this world and the beyond.

The manual labourer is particularly privileged within this image of spiritual work, because the experience of pain is direct and the grasp of connection between the Passion and bread-getting is not obscure once religious inspiration has been recognised as essential. Those who work with their bodies and experience the extension of the self in using a tool are closer to the truth of mediation. But as the distance between matter in contact with matter expands, so, too, the intuition that in labour all is means. She elaborates upon this in her reflections upon the path to salvation by means of circularity rather than in a progressive, horizontal line:

Work makes us experience in distressing fashion the phenomenon of finality being shot back and forth like a ball: working in order to eat, eating in order to work. If we look on either of these as an end, or each as an end separately, we are lost. Truth lies in the circle. (N 496)

Weil's rejection of progressive effort as a straight line is linked to the manual labourer's capacity to grasp an elemental truth that is otherwise ignored or disputed in the civilisation of the 'great animal'. If the daily lessons of the body extending beyond its limits, but respectful of nature's limitations, were to become popular truth, the self-evidence of rotational flow would infuse all work. Weil perceives that those who work closely with matter, encountering physical obstacles and knowing the body's capacities for response, are in a position to know more readily the truth of circularity. She writes that the labourer is like a squirrel revolving in a cage:

... on the one hand, supreme wretchedness; on the other, supreme splendour.
It is just when man sees himself as a squirrel revolving in a cage that, provided he doesn't lie to himself, he is close to salvation. (*N* 496)

In order to be affirmed in this glimpse of truth, physical labourers in the city and the countryside require education that encourages a sense of spiritual purpose. Weil inserts a call for educational renewal in her plan for civilisation's revitalisation. It bears little resemblance to traditional curriculum innovation. Her belief that science and religious inspiration go hand in hand extends to the novel design of education which will introduce symbolic forms from work experience into the context of an expanded meaning of work's purpose. In this way, the distance will close between everyday knowledge and the recognition of supernatural verities.

Another facet of the manual labourer's privileged spiritual status is the value of obedience freely given. Weil's identification of matter as the teacher of obedience again suggests proximity and direct connection that opens to imitation as essential. Force teaches the worker to become docile, and to accept violence as an ordinary expectation. But this form of submission is distinguishable from obedience, to the consent given by those whose lives have become spiritualised. It is an awesome challenge which is not prescribed as something that can be accepted without the structural changes and adjustments that shift human attention away from false incentive and inflated understanding of destiny.

Agnes Heller's vision is large, but does not compare with Weil's in scope. Her objective in writing 'radical philosophy' is to contribute to the lessening of technological threat and confusion about the capacity of the citizen to think values and render adequate decisions. She writes as a humanist who opts for justice and egalitarianism, who offers an alternative to the nihilism and active irrationality she associates with this period of late modernism.

Comparison can be made regarding Weil and Heller. Both philosophers share a commitment to the concrete world, to the common person and the claims of justice which are not always spoken by those left marginal by the power arrangements of modern and postmodern life. They focus upon human needs rather than legal rights for amelioration of the disequilibrium of society.[12] Weil approaches need in the largest context, offering an enumeration of the soul's needs, while Heller attempts to delineate needs in terms of the psychosocial pressures of an industrialised culture. In either case, the notion of entitlement is not abandoned, but subordinated to human yearning and requirements for dignity and freedom. In the naming of freedom and life as universals, Heller does not depart from Weil's vision. Their difference remains one of the emphasis upon ethical discourse, on the one hand, or spiritual integration on the other.

Heller's holistic view of the human person is particularly relevant in the drawing of parallels between her thought and that of Simone Weil. She does not trivialise the role of reason, but asserts that feeling/emotion and bodily knowledge must be considered.[13] Accordingly, her philosophical focus has been on questions of shame, concerns about satisfaction of needs, intergenerational cultural differences.[14] She contends that, in spite of the abundance of values seemingly detached from institutions in our everyday world, there are universals which can be named and clarified. The person Heller describes is fully capable of rational engagement in moral discussion, despite the value relativism that would seemingly rule out coherent exchange. She believes that a philosopher's task is to enable this discussion to take place. Not to pre-empt the content of the discussion, but to present cogent arguments for and against the values already circulating within the culture. In short, she would have a citizen of dignity whose efforts in the public realm would not be reduced to rote actions and fickle expression of this or that value.

Heller shares with Weil a sense of the integrity of the ordinary person who has been shunted to the side by cultural misunderstanding and discriminatory practice. Heller would rescue the ordinary person from the charge of apathy or irresponsibility by arguing for the power of education and a shift in assumptions regarding freedom. Perhaps the most convincing clue in discovering a parallel

---

[12] See the essays in this volume by Eric Springsted, Richard Bell, and Collins and Nielsen for further discussion of the issues surrounding 'rights', 'justice', and 'the law' in Simone Weil.

[13] Agnes Heller, 'The Discourse Ethics of Habermas: Critique and Appraisal', *Thesis Eleven* (1984/5), pp. 5–17; see also Richard Bernstein, 'Agnes Heller: Philosophy, Rational Utopia, and Praxis', *Thesis Eleven* (1987), pp. 22–38.

[14] See Agnes Heller, *The Power of Shame*, Boston: Routledge, and Kegan Paul, 1988; 'Towards an Anthropology of Feeling', *Dialectical Anthropology*, 4:1 (1979), pp. 1–20; 'Are We Living In a World of Emotional Impoverishment?' *Thesis Eleven*, no. 22 (1989), pp. 46–60.

between Weil and Heller is in the notion of satisfaction advanced by the latter in her critique of a dissatisfied society. She concludes that clarification of needs and wants allows us to accept the experience of dissatisfaction to the extent that destiny triumphs over contingency. In this vision Heller describes the importance of a 'Self-development' that is tolerant of abundance, but refuses the excess of want. The larger self, the self Heller places in capital letters, experiences a limit and can consent to 'enough'. I will say more of this below. In regarding how Weil rejects short-term remedies for labour the idea of satisfaction has not been lost, although she does not use the language of job satisfaction which is, and has been for more than a generation, a key measure of labour motivation and reward. Weil could not have settled for strategies designed to improve workers' sense of a worthy day's work based solely upon a set of hour and wage adjustments, and designated as job incentives for work satisfaction. This reduction of the problem which infests the soul with such grief would have been intolerable. One cannot ameliorate an evil by covering it with incentives that only add salt to the wound. Heller cannot accept political measures that allow value confusion to continue on the path to disorder. Neither woman regards satisfaction as the way to renewal; both demand depth in the struggle for a just society.

It was not Weil's understanding of her writing that it either contributed to a radical philosophical practice, or that it advanced a utopian perspective. Heller argues that the quest for truth must be a vocational commitment and 'only a quest like this can carry the promise of a utopian reality'. She offers a set of radical needs, as well as an assertion that our present age embraces two universals: freedom and life. The problem with both universals is that there is an ever-expanding production of goods which seemingly appropriates the notion of freedom as one that is tied to consumerism and the desire for as much as can be purchased. Freedom and life become confused with a short-term happiness that will do no more than satisfy the 'pluralization of tastes'.

Mistaken ends absorb the postmodern citizen who lives in an unstable, confusing culture of abundant choices. But choices are far removed from a common vision of the good life. What Heller advances is a culture of civil virtue where 'life tastes well', rather than one in which tastes dominate life's shape. Her vision lifts democracy as the most significant of the three 'logics' of modernity and asserts that three ideals are to shape this political form of governance. Freedom is the meta-virtue which cannot be realised, but must be the focus of moral discourse. How is freedom to be if it is not exclusively defined by individualism and liberalism? It is the ideal of the true, empowering citizens to enjoy the fullest possible participation in moral discussion and policy choice. The good experienced as recognition of the other is a second ideal. Self-development is the third, and Heller relates it to beauty. All three are interconnected as a unity. Although the good is an elusive notion in today's society, Heller argues that it can be reasoned.

The utopian dimension of Heller's perspective includes both ideals and needs. She writes of radical needs: 'We characterize as radical needs all needs which arise within a society based on relationships of subordination and superordination, but which *cannot be satisfied* within such a society. These are needs which can only be satisfied if this society is *transcended* (*RP* 138, her emphasis).

The enumeration of needs clearly refers to the universals of life and freedom, and includes: unitary humanity as a reality, equality, non-discrimination in institutions, the abolition of war and the development of personality. It is the final need that I want to briefly elaborate upon, because this need ties Heller's vision to the moral problem of domination and sociability, to her expression of 'universal gesture'. In overcoming contingency, Heller contends, a primary choice must be made to choose decency and honesty, which includes having to accept suffering in order to prevent another's harm. Neither exploitative nor dependent relationships encourage decency. A balance must be struck between 'developing endowments into talents' and the recognition of another's needs. 'If one does an injustice or wrong to others, one has violated the autonomy of others, one has withheld recognition of the needs of others, one has failed to co-operate with one's fellow creatures – in short, one has used others as mere means. (*PPC* 42)

The hope for a civilisation that fosters the best in its citizens, engaging as many as are ready to participate in the ongoing conversation of political priorities, is Heller's response to an unstable political arena, a confusing social order filled with the pressures to choose and negligible resources to guide a decision. In response to this expanding culture of possibility which causes much anxiety, Heller attempts to establish some signposts for rational discussion and decision making that enable the modern person to think and act with greater assurance that aspirations can be met. She tells us that the challenge is in resisting the temptation to withdraw into complete contingency. Rather, we seem to be prompted towards facing the scope of contingency, and working our way through it to a reasoned destiny.

CONCLUSION

Agnes Heller shares with a number of contemporary moral philosophers the concern for public moral ideals. These ideals have faded in our civilisation, requiring an acceptance of this condition or a commitment to turn things around. In her modified Aristotelian approach, the ancient questions of how we choose to be good, do good, and function responsibly towards a common good are recast by Heller who adds her existentialist notion of contingency to the moral stew.

Her starting place is in the assertion that there is a moral universal which shapes the specificity of choice. This universal is a commitment to be good. There are, then, no good persons as such; only variation on the ways in which people choose to express the universal in particular instances involving concrete choices. Heller distinguishes, as did Aristotle, the virtuous person from the engaged citizen. Decent persons, she adds, may not be good citizens, but they choose the world in which they live under the pressure of competing demands, conflicting possibilities and dilemmas that occur in the everyday world. The decent person needs a 'meta-norm'. Heller proposes that the 'universal orientative principles' that she has identified can serve in guiding choice. These guides include the civic virtues and ideals mentioned in an earlier section of this essay. 'Once the world is regarded as contingent', Heller asserts in advancing her vision, 'it becomes pregnant with possibilities, open-ended, bereft of an in-built telos and indeterminate' (*PM* 125). Such possibility is freedom, and its exercise is invariably practical. Heller warns that the decent person who chooses destiny has still to cope with the irrational forces that throw a long shadow across modern civilisation.

The good citizen is akin to Aristotle's political animal, a person concerned about the state of the polity, and anxious to see justice prevail over the many instances of injustice we encounter in everyday life. Most notable, in my opinion, is this good citizen's sense of responsibility for others. Some citizens work towards the good in the domestic sphere, and some are carried across national borders. A few 'reach out to transform the modern world, our contingent world, into a common destiny'.

Simone Weil, most certainly, was an exemplar of Heller's good citizen in this latter sense. Her life not only attested to the priority of engagement in the concrete issues of her world, but her writing consistently advanced a transformational vision of a common world. Whether in her letters to managers of factories, attempting to advance some reforms on behalf of labour, or placing herself in the unemployed protesters' lines. Weil reached beyond contingency on behalf of freedom for many.

Perhaps nothing speaks more powerfully to this transformational vision than the first ten or so pages of *The Needs for Roots*. In that text Weil lifts the claim of obligation as an eternal one which must be met concretely in this world. She anticipates Heller in advancing an imperative of respect which calls upon every human to respect another in his/her humanness. Heller's notion of 'universal gesture', which is defined as reciprocal responsibility for the human being as such, comes close to Weil's understanding, but is not rooted in supernatural reality. Both Weil and Heller, however, understand that the expression of respect, for Weil the singular obligation, must be exercised in concrete, practical existence. Both also refer to recognition of obligation/respect as a matter of general assent. Weil writes of 'verification in the common consent according to universal conscience'.

In providing a statement of needs, Heller chooses those which are principally associated with the civic order, except the first. The acknowledgement of a unitary human reality as a human need refers, I suspect, to the circumstances we find ourselves in as a globally connected people. When one society misuses a resource, another will sooner or later experience loss. Weil distinguishes physical, moral, and spiritual needs. The last meets the 'hungers' of the soul which must be fed as fully as the bodily need for food.

It strikes me that the labour reforms of Weil's vision are tied more integrally to the moral and spiritual needs, than to the obvious connection of physical needs which assure health, warmth, shelter, and safety from physical violence. To be protected from cruelty, the foremost moral need is for every worker to be assured of working conditions which will not demean and humiliate. Yet it is the guarantee of order, liberty, and responsibility – needs of the soul – which touch upon the deepest issues of the corrosive effects of labour organisation and process. To be relieved of an arbitrary milieu, which fosters constant fear and anxiety, is to be able to lift the head from a downcast position. It is a need which promises to bring certitude into the labourer's setting. Heller similarly identifies order, but not as a structural matter so much as one of a communication system in great disarray. Her hope is that opportunities will increase for more and better rational exchange among decent persons. Where liberty appears as Weil's second need of the soul, opening possibilities for unencumbered choice, Heller's notion of Self-development arises as a parallel, although this same expression of moving beyond contingency to destiny entails responsibility for another as well. Weil describes the need for responsibility in terms most critical to the worker, generalised as the sense of being useful. Neither the unemployed nor the physical worker enjoy this form of responsibility, the former deprived of opportunity to engage in socially useful activity, the latter deprived of initiative and interest in the efforts made at some cost to body and mind.

The needs of body, soul, and moral existence require action. Those societies which fail to respond are unhealthy societies. 'Every social organism', Weil writes, 'which does not provide its members with these satisfactions is diseased and must be restored to health' (*NR* 15). Civilisation's diseased state is a reflection, then, upon how well a social order attends to the basic needs of every human. Workers figure as pivotal in the examination of the societal response to disorder. Weil paints a gloomy picture of their condition. The woes of workers are multiple, but, according to Weil, can be assuaged or overcome through the reforms she advances in the pages of her final essay.

We must change the system concerning concentration of attention during working hours, the type of stimulants which make the overcoming of laziness or exhaustion – and which are merely fear and extra pay – the type of obedience necessary, the far too small amount of initiative, skill, and thought demanded of workmen, their present exclusion from any imaginative share in the work of the enterprise as a whole, their sometimes total ignorance of the value, social utility, and destination of the things they manufacture, and the complete divorce between working life and family life. (*NR* 54–5)

This is a large description of concern which continues to our day to call for implementation. Weil understands the consequences of such woe and argues for a radically modified civilisation which respects all work and those who labour with little hope. Although she proposes reforms that embrace the skills of artisans, she does not retreat into a nostalgia for medieval guilds. Her call for civilisation is a call for the unprecedented prominence of spiritual labour in a technologically advanced, but decentralised, industrial setting.

In my sketch of some comparative elements in the contemporary writings of Agnes Heller I have sought only to demonstrate that the sense of a disordered civilisation is not peculiar to Simone Weil, nor are her remedies anachronistic. This most preliminary effort invites further inquiry, especially in the area of universal consent and gesture. To the degree that Agnes Heller and Simone Weil notice and name the depth of oppressive conditions and do not despair of them, there is cause for celebration. The challenge remains urgent. Both women suggest beginnings, hoping for the greatest possible reduction of disequilibrium and social injustice.

CHAPTER 9

Reading Simone Weil on rights, justice and love

Richard H. Bell

The challenge of reading Simone Weil is to render her extraordinary thoughts and language into an ordinary idiom; to connect her uncommon insights to our common life.

One such uncommon insight of hers is that, when some words lose their meaning, the consequences may be morally and physically harmful to us (cf. *SE* 156ff.). 'Justice', she believed, is one such word that lost its meaning in modern times. It has been replaced by a vacuous notion of 'rights' with devastatingly harmful results.

An extraordinary thought of hers is that we must reclaim a meaningful sense of justice for our lives. If we could do this we would be doing no less than 'saving human lives'. This seems more than a worthy goal for our postmodern world. To reclaim a meaningful sense of justice, however, requires that we acquire a *new* virtue, a 'supernatural virtue', one she calls 'the supernatural virtue of justice'. How would we go about acquiring such a virtue?

First, we must recognise how we have reduced 'justice' to 'rights' and what this has done to the human spirit. One thing this reduction has done is to have blunted our *pursuit* of justice.

Second, one must do everything in one's power – everything that is humanly possible – to right wrongs, to prevent harmdoing, to struggle against error and evil ('short of a certain limit of violence' *OL* 146), remembering that when all *that* is done good may still not be restored. What is still required is some super-natural intervention.

Third, we must understand that the supernatural virtue desired is a gratuitous intervention of divine love when, and only when, our human practices are of the form which is unconditional love, and that this form of love is, understood from a human point of view, 'madness'.

Fourth, this means that the love which is the new virtue of justice is asymmetrical – that is, it originates in God, is measured out through specific acts of love carried out by human beings towards other human beings on this earth. Furthermore, this kind of love usually goes unnoticed because its effects are smothered or obstructed by the seeming disequilibrium of human force and power – or oppression numbed by affliction. When this love *is* noticed it is recognised as unusual and extraordinary – as 'mad'. It seems as a small light in darkness. This extraordinariness is sufficient, however, to keep us 'waiting' while we engage in our 'mad love' and 'hoping' that such madness will trigger this new virtue and recreate a more humane equilibrium on earth.

All along we are deluded into thinking that we can restore this equilibrium on our own, or through some ideology or entrepreneurial venture. Through most of her young life, Simone Weil thought this as well. When, however, she discovered an incarnate God she saw that, although we must continue to struggle against harmdoing, the struggle must have a different ally – a form of love that is God's love that is carried out against all odds by individual human beings, one act at a time, in this world, and seen as utter madness in the eyes of this world.

Now let us back up for a moment and start with a more common idiom; let us see how far we can see with the limited understanding we have inherited. Then we may be able to connect this uncommon insight to some aspects of our common life.

'RIGHTS' AND 'JUSTICE'

Among the more striking features of Simone Weil's work is her attention to the concreteness of human life; to people's anguish and pain, hopes and fears, aspirations and failures in their everyday life. She philosophically proceeds from the concrete to the theoretical; from specific human experience to the philosophically more general. This has recently been noted by both Peter Winch and David McLellan. Winch writes:

one of the most valuable features of Simone Weil's philosophical procedure is to root the concepts which are most important to her [and 'justice' is certainly one of these] in actual, very concrete, features of human life. Although she is no enemy of abstract theoretical considerations, she does not start with these, but with the circumstances of life which give rise to them.[1]

And McLellan points out that after her factory experience in 1934–5, her brief sojourn with the Republican forces in the Spanish civil war, and an important recovery and discovery period in Italy, she returned to teaching with a new outlook. He writes:

Instead of taking her pupils through the ordinary philosophical texts, she made them read the novels of Balzac and Saint-Exupéry and tried to move to the abstract from the very concrete. She told her students that for the Greeks the finite was more beautiful than the infinite, that the circle was preferable to the line, and that therefore the most important ideas, from painting and sculpture to economics and politics, were those of the equilibrium of forces, of proportion, and of balance – themes that were to be pursued in her Marseilles writings.[2]

This procedure was particularly manifest in her later, post-factory, essays, and was less obvious in the more theoretical attitude toward social oppression as critically developed in *Oppression and Liberty* (1934). It is through these later essays that we will focus our reading of Simone Weil on justice and love.

A good example of this philosophical procedure of hers runs through the 'Essay on the Notion of Reading'. There she shows how our ordinary encounters with letters from friends, images on a walk, a sudden noise, scenes in nature, evoke particular 'readings' – interpretations of expectation, joy, fear, calm – that lead to 'a corrected illusion of the senses'. 'I act according to what I read', she says.

... if in a noise I read honor to be won, I run toward the noise; if I read danger and nothing else, I run far from the noise ... all our life is made of the same fabric, of meanings that impose themselves on us one after the other, and of which each, when it appears enters into us by our senses, reduces to phantoms all the ideas that could stand against it. (*ER* 300f.)[3]

To understand such an abstract concept as 'justice', for example, requires 'readings' that visibly impact our sensibility. Fear, pain, cruelty, compassion, attention to the suffering of a human being are

---

[1] Peter Winch, *Simone Weil: The Just Balance*', Cambridge: Cambridge University Press, 1989, p. 190.

[2] David McLellan, *Simone Weil: Utopian Pessimist*, London: The Macmillan Press, Ltd., 1989, p. 134.

[3] I am using a translation done by my colleague David Wilkin of the French Department of The College of Wooster. The citation is to the published translation in the list of abbreviations.

the ordinary encounters that will go to make up our reading of 'the circumstances of life which give rise to' injustice or where some good can be done. It is such encounters, for Weil, that 'reduce to phantoms' all the abstract formulations of justice like 'rights based contractarian theories' (a phantom of John Rawls). We will see as we go along how this philosophical procedure will enable us to surface the meaning of justice in Weil's view.

Let us begin with an example from a recent experience. In the United States, in April 1989, there was a festive, though serious, march in Washington for women's rights. It was part of the backlash to the anti-abortion campaign by the so-called 'Right to Life' movement. Those who went on the Washington march returned satisfied with the thought that a blow had been struck in favour of women's rights. Nothing rankles more than the thought that some basic right may be denied us – 'Have I not a fundamental right to choose to do what I want and what is responsible with my own body or with my life?' But then we hear the response to this: 'what of the "rights" of a fetus – an unborn child maturing to term, dependent wholly on a woman's choices? Is life itself a right to be claimed or denied?' A clash of 'rights' erupts – women's rights, right to life! But we are convinced that our hallowed concept of 'rights' should be at the centre of such social conflicts. The inheritance of 'rights' talk seems so clear – two eighteenth-century revolutions fought to insure them, and the 'enlightenment spirit' has for two hundred years cemented human, political, and economic 'rights' for Western culture. It has become a 'sacred' cry – a fund to draw upon for any side of an argument.

Simone Weil, however, calls our attention to the concept of 'rights' in an unsuspecting way, and we must look again at this clash before our eyes. In the midst of World War II, when so many 'rights' were being abused, Simone Weil, writes in her essay 'Human Personality': '[to say] "I have the right ..." or "you have no right to ..." evoke[s] a latent war and awaken[s] the spirit of contention. To place the notion of rights at the center of social conflicts is to inhibit any possible impulse of charity on both sides' (*SE* 21). Then I think about the after-glow of the march and 'women's rights' and brace myself for the next counter charge of the 'right to lifers' – any 'impulse to charity' left this current discussion over 'rights' long ago. I read again in Weil: 'Thanks to this world ['rights'], what should have been a cry of protest from the depth of the heart has turned into a shrill nagging of claims and counter-claims, which is both impure and unpractical' (*SE* 21). Is 'rights' the correct concept to use here, I ask myself? Am I missing something deeper? Finally I read the following in Weil:

Relying almost exclusively on this notion [of rights], it becomes impossible to keep one's eyes on the real problem. If someone tries to browbeat a farmer to sell his eggs at a moderate price, the farmer can say: 'I have the right to keep my eggs if I don't get a good enough price.' But if a young girl is being forced into a brothel she will not talk about her rights. In such a situation the word would sound ludicrously inadequate. (*SE* 21)

But how do we keep our eyes on the real problem? It is not just a violation of rights this young girl has experienced – she has suffered an *injustice*, and we mean by this that she has had great harm done to her which cannot be understood as a 'right' taken. What has been taken and what could be returned in place of the sexual violation?

In answer to the question, 'what right has been taken?', one might hear the response from the legal community: 'the fourth ammendment "right to privacy"'. But this does not touch the nerve centre of this type of violation. An example used by Simone Weil similar to the offence of forcing a young girl into a brothel is that of rape. J. P. Little commented in her essay on this violation. She said, rape involves 'the destruction of the moral being of the individual, the infinitely small but precious capacity for consent'.[4] What is legally called a person's 'right to privacy' does not adequately cover such a moral destruction. 'Having the right to ...' always involves something a person has, and what is truly sacred, the seat of justice and one's moral being for Simone Weil, is wholly impersonal. What is lost is the sacred core of one's being, not something that can be replaced by a court of law or even by some compensatory action by the violator. Also following Little's discussion of the logic of decreation we see that justice relates to the 'uncreated' part of our being, that which does not easily consent to the necessity of events unless it is totally crushed; justice cries out to the extent that it is not being worn away by circumstances of force – 'Why am I being hurt?'

To have bought into rights language is to believe that power can be counter-balanced by power. To say 'if we could just achieve equal rights ...' means I must either snatch rights from someone else

---

[4] See Little's essay on 'Decreation', above.

(one who has a disequal amount) or impose an ideology by force of persuasion to 'guarantee' rights in a more or less coercive way (even by civil law). This way of thinking will not easily go away. But in Simone Weil's thinking the only substantial way to counterbalance force is neither through force nor through a more equitable distribution of rights, rather it is through a kind of justice that has as its most active ingredient love.

'Rights', Simone Weil says, 'have no direct connection with love' (*SE* 20), and justice has primarily to do with seeing that no harm is done to another human being. And this, of course, is her point: to contrast our use of 'rights' with 'justice', and to force us to see that, as she says, 'at the very best, a mind enclosed in language is in prison' and that 'to be unaware of being in prison' is to be 'living in error' (*SE* 26). Reading the details of situations in our human life helps us to move from 'error' to 'truth'. (We will return to this movement later in considering 'justice' as a 'supernatural virtue'.) Although our readings of all human texts are from a perspective, there are some readings that are more adequate, or truthful, than others. There are no perfect readings. (Here the notion of hierarchical readings and 'non-reading' discussed by Andic and Allen are relevant.)

We must ask: 'isn't there something fundamentally askew, in error, about our 'rights' talk when it lies so close to matters of life and death – when it no longer is linked to an exchange and a commodity?' Simone Weil even suggests that 'rights' talk is suited to the market place (the farmer and his eggs), and when applied to such issues as human violation it leads to a certain moral mediocrity – but then, I think, the clash of women's rights over abortion at best shows our mediocrity in thinking and in dealing with human lives. A different language is needed to move us from our mediocrity.

This moral mediocrity into which we have fallen runs very deep and we may not be able to extricate ourselves easily. To change the nature of our 'rights' talk, as Peter Winch says, 'concerns the whole language in which questions about justice are commonly raised, at least in the second half of the twentieth century'. Winch, in his discussion of Simone Weil's distinction between 'rights' and 'justice', reminds us that John Rawls' whole enterprise in *A Theory or Justice* (a theory that has become near canonical) uses 'rights' language, 'or at least deals in the conceptions that ['rights' language] expresses'.

Simone Weil's view of justice challenges Rawls' whole way of conceiving 'justice'.[5]

Winch continues this point as follows:

The *inspiration* for a demand for rights may well be a concern for justice; it may be that in some circumstances to struggle for rights is the best way of struggling for justice. But that does not mean that the struggle for justice is the same as the struggle for rights; the one struggle may be successful and the other not – maybe that is even more often than not the outcome. And if the distinction is forgotten, there is the danger that a concern for rights will take one farther and farther away from justice; or that the quest for justice will be entirely submerged.[6]

There is a clear and present danger, for example, in the South African situation that 'justice will be entirely submerged' in the new clamour to give blacks some 'rights'. It is not hard to see that this might be the desired outcome among many whites, while it is equally clear among many blacks that there must be no final settlement on 'rights' without 'justice' that includes 'charity' and genuine 'attention' to the decades of harm done to them. It would also be a striking advance in our thinking if those who are in the process of reforming the shape of Eastern Europe and the Soviet Union were to remember about the prison of language, (Vaclav Havel is among the few in Eastern Europe who seems well aware of this), and reconceive of 'human rights' with a stress on the implication of 'human justice' in the deeper sense in which Simone Weil wishes to move us.

If we take Simone Weil's point about the 'shrill nagging' of 'rights' talk, then we have even a harder task to move from error to truth. We have to see how turning over the concept of 'justice' in the sense that her philosophical procedure recommends might change our course and make us think differently.

We have before us in this powerful essay 'Human Personality' two distinct notions: 'rights' and 'justice'. She summarises the difference between them in this way.

The notion of rights is linked with the notion of sharing out, of exchange, of measured quantity. It has a commercial flavour, essentially evocative of legal claims and arguments. Rights are always asserted in a tone of contention; and when this tone is adopted, it must rely upon force in the background, or else it will be laughed at. (*SE* 18)

---

[5] Winch, *The Just Balance*, p. 180.   [6] Winch, *The Just Balance*, p. 181.

Justice consists in seeing that no harm is done to men ... [it is associated with the cry] 'Why am I being hurt?' (*SE* 30)

The other cry, which we hear so often: 'Why has somebody else got more than I have,' refers to rights. We must learn to distinguish between the two cries and to do all that is possible, as gently as possible, to hush the second one, with the help of a code of justice, regular tribunals, and the police. Minds capable of solving problems of this kind can be formed in law school.

But the cry 'Why am I being hurt?' raises quite different problems, for which the spirit of truth, justice, and love is indispensable. (*SE* 30)

Simone Weil says, 'If you say to someone who has ears to hear: "What you are doing to me is not just", you may touch and awaken at its source the spirit of attention and love' (*SE* 21). It, therefore, requires a much more detailed analysis of the concepts of 'attention' and 'love' in Simone Weil to begin to open out her reading of the concept of justice. Justice for her is related to the readings we give to the principalities and powers of our world and to individual persons. For Simone Weil a correct reading must focus attention on the 'whole human being', and on the faintest cry of those who are hurting all around us (cf. *SE* 9, 11 and *WG* 114f.).

Before we go on to her account of her new virtue of justice, let us step back in our analysis for a moment. We have become unaware of the prison language has placed us in. What is the error here? 'Rights' language has imprisoned the concept of 'justice'. They have been reduced to mean the same thing. Rights and justice have, as Simone Weil observed, been placed 'at the centre of social conflicts' and thus 'inhibit any possible impulse of charity'. In Simone Weil's own earlier conception of justice – before her factory experience in 1935 – social conflicts were at the centre of justice concerns. Pay disputes and work conditions were to be negotiated with the management to improve rights and offset or balance social inequities. Before her factory experience she was a leading advocate for social rights and was bent on changing things. Within two to three weeks of factory work she succumbed to 'the daily experience of brutal constraint' (*SL* 21). This she could only characterise as the condition of a slave. 'Slavery has made me entirely lose the feeling of having any rights' (*FW* 211 and *SL* 22). Neither negotiation nor revolt seemed possible for the workers.[7] She came to the startling

---

[7] This point is made in a number of places in both *Oppression and Liberty*, Amherst, MA: The University of Massachusetts Press, 1973, and in her 'Factory Journal'. David McLellan also makes this point, *Utopian Pessimist*, p. 109f.

revelation that, as a worker with the prevailing conditions she experienced first hand, she 'possessed no right to anything' (*SL* 22). This, she said, 'killed my youth'; it marked her for the rest of her life. After her factory year, it was clear to her that 'rights' talk could no longer sustain the moral debate regarding justice.

With the loss of rights so complete and so devastating, what meaning is there left for it? If neither rational negotiation nor revolution can restore one's rights, do we give up on justice as well? A new concept entered her soul as a result of this experience, that of profound humiliation. What she had thought to be a matter of loosening the workers from their oppressors' chains, was now under-stood to be a much more complex phenomena – one of restoring human dignity in the context of slavery. No longer was oppression seen as bound to social conflicts, but rooted in the suffering, humili-ation, and physical constraint placed on the human soul – a mark of what she now called 'affliction' (*malheur*).[8] She now had to rethink the concept of justice altogether.

To help us analyse the difference between 'rights' and 'justice', she turns our attention to classical Greek literature and offers us an alternative reading of the meaning of justice. She turns us to Creon and Antigone, to Hector and Achilles – object lessons in how 'justice' language works and how 'rights' language in Antigone's voice, for example, is so utterly unthinkable. Antigone can say, 'I was born to share, not hate, but love' (*SE* 20) – an expression foreign in an age of litigation and moral relativity.[9] Justice is 'companion of the gods'; it connects up with 'love', she says, and 'rights has no direct connection with love' (*SE* 20).

In 1939, she wrote her essay on the *Iliad*, where 'force' is shown to be the dominant pressure placed upon human beings – now not just those persons who might find themselves a victim of some form of oppression, but on all human beings. She writes:

Force is as pitiless to the man who possesses it, or thinks he does, as it is to its victims; the second it crushes, the first it intoxicates. The truth is nobody really possesses it. The human race is not divided up, in the *Iliad*, into conquered persons, slaves, suppliants, on the one hand, and conquerers and chiefs on the other. In this poem there is not a single man who does not at one time or another have to bow his neck to force. (*IL* 11)

8 McLellan, *Utopian Pessimist*, p. 116f.
9 See Ann Loades' discussion of Simone Weil's 'Antigone', below.

There is no reason to think that the circumstances of human life have changed for us as we continue to imprison our human world with the arms race, the nuclear threat, various forms of economic oppression, and multiple forms of human cruelty. We have, in Weil's terms, overstepped a limit and thus lost 'equilibrium which ought to determine the conduct of life' (*IL* 15).

If we stand in our human world in a state of disequilibrium, and have yielded to force as a way of life, is there anything that can restore our equilibrium? For the Greeks, Weil says, 'Justice and love' is the balancing factor. It is this necessity of human misery under the constraints of force that is a precondition to the recognition of justice and love. She says of the *Iliad*, 'Justice and love, which hardly have any place in this study of extremes and of unjust acts of violence, nevertheless bathe the work in their light without ever becoming noticeable themselves, except as a kind of accent' (*IL* 30). *All* of Weil's post-factory year works are 'accented by', and *many* are 'bathed in', the light of justice and love. So what is 'justice' if it cannot be reduced to 'rights'; if it cannot be rationally negotiated? – 'eggs for the right price', 'no increased productivity without better work conditions and wages'. Rather, as we have noted, justice 'awakens at its source the spirit of attention and love' (*SE* 21). We must now focus on the concepts of 'attention' and 'love' (two concepts seldom, if ever, heard in the vocabulary of 'rights' talk) in order to understand her notion of 'justice'.

'JUSTICE' AND 'ATTENTION'

Peter Winch has discussed the importance of 'attention' to justice very well, but has not said enough about the concept of love relative to justice. So, first let us look at part of Winch's critique.

Attention has to do with discernment – discernment of what someone is saying, discernment of the kind of protest a person makes who is being harmed, discernment of the social conditions which create the climate for injustice or even misunderstanding, and discernment of myself as an equal subject of affliction. Winch writes:

there are special obstacles *in the soul of the reader* in the way of recognizing protests at real injustice. 'Attention' is necessary; and the peculiar difficulty of my attending to someone in such a situation is that it requires me to understand that we are both equal members of a natural order which can at any time bring about such a violation of whoever it may be, including myself. That is, I cannot understand the other's affliction from the point of view of my own privileged position; I have rather to understand *myself* from the standpoint of *the other's* affliction, to understand that my privileged position is not part of my essential nature but an accident of fate.[10]

Then Winch quotes Simone Weil from 'Human Personality':

To acknowledge the reality of affliction means saying to oneself: 'I may lose at any moment, through the play of circumstances over which I have no control, anything whatsoever that I possess, including things that are so intimately mine that I consider them as myself. There is nothing that I might not lose. It could happen at any moment that what I am might be abolished and replaced by anything whatsoever of the filthiest and most contemptible sort.' [*SE* 27)

When Simone Weil says justice is 'seeing that no harm is done to men' (*LPG* 94), the 'seeing' here implies that one read both the nature of the harm being done and making certain that the particular harm is stopped. Both of these require a considerable degree of attention.

The cultivation of attention is a task that requires discipline, but it is something that any human being can acquire. At the most basic level attention can be cultivated in school studies, in attention to the natural world, and in a variety of forms of meditation.[11]

There is a more fundamental sense, however, in which attention can be cultivated and seen to be a basic part of one's pursuit of justice. Winch discusses this more fundamental sense in his chapter on 'The Power to Refuse'[12] primarily through Simone Weil's essays 'The *Iliad*' and 'Are We Struggling for Justice?' The central point is the focus given by Simone Weil to attention to human beings rather than to things or matter. Winch says:

To recognize the existence of another human being is to acknowledge a certain sort of obstacle to some projected actions: that is to say, it is to acknowledge that there are some things one *must* do and some things one *cannot* do in dealings with the other which hence constitute a limit to the ways in which we can pursue our projects.[13]

---

[10] Winch, *The Just Balance*, p. 182.

[11] Simone Weil has spelled this out powerfully in her essay on "Reflection on the Right Use of School Studies," in *Waiting for God*, and I discuss these forms of attention in greater detail in R. H. Bell, *Sensing the Spirit*, Philadelphia: The Westminster Press, 1984, ch. seven.

[12] Winch, *The Just Balance*, p. 105ff.   [13] Winch, *ibid.*, p. 107.

This very recognition and its consequent limiting affect on our projects, Winch argues, is the result of 'an initial primitive, unreflective reaction ... later refined into a mode of behavior'.[14] In other words, our human practices are governed by learning a series of moves and reactions to circumstances which range from stepping out of the way of a passerby to avoid being bumped, to involving the passerby in some mutual activity by gaining their consent. To do the latter I must have attended to the behaviour of the other sufficiently to have gained their trust. I could, of course, also coerce the other's behaviour by some threat or oppressive action. The point is, however, that from such 'primitive, unreflective reactions' we learn to stop and reflect, to be attentive to others. Winch sees this as related to Simone Weil's striking phrase from 'The *Iliad*', i.e., 'that interval of hesitation, wherein lies all our consideration for our brothers in humanity' (*IL* 14). Winch concludes that it is this 'tendency to hesitate in certain circumstances [that] is the seed out of which grow certain kinds of thinking about our fellow human beings',[15] and ultimately out of which can grow a 'geometry of human relations that embodies justice within the human community.[16]

A crucial factor in Simone Weil's conception of justice is that of consent, and consent requires a, more or less, condition of equilibrium. But such equilibrium is almost impossible, she notes, commenting on Thucydides. The actual human condition is more like our not waiting for others' consent, but in exercising the power we have or can get away with, or consenting out of fear of power or by promise of reward, (cf. *SJ* 1f.). 'Consent', she says, 'is made possible by a life containing motives for consenting. Destitution, privations of soul and body, prevent consent from being able to operate in the depths of the heart' (*SJ* 5).

If I have been given reason to distrust my parents, a friend, my school authorities, my government, why should I consent to their wishes or commands? They may coerce me with rewards or threat of punishment, but this further reduces my motivation to consent – or it changes consent to a kind of involuntary submission. Only if I can trust and believe whatever authority in which I willingly submit myself can I willingly consent 'in the depths of [my] heart'. This is illustrated clearly in Vaclav Havel's book, *Living in Truth*, and also

---

[14] Winch, *ibid.*, p. 107.   [15] Winch, *ibid.*, p. 108.
[16] Winch, *ibid.*, pp. 115–19. Eric Springsted's essay addresses these issues as well.

by the downfall of the Eastern European regimes in 1989 by virtue of the peoples' whole lack of trust and by withholding of consent. Havel writes, the price of 'living a lie', of living in deceit only to maintain some bearable life, is too high; it is a 'profane triviali-zation' of inherent humanity. 'To live in truth' requires a new realignment with the 'human order'. Havel says,

[The] task is one of resisting vigilantly, thoughtfully and attentively, but at the same time with total dedication, at every step and every where, the irrational momentum of anonymous, impersonal and inhuman power – the power of ideologies, systems, *apparat*, bureaucracy, artificial languages and political slogans.[17]

To be able to 'live in truth' is a precondition to consent. Simone Weil says to preserve consent religiously and 'to try to create conditions for it where it is absent, that is to love justice' (*SJ* 5). And, 'to the extent to which at any given time there is some madness of love amongst men, to that extent there is some possibility of change in the direction of justice: and no further' (*SJ* 5). I will say more on the 'madness of love' in a moment, but first we must return to the connection of love to justice.

'JUSTICE' AND 'LOVE'

It is in the connection of love to justice that we see most clearly why I call her return to the concept of justice a *new* virtue. In the classical, Aristotelian sense, a virtue is acquired through practice. For Simone Weil, justice is *not* acquired, it is given by God in the form of divine love. We will see, however, that it is *related* to human practices, even though not acquired by them. To have this new virtue – 'the supernatural virtue of justice' – one must consent to this love given by God, and this level of consent comes from the most sacred part of our being – the 'uncreated' part in us that desires God's love. Simone Weil says, 'human consent is a sacred thing. It is what man grants to God. It is what God comes in search of when like a beggar he approaches men' (*SJ*, 2). To grant this most sacred thing to God, however, requires that I renounce all those 'created' parts of myself that yield to power, that create motivations in me for *not* consenting.

---

[17] Vaclav Havel, *Living in Truth*, edited by Jan Vladislaw, London: Faber and Faber, 1989, p. 153. See especially his long essay 'The power of the powerless'.

The picture should be emerging that in this rather uncommon 'language game' of Simone Weil's concerning this new 'supernatural virtue', God holds all the cards, but needs our human consent to play out the divine hand. This is why I said at the beginning that the supernatural virtue of justice is the product of the gratuitous intervention of divine love, and that this love is asymmetrical. The qualification I placed on this intervention was that it could happen when, and only when, our human practices are *of the form which is love*. Any human practice which is of the form of love must presuppose mutual human consent, and thus what we, as human beings, call up by consent is that part of us which is one with God and is thus God. Justice, therefore, is consenting to God to have God made present in our human practices which are, themselves, of a form which is God's love, i.e. of a form of unconditional love, a love which we rarely, if ever, can recognise.

Let me try to illustrate this in another way, using two examples from Simone Weil. I believe these examples were used by her to make a different point than mine, but they may serve my concern to translate her uncommon idiom. The point I hope they will illustrate is that, while 'rights' always operates within a *horizontal symmetry* on a social scale, 'justice' operates within a *vertical asymmetry* on a cosmic scale.

The first illustration comes from 'Human Personality'. She says that the gram is inferior to the kilogram on the scales, then goes on to say:

But there can be a scales on which the gram outweighs the kilogram. It is only necessary for one arm to be more than a thousand times as long as the other. The law of equilibrium easily overcomes an inequality of weight. But the lesser will never outweigh the greater unless the relation between them is regulated by the law of equilibrium. (*SE* 33f.)

In relation to what I have called the cosmic scale, where human actions are related to divine love, the kilogram lies in the arena of human practice, and could only normally be balanced by a counter-weight on the social scale equal to it or overcome by a heavier weight. The gram, on the cosmic scale, however, is a non-material counter-weight – it is like the mustard seed or the pomegranate seed – and, when placed on the scales with the un-equal arm of supernatural justice, balance or equilibrium can be achieved. On this cosmis scale the asymmetry of God's love to our human action is evident. God, though unseen and not to be spoken of, can implicitly balance the scales on this earth through the genuine human practice of our unconditioned love to our fellow human beings.

Consider a second example. This comes from Simone Weil's essay, 'On Bankruptcy', written in 1937:

The payment of debts is necessary for social order. The non-payment of debts is quite equally necessary for social order. For centuries humanity has oscillated, serenely unaware, between these two contradictory necessities. Unfortunately, the second of them violates a great many seemingly legitimate interests and it has difficulty in securing recognition without disturbance and a measure of violence. (*SE*, 149)

The first (payment of debts), however, survives and it is considered scandalous to default on debts (see her example of Cephalus and Socrates, *SE* 148). Rights, it could be argued, rest on such balance of debts within society. To have a right to something, means that it cannot be taken away without equal compensation. Our courts of law are set up to oversee the enforcement of fair, if not equal, compensation. And it is necessary to social order that such balance is maintained.

But justice is not based on this symmetry of debt payment; it is, rather, based on the asymmetry of non-debt payment. One implication here is that sometimes debts must be cancelled or forgiven to maintain social order. If unfairness has resulted in gross imbalance, for example, between rich and poor, and the one who suffers from the unfairness cannot compensate loss, then to avoid revolt or risk further unfairness, a debt may be cancelled. (This has got the world economic community tangled up at present, owing to the enormous debts of poor nations to First-World banks and the inability, almost unthinkability, of the Western banks to write-off the debts. There is the growing awareness that such may be a necessity to survive globally. This, of course, is not an unconditioned forgiveness of debt, for the act of forgiveness is to preserve a possibly worse financial loss. It is, however, a kind of gratuitous act.) Simone Weil notes:

The revolt by which the Roman plebeians won the institution of the tribuneship had its origin in a widespread insolvency which was reducing more and more debtors to the condition of slavery; and even if there had been no revolt a partial cancellation of debts had become imperative, because with every plebeian reduced to a slave Rome lost a soldier. (*SE* 149)

There is a deeper sense to her notion of non-payment of debts regarding justice, however. This relates to the human scale of affliction where any notion of 'repayment' or 'compensation' seems totally meaningless (as in the case of the sexual violation of a woman, or of cruelty imposed by armed force to perpetuate fear). As we noted earlier with the case of the violated woman, what 'right' has been taken away and how could it be replaced? Or, in the second case, is repayment of cruelty to be some return of cruelty in kind?

The asymmetrical aspect of justice is created by the weight of necessity and how, given our equal vulnerability to misfortune, we all, at some time, bow our necks to force. This also means that we must all become acquainted with affliction, even to the point, as Weil suggests, of becoming slaves with no sense of rights whatsoever. Acquaintance here begins with attention – attention to things in the natural world, to school studies, and then to human beings through a succession of 'intervals of hesitation'. But it continues with love, that is, an unconditioned, non-compensatory act of compassion toward one who is afflicted. The human world, however, knows little of such unconditioned love, and thus the love has its source from outside the human world – it appears to be 'love from nowhere', a form of 'madness'. We can flatter ourselves that we will read a situation in the right way, says Weil, and thus act justly, but invariably we give a 'wrong reading of justice' leading to another exercise of our power (*GG* 122). 'Readings', she says – 'except where there is a certain quality of attention – obeys the law of gravity. We read the opinions suggested by gravity (the preponderant part played by the passions and by social conformity in the judgments we form of men and events). With a higher quality of attention our reading discovers gravity itself, and various systems of possible balance' (*GG* 122). And the 'system of possible balance' that we must look for in the case of bringing justice about lies outside the natural world. Simone Weil says:

Only by the supernatural working of grace can a soul pass through its own annihilation to the place where alone it can get the sort of attention which can attend to truth, and to affliction. It is the same attention which listens to both of them. *The name of this intense, pure, disinterested, gratuitous, generous attention is love.* (*SE* 28, my emphasis)

Balance or equilibrium here can neither be found in, nor function within, a social order. Rather it has its meaning in a larger cosmic order. The counterbalance to the weight of natural necessity is God's grace. For Simone Weil the model of such counterbalancing grace is the crucifixion. The cross represents the divine intersection with the world – our only pure example of an unconditioned love. The cross, in fact, is a sign of the Incarnation where God, having taken leave of the world to allow humans to act, re-enters by our consent. Here again, we have links with the concepts of 'decreation' and 'grace'.

The harmony and equilibrium that operates on the cosmic scale – a justice that embraces divine love – must recognise the asymmetry:

> that nothing in the world is the center of the world, that the center of the world is outside the world, that nothing here below has the right to say *I*. *One must renounce in favor of God*, through love for Him and for the truth, this illusory power which He has accorded us, to think in the first person. He has accorded it to us that it may be possible for us to renounce it by love. (*IC* 174, my emphasis)

Ultimately, then, justice is beyond human control, but it is also manifest within, and through, human action by attention and fellow-love. In this dual sense justice is possible within the world, but it is the supernatural virtue of justice that is manifest here. 'The criterion for those things which come from God', she says, 'is that they show all the characteristics of madness except for the loss of capacity to discern truth and love justice' (*FLN* 351). Our 'madness' from the perspective of the cosmic scale is *not* to recognise our limits and our abuse of power, and to read our actions as 'just' *by our own measures*. 'Madness' understood on the social scale is not to bow to power and risk becoming a slave. Simone Weil found few examples of how a human might understand justice as possible through human behaviour within the world. One that she did find compelling is in the Egyptian *Book of the Dead*, spoken by a soul on the way to salvation.

The model here for 'uncontaminated' justice – justice as far as is humanly possible – should show all the marks registered in *The Book of the Dead*:

> to show no scorn of God and to show reverence for the truth.
> to listen for and be attentive to words of right and truth.
> not to strike fear in any person.
> to make no person weep and let no one suffer hunger.
> to act without arrogance or expectation of favor.[18]

If we do these things, God's grace takes care of the rest.

This *new* virtue of justice, this supernatural virtue, understands the word 'justice' in the same way it understands 'God', 'truth',

---

[18] Cf. *SE*, 131f. and also *Letter to a Priest*, London: Routledge and Kegan Paul, 1953, p. 13f.

'beauty', and 'love'. These are words, says Simone Weil, which 'illumine and lift up toward the good'; they refer to 'an absolute perfection which we cannot conceive'; they are 'the image in our world of this impersonal and divine order of the universe' (*SE* 33f.). In another context she makes this very telling remark about these words of this 'impersonal and divine order'. 'Humanism was not wrong in thinking that [these words] are of infinite value, but in thinking that man can get them for himself without grace' (*SE* 53). To think we can get justice without grace is to remove the term from its divine order.

In her later reflections, Simone Weil goes so far as to say that there is 'no distinction between love of our neighbor and justice' (*WG* 139). In fact she says: 'Only the absolute identification of justice and love makes the coexistence possible of compassion and gratitude on the one hand, and on the other, of respect for the dignity of affliction in the afflicted' (*WG* 140). The important feature in what I am calling the asymmetrical aspect of justice is that, 'the supernatural virtue of justice consists of *behaving exactly as though there were equality* when one is the stronger in the unequal relationship' (*WG* 143, my emphasis). Thus, if you are in a position of power, or control, or wealth relative to another human being, there must be mutual consent between the parties, and the weaker party should in no way feel humiliated, or the stronger superior. The fact will remain, however, that the condition of inequality will persist by necessity. That is why a 'supernatural' virtue is required to bring about justice. 'In true love', says Weil:

it is not we who love the afflicted in God; it is God in us who loves them. When we are in affliction, it is God in us who loves those who wish us well. Compassion and gratitude come down from God, and when they are exchanged in a glance, God is present at the point where the eyes of those who give and those who receive meet. The sufferer and the other love each other, starting from God through God, but not for the love of God; they love each other for the love of the one for the other. This is an impossibility. That is why it comes about only through the agency of God. (*WG* 15)[19]

THE 'MADNESS' OF JUSTICE AND LOVE

Within the social scale, this higher justice requires a certain kind of 'madness', as Simone Weil notes – it requires thought and action

[19] Here is a perfect example of 'essential contradiction' being resolved in correlation as discussed by André Devaux in his essay, above.

that goes against the stream of the situation of power and oppression on the human level. When, within the social order, we take such contrary actions we are called 'mad'.

It is interesting to note here the way in which 'madness' is used by Simone Weil in light of the later and well-known view of Michel Foucault in his *Madness and Civilization*. Foucault differentiates (a) 'madness' as seen before 'the Renaissance', 'linked to the presence of imaginary transcendences' and ascribed to those who bore the 'stigmata' of coming 'from the world of the irrational', from (b) 'madness' in 'the classical age' – post his 'landmark' year of 1656 – where madness was perceived in a person because the person crossed 'the frontier of bourgeois order of his own accord, and alienate[d] himself outside the sacred limits of its ethic'.[20] It is clear that Simone Weil believed we must cross the frontiers of the current social order and ethics 'of our own accord', and also that we must alienate ourselves outside the bourgeois ethic, but 'madness' for her bore not the 'stigmata' of 'imaginary transcendences'; rather the 'stigmata' that her 'madness' bore was witness to God incarnate and crucified as love, the stigmata of the cross. Whereas Foucault's second madness, post 1656, is defined within a post-Renaissance secular context, Simone Weil combines and modifies his two notions to construe 'madness' as a concept which is out of 'sync' with our modern secular culture. Maybe hers is a 'postmodern' idea of madness, just as her idea of justice goes beyond our modern conceptions of justice.

Even though we may be deprived of consent 'in the depth of the heart' by all manner of 'privations of soul and body' (*SJ* 5), such privations must be challenged. Hope against hope, 'justice', she says, 'has as its object the exercise of the faculty of consent on earth. To preserve it religiously wherever it exists, to try to create conditions for it where it is absent, that is to love justice' (*SJ* 5). And she concludes, as was quoted earlier, 'To the extent to which at any given time there is some madness of love amongst men, to that extent there is some possibility of change in the direction of justice: and no further' (*SJ* 5).

Thus, when Simone Weil asks, 'Are we struggling for justice?' she is in essence asking us how 'mad' we are among our fellow human beings? And she answers: to the degree that we refuse harm doing

[20] Michel Foucault, in *The Foucault Reader*, edited by Paul Rabinow, London: Penguin Books, 1984, p. 136.

and prevent harm being done to other human beings (*SE* 31); to the degree that we resist all forms of evil and encourage conditions for the flourishing of the good; to the degree that we are willing to 'hurl' ourselves 'into risks'; and to the degree that we are grateful to God and love unconditionally we *are* mad and *are* engaged in the struggle for justice.

There are some clear and unequivocal examples of such 'madness', of true struggles for justice. One may think of Gandhi, or Martin Luther King jun., or Mother Theresa of Calcutta, but a most moving example shown through the lives of ordinary people is found in the story of the people of the village of Le Chambon-sur-Lignon, who, during World War II, placed themselves at risk out of gratitude to God and in unconditional love in order to save the lives of Jewish children.[21] They did so on their own accord and from the depths of their hearts, guided by the traditional aspirations of their religious faith – a belief in the Incarnate God of Jesus. Their actions were witness to what Simone Weil called 'the supreme and perfect flower of the madness of love'; they rekindled 'the smallest traces of ... the fragile earthly possibilities of beauty, of happiness and of fulfilment ... all with an equally religious care' (*SJ* 9).

Her programme for this struggle is, in the best sense *both pragmatic and idealistic* – hers is nothing short of a spiritual vision that would involve radical changes in the way we conceive of our social order and of our own human nature. She is quite explicit in what must be done in a just order. I conclude with remarks from her vision.[22]

What we need is something a people can love naturally from the depths of its heart, from the depths of its own past, out of its traditional aspirations, and not through suggestion, propaganda or foreign import ...

What we need is the forms of social life to be so devised as to remind the people incessantly in the symbolic language most intelligible to it, most in harmony with its customs, traditions and attachments, of the sacred character of this fidelity, the free consent from which it issues, the rigorous obligations arising from it ...

[21] See the account of this village's actions in Philip P. Hallie, *Lest Innocent Blood be Shed: The Story of the Village of Le Chambon and How Goodness Happened There*, Harper Torchbooks, New York: Harper and Row, Publishers, 1979.

[22] These passages from Simone Weil provide a suggestive pragmatic outline for the kind of transformation to a new civilisation of work detailed by Clare Fischer, above; for how we can 'root' ourselves within human community as discussed by Eric Springsted, above, and offer guidelines toward the 'new Renaissance' called for by H. L. Finch in his essay below.

We shall not find freedom, equality and fraternity without a renewal of our forms of life, a creativity within the social fabric, an eruption of new inventions . . .

What we need in addition is for the spirit of justice to dwell within us. The spirit of justice is nothing other than the supreme and perfect flower of the madness of love . . .

The madness of love draws one to discern and cherish equally, in all human milieux without exception, in all parts of the globe, the fragile earthly possibilities of beauty, of happiness and of fulfilment; to want to preserve them all with an equally religious care; and, where they are absent, to want to rekindle tenderly the smallest traces of those which have existed, the smallest seeds of those which can be born.

The madness of love imbues a part of the heart deeper than indignation and courage, the place from which indignation and courage draw their strength, with tender compassion for the enemy.

The madness of love does not seek to express itself. But it radiates irresistibly through accent, tone and manner, through all the thoughts, all words and all actions, in all circumstances and without any exception. It makes impossible those thoughts, words and actions through which it cannot radiate.

It truly is madness . . . But if the order of the universe is a wise order, there must sometimes be moments when, from the point of view of earthly reason, only the madness of love is reasonable. Such moments can only be those when, as today, mankind has become mad from want of love. (*SJ* 8–10)

CHAPTER 10

The spirit of Simone Weil's law[1]

Ronald K. L. Collins and Finn E. Nielsen

> It is the aim of public life to arrange that all forms of power are entrusted, so far as possible, to men who effectively consent to be bound by the obligation towards all human beings which lies upon everyone, and who understand the obligation.
>
> Law is the totality of the permanent provisions for making this aim effective. (*SE* 223)

Still wrestling with the philosophic side of existence, Simone Weil tried in the last year of her life to discover how 'the eternal and unconditional obligation "descends" or incarnates in this world' (*PR* 245). Could human obligation be expressed in a legal text? Could law – constitutional, statutory, and judicial – actually rearrange power without perpetuating its inhumane force? Could law serve the pursuit of truth in some authentic sense? Could penal laws ever be more than retaliatory? Could the keepers of the law, especially judges, be trusted to fix their 'attention' on a notion of justice rooted in human obligation? And finally, could law be made dialectical? Essentially, these were the questions with which the Free French philosopher grappled.

WEIL'S ENCOUNTER WITH LAW: THE PERSONAL AND POLITICAL CONTEXT

'Simone Weil's encounter with law was, on the whole, late, conjectural and finally rather brief' (*PR* 227). There are a handful of late writings with specific discussions of law, though she did not

---

[1] In addition to the standard abbreviations used throughout the text of this book, the following abbreviations will also be used in this essay:

SP Simone Pétrement, *Simone Weil: A Life*, trans. Raymond Rosenthal, New York: Pantheon, 1976;

PR Patrice Rolland, 'Simone Weil et le Droit', *Cahiers Simone Weil*, vol. 13:3 (September, 1990), p. 227.

regularly devote much ink to the subject. We shall, as we continue, identify and critique her essential writings on both the letter and the spirit of law, as well as various other law-related reports she drafted during the 1942–3 period of her life.[2]

Additionally, in her last years she wrote much about many things linked to law and legal systems. Consider, for example, her extended essays on liberty, rights, and obligations. Likewise, her conception of justice and her critique of oppression are practically and theoretically related to questions of law. Even her spirituality is, at some level, law-grounded in so far as the 'needs of the soul' are, of necessity, connected to law. From this vantage point, *The Need for Roots* – with its reflections and directives on liberty, obedience, judging, freedom of opinion, truth, and punishment, etc. – is a text penned in the light of law. The same holds true for her remarkable 1943 essay, 'Draft for a Statement of Human Obligations'.

At one point in a discussion of justice in her 'Human Personality' essay, also drafted in 1943, Weil flags the importance of law in the following grand way:

We must learn to distinguish between [the cries of the person ('why am I being hurt?') and those of personalism ('why has somebody else got more than I have?')] and to do all that is possible, as gently as possible, to hush the second one, *with the help of a code of justice, regular tribunals, and the police. Minds capable of solving this problem can be formed in a law school.* (*SE* 30, emphasis added)

The 'problem' to be solved here is nothing less than the puzzle of justice, in all its practical, political and transcendent forms. This crucial and largely overlooked passage – its message curiously directed to law students – suggests many conceptual relationships: i.e. between law and truth; law and liberty; law and equality; law and rights; law and obligations; law and punishment; and between law and the supernatural.

Between December of 1942 and April of 1943, this problem became increasingly pressing to Weil as she reflected on the state of affairs in her beloved France. Working for the fighting Free French Movement in London, Weil and others debated the question 'as to whether after the victory, the Vichy government, which had certain

---

[2] These reports dealt with: (1) 'responsibilities and sanctions for the mistakes committed by the French before the war, during the war, and under the Occupation'; (2) the 'bases for a statute regarding French non-Christian minorities of foreign origin'; and (3) the formation of a future party and the structure of government (*SP* 507–10).

elements of legality, should be supplanted in the normal manner or should be overthrown in order to re-establish true legality. This led to reflections on legitimacy' (*SP* 505).[3] And it was precisely this issue, what we might call the *crisis of legitimacy*, that became increasingly important to Weil in the last months of her life. It is not enough to talk or rhapsodise about '*légitimité*'. As Weil put it in her discussion of uprootedness:

> But giving a sentiment a name is not sufficient to call it to life. That is a fundamental truth that we are too apt to forget.
>   Why lie to ourselves? In 1939, just before the war, under the regime of decree laws, republican *légitimité* already no longer existed. It had departed like Villon's youth '*qui son partement m'a celé*,' noiselessly, without any warning, and without anyone having done or said anything to stop it. As for the feeling for *légitimité*, it was completely dead. (*NR* 180)

During the four months she spent at the Free French office on Hill Street, a 'worn out and tense' (*SP* 518) Weil wrote, among other things, night and day about the crisis of legitimacy. Acting in her official capacity, she focused on this problem when she reviewed and commented on various legal and political documents and reports prepared by Resistance committees in France. For example, she was asked to author a report on a draft for a new constitution prepared by the Commission for State Reform, a commission established by General de Gaulle. This report, entitled 'Remarks on the New Draft for a Constitution' (*EL* 85–92), was penned along with similar reports such as her 'Essential Ideas for a New Constitution' (*EL* 93–97), 'The Basis for Constitutional Reform' (*SP* 510), and 'The Legitimacy of the Provisional Government' (*LPG*).

These reports were wide-ranging and contained numerous comments on the Declarations of 1789 and 1793, the 1875 Constitution, and the Commission's proposals for change. This work prompted Weil to direct her attention to constitutional matters such as the structure of government and the separation of powers. Still, it was not a task executed in any mere technical or formulaic sense; rather, her discussion of these and related points was enveloped in a more philosophical analysis. The immediate crisis of legitimacy was a

---

[3] The immediate, but by no means sole, cause of this crisis was the question of whether or not the Constitution of the Third Republic was still in force in light of the changes wrought by the Vichy Regime. See generally David Thompson, *Democracy in France Since 1870*, London: Oxford University Press, 5th edn, 1969, pp. 213–15.

vehicle for examining an older crisis that had plagued the country since the Revolution.

Painting with a still broader brush, Weil dealt with the legitimacy question – often moving beyond constitutional law to statutory law, equity, and jurisprudence – on the larger canvas of the historical, cultural, philosophical, and spiritual points pertinent to the crisis of legitimacy. In her words: 'Seeing that we have, in fact, recently experienced a break in historical continuity, constitutional legality can no longer be regarded as having an historical basis; it must be made to derive from the eternal source of all legality' (*NR* 181). Against this backdrop, she approached the question of law and laws in two notable essays ('Human Personality' and 'Draft for a Statement of Human Obligations') and in *The Need for Roots*. In all of these works, constitutional and other, she was typically a stern critic of the existing French legal system.

Incredibly, maintained Weil, the political, legal, and educational systems of France had produced 'the degradation of the sentiment of justice' (*NR* 219) in the souls of the French. The legal system of the Third Republic, for example, was one of privilege, bureaucracy, corruption, and cruelty. As if to compound the problem of a relatively weak judicial system,[4] judicial advancement was grossly dependent on currying political favour. What judicial power there was, was arbitrarily exercised. Moreover, an arcane web of procedure increased the potential for injustice. The glory of 1789 had been entirely spent on a system at odds with fundamental fairness. It was this system of government and law to which Weil responded when she sketched the outlines of her own legal thought.

Weil's writings of this period, especially on law, were daring, provocative, and always fragmented. She herself once acknowledged that they tend to sound 'pretty fanciful, but [are] not' (*EL* 97). When Weil wrote on law for the Free French (and herself), she would not infrequently sacrifice precision for principle, clarity for commitment, and comprehensiveness for perspicacity. The strengths and shortcomings of these writings reflect the struggles

---

[4] In Weil's estimation, the courts of France had little if any meaningful power. For example, in her 'Remarks on the Proposed New Constitution' she wrote:

> [I]t is untrue that in the current system the courts constitute a power. There is no judicial power. The judges only automatically put into effect, with a margin of personal evaluation which in reality is very weak, what they are commanded to do by an informal mixture of texts handed down by the kings, the two empires and parliament, and stripped of any relationship with the spirit or the letter of the Declaration of 1789. (*EL* 87)

which engaged the 34-year-old Weil – struggles never confronted by the timid of her time.

FRAGMENTS AND COMMENTS

In what follows, we offer various fragments of Simone Weil's writings which deal with law in some explicit way.[5] A significant number of fragments appear in *The Need for Roots*, particularly in her discussions of liberty, obedience, freedom of opinion, and punishment. Accordingly, we have patterned this part of our essay after the fragmentary structure of Weil's thought.

Law and liberty

In the context of her discussion of liberty, Weil examines three law-related conditions necessary for liberty to be complete. They are: the forms of legal rules; the sources of the law; and the stability and number of legal rules of any political order. As to the first, the law's *forms*, she writes:

Rules should be sufficiently sensible and sufficiently straightforward so that any one who so desires and is blessed with average powers of application may be able to understand, on the one hand the useful ends they serve, and on the other hand the actual necessities which have brought about their institution. (*NR* 12–13)

From this statement emerges an idea of law that is: value-purposeful and not positivistic;[6] derived from the reality of necessity though quite different from the modern jurisprudence of Legal Realism; and, finally, a notion of law more akin to self-realisation in the classical sense than to self-representation in the modern sense.

    Beyond form, the *source* of the law is also crucial, both in origin and perception: Such rules 'should emanate from a source of authority which is not looked upon as strange or hostile, but loved as

---

[5] What little Weil wrote on law dwelled on constitutive and criminal law matters largely to the exclusion of the civil law. So far as *law* is concerned, we find virtually nothing in her writings about, say, civil liability, property, corporations or commercial transactions, etc. This is not to say that she did not have views on some of these topics, like, for example, her many observations on property. But those views never find any real legal expression in her works.

[6] In *The Need for Roots* Weil noted: '[O]bligation is not based upon any *de facto* situation, nor upon jurisprudence, customs, social structure, relative state of forces, historical heritage, or presumed historical orientation; for no *de facto* situation is able to create an obligation (*NR* 5).

something belonging to those placed under its direction' (*NR* 13). These rules of the regime are to be 'incorporated' into one's very 'being' (*NR* 13) and come, in time, to be accepted in much the same way that salutary habits of behaviour are accepted. Accordingly, while the source of the law is external, its process is more an internal one. Because this process is largely an internal one, it is vital that citizens *understand* their laws.[7]

According to this formula, arbitrary actions (unexplainable by definition) by lawmakers, jurists and/or executive officials, whether malevolent or benevolent, can never lay claim to real legitimacy. Moreover, this notion of law is, *at one level*, more horizontal than vertical, if only because it depends not on the sanctions of a powerful sovereign, but rather derives from a shared vision of the law which portrays superiors as symbols of the good.[8] Thus, '[l]iberty is the power of choice within the latitude left between the direct constraint of natural forces and the authority accepted as legitimate' (*SE* 225). The latter regulates (in the same kind of way that we regulate room temperatures) the domain of free choice. Generally speaking, nature compels whereas law counsels. Both, however, make demands upon the individual, but in significantly different ways.

Finally, laws may neither be erratic nor innumerable if they are to serve the goals of liberty: 'They should be sufficiently stable, general, and limited in number for the mind to be able to grasp them once and for all, and not find itself brought up against them every time a decision has to be made' (*NR* 13). Laws must not be so vague and numerous as to make this goal unobtainable. This is not simply to produce a due process of results, but more importantly to produce a *deliberative process* of fairness.

If the number of laws is to be confined, and if their meaning is to remain intelligible, certain things must follow. First, the regime

---

[7] In *Oppression and Liberty* Weil maintained:

True liberty is not defined by a relationship between desire and its satisfaction; but by a relationship between thought and action; the absolutely free man would be he whose every action proceeded from a preliminary judgment concerning the end which he set himself and the sequence of means suitable for attaining this end. (*OL* 85)

[8] In her account of 'hierarchism' in *The Need for Roots*, Weil noted:

Hierarchism ... is composed of a certain veneration, a certain devotion towards superiors, considered not as individuals, nor in relation to the powers they exercise, but as symbols. What they symbolize is that realm situated high above all men and whose expression in this world is made up of the obligations owed each man to his fellow men ... The effect of true hierarchism is to bring each one to fit himself morally into the place he occupies. (*NR* 19)

A related point, pertaining to dialectic, is made in André Devaux's essay, ch. 6 above.

cannot be a mass one (or a mass-oriented one) because the number of laws is at some point proportionate to the number of citizens. Second, law cannot be premised primarily on the rule of rights, either economic and/or civil, for such regimes must protect a plethora of claims. Special interest legislation and perpetual litigation – two hallmarks of the regime of rights – are an anathema to Weil. Third, and related, Weil's general notion of constitutive and statutory law appeals more to principles than to particulars. That is, if such rules are to be kept limited in number, lawmakers must resist the process of micro-contextualised legislation that attempts to suit law to a myriad of events. Lastly, citizens must play an active role in the legal process, rather than abandoning the process to professional rulers.[9]

There is yet another explanation, adds Weil, why the number of constitutive and statutory laws ought to be fixed: 'There is no reason at all why the sovereignty of the law should be limited to the field of what can be expressed in legal formulas, since that sovereignty is exercised just as well by judgments in equity' (*NR* 26).

This statement seems at odds with what we have just examined. That is, why would Weil press for sufficiently straightforward laws, limited in number, and then defend the open-ended rule of an ever-changing law of equity? At least two answers are possible. First, there is indeed a contradiction here – one that simply must be accepted.[10] Writing in her Marseilles notebooks, Weil said the following about the value of contradiction and its relation to law:

Bad union of opposites (bad because fallacious) is that which is achieved on the same plane as the opposites. Thus the granting of domination to the oppressed. In this way we do not get free from the oppression–domination cycle.

The right union of opposites is achieved on a higher plane. *Thus the opposition between domination and oppression is smoothed out on the level of the law –* which is balance. (*GG* 91, emphasis added)

---

[9] See e.g. Gabriella Fiori, *Simone Weil: An Intellectual Biography*, trans. Joseph R. Berrigan, Athens, GA: University of Georgia Press, 1989, p. 361, n. 20 (discussing Weil's views on popular referenda, which – in the words of the biographer – are always 'preceded by a long period of reflection and discussion').

[10] See generally *FLN* 134 ('Contradiction is the lever of transcendence.'); *GG* 89 ('The contradictions the mind comes up against – these are the only realities: they are the criterion of the real. There is no contradiction in what is imaginary. Contradiction is the test of necessity.'). See also André Devaux's discussion of 'transforming contradiction into correlation,' in ch. 6 above.

Applied to the issue at hand, the law-as-limited versus law-as-open-ended contradiction cannot be overcome on the plane of positive law. Rather, only when law becomes transcendent – when it rises above itself – can these two opposites coexist in a way salutary to the soul. Any blind and mechanical system of law, like Marx's systematic materialism, cannot resolve the contradiction, but can only give the allusion of having done so. And this, for Weil, is an illegitimate use of contradiction. (See André Devaux's essay, above.)

Second, perhaps the two points may be reconciled with one another, but in a slightly different way. For example, since the principles of law must be knowable to all, law's particular application, of necessity, depends on its interpretation by courts of equity. Put differently, there needs to be a certain domain (constitutional and perhaps statutory) where the principle, and maybe even the formula, of the law must typically be rendered in a clear and concise manner. Beyond that realm, however, the fair application of the law depends on flexibility, on a judge[11] seeing past law's letter to life's context. Thus, Weil was highly critical of the French Code, which she felt 'stripped Justice of its majesty' (*EL* 152). For her, the declared law serves as a *guide*, while equity declares the law of a given case.[12] In this latter regard the judge must pay particular attention to the needs (physical and spiritual) of those before the court. That is why '[h]uman attention alone', Weil wrote in her last notebook, is essential to the legitimate 'exercise [of] the judicial function' (*FLN* 351). This means, in Weilian terms, black-robed officials of state suspending their thought, keeping it detached, while waiting for it to be penetrated by the reality of those who come before the bench of justice (see Richard Bell's essay, above).

Law and obedience

Obedience, both to rules and rulers, is a vital need and a corollary to liberty. Yet this need is profoundly denied whenever laws turn obedience into any form of involuntary servitude. In Weil's legal lexicon, as elsewhere, the key word here is *consent* (see the essays by Clare Fischer, Richard Bell, and Eric Springsted, above). Obedi-

---

[11] There remains as well the area of regulatory or administrative law.
[12] See *SP* 507 ('they must always judge with equity. For them the law should only serve as a guide.').

ence 'presupposes consent, not in regard to every single order received, but the kind of consent that is given once and for all ...' (*NR* 14). The 'sole reservation, in case of need', she added, was that 'the demands of conscience be satisified' (*NR* 14). Again, the consent is to principles more than to particulars.

What in some countries are called 'technical' defences have no place in this legal order. This is *not* because there is some sovereign ruler who may break the rules *carte blanche*, or because individual liberty is at the mercy of the governing mob. When the consent is to principles, the idea is constantly to reaffirm their role in life's everyday affairs. Why, in other words, does the wearer of the ring of Gyges[13] (be he president or plumber) not steal and rape? To ask this question is categorically different from asking whether there was an infraction of the letter of a given positive law or judicial precedent. Similarly, it is to reject the idea that law may be dispensed with when utility makes it convenient to do so.

Consent, the 'mainspring of obedience', is not to be confused with 'fear of punishment or hope of reward' (*NR* 14). We will turn to the topic of punishment later. As to the hope of reward, note that Weil refuses to cast law in a 'cost-benefit', Adam Smith-like manner; and for much the same reason she does not hold law out as a utilitarian reward mechanism. The whole idea of law as something bartered or contracted for is foreign to her.[14] Additionally, and in rather cryptic terms, Weil declared: 'Those who encourage a state of things in which the hope of gain is the principal motive take away from men their obedience, for consent, which is its essence, is not something which can be sold' (*NR* 14).[15] Citizens need to comprehend in a full and fair sense *why* they must obey laws and not just that they must do so. Without this, one might do the 'right' thing for the wrong reason, for example in the same way that a jogger defeats her exercise programme by taking a short cut to reach her *goal*, which is not really a particular site, but rather a physical state. Again, more than

---

13 For Weil's comments on this matter, see, for example, *N* II, 348.
14 See generally Finn Nielsen, *The Political Vision of Simone Weil*, unpublished Ph.D. dissertation, University of California at Santa Barbara, 1976, p. 102 (Simone Weil rejected the idea that 'rights and obligations are ... on the same level and implicitly rejected recourse to the idea of a contract as an explanation of establishing a social or political order'). In Springsted's essay, above, he discusses the relationship of rights to obligation in a slightly different manner.
15 In her London notebook, Weil wrote: 'today, if a man sold himself as a slave to another, the contract would be juridically invalid, because liberty, being sacred, is inalienable' (*FLN* 346).

results count here. Law, properly realised, allows citizens to synchronise their actions with the rule of necessity;[16] hence, in a Weilian sense, obedience through law has an all-important (and unexpected) transformative quality. This in turn may suggest something akin to natural law,[17] but a natural law decisively *not* Aristotelian or Thomistic in character.[18]

Law and freedom of opinion

Of the fourteen needs of the soul listed in *The Need for Roots*, Simone Weil devoted the most space to the entries on 'freedom of opinion' and 'truth'. The latter, she tells us, 'is more sacred than any other need' (*NR* 37), whereas the former is an 'absolute need on the part of the intelligence' (*NR* 23).[19] The need for either is not, however, synonymous with that constitutive right of freedom of expression as known, for example, in the United States. There are crucial differences: (1) for Weil, freedom of opinion is absolute, but only while in the service of a single value; (2) freedom of opinion and association are importantly different, and thus enjoy different claims to legal protection; (3) there is a corresponding *duty* of the state to suppress certain kinds of expression; and (4) special courts must be created to dispense justice on these matters, even though precise *judicial* definition may be impossible. Collectively, these characteristics are far more radical than their American counterparts, both in affirming such constitutional protections and in withholding them.

Absolute legal protection for freedom of opinion has never won the approval of the high tribunals of France, Great Britain, Canada, and the United States, among others. Still, for Weil, who delighted in her Sundays in Hyde Park,[20] a certain category of speech may never be abridged by the state. For Weil, the essential reason for protecting such expression is to advance the development of the

[16] Stressing much the same point, Weil noted that '[p]erfect liberty cannot be conceived as consisting merely in the disappearance of that necessity whose pressure weighs continually upon us ...' (*OL* 84) Obedience to just laws serves as a salutary reminder that liberty cannot be unlimited.

[17] See generally *PR* 242 ('In a certain sense she may have reproduced the notion of natural law under a new name.').

[18] See e.g. *NR* 243–4 (highly critical of Thomistic thought).

[19] See also Simone Weil, *Letter to a Priest*, trans. A. F. Wills, NY: Putnam, 1954, p. 62 ('Complete liberty within its own sphere is essential to the intelligence.').

[20] In March of 1943, Weil wrote to her parents: 'I spend hours ... watching people listen[ing] to orators. [Perhaps] this is the last remaining trace in ... the world ... of the discussions of the Athenian Agora ... (*SL* 181).

intellect. Any speech which furthers this end in a meaningful way cannot be governed by the state. Accordingly, Athens acted illegitimately when it tried and sentenced Socrates; and contemporary regimes do likewise whenever they squelch truth-seeking discourse in the name of some so-called security interest.

The key idea here is this: 'There has been a lot of freedom of thought over the past few years, but no thought' (*NR* 33). How can this be? One answer is that modern Western culture has over-emphasised *freedom* while de-emphasising *thought*. From Weil's perspective, this is explainable in two ways: First, the power of intrinsically meaningless words, as she observed in a trenchant 1937 essay,[21] has taken a free and deadly hold in the political and cultural realms. Words like 'capitalism' or 'communism' or even today's 'feminist' or 'environmentalist', for example, tend to shut off real thought; these and other 'ism' or 'ist' words stupefy people more than they inspire deliberation. In fact, that is exactly their political mission. Second, and related, is the problem of propaganda in all its many forms. Propaganda, as Weil explained it, was akin to expression intended to influence *action* rather than to prompt *thought*.[22] Such expression, be it in political or literary form, conveys information in such a way as to lead its audience to believe that it can be certain about things without engaging the mind. To borrow from Weil's writings on science, we might call this 'quantum' communication (*SNLG* 49, 58, 63).

Freedom of opinion and association were importantly different for Weil, and the penal law should treat them so. Unlike the constitutions of several modern nations, Weil urged us to separate the domain of these two rights. Again, why?

When people attempt to speak as a group or political party, which is the rule in today's society, the threat of uniformity, collective imagination, group pressure, coercion, and/or propaganda is usually so great as to close off even the opportunity for real freedom

---

[21] See *SE* 154 ('[W]hen empty words are given capital letters, then, on the slightest pretext, men will begin shedding blood for them and piling up ruin in their name, without effectively grasping anything to which they refer ...' She continued: 'To clarify thought, to discredit the intrinsically meaningless words, and to define the use of others by precise analysis – to do this, strange though it may appear, might be a way of saving human lives.').

[22] Given Weil's strong reservations about public expressions which convey a conviction about some truth, it seems odd that she selected the phrase 'freedom of *opinion*' rather than the phrase 'freedom of *thought*', which she also used but less frequently.

of thought (*NR* 27–33; and Martin Andic's essay, above).[23] '[I]n the domain of thought', said Weil, 'there should never be any physical or moral pressure exerted for any purpose other than the exclusive concern for truth' (*SE* 225). Of course, this critique of collectivities tracks what Weil said about the corruption of language through meaningless words and propaganda. Thus, political parties are the prime offenders when it comes to subverting the search for truth. Hence, 'no group should be permitted by law to express an opinion' and political parties should be abolished (*NR* 27).

Consistent with what has been presented here, the more that any expression moves away from the pursuit of truth and towards the *persuasion* of the public, the more it may be treated as conduct and regulated proportionate to any harm it inflicts on the citizenry. Most of what appears in the popular press, and some of what passes as literature, would fall into this category of limited protection. In all likelihood, publications such as Thomas Paine's *The Age of Reason* (1794) and Camille Paglia's *Sexual Personae* (1990) would be entitled to even less protection, if any. Above all, this secondary level of freedom of opinion must never, directly or indirectly, deny the 'eternal obligations toward the human being, once these obligations have been solemnly recognized by law' (*NR* 24). Thus, 'race-hate' speech, for example, would be unprotected.

In order to prevent 'offenses against the truth' (*NR* 38), propaganda of all kinds needs to be outlawed. This would be done by injunction (prior and/or post-restraints of the press) and, if necessary, by criminal sanctions. Finally, group or associational communication could be regulated depending on the extent to which the association allowed for actual freedom of opinion within its ranks, and on the extent to which the group pressed for the real *needs* of its members instead of acting as an agent for the collective appetite (*NR* 32–33).

And just how is all of this 'repression' (Weil's word, *NR* 26) to be done in a manner that comports with basic fairness? – especially where, as she adds, a 'juridical definition is impossible' (*NR* 26). The answer depends, in good measure, on Weil's understanding of judicial justice.

---

[23] She added: 'What has been called freedom of association has been, in fact, up to now, freedom for associations. But associations have not got to be free; they are instruments, they must be held in bondage. Only the human being is fit to be free' (*NR* 33).

Law and judging

There is an office of the state whose object is justice: this is the judicial office. (*EL* 152)

'The faith of a judge is not seen in his behavior at church, but in his behavior on the bench' (*FLN* 146). This statement, entered in her New York notebook, might suggest that, for Weil, the divide between the judicial and the spiritual was (or should be) great. Quite the contrary. As has been said earlier, her notion of attention is extricably linked to her idea of judicial justice (*FLN* 351). Thus, the members of the 'special courts' instituted to protect the public from 'offences against the truth' had to be

drawn from very different social circles; be naturally gifted with a wide, clear, and exact intelligence; and be trained in a school where they receive *not just a legal education but above all a spiritual one*; and only secondarily an intellectual one. They must be accustomed to love truth. (*NR* 40, emphasis added)[24]

This represented the paradigm of the Weilian jurist. But beyond this elevated notion of the judiciary, or at least the judiciary as reflected in her special courts, Weil also saw the judicial role in more general constitutive terms. Thus, in her 'Essential Ideas for a New Constitution' she envisioned a very active judiciary with a key role to play in the affairs of the state. Judicial constitutional review of legislative enactments was essential. Only by this mechanism could 'governmental and citizen compliance with the Fundamental Declaration' of the country be assured (*SP* 506). For this reason, the requirement of a case (an actual controversy between two parties) could be dispensed with, and a judge could raise a point of fundamental law on his or her own motion (*SP* 506). Broadly speaking, maintains Patrice Rolland, this is a 'true "government of judges" that she is creating' (*PR* 250).

Perhaps the best single statement of Weil's thinking on the judiciary and its role in society is set out in her London report, 'Essential Ideas for a New Constitution', where she noted:

Judges must have much more of a spiritual, intellectual, historical education than a juridical one (the strictly legal domain should only be retained in relation to unimportant things); they [judges] should be much,

---

[24] See also *SP* 507 (quoting Weil's 'Essential Ideas for a New Constitution' report: 'Judges must have much more of a spiritual, intellectual, historical, and social education than a juridical one ...').

much more numerous; they must always judge with equity. For them the law should only serve as a guide. This should also apply to previous judgments [judicial precedents].

But there should be a special court to judge the judges, and it should dispense extremely severe punishments.

The legislators should also be able to summon before a court chosen from among their fellow members any judge guilty, in their eyes, of having violated the spirit of the laws. (*EL* 95)[25]

This lone statement reveals much about Weil's conception of the judiciary and the judicial role. Her judges are hierarchical[26] public figures who serve as one of the key moral voices of the community. Thus '[t]hey would be responsible for', among other things, 'publicly condemning any avoidable error ... in a printed text or radio broadcast' (*NR* 38, 39). In fact, so great is their position in this new constitutional order that she provided that they be the ones to choose the President (from among the highest judges), who would in turn select a Prime Minister (*EL* 96).

Weil's judges are certainly not restrained in a way subservient or largely deferential to majoritarian will, even when that will is expressed in direct or representative legislation. Commenting on a draft constitution prepared by De Gaulle's Commission for State Reform, she noted:

What do the words 'representation of the majority and the opposition' signify? It is the introduction of political passions in their most arbitrary form, the least legitimate, in an official capacity, into what should be the seat of impartiality. If three men are there in their quality of representatives of the majority they will consider themselves obliged to speak in terms of this quality and not according to the unique light of their conscience. (*EL* 88)

In Weil's legal universe the positive law is only a 'guide' for judges. Her judges are in some ways policy makers, lawmakers, law executors, and law interpreters all in one. Accordingly, in Weil's. society their number should be enhanced considerably. While judges are to assume an active role in the community's affairs, similar to the one exercised by country priests, neither their presence nor number is intended to foster excessive litigation of the kind so

[25] See also 'Remarks on the New Constitution' (*EL* 87): 'There can only be judicial power if: 1. the judges receive a spiritual formation; 2. it is accepted that judgment in *equity*, inspired by the Fundamental Declaration, is the normal form in judgment.'

[26] See discussion under 'Law and liberty' section, above.

popular in America. For such litigiousness is born out of a regime of rights, which Weil strongly opposed. Rather, judges were to act as mediators concerned with mutual obligations, and as cultural and spiritual mentors concerned with the common good.

This middle ground is made possible by the rule of equity. For Weil, the concept of equity – as discounted by Creon in Sophocles' *Antigone* – is central. It is this vast and fluid rule of law that permits her to discount standard legal formulas, judicial precedent, and even the idea that juridical definition is possible in the abstract (*NR* 24, 26). What this means, at least in the context of her 'special courts' presiding over speech crimes, is the possibility of partisan or even arbitrary rule.[27] Furthermore, the broad sweep of such legal power would undoubtedly have a 'chilling effect' on the dissemination of all forms of public information.

How, then, does one prevent unjust usurpations of judicial power? Clearly, the need to guard against such abuses is even greater when one considers the power of Weil's judges to try the Prime Minister,[28] sentence the President to death once he or she is duly removed from office (*SP* 506), and to sentence writers to 'prison or hard labor for [any] repeated commission' of offences against the truth, 'aggravated by proven dishonesty of intention' (*NR* 38). Then there is an even more sweeping power, namely, their duty to punish[29] '*everything which is evil*' (*EL* 95).

Weil hoped to curb the potential for such abuses of power and coercion in three key ways: first, by the judicial selection process; second, by an oversight process consisting of a special court to 'judge the judges' aided by a legislative check on judicial rule; and, finally, by 'severe' sanctions against any jurist who violated his or her sworn duties. As for the chilling effect on public expression, it is probably something Weil generally saw as a social good. After all, 'in every area', J. P. Little reminds us, 'she wanted to make people responsible for their words and actions, and the more power they exercise, the more responsibility they must show'.[30]

---

27 See e.g. *NR* 40 ('But, it will be objected, how can we guarantee the impartiality of the judges?'); J. P. Little, *Simone Weil: Waiting on Truth*, Oxford: Berg, 1988, p. 89 ('some of the distinctions she makes seem somewhat arbitrary').

28 'The Prime Minister, at the end of his five year term of office – if he has completed it without difficulty – would automatically pass before a High Court of Justice to give an account of his actions.' 'Essential Ideas for a New Constitution' (*EL*, 97).

29 See also *EL* 157 ('*Judicial mission*. Remove a man from his surroundings, put him in a center or intensely spiritual atmosphere, have him judged 3, 5 years, return him home.').

30 J. P. Little, *Waiting on Truth*, p. 90.

Law and punishment

'[W]e have lost all idea of what punishment is' (*SE* 31), argued Weil. She was highly critical of the retributive form of penal justice (the rule of fear) that had long been the norm in the Republic of France. '[R]epressive' (*SE* 31), 'irresponsible conduct' (*NR* 21) was how she characterised the penal law as formulated by the parliament and exercised by the police, courts, and prison officials. For her, they did no more than inflict *meaningless* suffering while failing to dispense *uplifting* punishment (see the essay by J. P. Little, above). Weil decried the inherent abuses of the system to the point that she found it virtually 'impossible for there to exist among us, in France, anything that deserves the name of punishment' (*NR* 22). Writing in her notebooks, she could not contain her outrage:

The apparatus of penal justice has been so contaminated with evil, after all the centuries during which it has, without any compensatory purification, been in contact with evil-doers, that a condemnation is very often a transference of evil from the penal apparatus itself to the condemned man; and that is possible even when he is guilty ... Hardened criminals are the only people to whom the penal apparatus can do no harm. It does terrible harm to the innocent. (*GG* 65)

The French penal system, as she saw it, was bankrupt in conception and corrupt in execution. Accordingly, her critique and recommendations were conceptual and constitutional in nature.

Above all, crime is a malady of the soul (*FLN* 140). Unless one understands this, it is impossible to comprehend how punishment represents an essential need of the human soul. Crime is a turning away from the good (why would anyone commit a crime if not for some spiritual malfunction?) and a corresponding renunciation of one's fundamental obligations towards others. Punishment, then, is a vital 'method of procuring pure good for men who do not desire it' (*SE* 31).[31] Because of some 'affliction' (*SE* 32) or disorder in the soul, the desire for the good is dormant. If this condition is to be cured, punishment must awaken 'in a criminal, by pain or even death, the desire for pure good' (*SE* 31).[32] In this way, punishment is thera-

---

[31] See also *NR* 20 ('Crime alone should place the individual who has committed it outside the social pale, and punishment should bring him back again inside it.').

[32] In an unpublished 1943 Free French report, Weil wrote:

Any punishment that is not, in regard to the culprit, a proof of respect is a worse crime than that committed by the criminal. It clearly follows that the punishment must aim, sooner or

peutic,[33] not retributive;[34] its value depends on attentive consent, not on passive submission. Ultimately, punishment, if truly legitimate, gives more than it takes. Without this, punishment is more than a failure – it is institutionalised terror. On this basic point Weil is emphatic:

> If one judges a criminal to be incurable, one has no right to punish him; one ought only to prevent him from doing harm. The infliction of a punishment is a declaration of faith that in the depths of the guilty there is a grain of pure good.
>
> To punish without that faith is to do evil for evil's sake. (*FLN* 345)

But the criminal justice system is antithetical to even the idea of such a declaration. Judges, for example, preoccupied with formulaic justice (i.e. the letter of the law or the rule of precedent) or pledged to retribution, desecrate the individual in the name of some perverse sense of justice. In the hands of such a judge, punishment can no longer affirm hope in the individual, it can only deny it systematically.

In matters of sentencing, penalties should not only reflect the nature of the crime, but also the *power* of the person who committed it. Weil called for a 'conception of punishment in which social rank, as an aggravating circumstance, would necessarily play an important part in deciding what the penalty was to be' (*NR* 17). This equality principle was not based on any formal equality of charges or uniformity of sentencing. Quite the opposite, for according to this principle equality recognises the 'inevitable differences between men', but never allows those differences to 'imply any difference in the degree of respect' (*NR* 16). For Weil, the concept of proportionality is necessarily tied to the concept of equality, particularly in criminal law.

At some important level, a person's obligations correspond to that person's power. Here too, the focus is on the individual. When a member of parliament or the president of a big corporation steals, it

---

later, at evoking in the guilty man a movement of the soul that will lead him to recognize that the punishment is just and to submit to it freely. (Quoted in *SP* 508)

33 See generally *N* 3 ('Punishment. [I]f there is to be a cure for sin, punishment must not be considered an affliction. A painful experience, yes, certainly. A breaking in. What sort of a breaking in?'); see also *FLN*, 332 ('[C]riminals ... should be cured by a hard and laborious but healthy and happy open-air life in unpopulated country, where they would be employed ... And only when cured, if they feel the need of it, should they be made to suffer.').

34 See *SE* 32 ('All talk of chastisement, punishment, retribution, or punitive justice nowadays always refers solely to the basest kind of revenge').

can never be treated the same as when a factory worker or waiter steals, notwithstanding the amounts taken. The former, given their social and economic stations, have greater obligations. (Criminal law, in Weilian terms, operates as sort of an *honour* code, where punishment mirrors the extent of one's public esteem.) Therefore, the 'severity of the punishment must ... be in keeping with the kind of obligation which has been violated, and not with the interests of security' (*NR* 21). The last point, societal security, shows how far Weil is willing to steer away from any utilitarian conception of criminal justice and move instead towards a conception grounded in individual responsibility. Correcting crime first and foremost means striving to correct the moral disorder within the individual. Everything else is secondary (*NR* 6–7).

SOME PRELIMINARY CONCLUSIONS

In a larger sense, what practical and theoretical conclusions do these fragments on law suggest?

Above all, law is a means for transforming the power of arbitrary rule into a system oriented towards the recognition and realisation of human needs, physical and spiritual. Integral to this idea is Weil's notion of obligation. Since her concept of obligation is two-dimensional, law serves both temporal and transcendental purposes (*NR* 6–7). As to the latter, law is also one means, along with education, whereby the 'reality *outside* of this world' might be implanted within the reality of *this* world. From this vantage point, law is not an end in itself; rather, it points beyond itself.

What are the (inevitable?) consequences of attempting to combine these two realities? Do they pose a clear and present danger to our tolerant and liberal pluralist society? Are they perforce a formula for tyranny? Connor Cruise O'Brien's words suggest a possible answer:

A France reconstructed on Weilian lines ... would have no political parties, no trade unions, no freedom of association. It would have had a rigid, primitive, and eccentric form of censorship – one that would permit Jacques Maritain to be punished for having said something misleading about Aristotle ... There would be liberty, or something so described, coming second after 'order' and just before 'obedience' among the needs of the soul, but guarantees of this liberty are in no way indicated.[35]

[35] Connor Cruise O'Brien, 'The Anti-Politics of Simone Weil', *The New York Review of Books*, 12 May 1977, 24:8, p. 23; reprinted in *Simone Weil: Interpretations of a Life*, edited by George

But the spectre of *this* tyranny is not the only one. That is, what of the tyranny of a tolerant and liberal pluralist society? For example, its 'tolerance' incapacitates it in the face of the tyrannical power of words – those words that condemn people and nations to death. Its 'liberality' allows for the image of *freedom* of thought in the absence of any genuine *thought*, or perhaps even the possibility of such. Is community possible in a regime obsessed with rights? Moreover, this pluralist society is virtually helpless to combat the tyranny of moral reductionism, and moral relativism. It is precisely because of this, one might add, that the 'tolerant' society unavoidably turns away from a rehabilitative ideal of penal justice to a retributive one. And, ultimately, there is a deeper philosophical, political, and legal question confronting modern liberals: Can liberty, in any of these senses, *actually* amount to freedom from restriction?[36]

The latter kind of tyranny, as much as the one described in O'Brien's charge, was of great concern to Simone Weil. In her own way she declared war on the various modern forms of tyranny, and likewise challenged the premise of liberty as the absence of any restraint. But in doing so she was not altogether unmindful of the potential for tyranny in her own ideal regime. That is why she stressed the importance of *attention* as an essential prerequisite for the exercise of judicial power; of *consent* as a necessary precondition for genuine punishment; and the value of a legal order rooted in a concept of *obligation*. Without these preconditions, judicial rule disintegrates into arbitrariness; punishment collapses into brutality; and law crumbles into brute force. Weil seemed astutely aware of these facts. On an even more pragmatic plane, she realised that her 'pretty fanciful' ideas might only come into existence 'after one or two generations' and would likewise require many 'transitional stages' (*EL* 97, 96).

Given all of these preconditions, is the legal order Weil described realisable in *this* world? We answer 'no', but with an explanation. For one thing, the obvious incompleteness of her writings in this area

---

A. White, Amherst: University of Massachusetts Press, 1981, p. 96. For one response, see Mary G. Dietz, *Between the Human and the Divine*, New Jersey: Rowman and Littlefield, 1988, pp. 181–5.

[36] See generally Lawrence A. Blum and Victor J. Seidler, *A Truer Liberty: Simone Weil and Marxism*, London: Routledge, 1989, pp. 84–8 ('Liberty understood as freedom from any restriction – the core of the liberal conception of freedom – is a fantasy, for it has no connection with the real conditions of human existence and therefore, Weil insists, can have no value or meaning.').

would alone render their application highly problematic, if not preposterous. For another thing, since so much of what Weil wrote was paradoxical and contrary to contemporary opinion, her 'foolish' message is likely to be seen as deserving not 'the slightest attention' (*SL* 200). Still, the transformative potential of her outsider's words (about law, labour, education, and politics, etc.) inheres in its generative capacity to stimulate new and bold thought, while at the same time offering some conceptual criteria by which to critique the status quo. Consistent with this, Weil insisted on no more than that her readers ask always: 'Is what she says true?' (*SL* 201).

Weil attempted to employ law so as to safeguard the individual, not by a regime of rights, but by one of obligations (see also the essay by Eric Springsted, above). On this score, her thought is radically different from the conception of law advanced by modern liberals. She defended the individual in ways that today's liberals simply have not. Equally telling, since her notion of law is rooted in the individual, it is a notion far different from the one championed by contemporary defenders of civic republican rule. Moreover, Weil openly criticised the collectivity in ways that defenders of civic republican thought have not. The crossing back and forth over this ideological divide is puzzling. Combining concerns about the individual (think liberal rule) with the notion of obligation (think civic republican rule) is, from a modern perspective, more than paradoxical – it is outright contradictory.

In assessing Weil's legal (and political) thought, it is useful to reflect on how she works with, and sometimes through, this apparent contradiction. For example, on the question of freedom of opinion she calls for certain absolute protections of individual liberty. This smacks of the liberal order. But she then goes on to stress, among other things, that freedom of opinion must never, directly or indirectly, deny the 'eternal obligations toward the human being, once these obligations have been solemnly recognized by law' (*NR* 24). This smacks of the civic republican order. Consider, by way of another illustration, her thoughts on law and obedience. On the one hand, she identifies consent (again, think liberal) as the key factor of legitimate order. On the other hand, she rejects the idea of law as bartered, and links the notion of obedience with that of obligations owed to the person (again, think civic republican).

Weil's notion of *community* is rooted in the *individual*, and vice-versa. Conceptually speaking, is this possible? Functionally speaking, how is this to be done? For the purposes of this essay, we can no more than sketch a few introductory and incomplete answers to these questions:

1 Dismantle the regime of rights; furthermore, arrange all forms of power so as to comport with human needs;
2 attempt to bridge the gap between the two realms; the notion of obligation can serve as one such bridge. In principle, the idea is to establish a reciprocal relation between the individual and the community;
3 redefine the public notion of hierarchy (for example in government, business, and social life); away from status by privilege and power and towards rank seen as a reflection of the magnitude and weight of burdens and risks assumed; and
4 formulate a structure of law compatible with rule by principles; principles which find expression at every level from the constitutional preamble down to the local court practice.[37]

Though somewhat tempered by a separation of powers principle, the judiciary is the bright star in Weil's constellation. Her judges are rather similar in practice to Plato's 'custodians of the law';[38] and, to some degree, the role of her special court judges is analogous in principle to that of the 'nocturnal council'[39] in Plato's *Laws*. What does such a vision of the judiciary imply?

Potentially, the judiciary may well be the most deliberative of the branches of government. Not surprisingly, this potential accounted for Weil's preference for the judicial institution. Moreover, the judiciary is typically the least democratic of the branches. So far as an antidote to rule by the collectivity, her judges needed to be above the reach of the crowd. Beyond this, Weil's trust in rule-by-judges reflects a real scepticism of both *executive power* and *legislative capacity*.

[37] Of course, still other key concepts are relevant to this general inquiry, concepts such as Weil's notion of tradition (see the essay by Eric Springsted, above).
[38] See Plato, *The Laws* 632c in *Plato: The Collected Dialogues*, edited by Edith Hamilton and Huntington Cairns, Princeton, NJ: Princeton University Press, 1963) (dialogue trans. by A. E. Taylor), p. 1233 ('When the lawmaker has completed his discovery he will set over the whole system a body of guardians endowed some with wisdom, some with true beliefs, to the end that intelligence may knit the whole into one, and keep it in subjection to sobriety and justice, not to wealth or self-seeking'). See also Paul Friedländer, *The Dialogues: Second and Third Periods*, trans. by Hans Meyerhoff, Princeton, NJ: Princeton University Press, 1969, III, pp. 440–3.
[39] See Plato, *The Laws* 951d sq., 961a sq.; see also Paul Friedländer, note directly above, vol. 3, pp. 441–3; *PR* 251 (Weil's judges remind us of the nocturnal council).

Recall, her judges are also policymakers and lawmakers. Drinking at once from the three fountains of power, her officially robed custodians possess the strength that 'James Joyce and his hero mediated upon: "to forge within the smithy of my soul the uncreated conscience of the race".'[40] But what if actualising their consciences means producing results comparable to Chief Justice Roger Taney's 1856 ruling legitimising the institution of American slavery? Weil's answer moves along two tracks: first, their character and backgrounds, as discerned in the selection process,[41] would most likely prevent such occurrences; and second, such transgressions, if they did occur, would be met with 'severe' punishment, presumably even the death penalty. But given their immense power, is this enough?

Neither the majesty nor fairness of the law can reside in a black-letter text detached from the realities of the person. 'Laws are texts', she said, 'characterized by a rather large generality, with the intent of serving as *guides* . . . for the government . . . [as well as] for judges' (*EL* 94, emphasis added). How, then, are judges to interpret or apply or even announce the law?

Two Weilian concepts are relevant here, 'reading' (see the essays by Allen and Andic, above) and 'attention'. As to the former, judges read not only texts, but, more importantly, persons and situations:

Justice. To be ever ready to admit that another person is something quite different from what we read when he is there (or when we think about him). Or rather, to read in him that he is certainly something different, perhaps something completely different, from what we read in him.

Every being cries out silently to be read differently. (*GG* 121)

Reading a code (or judge-made precedent) can never be the same as reading a man or woman entangled in the web of life. Yet there are similarities in these two realms: both kinds of reading require a certain detachment, though of radically different types. To read a codified text in a detached way means setting the *person* aside in the name of some abstract or formulaic rule, whereas to read a person means setting our indifference towards him aside in the name of the person himself. To apply the full force of the Napoleonic Code to

---

[40] Quoted in Max Lerner, *America as a Civilization*, 2nd edn, New York: Henry Holt and Co., 1987, pp. 1009–10.

[41] To the best of our knowledge, based on her published writings, Weil never said exactly how and by whom her judges were to be selected. Our guess is that they would be selected by other judges. Cf. *EL* 88 ('The Supreme Court of Political Justice (why this adjective?) is badly composed. It is nominated by the President of the Assembly. Why?').

punish a common thief is, for Weil, to read the lesser of two texts (i.e. codified text) as if it were of greater importance than the 'text' of the person. This is perforce illegitimate.

Judicial detachment born out of a faith in legal texts professes justice through *indifference*, whereas judicial detachment born out of a faith in the person professes justice through a *discernment* cognisant of real needs (see the essay by Andic, above). Detachment from the one realm must be transferred to the other. That is why '[h]uman attention alone', maintained Weil, is vital to the legitimate 'exercise [of] the judicial function' (*FLN* 351). On this point she was unyielding: 'Attempts have been made to find mechanisms for the maintenance of justice which would dispense with the need for human attention. It cannot be done' (*FLN* 351).

The notion of equity is most compatible with Weil's view of law. Of course, this also means, contrary to the evolving Western practice, that neither Weil's criminal laws nor her restraints on freedom of opinion are narrowly written. What are clear and concise are the principles of law set out in the Fundamental Declaration. Statutory laws help to sharpen the focus of these principles, but are likewise written with a relatively high level of generality. Equally telling, her notion of equity is not (contrary to English common law) bound to judicial precedent.

Equity, for Weil, is contextual (the realities of this world) and normative (i.e. the reality outside of this world). Practically speaking, her equitable 'system' of law is essentially *ex post facto* oriented. That is, where laws are not particularised, where they are not concise, they take on meaning only *after* the fact, after a judge has breathed life into them. Looking at the legal system from the 'front end', such rule by equity cannot put the citizenry on actual notice of *exactly* what conduct is, or is not, prohibited. Yet, for centuries *ex post facto* laws, at least in the case of penal matters, have been deemed synonymous with tyranny. How would Weil respond to such a charge?

Weil might have answered somewhat along these lines: law should not be, either in formulation or application, static. The more that it tends in that direction, the more it will defeat the high purpose of justice. Citizens, government officials, and judges are not unaware of the law; that is, they are abundantly cognisant of its declaration of principles. Living *in* the law means living *out* these principles, always attentively applying them to a myriad of situations. Always thinking;

always reading. In living out the law, what is most important is the process of continually orienting oneself towards the good. Written laws, seen as 'guides', point citizen and judge alike in this direction. In this sense, then, law may take on a concretive meaning after the fact, though it is imbued with meaning from the beginning. Conversely, when the legal realm of right and wrong is neatly packaged in black letter in a code or case, law (seen as a dialectical process) is sapped of its meaning.

'One finds in the *Écrits de Londres* a vocabulary of "punishment" that is particularly abundant and which did not exist in the earlier writings of Simone Weil' (*PR* 245). In reading her post-1942 writings, one cannot help but notice the presence of punishment. Why? What does this tell us about her legal thought?

Recall that, for Weil, the purpose of punishment is therapeutic. It is an inclusive concept (bringing people in), not an exclusive one (sending them out).[42] Punishment removes 'the stigma of ... crime' (*NR* 21). Punishment, she tells, us, can reveal one's mistake, much as a teacher does when helping a pupil to understand an error in geometry. Finally, punishment is redemptive.

Not surprisingly, Weil found it salutary to introduce her concept of punishment into an idea of law for *at least* two reasons: first, to make possible the dialectical process in the law; and second, to infuse law with an overtly moral purpose. As to the former, punishment operates as an essential corrective device in the process of 'working out' the law. That is one reason why it represents 'a vital need of the human soul'. As to the second point, Patrice Rolland has offered the following comment on Weil's notion of punishment and its operation in the political process:

Political responsibility, by abandoning all thought of a penal judgment of political acts, gives up judging them in moral terms, that is to say it gives up believing that it possesses the ultimate truth about historical and political acts. Penal sanctions define acts as wrongs, acts which themselves are defined on the basis of moral values. (*PR* 247)

In this context, Weil's notion of punishment reintroduced moral questions into politics, and thereby *rejects* the idea that there are no truths in this realm. Punishment compels us, and especially our

[42] See generally *N* II, p. 619 ('Through punishment the criminal ought to be made to feel himself reincorporated in the collectivity, not excluded from it').

leaders, to face up to the moral matter. If there are no political truths, then there can be no punishment. The converse is equally true. Nuremberg-type political trials cannot be confined to the horrors of a single kind of inhumane behaviour. Of course, utility – namely, the relative practical costs of identifying such truths – may counsel against punishment. Here again, Weil wanted these hard questions confronted, not evaded. So committed was she to this point that she was prepared *if necessary*, to punish even her beloved General de Gaulle (*EL* 72).

Simone Weil left much incomplete. Yet, in her writings we can discern an ideal of law labouring to be born – an ideal at once unbending and unbound ...

CHAPTER 11

Simone Weil on beauty

Patrick Sherry

Simone Weil's writings on beauty have not received much attention from students of her work, and still less from writers on aesthetics. In the latter case this neglect is caused largely by the fact that her very exalted view of beauty runs counter to most twentieth-century aesthetics (indeed, it might be doubted whether her writings on the subject should be classified as 'aesthetics'). Yet her work is distinctive, and deserves a closer look. Her treatment of beauty as a *seen* attribute of God is strikingly audacious; and her sketching of a Trinitarian account of divine beauty suggests lines of comparison with the work of theologians who have developed such an account, notably Jonathan Edwards, Paul Evdokimov and Hans Urs von Balthasar. In this paper I shall say something about her views on beauty in general, then discuss briefly her Trinitarian approach, and end by raising some questions about a theology of beauty.

BEAUTY AND GOD

Already in her early lectures on philosophy Weil had developed a very high doctrine of beauty, related to a metaphysical vision inspired by Plato. Everything beautiful, she says, has a mark of eternity, for beauty immediately suggests what is infinite (*LP* 197, 185); moreover, 'Beauty is a witness that the ideal can become a reality' (*LP* 189).

As time went on, she developed these ideas further by working out an explicitly theological account. In her later work she sees beauty not only as a miracle and as one of the three mysteries, along with justice and truth, which serve as standards for everything in the world (*FLN* 341, 292; *IC* 190, 196), but also as divine. Her starting-point is not the beauty of art, but that of the natural world. She regards the beauty of art as dependent on that of the world, for the latter is a work of art, and all other beauties are reflections of it (*IC* 183, 191). Art, she says,

is an attempt to transport into a limited quantity of matter, modelled by man, an image of the infinite beauty of the entire universe ... Every true artist has had real, direct and immediate contact with the beauty of the world, contact which is of the nature of a sacrament. (*WG*[1] 123–4)

Although truly beautiful works of art are indeed inspired by God, 'the only beauty which is the real presence of God, is the beauty of the universe' (*WG* 130). This beauty is the order of the world which science studies, so that scientific investigation is really a form of religious contemplation, the presence of wisdom in the universe (*IC* 148, 172; *NR* 250; *WG* 120, 124). It is one of the two reflections of the true good (the other one, the idea of the good, being in our souls);[2] and it is a reflection of God's love, for it is a sign of the Creator's love for His creation (*IC* 102–3; *FLN* 277, 139).

As the reference to science may indicate, Weil is more interested in the order of the world, than in particular beautiful landscapes, sunsets and so on. The beauty of the whole world is the co-operation of divine wisdom in creation, and it is manifested when we recognise the necessity of things, a necessity which is impersonal, though it is obedience to a perfectly wise love (*SNLG* 187; *GG* 135).

In the beauty of the world harsh necessity becomes an object of love. What is more beautiful than the effect of gravity on sea-waves as they flow in ever-changing folds, or the almost eternal folds of the mountains?
The sea is not less beautiful in our eyes because we know that ships are sometimes wrecked. On the contrary this adds to its beauty. (*SLNG* 178; *IC* 191)

Our love of beauty is marked by detachment, for although beautiful things are often vulnerable, we desire them without wanting to consume them;[3] and, in coming to love the beauty of the world, we renounce our own purposes and projects, and contemplate and love its impersonal order. The docility of matter is a form of obedience to God, and it is this that makes it beautiful (*SNLG*, 179); we should love matter as a lover cherishes the possessions of the beloved (*SNLG*

---

[1] Page references made by Sherry throughout his essay to *WG* and *NR* are to British editions of these texts, respectively, Fontana edition paperback, and Routledge, 1952.

[2] *SNLG* 131. The two are connected, for beauty is like a mirror which sends us back to our own desire for goodness (*WG* 121).

[3] *GG* 136–7; she suggests that vice, depravity, and crime may be attempts to consume beauty (*WG* 121).

178); and in coming to love the order and docility of matter, we love and imitate the divine love and wisdom which created it.

Beauty, however, is more than a creation of God; it is also a *metaxu*, an intermediary which reflects God's nature and attracts the soul to Him: 'Thanks to God's wisdom, who has printed on this world the mark of the good, in the form of beauty, one can love the Good through the things of this world' (*FLN* 139). The beauty which we encounter in the world, and which attracts us, is in fact the appearance of divine beauty; and thereby it is a snare through which God seizes the soul in spite of itself (*IC* 3; *GG* 135; *WG* 118). And, because worldly beauty reflects divine beauty, it can be described as a kind of incarnation of God:

In everything which gives us the pure authentic feeling of beauty there really is the presence of God. There is as it were an incarnation of God in the world and it is indicated by beauty.

The beautiful is the experimental proof that the incarnation is possible. (*GG* 137; cf. *FLN* 83, 341)

Thus, she says, the beautiful is the real presence of God in matter, and contact with it is a sacrament in the full sense of the word (*GG* 138). Echoing both Plato and Dostoevsky, she suggests that beauty has come down from heaven to save us (*FLN* 286); and she sees carnal love as a quest for the Incarnation, for in it 'we want to love the beauty of the world in a human being' (*FLN* 84; cf. *WG* 126).

We go yet a stage further when beauty is described not just as an incarnation of God, but as an attribute of God Himself, and as the attribute in which we *see* Him. Writing of the 'ladder of beauty' in Plato's *Symposium*, whereby the lover of beauty ascends from bodily beauty to beauty itself, she says that we are not dealing here with a general idea of beauty, but with an object of love and desire which is eternally real; it is 'the beauty of God; it is the attribute of God under which we see him' (*SNLG* 129; earlier, on p. 119, she has identified Plato's Forms with God's attributes). She makes the same point elsewhere; writing of *Phaedrus* 250D, where Plato says that beauty is the only one of the lovable realities that is seen, unlike for example wisdom, Weil says 'God's own beauty made manifest to the senses is the beauty of the world' (*IC* 150; cf. *WG* 164–5).

Of course, people may see and admire beauty, but not recognise that it is divine. But then we often love and pursue things without knowing what they really are. In the case of beauty Weil suggests that the ancients worshipped the divine beauty in the guise of

Aphrodite (*IC* 128). And the moderns too may be said to have what she calls a form of the implicit love of God in their love of beauty, for in her essay 'Forms of the Implicit Love of God' she suggests that in this love one may love God without knowing it, as one may also do in other ways, for example through a real love of one's neighbours (*WG* 95–6, 113 ff.). There she again describes the world's beauty as sacramental; and she regrets that in general Christianity has lost any sense of this beauty (whereas Stoicism inculcated love for our 'universal homeland', the world) (*WG* 120, 124, 116, 131–2). She also there hints at a Trinitarian analysis of beauty when she says

God created the universe and his Son, our first-born brother, created the beauty of it for us. The beauty of the world is Christ's tender smile for us coming through matter. He is really present in the universal beauty. The love of this beauty proceeds from God dwelling in our souls and goes out to God present in the universe. (*WG* 120)

It will be seen from this brief summary of some of the leading themes of Weil's aesthetics that in her work we have a very ambitious theology of beauty. If beauty is an incarnation of God, and indeed one of His attributes, then the world's beauty is a road to God. Moreover, this road is a direct one: it is not the route of most natural theology, that of inference, which proceeds by deducing God's existence or some of His attributes from, for example, the order of the world; rather, for Weil, it is a matter of 'experimental proof', for in beauty we *see* God. As H. G. Gadamer says, commenting on one of the passages of Plato alluded to by Weil (*Phaedrus* 250D), beauty is there in the visible world, yet it is experienced as the reflection of something supraterrestrial.[4] This means that those who ignore or deface beauty are committing a *religious* fault. In *Waiting on God* Weil, as we have seen, criticises Christianity for its philistinism; but she also there gives an interesting twist to the traditional Catholic view that sexual sins involve 'serious matter' when she argues that, since carnal love is essentially a longing for the Incarnation, such sins constitute a serious offence against God from the very fact that the soul is unconsciously engaged in searching for Him (*WG* 126–7). She regards what is commonly called 'aestheticism' as committing a similar sin: 'the aesthete's point of view is sacrilegious ... It consists in amusing oneself with beauty by handling it and looking at it' (*NR* 89). An even more serious sacrilege is committed

---

[4] *Truth and Method*, trans. G. Barden and J. Cumming, London, 1975, p. 438.

when beauty is so corrupted that it becomes diabolical: for Weil believes that there is an art which is of the devil, and that there are perverted aesthetes (*GG* 138; cf. *FLN* 341; *WG* 124) – though she allows that even a diabolically perverted beauty is still a reflection of the beauty of the world (*IC* 190–1). For her, then, there is no question of 'art for art's sake'.

Clearly Weil's views fly in the face of much contemporary think-ing, both amongst theologians and writers on aesthetics. At the American Academy of Religion meetings in 1987 a speaker at a symposium on Hans Urs von Balthasar (one of the few contempo-rary theologians to have attempted a theology of beauty) threw out the rhetorical question, 'Who these days cares about beauty?' Many of those who write about theological aesthetics today tend to shy away from the concept of beauty as being too problematical or as no longer a central one. And the attribute of divine beauty is almost wholly ignored; it is, as von Balthasar says, God's most neglected attribute.[5] Karl Barth, for example, describes the treatment of divine beauty in Pseudo-Dionysius' *The Divine Names*, so influential on many medieval thinkers, for example Aquinas, as 'hardly veiled Platonism', which was ignored by the Reformers and by later Protestant orthodoxy. He warns his readers that beauty is a risky concept in relation to God's perfections, because of its connection with the ideas of pleasure, desire, and enjoyment, and its secular and Greek associations (he does acknowledge it as a divine perfection, but treats it only as auxiliary to God's glory).[6]

Amongst writers on aesthetics, likewise, beauty is no longer quite as central a concept as it was once. In an article with the significant title 'The Great Theory of Beauty and its Decline' Wladislaw Tatarkiewicz says that 'in our own century we have been witnesses to a crisis not merely in the theory of beauty but in the very concept itself'.[7] Recent philosophical aesthetics has been preoccupied with a wide range of questions, such as the ontological status of a work of art, the phenomenology of aesthetic experience, and the nature of representation and expression. Even when it discusses the nature and grounds of aesthetic judgment, the concept of beauty often plays a minor role, and is regarded as unhelpful by many people: one finds J. L. Austin's comment 'if only we could forget for a while

---

[5] *Word and Revelation*, trans. A. V. Littledale, New York, 1964, p. 162.
[6] *Church Dogmatics*, II, Pt. 1, trans. T. H. L. Parker *et al.*, Edinburgh, 1957, p. 651.
[7] *Journal of Aesthetics and Art Criticism* 31 (1972–3) pp. 165–80. I quote from p. 169.

about the beautiful and get down instead to the dainty and the dumpy'[8] often quoted. This displacement of the concept seems to have started in the eighteenth century, when other concepts like 'sublime' and 'picturesque' were introduced into critical discussion. Of course, beauty continued to be a central concept in the aesthetics of both Kant and Hegel, and the latter gave a very metaphysically ambitious role to it in his philosophy; and many later nineteenth-century writers, for example Ruskin, had a very exalted and often, indeed, religious view of it. By then people's ideas of beauty had been much affected by Romantic art (which Hegel regarded as the highest form of art), and they had come to place a lot of stress on the content, rather than the form, of a work of art, and on its ability to move us emotionally through its meaning.

The twentieth-century depreciation of beauty is partly a reaction against such high-minded views of art and beauty, and partly a result of philosophical scepticism. The word seems to create so many problems: what is beauty, and why do we find it so hard to define and to judge, why do people disagree so much about it, is it in things themselves or rather, as people say, 'in the eye of the beholder'? Hence many philosophers, for example Ludwig Wittgenstein[9] and Mikel Dufrenne,[10] prefer to use other terms. This attitude is found not only amongst philosophers and critics, but also among many artists, who reject or disregard the traditional view that their role is to celebrate the beauty of creation. An extreme form of such a reaction is found in the 'anti-art' of Marcel Duchamp, exemplified in his famous *Fountain* – which is a urinal. This is perhaps just a case of shocking the bourgeoisie. But there are many more serious examples: Robert Morris disclaimed all aesthetic quality and content for his metal construction *Litanies*, whilst the painter Barnett Newman said 'here in America, some of us, free from the weight of European culture, are finding the answer, by completely denying that art has any concern with the problem of beauty and where to find it'.[11]

---

[8] *Philosophical Papers*, 3rd edn, Oxford, 1961, p. 183.

[9] See his *Culture and Value*, trans. P. Winch, 2nd edn, Oxford, 1980, p. 55 and *Lectures and Conversations on Aesthetics, Psychology and Religious Belief*, edited by C. Barrett, Oxford, 1966, p. 3.

[10] *The Phenomenology of Aesthetic Experience*, trans. E. Casey *et al.*, Evanston, 1973, pp. lviii-lx.

[11] Quoted by Nicholas Wolterstorff in his *Art in Action: Toward a Christian Aesthetic*, Grand Rapids 1980, p. 54. It is likely, however, that Newman was rejecting traditional 'painterly' ideas of beauty in favour of a more intellectual conception, rather than dismissing the whole notion.

Faced with such comments and examples, one is inclined to retort that, if many modern philosophers, critics, and artists find little room for the concept of beauty, so much the worse for them. Their attitude is just a matter of fashion, and against contemporary fashion we can quote the witness of over two thousand years. In any case, fashion is already changing: it is noticeable that, since Tatarkiewicz wrote the article from which I have quoted, there have been two important books by writers in the Anglo-American analytical tradition of philosophy, Guy Sircello's *A New Theory of Beauty*[12] and Mary Mothersill's *Beauty Restored*,[13] devoted to a consideration of the concept, both of them defending its retention; not to mention works by writers from the Thomist and other intellectual traditions.[14] It has also been remarked (by Tatarkiewicz himself,[15] among others) that some of the concepts which have replaced beauty, especially that of the 'aesthetic', run into similar difficulties of definition and analysis.

These more recent developments make it a little easier for us to grapple with Weil's writings than it would have been a generation ago, but they do not remove the difficulties. The problem is not so much the fact that she makes beauty so central, as the way in which she does this and the connections she makes. Unlike modern writers on aesthetics, she is relatively unconcerned with analysing beauty, discussing the criteria for its ascription or examining the nature of aesthetic judgment. For her, beauty is something we see directly, albeit with a special sight: 'Absolute beauty', she says, 'is something as concrete as sensible objects, something which one sees, but sees by supernatural sight' (*IC*, 147; *WG*, 165). Her affinity with Plato here marks a similarity with the treatment of the concept of beauty found in many early Christian Fathers. Similarly, her view that we *see* beauty, and see it as divine, bears comparison with, for example, Gerard Manley Hopkins, for whom 'The world is charged with the grandeur of God. It will flame out, like shining from shook foil',[16] and who saw the beauty of Christ as manifested in the stars or in a

---

[12] Sircello, *A New Theory*, Princeton, 1975.

[13] Mothersill, *Beauty Restored*, Oxford, 1984.

[14] E.g. Armand Maurer, *About Beauty*, Houston 1983, and some of the essays in H. G. Gadamer, *The Relevance of the Beautiful and other Essays*, trans. Nicholas Walker, Cambridge, 1986.

[15] Tatarkiewicz, *Journal of Aesthetics and Art Criticism*, p. 178.

[16] 'God's Grandeur', in *Poems* (4th edn, Oxford, 1970), no. 62, p. 98.

bluebell[17] (again, for Hopkins too, the connection between our awareness of beauty and God was not one of inference).

Now modern writers who employ the concept of beauty locate it in a large network of concepts, and treat it as supervenient on some of these concepts; and since they are influenced by Hegel, at least to the extent that most of them are far more concerned with the qualities of works of art than with natural beauty, the relevant concepts are usually ones like line, colour, balance, and so on. Thus beauty is regarded as an emergent quality which is supervenient on other characteristics. Sometimes it may be a single characteristic: the particular depth, richness or vividness of a colour may lead us to call it beautiful;[18] sometimes it is a whole complex of properties, so that the ascription of beauty to a work of art becomes an overall verdict requiring justification in terms of an analysis of several qualities. Either way, this approach is far removed from Plato, who brushed aside the question of whether qualities like colour and shape contribute to beauty, in favour of an explanation of the beauty of things in terms of their participation in beauty itself (*Phaedo* 100D).

Obviously Weil is nearer to Plato than to any of the twentieth-century writers whom I have mentioned (though she does not seem to manifest Plato's anxiety to mount from the bottom rungs of the ladder of beauty to transcendent beauty as quickly as possible, perhaps because she also absorbed from Stoicism a love for the world, our 'universal homeland', along with its sense of the inter-connectedness of things); and it is this fact, rather than her unfashionable emphasis on beauty, which partly explains the strangeness of her approach. We have seen already how she is more concerned with the beauty of the whole world than with particular beautiful people or things, with the order of the whole than with the 'radiance' of individuals, and that she thinks the former permits us to contemplate and to love necessity. Now this concern is far differ-ent from that of most modern writers on aesthetics, and it explains the distinctive features of Weil's writings on beauty. One does not discuss the beauty of the world as one might discuss that of a particular work of art: love of the former has no opposite, at least not in the way that love of a work of art may be contrasted with dislike

---

[17] *The Journals and Papers of Gerard Manley Hopkins*, edited by H. House, Oxford, 1970, no. 62, p. 98.
[18] Cf. Sircello, sect. 5.

or disdain. Moreover, her distinctive approach explains why Weil makes the connections between beauty and other concepts which she does. When she relates beauty to other concepts, it is often to very grand concepts like goodness and truth, rather than to other more particular aesthetic concepts. She describes the beautiful as 'the contact of the good with the faculty of sense' (*FLN* 98), for instance, and makes similar connections with the concepts of truth and eternity.[19] She also follows many Christian writers in paying tribute to the beauty of purity and sanctity: 'if the saints attract us, that is because we sense the beauty in them. Virtue only touches us in so far as it is beautiful' (*IC* 147; cf. *FLN* 139; *SNLG* 124). Such connections help to explain her refusal to separate art from ethics (*SNLG* chs. 14–15).

It was not, I think, laziness or pig-headedness which led Weil to ignore contemporary aesthetics in favour of her own Platonic approach; for her works are spattered with remarks, often perceptive, about classical French literature and twentieth-century writers like Proust, and she certainly appreciated classical painting, music, and architecture.[20] Her fundamental insistence is that we are dealing here with a religious matter, and this, again, marks off her work from most contemporary aesthetics and raises the question of whether it should be labelled as 'aesthetics' in the modern sense.[21] In one of the passages in which she links beauty and God, she describes beauty as an incarnation of God. She says, a few lines previously,

Whenever one reflects upon the beautiful one is brought up against a blank wall. Everything that has been written upon the subject is miserably and obviously inadequate, because it is a study which must take God as its starting point. (*FLN* 341)

She also, as we have seen, regards beauty as a mystery and a miracle; and this too perhaps explains her reluctance to analyse the concept in terms of other aesthetic concepts or to discuss criteria. A similar

[19] E.g. in *FLN* 194, 229, 341; *NR* 88–9, 224, 257; *SNLG* 131; *WG* 127. Likewise, she discusses the concept of the good in a similar way, e.g. when she says 'The true is the contact of the good with the intelligence' (*FLN* 98).

[20] See, for example, the description of her visit to Italy in David McLellan, *Simone Weil: Utopian Pessimist*, London, 1989, pp. 131–2.

[21] Von Balthasar regards modern aesthetics, which he traces back to Baumgarten and Kant, as but a fragment broken off from a larger, theological, whole, in which 'glory' is a more fundamental concept than 'beauty'. See *Herlichkeit III*. 1.2, *Im Raum der Metaphysik: Neuzeit*, Einsiedeln, 1975, especially section 6. Ruskin preferred the term 'theoria' to 'aesthetics' for the true perception of beauty, for '"aesthesis" properly signifies mere sensual

reluctance, and a suspicion of those who would seek to capture beauty in their theories and rational schemes, were expressed classically by Schiller at the beginning of his *On the Aesthetic Education of Man*, where he says of beauty 'its whole magic resides in its mystery, and in dissolving the essential amalgam of its elements we find we have dissolved its very being'.[22] Others, like Étienne Gilson,[23] have made a similar point in terms of the indescribability of beauty; or, like Baudelaire,[24] in terms of its strangeness. Kant too denied that there can be objective rules of taste whereby the beautiful can be defined by means of concepts (though he thought that judgments of taste are universal, because the beautiful pleases universally).[25] Sometimes a more practical consideration is operative: if we could set out a theory of beauty giving the necessary and sufficient conditions for its ascription, we would have a recipe for producing beauty. In his *L'Éducation sentimentale* Flaubert pokes fun at one of his characters, a painter, who lived with this hope: 'Pellerin used to read every book on aesthetics, in the hope of discovering the true theory of the beautiful; for he was certain that he had only to find it to be able to paint masterpieces.'[26]

BEAUTY AND THE TRINITY

Weil's approach raises questions not only about the nature of beauty but also about the relationship between divine and earthly beauty. The simplest answer to the latter question is to say, as she does, that the two beauties are the same, for in earthly beauty we see divine beauty; or more guardedly, that one is a reflection,[27] or image, of the other. But we also find, both in Weil and many other writers, an alternative approach spelt out in Trinitarian terms; this approach explains the relationship between earthly and divine beauty in terms of the roles of the three Persons of the Trinity.

The simplest such Trinitarian analysis is found in some modern Russian Orthodox writers, who base themselves on the

perception of the outward qualities and necessary effects of bodies' (*Modern Painters*, III, Pt. 3, ch. 2, sect. 1).

22 Trans. E. M. Wilkinson and L. A. Willoughby, Oxford, 1967, I, sect. 5.

23 *Painting and Reality*, London 1957, p. 209.

24 *Art in Paris, 1845–1862*, ed. and trans. by J. Mayne, London 1965, p. 124.

25 *Critique of Judgement*, sects. 6, 9, 16–17.

26 Part I, ch. 4 (Everyman edn, p. 36).

27 As Jonathan Edwards says, e.g. in *The Nature of True Virtue*, Ann Arbor, MI: University of Michigan Press, 1960, ch. 2.

Cappadocian Fathers, and see the glory of the Father as manifested in the Son, his Word and perfect image, and reflected in the Holy Spirit, like a series of lamps being lit one from another (a comparison made by St Gregory of Nyssa[28]); and then shown in the world through the complementary work of the Son and the Spirit. Thus Paul Evdokimov lays downs the principle that 'The Father pronounces his word and the Spirit manifests it, he is the *Light of the Word*' at the beginning of his book *L'Art de l'icône: théologie de la beauté*,[29] and then proceeds to develop his theology of beauty in terms of this principle. For him the Father is the source of beauty, which is reflected in the beauty of his image, the Son, and revealed by the Holy Spirit, who is the 'Spirit of Beauty'.[30] In the West more complicated analyses have been developed, for example in the works of Jonathan Edwards[31] and von Balthasar,[32] which make use of the Augustinian position that the Holy Spirit is the bond of love between Father and Son, and proceeds from both of them.

Weil's Trinitarian aesthetic, however, differs from these consciously Christian theological analyses. Again, she goes straight back to Plato for her fundamental position. In a brief passage in her essay 'God in Plato' she mentions Plato's trinity of the Artificer, the Soul of the World and the Model of creation, in his account of creation in the *Timaeus*, an account which she sees as drawing an analogy from artistic creation to divine creation; she then proceeds to the claim that Plato's three terms correspond, respectively, to the Father, Son, and Spirit.[33] She gives a fuller development of this correspondence in her paper 'Divine Love in Creation' (*IC* ch. 8), paying special attention there to the role of the Son. Again, she identifies Plato's Soul of the World with the unique Son of God, whom she identifies in turn with beauty itself, for, she says, he is the perfect image, the image of the Father, as the beautiful is the image of the good. The Son is also described by her as the Word, who gives order to the world, the order which science contemplates and art imitates. The third Person is described as the Model of creation, i.e. the eternal *paradeigma* which Plato says the Artificer had in view when he

---

[28] *Macedon.* 6 (Migne, *PG* 45:1308B); *c. Eunom.* 1.36 (Migne, *PG* 45:416C).

[29] Evdokimov, Paris 1970, p. 15.

[30] Evdokimov, p. 29.

[31] For instance, in his *Essay on the Trinity* edited by G. P. Fisher, New York, 1903.

[32] E.g. in his *The Glory of the Lord*, I, trans. E. Leiva-Merikakis, Edinburgh 1982).

[33] In *SNLG* 132–2. Earlier in the essay, when discussing Books VI and VII of Plato's *Republic*, she correlates the three Persons with the Good, being and truth (105).

created the world (*Timaeus* 28c–29a). Again drawing on the parallel with artistic inspiration, she points out that the model is the source of the artist's inspiration: 'As soon as one replaces model by the word inspiration, the appropriateness of this image when applied to the Holy Spirit becomes evident' (*IC* 92).

Weil does not pursue her Trinitarian analysis of beauty any further in her discussion of the *Timaeus*, for her main concern there is with providence: the purpose of her essay is to pursue the parallel between providence governing the world and inspiration governing the material of the work of art, between the absolute love displayed throughout the universe and the love in an artist which begets a similar love in the souls of those who contemplate his work. Her identification of beauty with the Son, the perfect image of the Father, is to be related to another essay 'The Pythagorean Doctrine', in which she explains the mediatorship of Christ in terms of Greek mathematics and philosophy, and concludes that the Son is God's thought and the image of the Father, but that, since God's thought is also the order of the world, the Word is also the orderer of the world. Again, beauty is explained in terms of the order of the world.[34]

Of course, in identifying beauty with the Son, as being the perfect image of the Father, Weil is following much of Christian tradition. This identification goes back at least to St Augustine.[35] Likewise, she follows this tradition in claiming that the Son gave order to the world, and also in identifying the presence of wisdom in the world, which she regards as the object of science, with the presence of Christ (*WG* 124; whereas an alternative identification is found in St Irenaeus, who, as we shall see, identifies wisdom with the Holy Spirit).

Weil also takes on board Augustine's understanding of the Holy Spirit as the bond of love between Father and Son, and sees the consequent understanding of the Trinity as exemplifying the Pythagoreans' conception of perfect harmony (*IC* 166–7, 169; cf. *SNLG* 176). But, strangely, she does not pursue her understanding of the Holy Spirit into aesthetics, except in the discussions of the *Timaeus* already mentioned, where she identifies the Spirit with the

[34] *IC* ch. 11, especially pp. 185, 190ff. Eric Springsted's *Christus Mediator: Platonic Mediation in the Thought of Simone Weil*, Chico, CA: Scholars Press, 1983, explains this aspect of Weil's thought very thoroughly.

[35] E.g. *On the Trinity* vi.x.11, anticipated by St Clement of Alexandria in *Stromateis* ii.5.

model used by the Father in creation and with inspiration, and also when she links the Spirit with our consent to the order of the universe (*IC* 195). In the former discussions she is approaching the view of some Christian theologians,[36] based on Gen. 1.2 and Ps. 33.6, that the Spirit has a role in creation. But she does not take the matter any further, nor does she discuss the many forms that inspiration may take (her own conception seems to be derived from the visual arts, and is less appropriate to music and literature). If she had developed a richer account of inspiration, or if she had pursued her own point about the role of the Holy Spirit in the harmony of the Trinity, she might have given a more central role to the Spirit in her thinking about beauty than she did.

Curiously, the first Christian writer to link the Holy Spirit with beauty, Irenaeus, did so in words reminiscent of an Orphic text which Weil quotes on a number of occasions, 'Zeus made all things and Bacchus completed them' (*WG* 120; *IC* 186). In Book IV of his *Against the Heresies* Irenaeus identifies God's Word with the Son and Wisdom with the Spirit, says that they were both with the Father before Creation, and that God 'made all things by the Word, and adorned them by Wisdom'.[37] In later Western Christianity the association between the Spirit and beauty, first suggested by Irenaeus, has usually been developed in terms of the Augustinian view of the Trinity which Weil accepted. Jonathan Edwards, for example, argues that, because the Holy Spirit is the harmony, excellence, and beauty of the deity, he has the particular function of communicating beauty and harmony in the world.[38] Von Balthasar puts forward a similar view, though using the concept of 'form' rather than that of 'harmony'. Since for him the Spirit is the bond of love between Father and Son, he argues that the Spirit gives form to the Trinity and thereby 'In this incomprehensible unity he is the locus of the beauty of God.'[39] This obscure, but pregnant, remark is to be related to a line of thought which, again, comes close to some of Weil's thinking; for von Balthasar the Holy Spirit, being the unity of mutual self-surrender of Father and Son in Love, unites them in a vital way, and so holds the love in a Trinitarian form. The most daring application of this idea occurs in his theology of Holy Satur-

[36] E.g. Augustine, *De Vera Religione* vii.13 (Migne, *P.L.* 34:129).

[37] *Adv. Haer.* iv.xx.2; cf. *Demonstration of Apostolic Preaching*, ch. 5.

[38] *Miscellanies*, sect. 293, in Harvey G. Townsend (ed.), *The Philosophy of Jonathan Edwards from his Private Notebooks*, Westport, Ct. 1972, p. 260. See also Edwards' *Essay on the Trinity*, p. 108.

[39] Balthasar, *The Glory of the Lord*, i, p. 494.

day, in which he depicts the Spirit as the uniting bond between the Father and Son when the latter underwent the experience of abandonment in his death and descent into Hell. In their extreme separation then 'the spirit unites Father and Son while stretching their mutual love to the point of unbearability'.[40] This theology is strikingly anticipated by Weil when she describes the Holy Spirit as uniting through infinite distance the Father and the incarnate Son, even in the latter's cry of forsakeness on the Cross (*IC* 169, 197; *SNLG* 176–7). She does not, however, make the transition from the role of the Holy Spirit in the unity of the Trinity to beauty, which von Balthasar makes through the concept of form.

CONCLUDING REFLECTIONS

Weil's work presents such a contrast to most contemporary writings on aesthetics that it is tempting to conclude that it should not be labelled as aesthetics at all. The danger of this argument, however, is that her writings on beauty may then be shunted off to a siding. In fact, her insistence that the study of beauty must take God as its starting-point, and her dismissal of aestheticism as sinful, raise disturbing questions both about modern aesthetics and its limitations, and about our attitude to nature. If Weil is right, most of us should not be behaving as we are! Similarly, her work raises questions about the limitations of much Christian theology. But beyond these radical challenges there are two more particular areas in her thinking about beauty which deserve further reflection, namely her interpretation of beauty as a divine attribute, and her sketch of a Trinitarian approach. Let me end by saying a little more about each of these issues.

(1) Divine beauty. I think that von Balthasar is right in saying that this is the most neglected of God's attributes: I do not remember ever hearing a sermon about it, and relatively few theologians have written about it. There are many reasons for this. Today people tend to think of beauty in terms of colours, shapes, sounds, bodies, and so on, i.e. things which we experience through our senses (though it should be noted that we do acknowledge intellectual beauty, for example in the elegance of scientific theories and mathematical

---

[40] 'Mysteries of the Life of Jesus (IV): Jesus' Death on the Cross-Fulfillment of the Eternal Plan of God', in *The von Balthasar Reader*, edited by M. Kehl and W. Löser, Edinburgh, 1982, p. 149.

proofs): so how can God, who has no body or matter, be beautiful? There is also, perhaps, a bit of a Puritan hang-up at the back of our minds: the feeling that beauty is a matter of pleasure, something not really important, and so not to be associated with the serious business of religion. Then the idea of divine beauty is sometimes dismissed as a Hellenistic import into Christianity, a bit of Platonism smuggled in by Pseudo-Dionysius (a charge which will not stand up historically: the attribution of beauty to God by Christian theologians long precedes Pseudo-Dionysius,[41] and probably owes a lot to the Psalms, for example 27:4, and 145:5, and to the concept of the glory of God, which is central both in the Old and New Testaments).

The problem I will want to focus on is that it is difficult to envisage what is meant by God's beauty, compared with some other divine attributes, for example wisdom, power, and love. The ordinary believer gets some handle on these other attributes by trying to discern the relevant divine actions, for instance God's providence or wise governance, His power manifested in natural phenomena, and His love shown in providence and especially, Christians say, in the life and work of Christ. But it is more difficult to find a corresponding way in which God 'acts beautifully', other than by His creating beautiful beings. Those who attempt to fill in the picture here tend to say that the divine beauty is inexpressible, for it surpasses any earthly beauty, or else to produce something rather formal (for example by arguing that Aquinas' analysis of beauty in terms of wholeness, harmony, and radiance is applicable to God[42]).

At the root of this problem, I think, is the fact that we lack a proper vocabulary to support our ascription of beauty to God. Normally our predications of 'beauty' are supported by a whole barrage of concepts: by other aesthetic ones like 'elegant' or 'graceful', or by particular words describing the qualities of colours, sounds, and so on. But most of this vocabulary is not applicable to God – what would a 'pretty' or 'elegant' God be like? In the case of divine beauty the neighbouring or supporting concepts are drawn from elsewhere: from the language of power (the Biblical term 'glory' suggests power as well as beauty, and goes along with terms like 'majesty', 'splendour' and 'strength'), from that of ethics (most

---

[41] E.g. St Augustine describes God as the beauty 'in imitation of which the rest of things are beautiful', *De Ordine* II.19; *P.L.* 32:1019.

[42] Cf. Armand Maurer, *About Beauty*, Houston, 1983, ch. 6.

people think of Christ's beauty in terms of his moral and spiritual qualities), or from the more general divine attributes of perfection, goodness and holiness. This does not invalidate our ascription of beauty to God, but it leaves us with the task of clarifying further its nature. And here, perhaps, the last mentioned term, holiness, may be the clue: for I notice that the biblical ascriptions of beauty to God occur mostly in the Psalms, and in the language of joyful praise, awe, and adoration. Hence some later writers, above all Jonathan Edwards, closely associate, and even identify, God's beauty and holiness[43] (likewise, he also regards true virtue as the highest form of human beauty[44]). Weil sees the connection, but more with regard to human holiness than divine, for example when she says that 'Beauty is to things what sanctity is to the soul' (*FLN* 139).

(2) Closely related to the task of explaining the nature of divine beauty is that of explaining the relationship between it and earthly beauty. Weil, as we have seen, has two answers here, one in terms of earthly beauty being an incarnation of God and, indeed, a divine attribute which is seen, the other in terms of a Trinitarian analysis based on the creation myth in Plato's *Timaeus*. It is difficult, at first sight, to see the relationship between the two accounts; and one recalls that in much theology discussion of the Trinity is dragged in almost as an afterthought. But in Weil's treatment one difference between the two accounts, I think, is that in the first case she is starting as it were from below, from earthly beauty, and asking about its relation to God; in the second case she is starting from above, from God Himself, or rather from His actions in creation and providence, which she analyses in Trinitarian terms. In both cases we are faced with ideas which are difficult and unfamiliar to people today, and in both cases Weil's treatment is brief and a little cryptic. One way in which we might continue at this point is by developing the hints about the Holy Spirit, which she gives both in her analysis of Plato's *Timaeus*, and in the passage which I quoted from *Waiting on God*, in which she says that our love of the world's beauty proceeds from God dwelling in our souls and goes out to God present in the universe (p. 120). If we put together those two passages, we have the Holy Spirit playing a role in creation, and also in the inspiration of artists and in our love of beauty. The next step would be to relate the role of the Spirit in these divine works *ad extra* to his role within the

---

[43] E.g. in his *Essay on the Trinity*, p. 97.
[44] See Edwards, *The Nature of the True Virtue*, ch. 3.

Trinity (I have noted that both Edwards and von Balthasar derive the Spirit's special role with regard to beauty in the world from his position in the Trinity as the bond of love between Father and Son, a relationship which Edwards explicates in terms of the concept of 'harmony' and von Balthasar in terms of 'form'). Weil has a pertinent comment in her notebooks:

The question of the *Timaeus* is that of God's relation to the world. But nothing proves that the triad of Father, Soul of the World, Model does not correspond to something outside of the relation to the world, in the being of God; that could be reserved for esoteric teaching.[45]

What she reserves for esoteric teaching has, in fact, become one of the leading issues in theology in recent decades, in discussions about the relationship between the 'economic' and the 'immanent' Trinity. So Weil's work brings us to two of the greatest theological developments of our time, theological aesthetics and the revival of Trinitarian theology.

---

[45] *Cahiers*, ii, Paris, 1953, pp. 189–90 (my trans.).

CHAPTER 12

Simone Weil and Antigone: innocence and affliction

Ann Loades

INTRODUCTION

Simone Weil made her own translations and decisions concerning the Greek texts that she wrote about. English readers then read her Greek translations from French as re-translated into English. These problems about translation, and the philosophical issues which they can give rise to, have been ignored for the practical purposes of the presentation of this essay.

There are also difficulties about meanings to do with certain parts of the Sophoclean text, which are probably insoluble in an important sense – for instance, the connection between the invocation of Bacchus by the Chorus, and Creon's collapse. I have concentrated only on the use Simone Weil made of the text, rather than on other interesting aspects of the Sophoclean text itself. Finally, this essay proceeds by way of example, rather than by abstraction from examples – such abstractions (interpretations) I leave largely to the reader.

ON ANTIGONE

George Steiner's book, *Antigones: the Antigone Myth in Western Literature, Art and Thought*[1] nowhere mentions Simone Weil, though he does refer to the work of some of her near contemporaries, and offers explanations for their preoccupation with *Antigone*. My reflections on Simone Weil's interest in *Antigone* (to put it no more strongly than 'interest' at this stage) are an attempt to place her in this tradition elaborated by Steiner. Her interest, like his, and the very different treatments of for example Martha Nussbaum, Hans Urs von

---

[1] George Steiner, *Antigones: The Antigone Myth in Western Literature, Art and Thought,* Oxford: Clarendon, 1984, paperback 1986.

277

Balthasar, and Donald M. MacKinnon, represent further 'provisional' readings. Of them all, however, Simone Weil's is closest to
that of an actor, a participant in the drama. To some extent, she,
like Kierkegaard, is wearing a self-confessional mask, which is what
one might expect from engagement with a text written for performance. Unlike Kierkegaard, she does not restrict herself to what he
called a 'spiritual stage' in his own appropriation of Antigone.

We might account for the omission of Simone Weil from Steiner's
work by noting that, if all we did was to turn up her short essay
entitled *Antigone*, we could easily dismiss it as a *very* minor footnote to
Hegel. If, on the other hand, we attend to her explicit references to
the play, and to other things she writes which illuminate her understanding of it, we see an integration between the text, her theology,
and her life. Her exegesis of the text of the play may not be
comparable, let us say, to Steiner's Hölderlin, but it may count as
more than that minor footnote.

Simone Weil should be of interest to a reader of the *Antigone*
tradition as Steiner interprets it. He himself claimed in a Remembrance Day address in Cambridge University in 1989[2] that the
'dehumanisation of man' in our century has been, and we may say
still is, enacted within the 'high places and institutions' of European
culture. He further suggests that there were links, fatalities of conso-
nance, between high culture and barbarism:

It is more than arguable that the genius for speculative abstraction, for
aesthetic formalism, for disinterested inquiry immune to the roughage of
common needs and pursuits which have marked European intellectual,
artistic, scientific eminence, disabled our humanity. Where sensibility and
understanding are schooled to respond most intensely to the cry in the
poem, to the agony in the painting or to the absolute in the philosophical
proposition or scientific axiom, the cry in the street may go unheard.

In Simone Weil, there is more to her project of making the
masterpieces of Greek poetry accessible to the mass of people, closer
to them, than may at first appear (*SL* 49). As she writes, '*Antigone* is
by no means a moral tale for moral children'. One of the services she
believes herself to be performing for the afflicted is 'to find the words
which express the truth of their affliction, the words which can give
resonance, through the crust of external circumstances, to the cry

---

[2] Steiner, 'Remembering the Future', *Theology*, 93 (1990), pp. 437–44.

which is always inaudible: "Why am I being hurt?" "[3] By 'affliction'
she means an appalling concatenation of pain, isolation from one's
companions or community, degradation, perhaps being actually
despised or attacked by others because of one's degradation, and the
feelings of self-disgust, horror, and guilt which the afflicted one may
feel, trying to provide some account, as it were, for the state they are
in.[4] Her readers come to know that she offers no comforting reply to
the question about hurt. Even the energy to attempt to construct
such a reply shows that one has not reached 'the specific degree of
affliction, just as water does not boil at 99 degrees centigrade'. She
both wants to give resonance to the cry of the afflicted, and yet to
insist that the world is empty of the finality, the point of it all, for
which they cry (*IC* 198f.).

Given that she is acutely sensitive to the cry in the street, and
believes that she knows how *not* to respond, as well as how to
respond, to it, we can go on to acknowledge her as one of the heirs of
that phase of European culture associated with the poets, philosophers, and scholars devoted to Hellenism from the end of the
eighteenth century until the turn of the twentieth. In the nineteenth
century they turned from Homer's *Iliad* to Athenian tragedy, *Antigone* being awarded the prize among Sophocles' plays, themselves
pre-eminent in the seventy or so years of Athenian life in which were
to be found also the works of Aeschylus and Euripedes. Sophocles'
material may in part have lain ready to hand, but Antigone's
defiance of Creon's edict immediately after the carnage, and the
tragedy provoked by her defiance, may have been his own idea.
Simone Weil claims that:

There exists a focal point of greatness where the genius creating beauty, the
genius revealing truth, heroism and holiness are indistinguishable. Already
as one approaches this point, one can see the different forms of greatness
tending to flow into one another. (*NR* 224f.)

In her evaluation, 'The *Iliad*, the tragedies of Aeschylus and those
of Sophocles bear the clearest indication that the poets who produced them were in a state of holiness.' This provides us with one
reason at least for someone turning outside Christian scripture, or
indeed tradition, for resources in terms of which to think about

---

[3] Simone Weil, *HP* as found in David McLellan, *Simone Weil: Utopian Pessimist*, London:
Macmillan, 1989, p. 282.
[4] See Diogenes Allen, 'Natural Evil and the Love of God', *Religious Studies*, 16 (1980),
pp. 439–56.

aspects of life. If she is correct, she asks, 'Why waste one's time admiring others?' One could make use of them, derive instruction and pleasure from them, 'but why love them? Why give one's heart to anything other than the good?' So much for canon-fire. These texts give her something of what she calls 'the density of the real', the density which life offers everyday, but which she says 'we are unable to grasp because we are amusing ourselves with lies' (*SNLG* 162).

So far as one can, it may be well to keep at bay the explicitly Christian cast Simone Weil, like others, has given to Antigone, though I think it is integral to her understanding. It may also be the case that women seeking for resources to understand a specifically female/feminine way of 'imitating' Christ, may have turned to Antigone as an example of a woman articulate out in public space, standing for values and loyalties they found in jeopardy, and unable to find a voice for them except to some very limited degree in a text such as that of the fourth gospel. Simone Weil, in any case, finds the 'resurrection' themes and narratives of that gospel, as of any others, acutely problematic, as will become clear. She knows from her own personal experience that it is possible to have contact with a Christ whose tender smile for her is made manifest, but this has nothing to do with altering the course of a world in which affliction is not merely possible, but common. 'Resurrection' can lead us to suppose that such affliction will not be likely, or can be transformed in a meaningful way, and she is determined to rule out these misleading expectations from the very beginning. So, keeping Christian connections on the periphery, it can be helpful to relate at least some of the preoccupations of the Hellenists to their political (i.e. non-domestic) context, following Steiner.

Throughout the period which begins with the revolutionary wars of the eighteenth century and into our own time there lies, as there always will, the possibility of the exercise of arbitrary power, represented by Creon. At his first entrance, it is true that he says:

> No other touchstone can test the heart of a man,
> The temper of his mind and spirit, till he be tried
> In the practice of authority and rule.
> For my part, I have always held the view,
> And hold it still, that a king whose lips are sealed
> by fear, unwilling to seek advice, is damned.[5]

---

[5] All quotations are from *Sophocles, The Theban Plays* trans. E. F. Watling, Harmondsworth: Penguin, 1947.

Yet in his self pre-occupation he identifies order with his own personal dignity. He comes to claim that he is responsible only to himself, that 'every state belongs to its ruler'. Haemon's challenge that he would be an excellent king on a desert island is an attempt to plead Creon's own cause (as well as his own) as Creon had first expressed it.

Such an exercise of power as Creon's, may render others, in Antigone's words, 'unfriended, condemned alive to solitary death'. Simone Weil, referring to herself as, 'Antigone as usual', had a relatively brief experience of imprisonment in 1942 on arrival in London (*SL* 161), but her description of Prometheus' bondage[6] (and those of Niobe and Danae in *Antigone*) would keep her alert to this possibility of 'live burial', not least for political prisoners. We might add that the conditions in which some prisoners are held may also compel us to revise our metaphors. For example one does not, presumably, pray 'Let light perpetual shine upon them' for those confined in a modern state's all-white isolation cells, unless the words insist on their remembrance, no matter what they actually have done, or are supposed to have done. Simone Weil wrote that 'the soul of genius is *caritas* in the Christian significance of the word; the sense that every human being is all-important. That, at least, is my creed' (*SL* 104f). Impartiality and partiality need to balance one another. As Helen Oppenheimer puts it, 'partiality' is no more and no less than the acknowledgement of individual mattering, 'the love that appreciates and minds about particular people for their own sakes'. If we were God, we could be as partial as we liked, as it were, without neglecting, spoiling, or abusing someone. Since we are not capable of that kind of partiality, we need to praise impartiality also, being more even handed whilst acknowledging that so much of what we have comes to us as a gift.[7] So also as a comment on 'charity', and in elaboration of what she called the Christian quality of Antigone, Simone Weil urges the imitation of the impartiality of God who watches over all. 'It is this that Christ bids us to imitate: the perfection of the Celestial Father who makes the rain to fall and the sun to shine over all creation' (*IC* 9). Power such as Creon's

---

6 Simone Weil, *IC*, p. 67: 'Left in a deserted place where none can speak to him or hear him ... secured by nails and chains in complete immobility, in an unnatural position, unable to satisfy the need to hide himself which is so terribly intense in humiliation and affliction, exposed to the sight of whoever may happen to come to mock his distress, he is hated by the gods, abandoned by men.'

7 Helen Oppenheimer, *The Hope of Happiness*, London: SCM 1983, p. 131.

depends above all on his 'capacity to send the young to their several deaths'.[8] It is Creon's wife, Eurydice, who in her dying words names him 'child-slayer'. She recalls not only Haemon, but her other son, Megareus. In another version of the tradition, Creon, at the climax of the battle and at Teiresias' bidding, sacrifices Megareus to the gods to obtain salvation for the city. In other versions another son is sacrificed or opts for self-immolation by jumping from the walls.[9]

Those like Simone Weil who grew up close to the battlefields of 1914–18 knew about the quarter or a third of a million mostly young men left unburied and mashed into no-man's land, dislodged in death, as in life, from hearth and city. Of World War II, Steiner notes especially what he calls the 'urban hell' of some of those cities in the 1940s: 'Deserters, adolescents half out of their senses with fear, soldiers separated from broken units, were strung up on ... lampposts. Any attempt to cut down their fly-blown bodies was punishable by instant execution.'[10] In other words, although we can distance ourselves from the predicament of Antigone and Creon, let us say by attending to Martha Nussbaum's summary[11] of what ought to have been Creon's sense of *conflict* in his own place and time, one might find illustration of what ought to be that sense of conflict in closer situations of extremity. Creon's lack of a sense of conflict between the values of the well-being city (albeit as narrowly construed by him) and the values of fidelity to his kin, expressed in the burial rites of both his sister Jocasta's children as well as his own, make his willingness to treat Polyneices as mere carrion all of a piece with the priority he gives to the exercise of his power.

In any case, Creon inherits his power from a pair of fratricidal young men. Polyneices had menaced his city like a bird of prey, and no one attempts to refute Creon's charges against him – that he had come intending to burn and ravage his country, to drink his kindred's blood, enslave survivors, burn down the temples of the gods, ransack their shrines, and lay waste their laws. For these are the idioms of war, not merely of war as waged by traitors and enemies as distinct from patriots. Creon, and probably Eteocles, would conduct war in the same way, as Simone Weil knows. In her examination of the *Iliad* Simone Weil explains the difference between the realm of

---

[8] George Steiner, *Antigones*, p. 247.   [9] George Steiner, *Antigones*, p. 147.
[10] George Steiner, *Antigones*, p. 142.
[11] Martha Nussbaum, *The Fragility of Goodness: Luck and Ethics in Greek Tragedy and Philosophy*, Cambridge: Cambridge University Press, 1986, p. 55.

war and the other world, 'the far-off world, precarious and touching, of the family, that world where each man is, for those who surround him, all that counts most' (*IC* 25).[12] She recalls particularly Hector's wife wanting to prepare a hot bath for him when he returns from the battlefield. She comments: 'Indeed he was far from hot baths, this sufferer. He was not the only one. Nearly all the *Iliad* takes place far from hot baths. Nearly all of human life has always passed far from hot baths' (*IC* 25). And consider as a possible comment on the Creons of this world her analysis of the relationship between the strong and the weak, and the way the strong can be oblivious to the principle that 'those to whom destiny lends might, perish for having relied too much upon it'.

He who possesses strength moves in an atmosphere which offers him no resistance. Nothing in the human element surrounding him is of a nature to induce, between the intention and the act, that brief interval where thought may lodge. Where there is no room for thought, there is no room either for justice or prudence. This is the reason why men of arms behave with such harshness and folly. Their weapon sinks unto an enemy disarmed at their knees; they triumph over a dying man, describing to him the outrages that his body will suffer. Achilles beheads twelve Trojan adolescents on Patroclus' funeral pyre as naturally as we cut flowers for a tomb. They never guess as they exercise their power, that the consequences of their acts will turn back upon themselves. (*IC* 34)[13]

If she is right, that 'violence so crushes whomever it touches that it appears at last external no less to him who dispenses it than to him who endures it', then victors as well as vanquished are indeed 'brothers in the same misfortune' (*IC* 39).[14] So there will be and can

---

[12] See also Jean Bethke Elshtain, *Women and War*, Brighton: Harvester, 1987, pp. 49–50.

[13] And see in her essay on 'Morality and Literature', p. 162, *SNLG*.

The man falling down the slope of cruelty or terror cannot discern what is the force that impels him or the relations between it and all the other external conditions. In the words assembled by genius several slopes are simultaneously visible and perceptible, placed in their true relations, but the listener or reader does not descend any of them. He feels gravity in the way we feel it when we look over a precipice, if we are safe and not subject to vertigo. He perceives the unity and diversity of its forms in this architecture of the abyss. It is in this way that in the *Iliad* the slope of victory and the slope of defeat are manifest and simultaneously perceptible, as they never are for a soldier occupied in fighting. This sense of gravity, which only genius can impart, is found in the drama of Aeschylus and Sophocles.

[14] See also G. W. F. Hegel, *Phenomenology of Spirit* trans. A. V. Miller, Oxford: Clarendon, 1977, p. 267:

The dead, whose right is denied, knows therefore how to find instruments of vengeance, which are equally effective and powerful as the power which has injured it. These powers are other communities whose altars the dogs or birds defiled with the corpse, which is not

be no argument about whether or not to bury Polyneices' body or ashes, return corpses to families and honour their common humanity. Since Antigone names Polyneices only once, she has also stood for a reference beyond her own kin to this more universal claim.

Of women who cannot stop the slaughter, they may, as Simone Weil writes, want to lessen the distance from the men they love and lighten their own heavy burden of 'impotent sympathy' by suffering some equivalent distress (*SNLG* 195). In her own case, she wrote to Maurice Schumann that: 'The suffering all over the world obsesses me and overwhelms me to the point of annihilating my faculties and the only way I can revive them and release myself from the obsession is by getting myself a large share of danger and hardship.' This alone could save her from the waste of sterile chagrin (*SL* 156). She did not have to worry about her own brother as it so happened, but the fate of those beyond her immediate kin is inevitably central to her. She wrote of two categories of men – those who think and love, and those 'whose minds and hearts are abased before power camouflaged as ideas'. Antigone's retort to Creon, 'I was born to share, not hate, but love', is the retort she makes her own to the latter (*SL* 91).

Simone Weil is also alert to 'sisterhood' in the sense of the extraordinary opening line of Antigone's polemic, 'O kindred, own-sisterly head of Ismene'. War and its aftermath for Antigone are a disaster within a far more important fabric of fidelity, *philia*, antecedent to any particular historical or political system. In the play itself, and in the myth of Oedipus, this fidelity is given its obsessive quality by the theme of incest, which inevitably complicates the relationship between Antigone and her kind, giving her fidelity some of its destructive power. *Contra* Kierkegaard, Simone Weil deals with the incest theme by affirming Antigone's purity, despite the impurity of her birth. So in her appeal to Ismene we might think that Antigone looks for what Simone Weil calls 'a search for mutual consent' (*IC* 177), the 'imitation of the incomprehensible charity which persuades God to allow us our autonomy'. She does not find it. Simone Weil may also have been well aware of the pre-Freudian discussion of sister–brother love and its privileges and burdens.[15] In

raised into unconscious universality by being given back, as is its due, to the elemental individuality [the earth], but remains above ground in the realm of outer reality, and has now acquired as a force of divine law a self-conscious, real universality. They rise up in hostility and destroy the community which has dishonoured and shattered its own power, the sacred claims of the Family.

[15] George Steiner, *Antigones*, p. 17.

his *Phenomenology* Hegel wrote that the recognition of a sister in her brother is 'pure and unmixed with any natural desire':

... the moment of the individual self, recognizing and being recognized, can here assert its right, because it is linked to the equilibrium of the blood and is a relation devoid of desire. The loss of the brother is therefore irreparable to the sister and her duty to him is the higher.[16]

This stands in effect as Hegel's comment on the argument wrenched from Antigone when she flinches from her death. 'Father and mother lost, where would I get another brother?' Fidelity is to those born from the same womb in the first instance, but her particular way of putting it is also a rejoinder to Creon's brutal denial of the importance of Haemon's love for Antigone. 'Oh there are other fields for him to plough.' Husbands and sons even, may be replaceable, but not brothers.

In Simone Weil's writing this is also articulated in her piece on 'The laments of Electra and the recognition of Orestes', in which Electra recalls how her brother had come to call for her first, how she had sent him forth in splendour, and how she should have been the one to wash his body and lay it on the funeral pyre (*IC* 13). This in turn can be juxtaposed with the point in *Antigone* when the uncanny dust cloud settles, and Antigone is found at her brother's body, screaming 'like an angry bird/When it finds its nest left empty and little ones gone'.

Antigone also offends Creon by her challenge to his understanding of masculinity, acting outside the confines of her household as he should have done, if he, like her, had been the last of kin. And consider, as Steiner does, an appalling actual example of such behaviour, from enemy occupied Riga in September 1941. A girl described as 'entirely unpolitical in her sentiments' is caught doing what has been forbidden, which is trying to sprinkle earth on the publicly exposed body of her executed brother. When asked why she was doing so, she replied, 'He was my brother. For me that is sufficient.'[17]

Where then will Simone Weil stand in relation to Hegel's treatment of the powerplay between Creon and Antigone? There is more to Hegel's reflections, which have had such determining force, than the passage in the *Lectures on the Philosophy of Religion*.[18] Hegel,

---

[16] G. W. F. Hegel, *Phenomenology*, p. 275.   [17] George Steiner, *Antigones*, p. 108f.
[18] G. W. F. Hegel, *Lectures on the Philosophy of Religion*, edited by P. C. Hodgson, II *Determinate Religion*, Berkeley: University of California Press, 1987, pp. 665–6.

like others, has transposed the conflict from the very limited scale of the Greek *polis*, beyond that of the city, to the state: 'For example, in the *Antigone* the love of family, the holy, the inner, what is also called the law of the lower deities because it belongs to sentiment, comes into collision with the right of the state.' As Genevieve Lloyd[19] has explained, Hegel's treatment of femininity is double-edged. It rationalises women's exclusion from the political domain, whilst allowing men to maintain feeling while flourishing as self-conscious ethical beings. Women on the other hand can make of feeling and particular relationships something genuinely ethical. So, in Hegel:

Creon is not in the wrong; he maintains that the law of the state, the authority of the government, must be preserved and punishment meted out for its violation. Each of these two sides actualizes only one of the two, has only one side as its content. That is the one-sidedness, and the meaning of eternal justice is that both are in the wrong because they are one-sided, but both are in the right.

In what Hegel refers to as 'the unclouded course of ethical life', whatever that might be, both are acknowledged. Each has validity, but is counterbalanced by the other's validity. Hegel then thinks of the possibility of a reconciliation which would obviate the 'unhealed sorrow ... because an individual perishes', and this reconciliation would require the overcoming of one-sidedness. This has to do with divesting the subject of what he calls 'its unrighteousness in its own heart', presumably its thinking that its one-sidedness needs no counterbalance, so not even recognising one-sidedness.

His remarks on the tragedy, in the *Lectures on the Philosophy of Fine Art*, are equally succinct discussions of the theme.[20] The major piece of dialectic on the tragedy in the *Phenomenology*[21] precipitates a portrait of Antigone with special reference to her lines on 'the unwritten unalterable laws/Of God and heaven ... They are not of yesterday or today, but everlasting. Though where they come from, none of us can tell.' Antigone knows what they are, and what they mean. Creon may also have the same knowledge, but displaces it by giving greater weight to other priorities.

What Hegel calls ethical substance may become the essence of

---

[19] Genevieve Lloyd, *The Man of Reason: 'Male' and 'Female' in Western Philosophy*, Minneapolis: University of Minnesota Press, 1984, pp. 84–5.

[20] G. W. F. Hegel, *On Tragedy*, edited by A. and C. Paolucci, Newgate: Anchor, 1962, *passim*.

[21] George Steiner, *Antigones*, p. 30f.

self-consciousness, and this in turn becomes 'the *actuality* and *existence* of the substance, its *self* and *will*'. Such beings are

unalienated spirits transparent to themselves, stainless celestial figures that preserve in all their differences the undefiled innocence and harmony of their essential nature. The *relationship* of self-consciousness to them is equally simple and clear. They *are*, and nothing more.[22]

Hegel must, of course, take his Antigone into conflict, and in her action she cannot maintain her innocence. Hence he quotes 'Because we suffer we acknowledge that we have erred.' The translation of Simone Weil's version of this part of the Antigone reads:

> What crime have I committed before God?
> Why must I, unhappy one, still turn my eyes
> toward God, Whom may I call to my aid? Ah!
> It is for having done what is right that so much wrong is done to
>   me.
> But if before God my affliction is legitimate,
> then in the midst of my suffering I will recognize my fault,
> But if it is they who are at fault, I shall not wish
> them more sorrows than they make me suffer unjustly.   *(IC 23)*

It would be easy to spell out elements in her guilt, such as her response to her sister's hesitation, her dismissal of Haemon's claims, her sheer incomprehension of Creon which triggers his fury and their mutual downfall.[23] Despite these possibilities, Hegel more thoroughly ultimately undermines the 'dialectic of equilibrium'[24] between the two in one place in his *Aesthetik*. Quoting the same text about suffering, he sees in Sophocles' writing 'the heavenly Antigone, that noblest of figures that ever appeared on earth, going to her death' – nobler than both Socrates and Jesus. At this point Antigone is doubly a 'surrogate for reality', in Steiner's phrase.[25] Feminine emancipation in the nineteenth century had not yet been honoured; and, in Hegel's phrasing, the 'myth' of Antigone has overtaken the 'historicity' of two men, and what their followers had recorded of their words and deeds.

---

[22] G. W. F. Hegel, *Phenomenology*, p. 261.
[23] D. M. MacKinnon, *Explorations in Theology*, v, London: SCM, 1979, pp. 187–9, and D. M. MacKinnon, 'The Transcendence of the Tragic', pp. 122–35 of *The Problem of Metaphysics*, London: Cambridge University Press, 1974.
[24] George Steiner, *Antigones*, p. 41; G. W. F. Hegel, *On Tragedy*, p. 360.
[25] George Steiner, *Antigones*, p. 10.

Steiner's view is that Kierkegaard's conjuring of Antigone[26] is a direct challenge to Hegel's elevation of her. Noting Antigone's line: 'alive to the place of corpses, an alien still, never at home with the living or the dead', Kierkegaard addresses himself to the 'Symparanekromenoi', fellow moribunds: 'come closer to me, form a circle around me as I send my tragic heroine out into the world'. His necromantic fantasy allows him to suppose that: 'She is my creation, her thoughts are my thoughts, and yet it is as if in a night of love I had rested with her, as if she in my embrace had confided a deep secret to me.' Kierkegaard both assimilates her to himself, but also puts her firmly in her place in a Christianised scheme. She is for him a 'bride of God' or, rather, a 'virgin mother', carrying a secret under her heart, dedicated in her case to sorrow for her father and for her brother.[27] She cannot be guiltless, and there can be no assimilation of her identity to that of Christ's, let alone of her superseding him. Teasing the two apart Kierkegaard argues:

The identity of an absolute action and an absolute suffering is beyond the powers of the aesthetic and belongs to the metaphysical. In the life of Christ there is this identity, for his suffering is absolute, since it is absolutely free action, and his action is absolute suffering, since it is absolute obedience.[28]

In so far as Simone Weil is an orthodox Christian, and for what that is worth, she too must resist Hegel's final evaluation of Antigone, but Antigone remains on her 'list of images of Christ' (*FLN* 321f.). Her death song is readily assimilated to Christ's flinching from death (*IC* 52) and to his cry of dereliction. Antigone's suffering can also be assimilated to his, and attain what Simone Weil called 'a sort of equality with God, an equality which is love' (*IC* 170). Prometheus had pity and received none. 'Antigone also says, in Sophocles' play, that having shown piety she suffered impious treatment. The Greeks were haunted by the thought that caused a saint of the Middle Ages to weep: the thought that Love is not loved' (*IC* 65).

And on Antigone's appeal to the 'unwritten and inscrutable laws of God' she herself writes:

The good begins at a point beyond the reach of will, as truth begins at a point beyond the reach of intelligence. Beyond the intelligence, and therefore beyond the law. The true law is an unwritten law, as Sophocles knew. For the letter kills. So Moses did not come from God. (*FLN* 262)

[26] Søren Kierkegaard, *Either/Or*, 1, trans. H. V. Hong and E. H. Hong, Princeton: Princeton University Press, 1987, p. 153.
[27] Kierkegaard, *ibid.*, p. 157.   [28] Kierkegaard, *ibid.*, p. 158.

These remarks also signal her profound ignorance of, or her hostility to, the immense range and flexibility of Jewish reflection on the 'written', notwithstanding its origin with 'Moses'. So, she claims Sophocles as one whose quality of inspiration is the most visibly Christian, especially in Antigone, illustrating, 'We ought to obey God rather than man' (*IC* 8f.). In her treatment of the point in the essay 'Human Personality' she made yet another contrast, between 'unwritten law' and 'rights':

the unwritten law which this little girl obeyed had nothing whatsoever in common with rights, or with the natural; it was the same love, extreme and absurd, which led Christ to the Cross.

It was Justice, companion of the Gods in the other world, who dictated this surfeit of love, and not any right at all. Rights have no direct connection with love.[29]

Given that the language of 'rights' does not exhaust the possibilities of what human beings need to respond to and respect in others, 'rights' may none the less have their place in civil life.[30] More to the point here, however, is that just as affliction has its 'boiling point' so has love. Then there would be a further question about what sort of person could exhibit this love, without precipitating further violence, without acting beyond his or her moral level, forcing his or her talent. Criticising others or oneself for mediocrity leaves entirely open the question of whether it is actually possible to *live* the extreme and absurd love of which she writes, or whether it is inextricably bound up with a pressure towards transcendence expressed in the 'counsels of perfection', which may precipitate one towards death. Certainly, like Kierkegaard, Simone Weil knows of the fellowship with the dead where one is free to love, but it by no means follows that to be free to love the living is to be mediocre. Antigone, in any case, perished for having loved beyond reason and, if she must, and if that is all that is possible, will indeed love the dead (*IC* 10).

Simone Weil also compares the penalty of immuring inflicted on Antigone with that of the cross as due to the same motive, the search for an alibi. 'One doesn't actually kill; one places the condemned person in a situation in which he or she must necessarily die' (*N* 517f.). And there is a sense in which she writes in anticipation of

---

[29] As quoted in McLellan, *Utopian Pessimist*, p. 280. Richard Bell's essay above deals with this notion at length.

[30] Three essays in this volume deal with this – see Eric Springsted, Richard Bell, and Collins and Nielsen, above.

René Girard's *Violence and the Sacred*,[31] although his references to *Antigone* are surprisingly sparse. The point is that Creon cannot deal with the violence of his city because he cannot establish his difference from it, whereas further assimilation of Christ to Antigone is implicit in her claim that a crime producing a curse 'cannot be destroyed except by the suffering of a pure victim obedient to God' (*IC* 10). Another connection is that it is never to the gods of civic religion, but always to the presence of 'other gods' to which she appeals. Simone Weil simply assimilates the God who presides over the tragedy known as being 'beneath the earth' to the one 'known as being in heaven' (*IC* 9). It is the 'otherness' of the divine which counts, not being 'above' or 'below'. So she roundly asserts that 'It comes to the same thing. It is always to the true God, the God who is in the other world, that reference is made.'

This seems at once both profound but exasperating, unless we recognise in her a Sophoclean capacity for indirect, if not explicitly negative, theology[32] about a God who does not act in the world but who is obliquely present, and whose presence stands as a kind of absolute by which all else is found to be wanting. For Simone Weil writes that over Attic tragedy 'the idea of justice sheds its light without intervening' (*IC* 52), and it is worth attending to her Antigone-like view of stories of empty tombs etc:

The crucifixion of the Christ has almost opened the door, has almost separated on one side the Father and the Son, on the other Creator and creation. The door half opened. The resurrection closed it again. Those who have the immense privilege of participating with their whole being in the cross of Christ, go through that door, they pass to the side where the secrets of God himself are to be found. (*IC* 195f.)

It must be acknowledged, however, that in her comments on Electra's recognition of Orestes, she links it with the theme of recognition common in folklore. 'One believes a stranger is before one, but it is the most loved being. This is what happened to Mary Magdalene and a certain gardener' (*IC* 7), though of course Orestes says, 'Do not hold me'. One important difference might at first be picked out, even if Simone Weil were to acknowledge with clarity

---

[31] René Girard, *Violence and the Sacred*, trans. F. Gregory, Baltimore: John Hopkins, 1977). For some original applications of Girard, see also G. Pattison, 'Violence, Kingship and Culture', *Expository Times*, cii:5 (1991) pp. 135–50.

[32] Hans Urs von Balthasar, *The Glory of the Lord: a Theological Aesthetics*, iv, *The Realm of Metaphysics in Antiquity*, trans. O. Davies *et al*, Edinburgh: T. and T. Clark, 1989, p. 122.

'resurrection' appearances of which she is clearly suspicious, in that she specifically notes that 'Electra marvels at the presence of her beloved with three senses successively: sight, hearing *and touch*' (*IC* 16f. my emphasis). Orestes reveals himself to her only after she has 'let go the urn', has let go the very last tangible reminder of his 'dead' physical presence. One suspects that for her one has also to let go, even of the resurrection appearances themselves, even of sight and hearing, for Christ to be present to her as to others.

Of the theologians, it is von Balthasar who has made a constructive theological use of Sophocles which has an affinity with Simone Weil's position here. Confronted by the divine will, the barrier to the divine seems to break open, 'here earthly life has already been left behind and death is present in seed and essence'. Herein lies the 'true *imago dei* of man', with pain becoming the very medium of transcendence.[33] The invocation to Bacchus as soon as Creon agrees to free her is pointless in relation to her life, for Creon stops on the way to wash what is left of Polyneices, burn his body, and bury his ashes. The price of returning the dead to the earth is that the living also die, Antigone by hanging herself, and Haemon by falling on his own sword, having chosen to be immured with her rather than be parted from her. Since Eurydice also kills herself, Creon's pride is finally stricken, but Sophocles draws no clear connection between Antigone's fidelity and any possible peace which Creon may eventually find. It is because he does not do so that we may suppose Simone Weil finds his writing so appropriate.

We could also say of her that she resists disorder in her own society like a medieval mystic, by fasting and by the intensity of her desire to merge herself with the humanity of a suffering Christ.[34] Inevitably she risked death by doing so:

It is not in the power of a being to destroy himself. The true reply consists only in consenting to the possibility of being destroyed, that is to say, in the possibility of total disaster, whether that disaster actually happens or not. No one ever inflicts disaster on himself, neither out of love nor perversity. At the most one can, under one or the other inspiration, take distractedly and as if unconsciously two or three steps leading to the slippery point where one becomes a prey to gravity and from which one falls on stones that break one's back. (*IC* 183)

[33] Hans Urs von Balthasar, *The Glory of the Lord*, IV, p. 127.
[34] See for instance Martha J. Reineke, '"This is my Body", Reflections on Abjection, Anorexia and Medieval Women Mystics', *Journal of the American Academy of Religion*, 58:2 (1990), pp. 245–65.

So writing to her parents, using her London address, though actually dying in the sanatorium in Ashford, she could hardly bring herself to warn them of its imminence, except by indirect suggestion. 'Antigone has gone through a few bad patches, it's true. But they didn't last. It's all far away now' (*SL* 191).

Steiner claims that:

It is a defining trait of western culture after Jerusalem and after Athens that in it men and women re-enact, more or less consciously, the major gestures, the exemplary symbolic motions, set before them by antique imaginings and formulations. Our realities, as it were, mime the canonic possibilities first expressed in classical art and feeling.[35]

From this it follows that if we do not want people to behave or die in certain ways, we should change the canon, if we can. Since it is as it is, and if Simone Weil can properly be seen to be located in relation to these canonic possibilities, we might go on to ask where those of like implacable conscience should be found, some fifty years after her death? Some, in line with Bultmann, following his own essay on 'Polis and Hades in Sophocles' Antigone' and in a related essay, will insist on acknowledgement of the transcendent powers which limit, and give a relative value to, the human, reminding the state of its mere secularity, and its incapacity to render to us a security not within its power to deliver.[36] Rowan Williams' analysis of Barth's struggle with questions of appropriate patriotism and citizenship begins with the example of the 1958 German Evangelical Church's ten theses on the question of atomic warfare and the possession of nuclear weapons.[37] These theses insistently spell out the sheer incompatibility between Christian faith and the possession, let alone the use, of such weapons, and we might nowadays add modern *non*-nuclear weaponry too. So, too, Donald MacKinnon's critique of present-day power relations insists on our attending to:

the sense of personal defeat which may invade the spirit of a man or woman who is told that the condition of his or her survival, and that of the institutions under which he or she lives, is a willingness to perpetuate horrors of a sort that seem morally prohibited by any system of ethics,

[35] George Steiner, *Antigones*, p. 108.

[36] Rudolf Bultmann, *Essays Philosophical and Theological*, trans. J. C. C. Greig (London: SCM 1955), pp. 22–35; pp. 67–89 on 'The Understanding of Man and the World in the New Testament and in the Greek World'.

[37] Rowan Williams, 'Barth, War and the State', pp. 170–90 of *Reckoning with Barth*, edited by N. Biggar, London: Mowbray, 1988.

whether religious or humanist, which the individual may profess, however little his or her life may accord in detail with its Credo.[38]

So, acknowledging the statesman's genuine responsibilities, he none the less suggests that one might be driven to advocate courses of action which would require a very high cost in terms of apparent waste, for oneself if not for others, albeit as the fruit of austerely disciplined self-knowledge. However, much though Simone Weil distrusted large scale organisations, there seems to be no reason in principle why churches may not prompt individual conscience, rather than suppose those consciences to be formed in isolation from them or in antithesis to them.

Political philosopher Jean Bethke Elshtain[39] urges today's Antigones to beware of the problems facing us in trying to make accountable the bureaucratic hierarchies of the modern state and of our new political orders. In particular, she urges the importance of re-evaluating particular ties, loyalties, and traditions which are life-giving and preserving, though she has much more confidence than someone like Simone Weil in what Roman Catholic social thinking would indicate as the subsidiary, intermediate institutions lying in the region between the individual and the bureaucracy. These institutions may be most important for their capacity to nurture and protect people, as important goals for Simone Weil as obedience to properly constituted authorities. Yet Barrie Paskins, finally, is not prepared to concede despair even of the state. From a couple of notes Simone Weil made about the proper pride and humility of a worker, he derives a question of radical criticism, both for the international arena and within a state, of its existing practices: how must the state be organised to be a proper object of pride among its citizens?[40] His suggested criteria include ministering to the real needs of others, certainly among her objectives, but easily obliterated by the essential confrontational drama of an Antigone. We need to be open to what Steiner calls:

---

[38] Donald M. MacKinnon, 'Creon and Antigone', pp. 110–34 of *Themes in Theology: The Three-Fold Cord*, Edinburgh: T. and T. Clark, 1987, p. 14. See also in the same volume, pp. 87–109 'Power Politics and Religious Faith'.

[39] Jean Bethke Elshtain, 'Antigone's Daughters', *Democracy* (1982), pp. 46–59; and 'The Vexation of Weil', *Telos*, 58 (1983–4), pp. 195–203.

[40] Barrie Paskins, 'Pride and International Relations', pp. 146–60 of *Christ, Ethics and Tragedy: Essays in Honour of Donald MacKinnon*, edited by K. Surin, Cambridge: Cambridge University Press, 1989, pp. 156, 160.

the very delicate yet insistent possibility that Creon's intelligence is of a kind which might lead him to apprehend the necessary claims of Antigone's stance; that Antigone is possessed of a force of empathy which might lead her to perceive the rationale of Creon's position.[41]

There must be a place for the implacable conscience, but also for the energy and intelligence which will search out the middle ground, institutionalise compromises, and insistently fight for better ones, ever open to the scrutiny of transcendent other possibilities.

[41] George Steiner, *Antigones*, p. 299.

CHAPTER 13

Simone Weil: harbinger of a new Renaissance?

H. L. Finch

INTRODUCTION

Simone Weil laments the loss of civilisation since the Renaissance –
'all our spiritual ills', she says, 'come from the Renaissance' (*N* 465).
It seemed to her that the situation was this: for the sake of a worldly
individualism and power, connected with a misunderstanding of the
spirit of ancient Greece, the Renaissance sacrificed the indispensable
place of the supernatural in human affairs. Life and culture were
given a wholly worldly orientation: to take possession of the world
for the sake of mundane human desires and needs. Having brought
about the vast material changes of modern science and technology,
we now find ourselves threatened by forces of destruction, disinte-
gration, totalitarianism, and chaos, released by a far too narrow and
impoverished egocentric conception of human life.

The Renaissance, believing itself to be returning to Greek roots,
fell under the spell of a false individualism. Instead of a science and
culture based on piety and reverence, we had one based on power
and possession. We have made a five centuries experiment of trying
to live in a world in which the most important business of human life
was seen as seizing and grasping the kind of knowledge which is
power. 'We are', says Simone Weil, 'living in a world in which
nothing is made to man's measure; there exists a monstrous discrep-
ancy between man's body, man's mind and the things which at the
present time constitute the elements of human existence; everything
is in disequilibrium' (*OL* 108). It is what has been called 'humanism'
(but not what some 'humanist' scholars in Italy and Northern
Europe in the fifteenth and sixteenth centuries thought it to be).
And just this (strange as it may seem to some) has led to the denial of
humanity in new religions of nationalism and totalitarianism, and
outbreaks of cruelty on an unprecedented scale. The century of two

world wars, Auschwitz and Hiroshima, preventable starvation and dislocation of millions, and the agony and heart-break of millions of others marks the end of this bold experiment gone wrong – it marks the end of the Renaissance.

Our world seems one constructed solely for power and by our imaginations. It is a 'false' world for Simone Weil, as Martin Andic has so clearly shown in his essay on 'Discernment and the Imagination' above. Our question is: Do we have a way forward? Furthermore, does Simone Weil, in rejecting our 'Renaissance' culture, provide us with suggestions for a new way forward? As the Renaissance we have known – still *our* Renaissance – comes to an end, will this ending be even more catastrophic than our century suggests, or more gradual? We find in the writings of Simone Weil the spirit and point of view, hints and stirrings, outlines and beginnings of a new era, a new Renaissance, which contains the possibility of a new kind of life which may yet emerge. It is to this side of Simone Weil that we now turn.

THE FOUR DRAGONS

Even presenting any new ideas of Simone Weil proves a difficult task in *our* Renaissance culture – as Wittgenstein once remarked, 'Nothing is so difficult as not deceiving oneself.'[1] So, amidst so many deceptions – false imaginings – including our own, understanding Simone Weil is not easy. She baffles, and goes against, our 'modern' philosophical stream of thinking. Thus, before presenting her ideas, let me dispel some obstacles in understanding her thought. These obstacles I call the four dragons – what I believe are mistakenly regarded as *psychological* problems posed by her. It is the fate of many great thinkers to be almost immediately misunderstood. With Simone Weil certain prejudices are at once aroused which turn people away, perhaps protecting her from misunderstandings. Those who persist will almost certainly find their prejudices being shaken, and we will learn from her if we are capable of learning. As we will see, most of these prejudices centre around the modern myth of what may be called *psychologism* – that is, the idea that spiritual things may be 'explained' or understood in terms of psychology,

---

[1] Wittgenstein, *Culture and Value*, edited by G. H. Von Wright, Chicago: University of Chicago Press and Oxford: Basil Blackwell, 1980.

often a psychology which is from the outset hostile to spirituality, as in the case of Freud, *all* spirituality.

The four dragons in this case are *anorexia*, the claim of a *religious significance for affliction, anti-Judaism*, and the seeming autism of the famous '*paralysis prayer*' or the 'Example of Prayer', in which Weil prays to be made deaf, dumb, blind, and unable to move (*FLN* 243–5). Each one of these 'dragons' stirs up particular resistances among those under the spell of psychologism.

To begin with *anorexia*: not eating may be regarded as a psychological illness or a spiritual discipline. Difficulties arise when it is carried to an extreme, as in the case of the Cathars, with whom it was an accepted religious ritual, and of Simone Weil herself. In a recent book called *Holy Anorexia*, a professor of history at Rutgers University, Rudolph Bell, distinguished between secular anorexia, which is the pursuit of thinness, and holy anorexia as seen in some saints, which he calls the pursuit of holiness. The distinction vanishes when he regards both as a search for self-autonomy in terms of culturally defined desiderata.[2]

Suppose that Simone Weil were here and should say: 'The reason I am not eating, though it may lead to my death, is that I feel so much kinship with all those who are starving in the world during the World War that I am not able to eat.' Now a psychologist comes along and says:

No, that is not the real reason. We [psychologists] know more about this than you do. The real reason is that you are trying to establish and assert your own identity in a world which does not permit you to do that. And when this gets out of control, you will become your own victim. Furthermore, what you are doing does not really help starving people at all. And besides, if everybody did this, it would be bad for society. We might not be able to win wars. Your behaviour is psychologically unacceptable.

The first question is: whom should we believe as to the reasons why Simone Weil is doing what she is doing? Should we accept Simone Weil's reasons or the psychologist's? The psychologist probably does not consider the killing of millions of people in war normal

---

[2] *Holy Anorexia*, Chicago: University of Chicago Press, 1985. Bell calls the anorexia of Clare of Assisi and Catherine of Siena 'a positive expression of self by a woman in response to the world that attempted to dominate her' (p. 178). This is an excellent example of a modern academic turning what these two women themselves would have said (that they were transcending the self and the world in obedience to God) to fit into the framework of modern psychology. Here the 'psychological' is destructive of the 'spiritual' for the sake of 'pseudo-explanations'.

either, but would not let sympathy for the suffering of others carry her to the same extreme. That would be pathological in her terms.

Two different worlds are in conflict here. On the one hand, we have Weil's personal testimony, her inner experience, her spiritual act which includes what she says about it. And, on the other, we have the psychologist with his or her pseudo-scientific 'explanations', which establish or support what is the conventional wisdom as to what is healthy and what is not healthy. Is it not an understandable response to the manufacture and dropping of bombs on tens of thousands of people for a single woman to die by refusing to eat out of sympathy for these victims? What is it that needs psychological explanation as an act of *egotism* here? Is it not the 'psychology' which is pathological?

Now we turn to the question of *affliction* and its spiritual value which produces among psychologists murmurings about masochism. Once again we will learn more from going to actual religious testimony. There is a striking parallel to the experience of Simone Weil in the life of the seventeenth-century British philosopher, Anne Conway (1631–79), the author of the philosophical treatise called *The Principles of the Most Ancient and Modern Philosophy*, just now being rediscovered. Like Weil, Conway suffered all her life from the most agonising headaches. Doctors, healers, religious teachers from all over Europe came to her estate at Ragley Hall in England to try to help her, unsuccessfully. Among her closest friends were the Platonist Henry More and the chemist-doctor Van Helmont, who remained with her at Ragley.

What Conway, who was never cured of her headaches, writes about suffering is first-hand testimony. In one place she describes her room as a 'dungeon-chamber', and we are told by More's biographer that 'her Devotion was infinitely hindered by her Pain; and that the very Faculties in her, which should be applied to Humility and self-resignation, were swept away by the Violence of these pains as in a Storm'.[3] In her philosophical treatise, however, we also find the following:

because every Pain and Torment excites or stirs up an operating Spirit and Life in every thing which suffers; as we observe by continued Experience, and Reason teacheth us, that of necessity it must be so; because through Pain, and the enduring thereof, every kind of crassitude or grossness in

---

[3] Anne Conway, *The Principles of the Most Ancient Modern Philosophy*, edited by Peter Loptson, The Hague: Martinus Nijhoff, 1982, p. 236.

Spirit or Body contracted is attenuated and so the Spirit captivated or detained in that grossness or crassitude is set at Liberty, and made more Spiritual, and consequently more Active and Operative, through suffering. Now seeing a Creature cannot proceed infinitely to Evil, nor slide down into Inactivity or Silence, nor yet also into mere Eternal Passion, it uncontestably follows, that it must at length return unto Good; and by how much the greater its sufferings are, so much the sooner shall it return and be stored.[4]

Simone Weil's teaching that affliction is one of the forms of the love of God is in essence no different from Conway's.

With regard to the third dragon, Simone Weil's *anti-Judaism* (which we will return to later in terms of the philosophical issues involved), something similar arises. Anna Freud, for example is reported to have said that Simone Weil was drawn to Christianity by Jewish self-hatred.[5] If we had asked Simone Weil herself, she would have said she was drawn to Christianity by the love of Christ – such an account is given in her 'Spiritual Autobiography' (*WG*). Once again we have a psychologist claiming to know more about it than the human being involved – especially a human being who was extraordinarily free from self-deception, perhaps more free than Anna Freud. Simone Weil had a remarkable amount of insight into her own condition.[6] What are the reasons for believing what Anna Freud has to say about this, rather than what Simone Weil herself says? Is it any more than the prestige which attaches to a famous psychologist in an age which has made psychology a ruling myth? Is it a principle that no Jew can be drawn to another religion without it being an expression of Jewish self-hatred?

Wittgenstein tells the story of a woman who had a beautiful dream about a garden and the unpleasant explanation of it given by Sigmund Freud. Wittgenstein said Freud had done something very wrong. If the woman had a beautiful dream, then it was a beautiful dream and Freud should not have told her otherwise.[7] Freud's explanation tells us more about Freud than it does about the

---

[4] Anne Conway, p. 193.

[5] Anna Freud is quoted to this effect in Robert Coles, *Simone Weil: A Modern Pilgrimage*, Reading, MA: Addison-Wesley, 1987, ch. 3, 'Her Jewishness'.

[6] See the discussion of her death in J. P. Little's essay, above. Little also discusses her view on why suicide is not a legitimate 'way out'.

[7] This story is found in Wittgenstein, *Lectures and Conversations on Aesthetics, Psychology, and Religious Belief*, edited by Cyril Barrett, Oxford: Basil Blackwell, 1978, p. 24. Ray Monk, in his recent biography of Wittgenstein, discusses this story in the larger context of Wittgenstein's view of Freud, pp. 405ff.

woman, as Anna Freud's comments about Simone Weil tell us more about Anna Freud than they do about Simone Weil.

Finally, the fourth dragon is probably the most formidable of all, the *'example of prayer'*. What are we to think of a woman who prays to God to be rendered blind, deaf, dumb, and unable to will any bodily movement like a total paralytic?[8] This is something which seems like a blasphemy against all human life, asceticism in its worst form, like hair shirts and self-torment. Yet even here there is a spiritual meaning, and we have to try to understand what kind of spiritual experience it corresponds to.

Simone Weil is praying to be one, not only with the most unfortunate, but, it seems to me, with the material world, in the dumbness and obedience of matter which we share in also. There is a hint of a definite experience in what the Sufis call the 'animal unveiling', for animals are already in the presence of God in their way, and we can enter into the silent, speechless animal enlightenment through identification of our consciousness with it. Similarly perhaps we might enter into a purely material enlightenment or, as Simone Weil would see it, the most simple level of possible relation to the love of God. If there is a kinship of all creations, what Anne Conway called a *universal sympathy of all things*, then we may be able to experience the passivity and obedience of matter. Simone Weil's spiritual adventure took her right up to the inner frontiers of that. The 'paralysis prayer' is the result – not a repudiation of what is human, but a reaching out for the *universal sympathy of all things*, our kinship, our oneness even with dumb, insentient matter, for it too shares in the universal obedience.

Here is an example of what looks, from one standpoint, like a refusal of the greatest gifts of human life – mobility, sense experience, speech – but from another point of view is an inner experience of spiritual unity with the world, subject to the most brutal necessity and absence of God. There are, we could say, two 'readings' – a 'psychological' one, and a 'common-sense' spiritual one.

With each dragon some new 'explanation' is offered (psychological or ideological). Yet, Simone Weil directs us to an action or experience in each example which does not require these pseudo-explanations. She is expressing a form of life that is concretely lived with and towards God and other human beings.

---

[8] The 'paralysis prayer' is often cited. Cf. Eric Springsted, *Simone Weil and the Suffering of Love*, Cambridge, MA, 1986, pp. 80–1. J. P. Little has discussed this prayer at length in her essay on decreation in this volume, above, pp. 46–50.

Simone Weil, since her death in 1943 and growing public avail-
ability of her writing, has been the target and victim of such
'psychologic' explanations. In this we can see just the differences
between the Renaissance, which ended up producing such
'sciences', and a 'new' Renaissance in which Simone Weil would
want to make *the spiritual* the air which we breathe, not as a
substitute set of 'objects' to be *controlled*, but as the 'gifts' of an open,
freer, and wider intellect. The psychologist falsifies and trivialises
the spiritual by trying to deal with it 'scientifically', and not the least
of all trying to deal so with Simone Weil herself. (Some day soon this
'psychologising' of the spiritual will appear as condescending as the
way in which we now look, for example, upon Frazer's insufferably
'superior' tone toward primitive religions, which, as Wittgenstein
pointed out, are spiritually on a far higher level than was Frazer
himself![9]) Spiritually, Simone Weil is far in advance of her condescending 'psychological' critics.

THREE ULTIMATE PRIORITIES

What we have in the four dragons examples are different ways of
seeing the world – a whole new aspect of reality is revealed to us
simply by rejecting the conventional opinions on voluntary fasting,
human suffering, religious denial, and radical asceticism. We might
say that any 'new' Renaissance will hinge on 'reversing' perspectives, 'composing' perspectives or giving up perspectives altogether,
to use Simone Weil's language. We have through it all three ultimate priorities in Simone Weil's philosophy. These are found most
usefully presented in her essay 'Human Personality', but are generally expressed through her later writings. The priorities are:

1 the priority of love over power, which has as a corollary the
   priority of love over justice;
2 the priority of the individual over the collective; and
3 the priority of the impersonal over the personal.

These define Simone Weil's philosophy and religion, both culturally
and individually.

In her philosophy God is completely power-free, beyond all

---

[9] Cf. Wittgenstein, 'Remarks on Frazer's Golden Bough', trans. A. C. Miles and Rush Rhees,
The Human World, 3 (May 1971), pp. 18–451. An extended discussion of this point can be
found in R. H. Bell, 'Understanding the Fire-Festivals: Wittgenstein and Theories in
Religion', *Religious Studies*, 14, March 1978, pp. 113–24.

power. She finds nothing noble or worthy of reverence in power, in the sense of authority or lordship. Since the act of creation itself was traditionally understood as an act of power and God as an all-powerful ruler, we require a completely different creation-myth if creation is to be understood as an act of love. We need to invoke Isaac Luria's (1522–70) kabbalistic idea of creation as withdrawal (in Hebrew *Tsim-tsum*) or making-room-for-the-world – an idea embodied in 'decreation', as J. P. Little has so carefully detailed. As Weil expresses this, it is an abandonment in order to permit the creature to be.[10] Creation is an act of hospitality and sacrifice. Through it the world is turned over to a necessity which serves as a kind of screen or protection against the blindness of eternal love!

Justice has an affinity to power through law imposed by force and punishment. We cannot, on the other hand, speak of love as being imposed by force. This has led, in the traditional view, to the idea that justice somehow is more fundamental than love: a just society has to be created before there can be a loving society. In this patriarchal view, love becomes *mercy* which is thought of as *added* to justice.

Simone Weil's philosophy reverses this completely: the foundation and essence of justice for her is love or respect and consideration for other persons as human beings *which makes possible justice*. Justice, in the end, does not rest upon force, which can always be abused, but upon human respect. This, too, we have seen in earlier essays (see especially Richard Bell's essay, above).

Vladimir Soloviev (1853–1900), the Russian Christian philosopher, said to be the model for Dostoievsky's Alyosha Karamazov, now being republished in post-Gorbachev Russia, once observed that there is no moral content in people struggling for their own rights. It is only in struggling for *other* people's rights that we can talk about morality. *Common humanness* rather than common law, however enforced, is *the basis of justice*.

---

[10] The human image of divine love for Simone Weil is mother-love, she writes:

> Love is supernatural when it is unconditioned. An unconditional love is a madness. A mother's love is the best image of it here below. But it is only an image. Even a mother's love wears out if all the conditions for its renewal are lacking.
>
> Only the love of God and the anonymous love of one's neighbor are unconditioned. One may add the love (friendship) between two friends of God who have traveled the road of sanctity beyond the point where sanctity is something final . . .
>
> It is this friendship which Christ added as a third commandment. That is to say as a third perfectly holy love alongside the love of God and the love of one's neighbor. (*FLN* 127–8)

What prevents me from gouging another person's eyes out if I feel so moved and believe that no one else will ever know? This question was asked in the first book of Plato's *Republic*. Weil's answer is that it is not because of the other person's rights nor because of the law. It is because, she says, I would be violating something sacred in the other person, in fact the only thing sacred – the expectation we are all born with and, at some level, never lose, *that good will be done to us*. This is the primal sacred innocence of every human soul, arising from the fact that we are all born totally dependent upon the care of others. We are born in a situation in which we will not survive unless food and care are provided, *which we have done nothing to deserve*.

This brings us to the subject of Simone Weil's conception of the essential human condition. It is made very clear that, supernaturally speaking, love is the basis of justice and not the other way around. The love of God, like the love of a mother, comes before the fear of the Lord, as it does before the fear of a father. We are born into a situation of complete dependence upon a human being, principally the mother or primary carer. It is our original connection with the good. We are not born into a *quid pro quo* relation or with 'rights'. Even if born in pain, or without adequate care, or after long suffering in the womb, we will always find ourselves at birth entirely in the hands of others. From start to finish this is our primary relation: needing someone to help us, and having to expect that good will be done to us. Here is the human bond upon which all hope for justice eventually rests. What we receive comes as a gift, a grace, and not as something earned or entitled.

The initial situation is not a power relation. Mother-love is not initially enforced by law. This philosophy is so squarely based on the primacy of love that it is inevitably also based on the primacy of the mother–child relation. While the desire for the good is often thought of as the desire to *possess* the good (something which Plato shows is not possible since the good is not an 'object'), it is expressed by Simone Weil as the desire to *receive* the good. As the mother's love is a gift or a grace (even if the baby 'searches for', or 'roots for', the nipple), so everything supernatural in human life is a gift. We cannot force another person to give us a 'gift', any more than we can force them to give us friendship or love. These lie beyond the limits of force by which we try to enforce relative justice (*quid pro quo* or 'fairness' or rights). If the essential human situation is the receiving of gifts (as in the cases of the infant, the genius, the wise man, and the saint), then this indeed lies in a different dimension from force and power. Even if it is able to kill or reduce both giver and receiver to inert matter, it still cannot 'control' gifts, least of all the divine–human gifts.

This is the *human bond*, our original 'innocence' which, however betrayed, never seems to desert us (because there is nothing we can do but to keep on depending on it). Justice does not then reside in law imposed from above (God, state, father or superego) but rather in this common humanness, going back we must suppose, to the universally shared dependency in infancy. *This* is the first reality.

It is important because it shows us where the only answer that is broad enough and deep enough, if it were recognised and honoured, is to be found – to stand up to the naked power of the world. What is sacred and divine is thus what belongs to this humanity, not what links us to any nation or people or church, or reason or will. Why should human beings not be divinely defined by such humanity? Would this not be a *genuine* humanism?

We turn now to our second priority, the individual before the collective. As has frequently been pointed out, 'triumph of the will' in this century coincides, not only with ideology and totalitarianism, but also with scepticism and technological hubris. The attempt to 'conquer nature' by imposing the human reason and will upon it, the upshot of our post-Renaissance science, has resulted, as Weil points out, in an enormous increase in collective power, and a corresponding decrease in the role and significance of the individual. The individual has become the pawn of state and social forces about which he or she has no say. It is the triumph of the collective over the individual.

It is a violation of the Western tradition, as it is of Christianity. The intrinsic superiority of the individual to the collective is a cardinal principle of Western thought, as it was in Greece prior to Christianity. The Christian revelation of the divinity, or potential divinity, of the individual fulfills this. When Jesus spoke in the first person as an individual to individuals, he stepped outside the limits of traditional Judaism by putting the individual ahead of the people, the divinity of the individual above the holiness of the people.

For Weil there is not, and cannot be, ultimate spiritual significance in *any* group. A people can make war and it can experience mass emotions, but it cannot think and it cannot make free decisions. The concept of a 'holy people' is an illusion in her view, because it is bound to be infected with collective egotism. The collective soul takes the place of God, as it is likely to do in every kind of nationalism.

Because no nation or people or church can be holy, unconditional love of any social group or organisation is a form of idolatry and of evil:

God can become a piece of bread, a stone, a tree, a lamb, a man. But He cannot become a people. No people can become an incarnation of God. The Devil is the collective ... Pride is the devil's characteristic attribute. And pride is a social thing. (*FLN* 304)

Nationalism in its extreme form appears as a glorification of the collective soul. Weil suggests that the Old Testament God was such a glorification of a single people who called *their* collective soul the creator and ruler of heaven and earth, implying thereby what she calls a 'terrifyingly imperialist outlook', later taken over by the Roman Empire and then the Christian Church (*FLN* 214).

For Simone Weil there are no qualities, superior or inferior, which belong to a people or a collective soul, that offset its tyrannical power over the individual. Whatever its qualities, they pale into insignificance beside the individual spiritual qualities of humility, intelligence, and love which do not, and cannot, belong to social groups.

This, it seems, is a genuine intellectual issue between Jews and Christians as to which comes first, the collective or the individual – the holy people or the divine individual. If Jews believe, as many do, that the collective soul is more important than the individual soul, they must still accept the possibility that, in a world which does not believe this, there will be individual Jews who do not agree with it.

Baron Nathaniel Rothschild, after being admitted to the British House of Lords, is said to have prayed that individual freedom would not remove him from the Jewish people.[11] Simone Weil's prayer was opposite. She did not choose to be bound by peoplehood. She wished instead to be emptied of all such attachments, and demonstrated in this way the authority of individual choice and the possibilities of individual genius and grace.

We now turn to Simone Weil's conception of the individual, including her rejection of the 'personal self'. There are for her, we

---

[11] The story about Baron Rothschild is told in Yaacov Herzog, *A People That Dwells Alone*, New York: Sanhedrin Press, 1975, p. 145f.

may say, two selves: the essential impersonal self, which might be described as the truly unique individuality with which we are born, and a secondary acquired 'social self', a personal ego shell which comes in time (around the age of four, five, or six) to overlay and 'imprison' it. It is in terms of the differences between the two selves that she distinguishes (in a way not unreminiscent of D. H. Lawrence)[12] what is valuable and not valuable in each of us. It serves to define also what she means by *humility*;

Humility is not a bad opinion of one's own person in comparison to other people. It is a radically bad opinion of one's own person in relation to what is impersonal in oneself. When once the impersonal has implanted itself in a soul and begins to grow there, it draws all the good to itself. The person retains as its own property only the evil. (*FLN* 182)

We should be clear that *impersonal* does not mean cold, detached, inhuman or unfeeling. It means intense feeling, but freed from pride, vanity, prestige, and power. The mother's attitude towards the baby might be described as intensely impersonal, as is the baby's attitude towards her. Both are not personal in an ego sense because neither normally is concerned with self-interest, self-promotion or self-defence. This is the way in which they transcend the personal.

When Simone Weil says *only the impersonal in us is sacred*, others might prefer the word *essential*. Jesus' relation to individuals, we feel, enhances their individualities, but not their egos. (Jesus was not addressing a people-self, as he might in Judaism, or an Hindu *atman* universal self, or a Buddist no-self. He was talking to essential individuals, impersonal friends.)

The *impersonal* is, for Simone Weil, the mode of grace, as distinct from the *personal* which is the mode of the will. (We feel the will *belongs* to us, whereas grace does not 'belong' to anybody.) We need to be detached from ourselves (i.e. from our social selves) and only a kind of self-emptying God can do that. To carry it all the way is *kenosis*, or the acceptance of the void (in her language), which underlies the inspirations of the artist as well as the illuminations of the shaman or prophet. What is emptied is what comes from self-image, persona, and social conditioning. This is what we must learn to do without.

---

[12] The comparison of Simone Weil with D. H. Lawrence has often been made, most effectively by Richard Rees, *Brave Men* [sic] – *A Study of D. H. Lawrence and Simone Weil*, Carbondale: Southern Illinois Press, 1958. An important distinction is that Lawrence had far more to say about the soul and Simone Weil about the Spirit.

Joseph Klausner, the Jewish biographer of Jesus, once observed that one of the most extraordinary things about the Jesus of the gospels was the extent to which he seemed to be able to separate himself from his emotions. We might hazard the guess that his very intimate relation to God altered the quality of all his other relations. This is why the term 'objective love' (borrowed here from A. R. Orage) seems appropriate for the New Testament, to distinguish it from emotional selfishly tinged 'subjective love'. The former is a total attitude, made possible by grace, not an emotion or a fixation or fascination.

To lay hands on the world and possess it collectively and egotistically has been the theme of the modern age since Renaissance, the age which culminated in Nietzsche's formula of the *Will to Power* or *Will to Will*. What Nietzsche saw beyond this was nihilism, which indeed is all that can remain from more willing. The reversal gives rise to philosophies of receptivity and response, of which Simone Weil's is one of the most prominent. (Later Wittgenstein and later Heidegger are two others).

CONCLUDING REMARKS: TOWARD A DIVINE HUMANITY

The European Renaissance of the fifteenth and sixteenth centuries failed, Weil said, because it was not of Christian inspiration. This was her analysis of what has gone wrong with the world. As a result, our science has been cut off from the good and the deeper levels of the human spirit. It has envisaged a world entirely of forces and power with no room for human freedom and choice. In this situation, Weil said, the task is to go back and find the point at which the compact between the human mind and the world was broken, or, as she also put it, we became the victims of our own creations and means took over as controlling ends. This task should be done even if it is already too late to prevent a catastrophe.

How did the misstep occur? Weil suggests that there are three aspects of the modern world which epitomise it: algebra, money, and machines (*FLN* 25, 27, 30, 39). What algebra, which now includes computer algebra, money, and machines have in common is that we cannot see clearly how they are working in relation to the human situation. And if we can see a part, we cannot see the whole. Imagine a vast collective governmental structure like the Pentagon, the interlocking computer systems it relies on, or the vast sums of borrowed money that debt-ridden countries (rich and poor) depend on, or the mass-destruction arms machines possessed world-wide – all this is beyond the comprehension of the individual mind. No individuals, at the bottom or the top, have any idea of what consequences flow from these.

An immeasurable distance still seems to separate us from an era free from collective and individual ego. The social and individual power-illusions which have made human history, and particularly twentieth-century history, such a long troubled sleep, still dominate us. But is the dawn coming?

Simone Weil's philosophy of history begins with ancient Greece and the gospels; it goes beyond both, however, as it absorbs certain Eastern philosophies and a 'kenotic' theology. Though the spirit of Simone Weil is basically the spirit of the gospels, she belongs with the 'outside Christians' (as do Tolstoy and Wittgenstein, who also had 'no official religion') though in love with the New Testament. For her the gospels are seen through the eyes of Homer and Euclid, and broadened by Eastern thought, all of which share the same impersonal sense of the divine in individual terms as Jesus Christ did.

The 'communality of humanity' will not be found in the old sense of an 'enlightenment' metaphysics of empty liberalism, but rather in the new sense of 'survival metaphors' which we need as a dying man needs a drink of water. The centre of a future civilisation – a 'new' Renaissance – must be freedom of the thinking spirit in poetic and discerning genius, the intimate work relation between the human body and its environment, and the common human bond arising from every human's root expectation that good will be done to him or her.

It is very necessary (above all for the sake of the next few generations, Simone Weil says) to change our conception of human greatness so that we no longer think of mass-fixated, mean-spirited men of power, like Hitler and Stalin, as 'great' men, nor of 'empires' (economic or militaristic) as 'great' societies, but reserve the term of 'greatness' for those humans and those smaller communities who truly deserve it. We must each become more like educators and spokespersons of *a divine humanity* – receptive to God coming into our midst so that we may be truly lifted up. Because we are not open and attentive to this, Simone Weil's prediction is not an optimistic one.

When chaos and destruction have reached the limit beyond which the very functioning of the economic and social organisation becomes materially impossible, our civilization will perish; and humanity, having gone back to a more social life dispersed into much smaller collectivities, will set out again along a new road which it is quite impossible for us to predict. To imagine that we can switch the course of history along a different track by transforming the system through reform or revolutions, to hope to find salvation through a defensive or offensive action against tyranny and militarism – all that is just day-dreaming. There is nothing on which to base even attempts. (*OL* 116f.)

Select bibliography

Allen, Diogenes. 'Natural Evil and the Love of God', *Religious Studies*, 16 (1980).
  Three Outsiders: Pascal, Kierkegaard and Simone Weil, Cambridge, MA: Cowley, 1983.
Bell, Richard H. *Sensing The Spirit*, Philadelphia: The Westminster Press, 1984.
Bell, Richard H. (ed.). *The Grammar of the Heart: New Essays in Moral Philosophy and Theology*, San Francisco: Harper and Row, 1988.
Bell, Rudolph. *Holy Anorexia*, Chicago: University of Chicago Press, 1985.
Blum, L. A. and V. J. Seidler. *A Truer Liberty: Simone Weil and Marxism*, London: Routledge, 1989.
Bultmann, Rudolf. *Essays Philosophical and Theological*, trans. J. C. C. Greig, London: SCM, 1955.
Caubaud, Jacques. *Simone Weil: A Fellowship in Love*, New York: Harvill, 1965.
Caussade, Jean-Pierre de. *Self-Abandonment to Divine Providence*, trans. Kitty Muggeridge, London: Collins, 1981.
Coles, Robert. *Simone Weil: A Modern Pilgrimage*, Reading, MA: Addison-Wesley, 1987.
Conway, Anne. *The Principles of the Most Ancient Modern Philosophy*, edited by Peter Loptson, Hague: Martinus Nijhoff, 1982.
Devaux, André A. 'Simone Weil et Blaise Pascal', in *Simone Weil: La Soif de l'absolu*, edited by J. P. Little and A. Ughetto, *Sud* (Marseille), no. special, 1990.
Dewey, John. *Individualism: Old and New*, New York: Capricorn Books, 1962.
Dietz, Mary G. *Between the Human and the Divine: The Political Thought of Simone Weil*, New Jersey: Rowan and Littlefield, 1988.
Eckhart, Meister. *Sermons and Treatises*, trans. and edited by M. O'C. Walshe, Shaftesbury: Longmans, 1987.
Edwards, Jonathan. *Essay on the Trinity*, edited by G. P. Fisher, New York, 1903.
Elshtain, Jean Bethke. *Women and War*, Brighton: Harvester, 1987.
Finch, H. L. *Wittgenstein: The Later Philosophy*, New York: Humanities, 1977.

Fiori, Gabriella. *Simone Weil, An Intellectual Biography*, trans. Joseph Berrigan, Athens, GA: University of Georgia Press, 1989.

Fischer, Clare B. *Our Mother Country is Hope*, Albany: SUNY Press, forthcoming.

Foucault, Michel, *The Foucault Reader*, edited by Paul Rabinow, London: Penguin Books, 1984.

Gadamer, H. G. *Truth and Method*, trans. G. Barden and J. Cumming, London, 1975.

The Relevance of the Beautiful and other Essays, trans. Nicholas Walker, Cambridge, 1986.

Girard, René. *Violence and the Sacred*, trans. F. Gregory, Baltimore: Johns Hopkins, 1977.

Hallie, Philip P. *Lest Innocent Blood be Shed: The Story of the Village of Le Chambon and How Goodness Happened There*, Harper Torchbooks, New York: Harper and Row, Publishers, 1979.

Hauerwas, Stanley. *A Community of Character*. Notre Dame: University of Notre Dame Press, 1981.

Havel, Vaclav. *Living in Truth*, edited by Jan Vladislaw, London: Faber and Faber, 1989.

Hegel, G. W. F. *Phenomenology of Spirit*, trans. A. V. Miller, Oxford: Clarendon, 1977.

On Tragedy, edited by A. and C. Paolucci, Newgate: Anchor, 1962.

Heller, Agnes. *A Radical Philosophy*, Oxford: Basil Blackwell, 1984.

A Philosophy of Morals, Oxford: Basil Blackwell, 1990.

The Power of Shame, Boston: Routledge, and Kegan Paul, 1988.

Heller, Agnes and Ferenc Féher. *The Postmodern Political Condition*, Oxford: Polity Press, 1988.

Hellman, John. *Simone Weil: An Introduction to Her Thought*, Waterloo: Wilfred Laurier University Press, 1982.

Ignatieff, Michael. 'The Limits of Sainthood', *The New Republic* (June 1990).

Kierkegaard, Søren. *Concluding Unscientific Postscript*, trans. David F. Swenson and Walter Lowrie, Princeton: Princeton University Press, 1941.

Works of Love, trans. Howard Hong and Edna Hong, New York: Harper and Row, 1962.

Kühn, Rolf. 'Le Monde comme texte: Perspectives herméneutiques chez Simone Weil', *Review de Sciences Philosophiques et Théologiques*, 64:4, 1980.

Larmore, Charles. *Patterns of Moral Complexity*, Cambridge: Cambridge University Press, 1987.

Little, J. P. *Simone Weil: Waiting on Truth*, Oxford: Berg, 1988. (Berg Woman's Series).

Simone Weil: A Bibliography, London: Grant and Cutler, Research Bibliographies and Checklists, no. 5, 1973. *Supplement No. 1* to the foregoing, 1979.

Little, J. P. and A. Ughetto. *Simone Weil: La Soif de l'absolu, Sud* (Marseille), no. special, 1990.

Lloyd, Genevieve. *The Man of Reason: 'Male' and 'Female' in Western Philosophy*, Minneapolis: University of Minnesota Press, 1984.

Loades, Ann. *Searching for Lost Coins: Explorations in Christianity and Feminism*, Pickwick, 1987.

MacKinnon, D. M. *Explorations in Theology 5*, London: SCM, 1979.
  The Problem of Metaphysics, London: Cambridge University Press, 1974.
  'Creon and Antigone', *Themes in Theology: The Three-Fold Cord*, Edinburgh: T. and T. Clark, 1987.

Maritain, Jacques. *Scholasticism and Politics*, New York: The Macmillan Co., 141.

McLellan, David. *Simone Weil: Utopian Pessimist*, London: Macmillan, 1989.

Miles, Sian (ed.). *Simone Weil: An Anthology*, London: Virago, 1986.

Mothersill, Mary. *Beauty Restored*, Oxford, 1984.

Murdoch, Iris. *The Sovereignty of Good*, London: Routledge, 1970.
  'The Darkness of Practical Reason', *Encounter* (July 1966).

Nielsen, Finn E. *The Political Vision of Simone Weil*, unpublished Ph.D. dissertation, University of California at Santa Barbara, 1976.

Nussbaum, Martha. *The Fragility of Goodness: Luck and Ethics in Greek Tragedy and Philosophy*, Cambridge: Cambridge University Press, 1986.

Oppenheimer, Helen. *The Hope of Happiness*, London: SCM, 1983.

Panichas, George (ed.). *The Simone Weil Reader*, New York: David MacKay, 1977.

Perrin, J. M. and G. Thibon. *Simone Weil As We Knew Her*, trans. Emma Craufurd, London: Routledge and Kegan Paul, 1953.

Pétrement, Simone. *Simone Weil, A Life*, trans. Raymond Rosenthal, New York: Pantheon, 1976.

Phillips, D. Z. *Through a Darkening Glass*, South Bend: University of Notre Dame Press, 1982.
  From Fantasy to Faith: The Philosophy of Religion and Twentieth-Century Literature, London: Macmillan, 1991.
  Faith After Foundationalism, London: Routledge, Chapman and Hall Ltd., 1988.

Plato. *Plato: The Collected Dialogues*, eds. Edith Hamilton and Huntington Cairns, New Jersey: Princeton University Press, 1963.

Rees, Richard. *Brave Men – A Study of D. H. Lawrence and Simone Weil*, Carbondale: Southern Illinois Press, 1958.

Rorty, Richard. *Contingency, Irony, and Solidarity*, Cambridge: Cambridge University Press, 1989.

Sandel, Michael. *Liberalism and the Limits of Justice*, Cambridge: Cambridge University Press, 1982.

Sherry, Patrick. *Spirit and Beauty: Introduction to Theological Aesthetics*, Oxford: Oxford University Press, 1991.

Sircello, Guy. *A New Theory of Beauty*, Princeton, 1975.

Söelle, Dorothee. *Beyond Mere Obedience*, trans. Lawrence Denef, Augsburg, 1970.

Suffering, trans. Everett Kalin, Philadelphia: Fortress Press, 1975.

Sophocles. *The Theban Plays*, trans. E. F. Watling, Harmondsworth: Penguin, 1947.

Springsted, Eric. *Christus Mediator: Platonic Mediation in the Thought of Simone Weil*, Chico, CA: Scholars Press, 1983.

Simone Weil and the Suffering of Love, Cambridge, MA: Cowley, 1986.

Steiner, George. *Antigones: The Antigone Myth in Western Literature, Art and Thought*, Oxford: Clarendon, 1984.

'Remembering the Future,' *Theology*, 93 (1990).

Terkel, Studs. *Working*, New York: Pantheon, 1972.

Vetö, Miklos. *La Métaphysique religieuse de Simone Weil*, Paris: Vrin, 1971.

Von Balthasar, Hans Urs. *Word and Revelation*, trans. A. V. Littledale, New York, 1964.

The Glory of the Lord: a Theological Aesthetics, trans. E. Leiva-Merikakis, Edinburgh, 1982.

Weil, Simone. (additional works noted, but not listed in abbreviations cited in text).

Sur la science, Paris: Gallimard, 1966.

Poèmes, suivis de 'Venise sauvée', Paris: Gallimard, 1968.

La Source Grecque, Paris: Gallimard, Coll. *Espoir*, 1979.

Oeuvres Complètes, co-edited by André A. Devaux and Florence de Lussy, Paris: Gallimard, 1988– .

Williams, Rowan. 'Barth, War and the State', in *Reckoning With Barth*, edited by N. Biggar, London: Mowbray, 1988.

The Wound of Knowledge, London: Darton, Longman and Todd Ltd., 1979.

Winch, Peter. *Simone Weil: 'The Just Balance'*, Cambridge: Cambridge University Press, 1989.

Wittgenstein, Ludwig. *Culture and Value*, edited by G. H. Von Wright, Chicago: University of Chicago Press and Oxford: Basil Blackwell, 1980.

Lectures and Conversations on Aesthetics, Psychology and Religious Belief, edited by Cyril Barrett, Oxford: Basil Blackwell, 1978.

Philosophical Investigations, trans. G. E. M. Anscombe, Oxford: Basil Blackwell and Mott, 1958.

The Blue and Brown Books, Oxford: Basil Blackwell, 1958.

Index

In this index I have identified all Author/Names in the text and notes and the most important proper nouns like *Bhagavad Gita*, as well as central concepts when those are particularly being critically analysed or used in an extended way. Because of the frequency of use by Simone Weil and throughout these essays of terms like: *God, love, will, desire, need, good, self, work/labour, obedience, necessity, soul, supernatural, justice,* and *truth*, these have not been indexed unless they are the subject of analysis. I have not indexed the proper names *Christ* or *Jesus* or scriptural books because of their frequency of use, but have focused on the critical use of the concept *incarnation*.